The
Holocaust, Religion,
and Politics of
the
Collective Memory

The Holocaust, Religion, and the Politics of Collective Memory

Beyond Sociology

Ronald J. Berger

Transaction Publishers
New Brunswick (U.S.A.) and London (U.K.)

First paperback printing 2013
Copyright © 2012 by Transaction Publishers, New Brunswick, New Jersey.

This book is printed on acid-free paper that meets the American National Standard for Permanence of Paper for Printed Library Materials.

Library of Congress Catalog Number: 2011014058
ISBN: 978-1-4128-4304-1 (cloth); 978-1-4128-5255-5 (paper)
Printed in the United States of America

Library of Congress Cataloging-in-Publication Data

Berger, Ronald J.
    The Holocaust, religion, and the politics of collective memory : beyond sociology / Ronald J. Berger.
        p. cm.
    Includes bibliographical references and index.
    ISBN 978-1-4128-4304-1
    1. Holocaust, Jewish (1939–1945)—Historiography.   2. Holocaust, Jewish (1939–1945)—Influence.   I. Title.
    D804.348.B474 2011
    940.53'1801—dc22

                                                2011014058

To the victims and survivors of the Holocaust,
among them, my extended family

Contents

Preface

I have been steeped in the Holocaust since the late 1980s. That this interest was late in coming may seem odd, given that my father was a Jewish survivor of the Holocaust. But growing up in Los Angeles, California, in the 1950s and 1960s, we did not talk much about it. As a child I did ask my father about the absence of my grandparents, who were killed, and about the concentration camp number that was tattooed on his left arm, but with a short matter-of-fact answer, all was said and done. Neither did I learn anything about the Holocaust during my years in public school, Hebrew school, or my undergraduate and graduate studies at UCLA. It was only in the late 1980s, after a social movement of second-generation children of survivors had been underway for some time (Epstein 1979), that my father recounted his story in detail to me.

I am a sociologist, not a historian, but this experience led me to pursue a professional interest in the Holocaust. With *The Holocaust, Religion, and the Politics of Collective Memory* I have an opportunity to bring together in one place the fruits of my reading and study of this subject, a comprehensive synthesis of what one sociologist thinks is most important to know about the origins, implementation, and postwar legacy of this archetypal genocide of human history. My aim as well is to contribute to the intellectual project, begun by Irving Louis Horowitz, Zygmunt Bauman, and others, of bringing the Holocaust (and genocide studies more generally) into the disciplinary mainstream of sociology, countering the tendency to marginalize these subjects from conventional sociology courses and general concerns of sociological inquiry.

Chapter 1 considers the reasons for sociology's relative neglect of the Holocaust, a neglect I experienced in my own sociological education. It also provides introductory background on German history to set the stage for a consideration of important lines of sociological inquiry derived from the work of classical social theorists. And it introduces the concept of collective memory, which anticipates a later examination of postwar mnemonic disputes about the legacy of the genocide.

Chapter 2 addresses the question: Why the Jews? In doing so, it reviews the biblical history of the Jews and then the emergence of Christianity and the ensuing Christian anti-Semitism that marked the Jews as a pariah people of Europe, including Martin Luther's contribution to German anti-Semitism. Having identified the religious basis of social animosity toward Jews, it considers the pseudoscientific view of Jews as an inferior biological race that was polluting German society, and the associated eugenics movement, which advanced a pernicious ideology aimed at social intervention to regulate the genetic composition of the population. It also examines the Nazi's eugenics campaign of compulsory sterilization and euthanasia.

Chapter 3 turns more directly to Adolf Hitler's rise—the emergence and mobilization of the Nazi movement and Hitler's acquisition of political power. It then traces the evolution of Nazi anti-Jewish policy through its legislative initiatives, emigration and deportation policies, plundering of Jewish assets, and lastly, the Final Solution of total extermination. Chapter 4 covers the social structure of the genocidal regime, examining the key elements of Nazi culture, the state and corporate enterprises that profited from Jewish persecution, the bureaucratic mechanisms of destruction, and the apparatus of killing, including the concentration camp system.

Chapter 5 addresses the Jewish response to the Holocaust and raises the question of how some Jews managed to survive their ordeal. It also considers the role of the Jewish councils and Jewish resistance. Chapter 6 turns to the bystanders and third-party resisters, beginning with an examination of German resistance to the Nazi regime and the role of the Christian churches. It then considers the question of altruism and the "righteous Gentiles" who risked their lives to help Jews. Finally, it addresses the role of the United States, the Allies, and neutral countries.

Chapter 7 and chapter 8 shift the focus to the postwar period and the varying collective memories and mnemonic disputes that emerged as groups with different interests and present concerns attempted to grapple with the legacy of the Holocaust. Chapter 7 deals with postwar European memories in Germany and Poland, while chapter 8 deals with postwar Jewish memories in Israel and the United States.

Lastly, chapter 9 discusses the postwar emergence of a new international norm aimed at the prevention of genocide, embodied in the United Nations Genocide Convention, and the failed promise of genocide prevention in the postwar period. It also contextualizes the norm in terms of the more general problem of social solidarity and the exclusionary social processes that deny the full humanity of all too many human beings. In doing so, it examines the ongoing dilemma of Christian-Jewish coexistence as a representative case of the challenges that confront efforts to construct inclusionary societies that are fully incorporative of social differences.

* * *

There are several people I wish to thank for their insights and suggestions on my previous work that have informed this book: Deborah Abowitz, Norman Denzin, Stephen Gaies, James Holstein, Richard Koffler, and Kent Sandstrom. I'm also appreciative of the encouragement to undertake this project that I've received from Irving Louis Horowitz, Mary Curtis, and Lynne Rienner; and I'm especially appreciative of Irving's sagely advice on ways to improve the manuscript. Of course, the scholarship of Holocaust historians and other social scientists, from whom I have learned so much, deserves mention as well. They are too numerous to single out by name, but a perusal of the bibliography of this book will identify some of the most notable individuals. I would be remiss if I did not also mention my indebtedness to my father Michael Berger, and my uncle Sol Berger, the only two survivors of our prewar Jewish family in Poland, who have given me an intimate understanding of what it was like to experience the Holocaust. Finally, as always, there are my wife Ruthy, whose love and friendship has sustained me throughout the years; and my daughter Sarah, for whom everything I care for is about.

1

Sociology and the Holocaust

The Holocaust—the genocidal program of extermination that the Nazis called the Final Solution—took the lives of some six million Jews.[1] This amounted to about 60 percent of European Jewry and a third of the world's Jewish population (Gutman and Rozett 1990). To be sure, all too many other groups suffered at the hands of the Nazis as well. When one adds the murder of Gypsies, Poles, Slavs, Soviet civilians and prisoners of war, gay men, the disabled and mentally ill, among others—the number of innocent dead is far greater (Berenbaum 1990; Bloxham 2009; Gellately 2001; Lukas 1986).[2]

Some analysts, therefore, argue against the common focus on the particularity of the Jewish experience during the Holocaust, noting that the Nazi assault on the Jews took place in the context of a more general attempt to construct a racial utopia in which persecution was extended to a wide range of "impure" or "undesirable" groups (Burleigh and Wipperman 1991; Hancock 2009; Milton 1990). Others insist, however, that the Jews were the only group targeted by the Nazis for total annihilation and that this fact makes what happened to them unique. This observation is not intended to create a hierarchy of pain or to minimize the suffering that so many endured. Rather, it is meant to point out that the Final Solution "happened to a particular people for particular reasons" and that "the Jews were, for the Nazis, the central enemy" (Bauer 2001:63, 67).[3] Indeed, as Germany's military defeat "by the Allied powers became manifest, the *raison d'être* of World War II increasingly shifted . . . toward a war against Judaism in the bowels of Europe" (Horowitz 2009:495; see also Dawidowicz 1976; Friedländer 2009; Goldhagen 1996).

Ironically, for over a decade after the war, Jews did not have a preeminent place in public discourse about the Holocaust. According-ing to Jeffrey Alexander, "In the beginning, the Holocaust was not the 'Holocaust.' . . . In the torrent of newspaper, radio, and magazine stories, reporting the discovery by American infantrymen of the

Nazi concentration camps, the empirical remains of what had transpired were typified as 'atrocities,'" part of the general horror of war (2004:197). The particularity of Jewish victimization and the suffering of Jewish survivors were opaque; and the photographic and film images that were taken by the Allies presented the victims (dead and alive) as a "petrified, degrading, and smelly" depersonalized mass of misery that generated revulsion rather than compassion (p. 199).

During the postwar trials of the International Military Tribunal conducted by the Allies in Nuremberg, Germany, Jewish victimization was certainly acknowledged, but it was subsumed under the broader categories of "war crimes" and "crimes against humanity" and soon half forgotten (Hilberg 1991; Osiel 1997; see chapter 7). The word "Jew" was not even mentioned in Alain Resnais's otherwise brilliant 1955 documentary film *Night and Fog*. William Shirer's *The Rise and Fall of the Third Reich*, a 1960 bestseller, devoted just two to three percent of its some 1,200 pages to the Jewish genocide (Novick 1999). In his autobiography, the eminent Holocaust historian Raul Hilberg (1996) recalls how difficult it was to find a publisher for *The Destruction of the European Jews*, his groundbreaking account of the bureaucracy that implemented the Final Solution. Eventually, he found Quadrangle Books, a small independent company, which agreed to publish the book in 1961 after a Jewish-survivor family promised to subsidize the project with $15,000 to pay for books that would be donated to libraries.

Even classic works by Jewish writers such as Elie Wiesel's *Night* and Anne Frank's diary had inauspicious beginnings. Wiesel (1995) reports that his book, pared down from a much longer version that was first published in Yiddish, was initially considered too slender or too depressing for an American audience; and when it was eventually published in 1960 by Hill & Wang, it was not a commercial success. And were it not for *The Diary of Anne Frank* screenplay written by Frances Goodrich and Albert Hackett, which was made into a highly acclaimed Broadway play (in 1955) and an Academy Award caliber film (in 1959), Anne's diary might have lingered in obscurity for many more years (Novick 1999; Rosenfeld 1991, 1997; see chapter 6).

All this, of course, eventually changed, for reasons we will explore later in this book. As historical scholarship on the Holocaust proliferated, Wiesel observed that perhaps "no other tragedy or . . . event has been as [thoroughly] documented" (quoted in Cargas 1986:5). At the same time, he still views the Holocaust as a phenomenon that defies comprehension. Although his own writings have achieved much acclaim, Wiesel has said that he writes about the Holocaust to denounce writing, for words can never truly portray the nature of the evil and suffering that constituted this event (Freeman 1991; Sachar 1992; Weissman 2004).

Historians are respectful of this position, but argue against mystifying the Holocaust as beyond comprehension (Bauer 1989a; Marrus 1987). "The Holocaust was a human event," observes Yehuda Bauer, "perpetrated for human reasons which can be historically explained" (1987:209). Historians have by now succeeded in integrating the Holocaust into the mainstream of their discipline. Sociologists, on the other hand, have paid much less attention to the Holocaust and have been slower to fully integrate the genocide into sociology's corpus of disciplinary knowledge, ignoring opportunities, as Zygmunt Bauman suggests, to "show its relevance to the main themes of sociological inquiry . . . [and] feed them back into the mainstream of [the] discipline" (1989:xiii). The cause of sociology's neglect is a matter we will take up shortly, but it is arguably disconcerting to not only note sociologists' professional disinterest in the Holocaust, but also its absence in the sociological curriculum of higher education. In a survey of Holocaust courses taught in U.S. colleges and universities, for example, Stephen Haynes (1998) found that history departments accounted for more than half of the offerings, with religion/philosophy departments and foreign language/English departments each accounting for about 10 percent. The rest of the courses were divided among several other programs: Judaic studies, humanities, psychology, political science, and sociology.

The contributions of historians to the study of the Holocaust are sophisticated and vast. Their perceptive analyses and empirical documentation of the genocide constitute the primary corpus of knowledge for this book. This book represents one sociologist's engagement with this incredibly complex subject, an engagement that was first sparked in the late 1980s by an exploration of my father's story of Holocaust survival.[4] It represents a reading and comprehensive synthesis, imbued with a sociological sensibility, of the social science literature on the Holocaust. My aim is not to add to specialist knowledge of the field but to provide a disciplinary-informed selection and interpretation of the extant literature. In doing so, I focus not simply on Adolf Hitler and his coterie of Nazi collaborators as the key movers of the genocide, but also on the broader range of responsibility and participation of ordinary citizens, opportunistic businessmen, and compliant state

3

personnel, a phenomenon that Hannah Arendt (1963) referred to as the "banality of evil," which I appropriate less as a psychological construct that describes the state of mind of the perpetrators and more as a sociological construct that highlights the organizational and institutional mechanism of annihilation.[5] I will also be concerned with the aftermath of the genocide, that is, the social and political ramifications of varying postwar collective memories of the Holocaust.

This book is thus a collaboration of history and sociology, an attempt to engage the sociology of the "big range," as Irving Louis Horowitz (1964) has called it, a sociology that is historically anchored, both in its knowledge of its own disciplinary heritage and in its aim to advance sociological interpretation of historical events (see also Hall 1992; Skocpol 1987). It will be comprehensive, concerning itself with the origins, implementation, and legacy—the before, during, and after—of the archetypal genocide of our times. And it aims to counter the disciplinary segregation of "Holocaust studies as an area of inquiry onto itself," as a topic that is marginal to conventional sociology courses and general concerns of sociological inquiry, creating an "intellectual bifurcation [that] impoverishes both Holocaust studies and sociology" (Gerson and Wolf 2007:6; see also Bauman 1989; Horowitz 1993, 2002).

In this introductory chapter, I provide some additional background to American sociology's historical neglect of the Holocaust. I then consider the question of Germany's so-called special or separate path in history, and situate Nazism in the context of the broader phenomenon of totalitarianism and fascism. Next, I return to and draw upon the tradition of classical social theory to raise several sociological themes that will provide an overview and help illuminate some key issues in the study of Nazism and the Holocaust. Finally, I introduce the concept of collective memory in anticipation of our later consideration of postwar mnemonic disputes in four nations: Germany, Poland, Israel, and the United States.

Understanding Sociology's Neglect

The sociology of knowledge, popularized most notably by Karl Mannheim in his seminal work *Ideology and Utopia* (1936), has provided a framework for sociologists to interpret their own disciplinary tradition. As Louis Wirth wrote in the preface to *Ideology and Utopia*, Mannheim was concerned with "searching out . . . the motives that lie back of intellectual activity and . . . the manner and the extent to which the thought processes themselves are influenced by the participation of the thinker in the life of society. . . . [How do] the interests and purposes of certain social groups come to find expression in certain theories, doctrines, and intellectual movements?" ([1936] 1985:xxviii). As a general proposition, the sociology of knowledge offers a framework for understanding sociology's neglect of the Holocaust as an object of sociological inquiry.

In the introduction to their anthology *Sociology Confronts the Holocaust* (2007), Judith Gerson and Diane Wolf wonder whether sociology might have a "Jewish problem." "Few sociologists," they observe, "have focused their academic work on the Holocaust or post-Holocaust life. Those who have tend to be in Jewish studies programs, and thus their work is often regarded as marginal to most disciplines" (p. 3). It is arguably true that the majority of scholars who study the Holocaust are of Jewish background, but the most interesting question, Gerson and Wolf ask, is why so few sociologists, "regardless of their religious or cultural identity," have not taken up such work.

In his appraisal of sociology's historical neglect, Burton Halpert (2007) focuses on the anti-Semitism of leading American sociologists of the prewar and war years, an anti-Semitism that was a reflection of American society as a whole, during a time before and during World War II when employers, universities, and neighborhood covenants widely discriminated against Jews. Many of the founders of American sociology in the early part of the twentieth century, Halpert observes, were either clergy or sons of clergy who "advocated a social gospel calling for a Christian sociology to create a better Christian America" (2007:8). But accompanying this view were a host of common anti-Jewish stereotypes and negative attitudes toward Jews, who were viewed as unworthy people who had killed Jesus Christ and who were therefore deserving of the persecution they had endured throughout the centuries (see chapter 2).

Edward Alsworth Ross, for instance, the last president of the American Sociological Society (ASS, now the American Sociological Association) to serve two terms (1914–1915), characterized immigrant Jews as "insoluable clots" who were overrunning America and undermining the racial purity of the country (quoted in Vidich and Lyman 1985:164). Thomas Nixon Carver, an economist/sociologist who served as chair of the sociology department at Harvard University, derided the children of Jews as dirty and ill mannered (Vidich and Lyman 1985). To be sure, there were sociologists such as Charles

5

Ellwood (ASS President, 1924) and Emory Bogardus (ASS President, 1931) who spoke out against the anti-Semitism of their colleagues, but "Ellwood's fear of fascism and the danger that it portended for democracies was ridiculed within American sociology circles" (Halpert 2007:11; see also Bannister 1992; Turner 2007).

By the 1930s, the Christian reformism of this early American sociology came under criticism from within the profession as too value-laden. Edward B. Reuter (ASS President, 1933) urged his colleagues to move beyond "do-gooder" sentiments and become more scientific by emulating the natural sciences. While abandoning the reformist goal of creating a better Christian society, for the most part these scientifically minded sociologists disengaged from the central political debates of the day, most notably the rise of European fascism in the 1920s and 1930s (Gerth and Landau 1963; Mannheim 1936).

Stephen Turner notes that "[t]here is a well-entrenched belief that sociology is intrinsically an 'oppositional science,'" but cross-national analyses of sociology's engagement with fascism was anything but critical (1992:1). In the United States, the anti-Semite William Ogburn (ASS President, 1929) was a chief advocate of value neutrality, while also dismissing reports of Germany's harsh treatment of Jews with the remark, "the true enemy is emotion" (quoted in Bannister 1992:189). Ogburn "praised totalitarian regimes for their efficiencies" and rationalized "German atrocities as an unfortunate byproduct of war" (Halpert 2007:15). In a similar vein, George Lundberg (ASS President, 1943) asserted that as "a value-neutral social scientist he could function as well in Hitler's Germany as in [Franklin] Roosevelt's America" (Halpert 2007:15). When accused by his colleague Read Bain of being a Nazi, Lundberg replied that he disliked the Nazis as much as the Hebrews (Bannister 1992). After learning of the extermination of Jews, Lundberg reasserted his opposition to the intrusion of values and morality into social science: "[W]e find ... large numbers of organized and articulate Jews in their unhappy predicament devoting themselves to legalistic and moralistic conjurings so that their attention is entirely diverted from a realistic approach. . . . [T]hey demand international action outlawing anti-Semitism instead of reckoning with the causes of the antagonism in a purely scientific way" (Lundberg 1944:3).

On the other hand, there were notable sociologists such as Robert Merton (ASS President, 1957) who broke with this tradition. Merton wrote an early essay in 1937 on the responsibility of science to engage moral issues, using the case of Nazi science to illustrate the abandonment of this principle (Merton 1968).[6] There were other sociologists, too, who turned their scholarly gaze on Nazism. In *Nazi Germany: Its Women and Family Life* (1938), Clifford Kirkpatrick conducted extensive interviews with German citizens, including Nazi Party members, and concluded that Germany was embroiled in "an experiment in regression to tribal-group intimacy on a national scale by means of modern agencies of communication" (cited in Bannister 1992:195). Kirkpatrick also noted that he had "no illusions about his capacity for purely objective description." In his political outlook, he wrote, the sociologist "is liberal in the sense that he values reason, toleration and co-operation" (cited in Bannister 1992:195).

Theodore Abel was another early contributor to sociological reflection on the Holocaust. In *Why Hitler Came to Power* (1938), Abel reported on data he had collected through a contest he sponsored to find the "Best Personal Life History of an Adherent of the Nazi Movement," for which he received 683 manuscript submissions. Abel concluded that Nazism was a highly differentiated social movement that drew adherents from across the class spectrum of German society (Baehr 2002; Bannister 1992).[7]

Talcott Parsons (ASS President, 1949) is also notable for speaking out against Nazism, helping to establish the Harvard Defense Committee to mobilize public opinion against Germany, and publishing several articles and book chapters that critically analyzed the impact of Nazism on German society (Gerhardt 1993, 2002). In an analysis of Nazi scapegoating of Jews, Parsons concluded that "the most important source of virulent anti-Semitism is probably the projection of the Jew, as a symbol, of free-floating aggression, springing from insecurities and social disorganization" (cited in Bannister 1992:200).[8]

At the same time, as Halpert suggests, Parsons's critique of Nazism "seems to have derived more from his disdain of totalitarianism, which threatened academic freedom and democratic institutions, than from his sympathy" for the plight of the Jews (2007:17). After the war, he apparently helped recruit Russian collaborators of the Nazis to Harvard's Russian Institute (Wiener 1989).[9] And he never said a word about the Holocaust until just before his death in 1979, when he expressed regret for his silence in a letter to a colleague (Halpert 2007).

Even as the discipline of sociology was opened up to the value-laden civil rights, women's and other social movements of the 1960s, and internal critiques of the discipline were underway (Gouldner 1970; Horowitz 1964, 1967, 1968, 1972), the "normative order of neglect" of the Holocaust was so institutionalized as to isolate sociology from an engagement with one of the most significant events of the twentieth century (Halpert 2007:17). Bauman, who called for a reversal of this state of affairs in his 1989 book *Modernity and the Holocaust*, admits that at one time even he "believed (by default rather than by deliberation) that the Holocaust was an interruption of history, a cancerous growth . . . [or] momentary madness" that should be left to the "professional pathologists" (1989:viii).

It is disheartening to read the 900-plus page anthology *Sociology in America: A History* (2007), edited by Craig Calhoun, an American Sociological Association Centennial Publication, which mentions the Holocaust in passing in an inconsequential manner on just one page, and Nazism on just seven other pages, with none of the twenty-one contributors making these subjects the primary focus of their inquiry. The more general question of genocide, too, is mentioned on but one page, in Michael Kennedy and Miguel Centeno's chapter on "Internationalism and Global Transformation in American Sociology," where the authors note that "[m]ore scholars working on genocide identify with political science and history than with sociology. . . . Although one might argue that genocide should not be central to the American sociological imagination, it is hard to appreciate why the study of this most basic kind of inequality is not at the center of a discipline focused on power, privilege, and destitution" (2007:685).

As far back as *Genocide: State Power and Mass Murder*, published in 1976, Horowitz critiqued sociology as a secondary social science that was squeamish about fundamental issues of life and death. "Many sociologists," he wrote, "exhibit a studied embarrassment about life and death issues, feeling that intellectual issues posed in such a manner are melodramatic and unfit for scientific discourse" (1976:9–10). But it is precisely the study of genocide, he later added, which "gives to the social sciences a tool for the analysis of whole societies" (2002:43) and constitutes a necessary step in reaffirming "the worthwhileness of social-science analysis" (1993:149). Indeed, "[t]he measure of a civilization's worth is its promulgation of life or its promotion of death. This becomes a continuum for the study of human beings" (2002:258–259).

We now know that the Holocaust is too fundamental to be ignored, too traumatic an event—not just for those who experienced it, but for the entire world—to allow this state of affairs to continue. But, it is fair to ask, why yet another book? The field of Holocaust studies is replete, one may even say cluttered, with an abundance of empirical and interpretive studies, memoirs, and other literatures. It is the aim of this book to condense and distill a large portion of the social science work, boiling it down, if you will, to some of the essentials, without abandoning either sociological interpretation or empirical elaboration. I envision this effort as part of a broader intellectual project—initiated by Horowitz, Bauman, and others—aimed at remedying the marginalization of the Holocaust in the discipline to which I have devoted the whole of my professional life. I also write this book for my students, and to the students of others, who deserve to learn more about this most haunting event in human history.

Is Germany a Special Case?

For the purpose of providing historical background, and as a preface to our sociological inquiry, we begin by examining an historical interpretation that isolates Germany as a nation that lagged behind other Western countries such as Great Britain, France, and the United States in developing an Enlightenment tradition of political liberalism that valued democratic institutions and individual rights. This *Sonderweg* (special or separate path) interpretation is viewed by some historians as key to understanding the eventual rise of Nazism in Germany (Fischer 1995; Herf 1984; Maier 1988). Saul Friedländer (1989) characterizes this approach as macroscopic or "global" in orientation, as opposed to a microscopic approach that focuses on the specific events that gave rise to the Final Solution, the latter of which we will take up in later chapters.[10]

Prior to unification as a nation in 1871, Germany consisted of several independent states. Among them Prussia was the only one that had an army comparable to those of any Western European power. In 1862, Prussian King Wilhelm I appointed Otto von Bismarck as Prime Minister of Prussia. Bismarck wielded a coalition of Germanic states that fought four successful wars, established Germany as a military powerhouse, and culminated in unification. Wilhelm I became the Kaiser (emperor) of Germany and appointed Bismarck as chancellor to head the government. A parliament was established with jurisdiction over domestic matters, but the Kaiser retained control of the army and foreign policy. The chancellor served at the pleasure of the Kaiser, not the parliament (Fischer 1995; Shirer 1960).

In this way, Klaus Fischer (1995) argues, German nationhood was born not from a broad, democratic consensus arising from the grass-roots, not from a yearning of a people wishing to be free. Rather, it was imposed by the "force of superior Prussian arms" and imbued with a militaristic spirit that valued authority over democracy and obedience over autonomy (1995:19). Thus, as the country began to industrialize in the late eighteenth and early nineteenth centuries, political modernization lagged behind economic modernization and made Germany especially vulnerable to the appeals of fascist totalitarianism (Herf 1984; Maier 1988).

Donald Bloxham (2009), on the other hand, notes an important limitation of the *Sonderweg* thesis: its failure to locate the emergence of German fascism in the context of "a longer history of mass killings prompted by the rise of nationalism and the collapse of older empires" throughout Europe and the Eastern Mediterranean region in the last quarter of the nineteenth and the first half of the twentieth centuries (Mazower 2010:8). In these emergent nation-states, Bloxham observes, majority ethnic groups began a process of excluding ethnic minorities through practices that ranged from sporadic violence to forced assimilation by means of language policy, expropriation of property, and restrictions (even prohibition) of minorities from participation in various occupational, political, and administrative positions. The most genocidal of these exclusionary campaigns was arguably the state-sanctioned murder of 1 to 1.5 million Armenian Christians by the Muslim majority in Turkey in 1917 (Horowitz 2002; Mazian 1990; Rosenbaum 2009).

At the same, Bloxham (2009) acknowledges, the specificity of what transpired in Nazi Germany needs to be addressed. To begin with, we should first note a distinction between *totalitarianism* more generally and *fascism* in particular. In *The Origins of Totalitarianism*, Arendt (1951) was among the first to advance a unitary approach, viewing the differences between Nazism and Communism "as of lesser significance than the organizational and cultural linkages that such systems have with each other" (Horowitz 2002:230). As such, Fischer defines totalitarianism as "the monopolizing of human activities, private and public, by a modern technocratic state," a political system where the means of control and domination are centralized in an all-powerful government, a one-party state, where personal liberties are suppressed and social institutions such as the media and schools are compelled to serve the interests of the state (1995:4). Horowitz adds, following

Arendt, that totalitarian states exhibit "a near insatiable desire to expand from nation to empire—whether directly through military adventure or indirectly through political infiltration" (2002:230).

Martin Jay, on the other hand, makes a distinction between *right-wing* totalitarianism and *left-wing* totalitarianism, with right-wing fascism being the "counter-revolutionary rival" of left-wing Communism (1993:38). The term "fascism" has its root in the Italian *fascio*, which literally translates as a bundle or sheaf. "More remotely," as Robert Paxton explains, "the word recalled the Latin *fasces*, an axe encased in a bundle of rods that was carried before the magistrates in Roman public processions to signify the authority and unity of the state" (2004:4). Unlike Communism, fascism as a political-economic system is hospitable to private ownership of industry, as long as economic production is consistent with state objectives, which includes limits on imports to promote national economic independence, and it is restrictive of labor unions and workers' right to strike. Additionally, fascism conflates militarism and cultural nationalism, glorifying violence while expressing a nostalgic longing for the restoration of an exclusive lost community that is rooted in a people's common heritage. At the same time, it is forward-looking in its messianic vision of a glorious new day that will come about as a result of the fascist revolution (Herf 1984; Laqueur 1996; Paxton 2004; Payne 1980).

Because fascist movements are intensely nationalistic, they give rise to distinct orientations that reflect the particular circumstances and aspirations of each nation-state (Deák 1983; Paxton 2004; Payne 2001). What was characteristic of German fascism (Nazism) in the period between the two world wars—what distinguished it, for example, from Italian fascism—was the centrality of anti-Semitism to its political program and worldview. In Italy, anti-Semitism did not figure prominently in Benito Mussolini's rise to power in 1922, which preceded Hitler by over a decade, and in the ideology of Italian fascism. While Mussolini was arguably a racist and anti-Semite, his government did not openly advocate discriminatory policies against Jews until the latter part of the 1930s, when German fascism was exerting greater influence. Moreover, these policies never achieved the broad consensus of popular support that they did in Germany (Carpi 2001; De Felice 2001; Paxton 2004; Zuccotti 1987).

In Nazi Germany, on the other hand, anti-Jewish policies played a predominant role. Nazi ideology asserted that the "spiritual, moral, and physical redemption" of the German people, the German

Volk, required the purging of the Jewish blight, for "the Jew" (*der Jude*) was the source—the very essence—of all that was vile, corrupt, and evil (Bauer 2001:115). This redemptive anti-Semitism, as Friedländer (2009) calls it, envisioned a radical reordering of society premised on the elimination of Jews. It had its roots, as we shall see, in Christian anti-Semitism and in secular notions of a Jewish culture that was "spiritually inferior" (Hertzberg 1968:274). In the nineteenth century, these views were given a modern foundation through pseudoscientific theories of race. In the twentieth century, they were carried to messianic heights through Hitler's charismatic leadership (Bauer 2001; Bloxham 2009; Rose 1990; Volkov 1989).

Sociological Frameworks: The View from the Classics

Although the Holocaust begs for sociological insight, sociologists, as we have seen, have lagged behind historians in grappling with this subject matter. In the remainder of this chapter, I suggest several avenues of sociological interpretation derived from the classical tradition of social theory that will help illuminate some key issues in the study of Nazism and the Holocaust. This point of departure seems appropriate, for as Alexander suggests, "Classics are earlier works of human exploration which are given a privileged status vis-à-vis contemporary explorations in the same field. The concept of privileged status means that contemporary practitioners in the discipline in question believe that they can learn as much about their field through understanding this earlier work as they can from the work of their own contemporaries" (1989:9).

In one way or another, all classic formulations posit a theory of *social structure* and *social action*. Social structure refers to social relations that are external to individual actors, to forces that constrain behavior "by fixing in advance its material environment" (Alexander 1984:10). Social action, often referred to as human agency, suggests activity that responds to these constraints, most often conforming to or reproducing predominant structural patterns, but sometimes challenging or modifying these patterns as well (Emirbayer and Mische 1998; Sewell 1992). It entails motivated behavior, whether it is rational (instrumental) behavior based on calculation of self-interest or the means to achieve goals, or nonrational (normative) behavior based on values, moral concerns, or emotional needs that are imbued with collective symbolic meaning. We now turn to some important themes associated with the work of three classical theorists: Karl Marx, Max Weber, and Émile Durkheim (Alexander 1984; Giddens 1971; Ritzer 1992). Although these sociological giants offered different and often conflicting interpretations of society, they were all committed to the use of social science to improve the human condition (Horowitz 1993).

From Karl Marx: Capitalism and the Nazi State

Alexander considers the German social theorist Karl Marx (1818–1883) to be the "greatest theorist of social structure in the [rational] tradition" (Alexander 1984:184), and some analysts believe that much social theory has developed as a debate with Marx (Zeitlan 1990).[11] For Marx, the relationship between economic classes constitutes the basic element of social structure that constrains individual action. Members of different classes have different and often opposing economic interests, and they tend to act rationally in pursuit of these interests.

In the Marxian tradition, capitalism is understood as an economic system based on private rather than public ownership of the determinative means of production (factories, technology, raw materials), one that pits owners of capital, who wish to lower labor and production costs, against workers, who wish to improve wages and working conditions. In the aftermath of World War I, rebellious mobs of German workers were echoing their Russian counterparts in calling for the confiscation of private property and workers' control of large-scale enterprises. German elites were fearful that their country might suffer the same fate as Russia had in 1917, when the Communists seized the apparatus of the state (Fischer 1995; Poole 1997b; Shirer 1960).

As an aggressor and defeated nation of World War I,[12] Germany paid a heavy price. Under the terms of the Treaty of Versailles, the Allies forced it to accept full responsibility for the war, relinquish considerable territory, pay $33 billion in reparations, and dramatically limit the size of its armed forces. In 1919, a democratic constitutional government was established in Weimar, Germany—the Weimar Republic—but it was an unstable government that never received full popular support (Botwinick 2001; Fischer 1995; Shirer 1960). Capitalists were especially concerned about the apparent erosion of their economic power vis-à-vis the state, as the Weimar constitution guaranteed "every German a living through productive work," and if no work was available, "would provide the means necessary for a worker's livelihood" (Fischer 1995:184).

Thus Marxian interpretations of German fascism view it as the final outcome of a capitalist system in crisis, where owners of big business supported extreme measures to subvert their political opposition and secure conditions that would allow for the unfettered accumulation of profits (Brady 1937). According to R. Palme Dutt, the "open and avowed supporters of Fascism in every country are the representatives of big capital . . . [whose aim is] to defeat the working-class revolution and smash the working-class organizations" (1935:100, 102). During the Nazi period these capitalists went even further, hoping to exploit the Jews and others as slave laborers. This interpretation, of course, leaves unanswered the question of why capitalists would favor a policy of extermination that destroyed this slave labor pool. Nor does it account for the virulent nature of Nazi anti-Semitism (Friedländer 1989).

Moreover, this Marxian thesis lacks empirical support. In his book *German Big Business and the Rise of Hitler*, Henry Ashby Turner (1985) notes that the leaders of the largest German corporations did not as a rule support Hitler's quest for power. Turner defines German "big business" as "large-scale private enterprises owned and operated by Germans in the fields of commerce, finance, industry, and insurance" (1985:xv).[13] The early growth of the Nazi Party took place without significant support from these corporate enterprises, and throughout the 1920s the Nazis "languished in disrepute in the eyes of most men of big business" (1985:342). Only two major industrialists—Ernst von Borsig and Fritz Thyssen—stand out as significant financial contributors to the Party. And many capitalists were apprehensive about the Nazis' tax policies and support of price controls, trade restrictions, and job creation through deficit spending that they thought were contrary to their interests (Fischer 1995; James 2001; Spielvogel and Redles 2010).

Richard Hamilton adds that big business is "not ordinarily . . . interested in radical transformation of existing institutional arrangements" but in the preservation of social order (1982:429). Before Hitler acquired power, most capitalists who were sympathetic to the Nazis viewed them primarily as "support troops in a broad conservative nationalist alliance" (1982:429). They did, on the other hand, eventually allow the Nazis into this alliance and grant them legitimacy by "inviting Hitler and other party spokesmen to address their gatherings" (Turner 1985:348).

Still another Marxian interpretation views disunity within the German capitalist class and conflict between the capitalist class and working class as creating a "class stalemate [that] allowed the state to escape domination by a ruling [economic] elite and to emerge with autonomous power as a dictatorial apparatus" (Maier 1988:88).[14] Marx ([1852] 1963) first advanced an interpretation like this in his study of Napoleon Bonaparte's rise to power in France in 1799. According to this view, Bonapartism, which some consider an early fascist state, imposed a dictatorship precisely in the economic elites' own interests, which it could not guarantee under a democratic political regime (Maier 1988:88; see also Abraham 1981). This view of Nazism, however, is contradicted by the fact that the Nazis had their own political and ideological agenda that was not subservient (and was often contrary) to capitalist interests (Turner 1985).[15]

In a study of IG Farben, a German chemical conglomerate that was the largest European corporation of that era, Peter Hayes (1987) observes that capitalists tended to follow rather than lead Nazism. "To a mounting degree," especially after the war broke out, IG Farben "became a mere executor of government orders; and technical possibilities, not financial or commercial considerations, dominated the [managing board's] decisions" (1987:326). Nevertheless, German industry proved itself capable of pursuing its ordinary profit-making ambitions under rather extraordinary conditions (the banality of evil), as it exploited Jewish and other slave laborers and manufactured whatever was necessary for the war effort and the Final Solution (such as poisonous gas and crematory ovens) (see chapter 4). Nazi economic policy was based on the recognition "that so long as a state displays its determination but permits businessmen to make money, they will let themselves be manipulated as to how" (1987:379). Thus the Nazis understood that business "interests are not immutable . . . but . . . capable of restatement according" to the political context (1987:379). Indeed, many big businesses not only survived but thrived during the Nazi era (Fischer 1995; Hayes 1998; Simpson 1993; Spielvogel and Redles 2010).

Even the record of non-German international firms is instructive here, with the United States offering numerous examples. According to Christopher Simpson's account, in the 1930s U.S. corporate investment in Nazi Germany "was expanding more rapidly . . . than in any other country in Europe . . . as U.S. companies sought to buy into European markets at bargain prices" (1993:11, 47). Major U.S.

15

corporations—Anaconda, Ford Motor Company, General Motors, Goodrich, International Business Machines,[16] International Harvester, International Telephone and Telegraph, Standard Oil of New Jersey, Texaco, and the United Fruit Company—were involved as well. Some of these companies invested heavily in German military vehicle and weapons production, operated German subsidiaries during the war years, and even had joint investments with German corporations that exploited concentration camp labor and profited from the plunder of Jewish property (Billstein et al. 2001; Black 2009; Matthews 2006). In 1937, the U.S. Ambassador to Germany, William Dodd, complained:

> A clique of U.S. industrialists is hell-bent to bring a fascist state to supplant our democratic government and is working closely with the fascist regime in Germany and Italy. I have had plenty of opportunity in my post in Berlin to witness how close some of our American ruling families are to the Nazi regime. On [the ship] a fellow passenger, who is a prominent executive of one of the largest financial corporations, told me point blank that he would be ready to take definite action to bring fascism into America if President Roosevelt continued his progressive policies. (quoted in Higham 1983:167)

Indeed, some prominent figures in major U.S. corporations were known Nazi sympathizers. In 1933, William Knudsen, president of General Motors called Hitler's Germany "the miracle of the twentieth century" (quoted in Higham 1983:63). By the mid-1930s, according to Charles Higham's account, his corporation "was committed to full-scale production of trucks, armored cars, and tanks in Nazi Germany" (1983:166). Walter Teagle, chairman of Standard Oil of New Jersey and director of a U.S. subsidiary of IG Farben, was a close friend of Henry Ford, whose anti-Semitic publications inspired Hitler (see chapter 2). In the early war years, between 1939 and 1941, Standard Oil provided Hitler's regime with much needed synthetic rubber, and even after the United States entered the war, it shipped gasoline to Spain that was transferred to Germany, in spite of desperate fuel shortages that existed in the United States at the time (Black 2009; Matthews 2006).

Six months before the outbreak of World War II, Chase National Bank (later named Chase Manhattan Bank) offered Nazi sympathizers in the United States an opportunity to buy German marks with dollars at discount rates. Pamphlets were sent out informing potential investors that "Germany could offer glorious opportunities to them and that marks would provide a hedge against inflation and would have much increased value after victory in the expected war" (Higham 1983:23). During the war, Chase kept its European branches open in "neutral" countries and in France. Its Paris branch "poured millions of francs into various French companies that were collaborating with the Nazis" (pp. 26–27). Its branch in the Vichy region of France enthusiastically enforced measures to expropriate Jewish property, "even going so far as to refuse to release funds belonging to Jews because they anticipated a Nazi decree with retroactive provisions prohibiting such release" (p. 25). Chase also acted as an intermediary for Nazis wishing to launder money into South America, handling transactions for the Nazi Banco Aleman Transatlantico, which was, according to a report by the Uruguayan embassy, "the actuality treasurer or comptroller of the Nazi Party in South America" (cited on p. 26).

From Max Weber: Bureaucracy and the Nazi State

More than Marx, the German theorist Max Weber (1864–1920) understood that the actions of the state are not simply derivative of economic relationships and that political power could be "sharply differentiated from economic power" (Alexander 1984:3; Gerth and Mills 1946).[17] Moreover, as Horowitz (2002) notes, the intentional involvement of the state in the killing of innocent people is the *sin qua non* of the phenomenon of genocide, what distinguishes it from other forms of mass atrocity and disaster.

Weber's full body of work is wide ranging, but for our purposes his most important contribution is his emphasis on the predominant role of bureaucracy in modern social life. According to Weber, bureaucracy is not simply a mode of organization but an apparatus that can be used to exercise power, including, as Horowitz suggests, the power to commit genocide. It does this by demanding efficiency and impersonality in the achievement of goals, by providing subordinates with authorization from superiors, by separating and diffusing responsibility, and by routinizing tasks (Bauman 1989; Kelman and Hamilton 1989; Markle 1995).

Hilberg (1961, 1985) argues that it was the bureaucratic administration of death that made the Holocaust unprecedented and distinguished it from a pogrom or mob action. Instrumental rationality supplanted rage, and it was "the technology of action, not its substance" that was "subject to assessment as good or bad, proper or improper, right or wrong" (Bauman 1989:160). Personal feelings—of both the bureaucrat and the target of his actions—were set aside, as

17

the obligation to follow bureaucratic rules was "substituted for moral responsibility" and as authorization from superiors negated the "authority of the private conscience" (Markle 1995:72). Rudolf Höss, the commandant of Auschwitz, explained it this way: "It didn't even occur to me . . . that I could be held responsible. . . . [I]t was understood that if something went wrong, then the man who gave the orders was responsible" (quoted in Gilbert 1950:255). Similarly, a Gestapo interrogator recalled: "I was simply doing my duty—no more no less! I had nothing to be ashamed of" (quoted in Engelmann 1986:280).

In the bureaucratic division of labor, each individual is delegated a small portion of responsibility, and the interconnections between the coordinated actions are often unclear (Bauman 1989). During the Holocaust, this made it easier for participants to forget "the nature of the product" (that is, death) that emerged from the process and to rationalize that what they were doing was not so egregious (Kelman and Hamilton 1989:18). Thus Franz Grassler, the deputy commissioner of the Warsaw Jewish ghetto, could contend: "Our job was to maintain the ghetto and try to preserve the Jews as a work force. . . . [The] goal . . . was very different from the one that later led to extermination" (quoted in Lanzmann 1985:182). And Walter Stier, who booked Jews on the *Reichsbahn* (German State Railways) so they could be transported to Treblinka, claimed he did not know that Treblinka was in fact a death camp: "Good God, no! . . . I never went to Treblinka. I stayed in Krakow, in Warsaw, glued to my desk. . . . I was strictly a bureaucrat!" (quoted in Lanzmann 1985:135–36).

To a large extent, it was the routinization of tasks, the very mundaneness of the work, that allowed some to convince themselves that what they were doing was "perfectly normal, correct, and legitimate" (Kelman and Hamilton 1989:18). Stier recalled that his "work was barely different from . . . [any other] work, . . . preparing timetables [and] coordinating the movement of . . . trains" (quoted in Lanzmann 1985:133). Writing of the so-called desk murderers, Hilberg observes: "The questions with which these [bureaucrats] were concerned were almost always technical. . . . How were the borders of a ghetto to be drawn? What was to be the disposition of pension claims belonging to deported Jews? How should the bodies be disposed? These were the problems [they] pondered in their memoranda, correspondence, meetings, and discussions" (1989:120–21). Knowing all this, the phenomenon of the banality of evil can be understood more fully: Ordinary bureaucratic processes were used to accomplish extraordinary deeds.

From Émile Durkheim: Social Solidarity and the Civil Sphere

In one way or another, both Marx and Weber were concerned with the ways in which external social structures affected the rational nature of social action (Alexander 1984). In doing so, they downplayed the ways in which actors' internal (psychological) dispositions were constituted by nonrational considerations. It was the French sociologist Émile Durkheim (1858–1917) who better understood that "social structure is located as much within the actor as without" and that a normative "collective conscience"—the "totality of beliefs and sentiments common to average citizens of the same society" (Durkheim [1893] 1964:79)—provides the normative glue that holds society together by "penetrating and socializing individual consciences" (Alexander 1984:9, 15).[18] The collective conscience, according to Durkheim, consists of "collective representations"—culturally shared symbols, systems of meaning, or categorization systems—that divide the world "into contradictory patterns of sacred and profane," into that which is good and that which is evil (Alexander 1984:5; see also Douglas 1966; Durkheim [1915] 1965). Alexander (2006) characterizes this normative order as the "civil sphere," the arena of social solidarity that exists outside the economy, state, and other social institutions, which constitutes the sense of "we-ness" or connectedness that members of a society feel for one another, the sense of who belongs and who does not belong to the group.

Earlier we noted that Nazi anti-Semitism characterized the Jew as the very essence of the profane, of all that was vile, corrupt, and evil. Nazism, however, did not create this representation out of "whole cloth." As we will explore in more detail in chapter 2, anti-Semitism was pervasive throughout Christian Europe, and the "Jewish question" was arguably the central question facing nations that were grappling with the issue of how to absorb (or not absorb) marginalized minorities who were unwelcome in the civil sphere of solidarity as defined by the core majority of the nation (Alexander 2006). In Germany in particular, even before the Nazis, Jews were viewed as the "malevolent and corrosive . . . opposite of the German," and German anti-Semitism provided the Nazis with a powerful symbolic code that expressed reverence for German culture by rejecting all that was not of it (Goldhagen 1996:55). Although a distinction should be made between the violent anti-Semitic impulses of the Nazis and the moderate anti-Semitism that was commonplace among Germans, all too many were indifferent to the Jews' plight and readily accepted their legal disenfranchisement (Browning 1998; Volkov 1989).[19]

Daniel Goldhagen (1996) argues that explanations of the Holocaust often fail to acknowledge the fundamental fact that the Nazis' primary victims were Jews, and that Jews were not considered to be legitimate Germans. Many explanations, he observes, do not "emphasize the autonomous motivating force . . . of antisemitism, . . . [as if] the perpetrators would have treated any other group of intended victims in exactly the same way" (p. 13).[20] While Goldhagen has been critiqued for his claim that German anti-Semitism was constituted by an "eliminationist" strain that was not typical of most Germans who were attracted to Nazism for other reasons, such as their economic program, appeal to nationalism, or anticommunist stance (Augstein 1998; Browning 1998; see chapter 3), like Durkheim, he wants us to understand individuals' beliefs and values as central factors that account for their conduct vis-à-vis others.

If social action is understood as nonrational behavior imbued with symbolic meaning, then the perpetrators of the Holocaust can be viewed as not entirely coerced, as not simply following orders, but as acting out of conviction that what they were doing was right, or at least not thinking that what they were doing was wrong. As Goldhagen notes, many explanations treat the perpetrators as if they were "people lacking a moral sense, lacking the ability to make decisions and take stances" (1996:13). Although they "were working within institutions that prescribed roles for them and assigned them specific tasks, . . . they individually and collectively had latitude to make choices regarding their actions," and thus to some degree their participation may be considered voluntary (p. 15).

Comments from members of the Order Police (*Ordungspolizei*), who participated in the shooting of innocent Jewish men, women, and children are instructive on this point. The Order Police, who were deployed in Nazi-occupied Poland, were comprised largely of ordinary Germans who were not Nazi Party members and who had received no training in the killing of civilians (see chapter 4). As one man remarked, "Under the influence of the times, my attitude to the Jews was marked by a certain aversion" (quoted in Browning 1992:182). Another admitted, "Truthfully I must say that at the time we didn't reflect about it at all. Only years later did any of us become truly conscious of what had happened then. . . . Only later did it first occur to me that [the killing of Jews] had not been right" (p. 72).

Although Durkheim believed that "[m]an is a moral being only because he lives in society," Bauman thinks that Durkheim was entirely too sanguine about the positive functions of morality in reinforcing social solidarity (quoted in Bauman 1989:172). To the contrary, Bauman suggests, morality may reside not in the observance of the normative moral order but in the subordination of it, "in action openly defying social solidarity and consensus" (1989:177). In Nazi Germany, however, all too many Germans lacked the moral socialization to extend their feeling of connectedness to Jews, who remained outside "the circle of people with reciprocal obligations to protect each other" (Fein 1979:4).

Collective Memories of the Holocaust

The Holocaust, as noted earlier, was not only a traumatic event for those who experienced it, but for the entire world. And in the ensuing postwar decades, individuals, groups, and nations as a whole have tried to grapple with its meaning. Taken together, these efforts can be understood in terms of the phenomenon of collective memory, a concept first developed by Maurice Halbwachs (1877–1945), a disciple of Durkheim, to advance understanding of the collective conscience and the social and political mechanisms for accomplishing social solidarity ([1950] 1980, 1992).

In general, collective memory entails the ways in which historical events are recollected in group context, if they are recollected at all, for collective memory entails both the remembering and the forgetting of the past. While collective memory is constructed, in part, by members of a society who actually lived through an event, it is also constructed by subsequent generations who represent the past vicariously through books, films, memorials, museums, and so forth. These cultural representations infuse disparate individuals' memories with common symbolic meaning, creating a sense of shared values, ideals, and solidarity that connects "successive generations with one another" (Durkheim [1893] 1964:80). As Robert Bellah and colleagues observe, communities (including nations) have a history and "in an important sense are constituted by their past. . . . [F]or this reason we can speak of a real community as a 'community of memory' . . . [that is] involved in retelling its story, its constitutive narrative" (1985:153).

At the level of the nation-state, it creates what Pierre Nora (1986) calls a "memory-nation."

According to collective memory theory, varying collective agents, or social carriers of memory, often compete with each other in both national and international arenas to establish particular narratives of the past as the "master frame" that foregrounds certain elements and backgrounds or erases others. These memories are constructed in light of present concerns and interests, which are not so much "*causes* by which memories are produced, but *contexts* in which memories are contested, selected, and cultivated" (Schwartz 1991:317, my emphasis). As such, collective memories often become embroiled in political disputes as they are strategically manipulated by social actors to alter the balance of power between groups (Berger 2002).[21]

In the later chapters of this book, we will examine these processes at work in four postwar national contexts of Holocaust memory construction: Germany, Poland, Israel, and the United States. We will see how the manner in which the Holocaust has been remembered has by no means been self-evident from the facticity of the event itself, and how the "relationship between remembered pasts and constructed presents is one of . . . perpetual renegotiation over time" (Olick and Levy 1997:934). We will also see how collective memories of the Holocaust have become globalized, as the memories of individual nations interpenetrate with each other (Berger 2002; Levy and Sznaider 2006).

Notes

1.   According to data compiled by Israel Gutman and Robert Rozett (1990), the Holocaust took the lives of 5.6–5.9 million Jews out of an initial population of about 9.8 million living in Europe and the Soviet Union. Their data "are of special importance because they are not the work of a single researcher trying to encompass all of Europe; rather, they are the work of a number of scholars, each working in his own area of expertise" (p. 1798).

The Nazis, of course, did not use the term Holocaust to describe the Final Solution, and postwar German historians are more likely to employ "descriptive terminology such as 'Nazi policy' (*Judenpolitik*) or the 'policy/policies of annihilation' (*Vernichtungspolitik*)" (Bloxham and Kushner 2005). Zev Garber (1994) credits Elie Wiesel with first bringing the term "Holocaust" into popular discourse when he began using it in print in the late 1950s. It has its etymological roots in Greek and the Greek translation of the Hebrew Bible where the terms *holokaustos, holokaustuma*, and *holokaustosis* (based on the Hebrew *'olah*) are used to refer to a sacrificial burnt offering made to God. For this reason, some people object to it being used to describe the genocide of the Jews. It is now generally taken to mean total destruction by fire, thus alluding to the open-air pits and crematoria that the Nazis used to dispose of the dead bodies of Jews (Laqueur 1980; Rubenstein and Roth 1987). When used with a lower case "h," holocaust is employed by some to refer to genocide more generally, but Yehuda Bauer (2001) prefers to limit its application to an analytical category that designates genocides that target an entire group for complete annihilation. In Israel and among many religious Jews, the term *Shoah* is preferred, which in Hebrew means "catastrophic destruction." Shoah also has a connotation that adds an element of doubt and even despair regarding the role of divine judgment and retribution (Rubenstein and Roth 1987).

2. Five million is the figure most often used to refer to the number of noncombatant Gentiles who were killed. This number is attributed to an assertion by Simon Wiesenthal, but it substantially underestimates the number of non-Jewish deaths (Bloxham 2009; Novick 1999; Rubenstein and Roth 1987). Moreover, various demographic projections of Jewish birth and death rates suggest that, if not for the Holocaust, the number of *additional* Jews who would have been alive in the year 2000 would have been 7.3 to 20 million (DellaPergola 1996).

3. Following the Jews, the Gypsies are the group that the Nazis appear to have targeted for the most thorough elimination (Bloxham 2009; Hancock 2009; Lewy 1999).

4. My father and uncle were the only two survivors of our extended Jewish family in Poland who had not immigrated before the war to survive. As was true of many other survivors, they did not talk about their experience for many years, in their case, for over four decades (Berger 1995, 2011).

5. Arendt, as is well known, advanced the "banality of evil" construct in her book *Eichmann in Jerusalem* (1963), a report on the trial of Adolf Eichmann held in Israel in 1961 (see chapter 8). Eichmann, a former traveling salesman, was the leading Nazi expert on Jewish affairs and a key engineer of the Final Solution. Psychiatrists at the trial remarked that he seemed clinically well-adjusted and had positive relationships with family and friends. Eichmann denied that he held any ill-feeling toward Jews and claimed that he joined the Nazi Party to further his career, not to pursue an anti-Semitic ideological objective, representing himself as a man who "would have done the same job if he had been ordered to kill all men whose name began with P or B, or all who had red hair" (Askenasy 1978:27). This representation, however, misrepresents Eichmann's ideological fanaticism, "his obsessive determination to hunt down and destroy every last Jew he could get his hands on, even when, as the tide of war turned, both the time and power to do so were deserting him" (Clendinnen 1999:103).

6. Robert Lynd and Robert MacIver are also noteworthy for their concerns about value neutrality (Kuznick 1987; MacIver 1941).

7. After the war, Abel (1951) was one of the first sociologists to study human behavior in the concentration camps (see also Adler 1958; Bloch 1947).

8. Parsons also had an influence on Seymour Martin Lipset's *Political Man* (1960), which has been described as one of "the fullest account[s] of fascism by an American-born sociologist" (Bannister 1992:201).

9. Parsons's defenders note that it was Harvard anthropologist Clyde Kluckholm, not Parsons, who initiated these recruitment efforts, and

that some of the alleged collaborators were not pro-Nazis but anti-Soviet Communists who sought a German alliance for their opposition to Joseph Stalin (Banister 1992).

10. Horowitz identifies four stages in the evolution of Holocaust studies: "The first stage is biographical and autobiographical, followed by a second stage of ethnographies of survivors and victimizers. The third stage is dominated by historians and social scientific efforts to examine the 'logic' of mass murder. The fourth stage . . . is microanalysis, in which sharp and clear distinctions are made between different treatment of victims in a variety of regions, states, nations, and even concentration camps. . . . [T]hese four stages do not negate one another but co-exist in the lasting if uneasy effort to understand the Holocaust" (2009:493).

11. Both of Marx's parents were from rabbinical families, but for business reasons his father converted to Lutheranism, and Marx was baptized as a Christian. In his writings, Marx disparaged religion and Judaism in particular. In his rather anti-Semitic essay, "On the Jewish Question," he characterized Jews as a parasitic group whose religiosity and class outlook needed to be transcended (Ritzer 1992; Rose 1990).

12. The backdrop of World War I, as Bloxham (2009) observes, was the quest for contested territory among the emergent European nation-states. In this quest, Germany was arguably a leading aggressor. In 1914, Francis Ferdinand, the Archduke of Austria-Hungary, was assassinated while traveling through Sarajevo, Serbia. With a promise of support from Germany, Austria-Hungary used this incident as an excuse to attack Serbia, its long-time enemy. Russia, Serbia's ally, began mobilizing troops on the Austria-Hungary border. Germany then declared war on Russia and also invaded Belgium and France. (France and Russia were allies.) Soon Great Britain and eventually the United States were drawn into World War I, and Germany was defeated in 1918.

13. This sector of the economy was marked by a high degree of capital concentration, with comparatively few corporations owning a disproportionately large percentage of economic assets. These companies were also characterized by a high degree of vertical integration, as many produced their own sources of energy as well as the raw materials needed for their products (Turner 1985).

14. The capitalist class is not a unified group and is itself composed of different segments or factions that may have competing interests (Jessop 2002; Wright 1978). Poole (1997b) argues that in Germany between the two world wars, *light industry* (e.g., electrical, chemical, textiles) and *commercial establishments* (e.g., department stores, retail merchants) that produced or sold consumer goods, favored "a policy of collaboration with organized labor" that would improve economic "prosperity by restoring the purchasing power of the people" (1997b:135). *Heavy industry* (e.g., iron, steel, and mining), on the other hand, "wanted lower labor costs that would give them an advantage in world markets" (1997b:36). Heavy industry also favored an expansionist foreign policy that would allow them to profit from government munitions orders and help them obtain needed raw materials. However, as Turner (1985) points out, some of the major firms were conglomerates, owning companies in diverse areas of the economy,

thus making the distinction between heavy and light industry somewhat obsolete.

15. In addition to its focus on big business, Marxian interpretations posit a class-based theory of fascism based on the thesis of a declining lower-middle class (see Marx and Engels [1848] 1948). According to this view, members of the lower-middle class (such as small shopkeepers, artisans, farmers) live at the margins of the middle class and are anxious about falling into the ranks of the working class or unemployed (Lipset 1960). In Germany, members of this class blamed their precarious position on competition from Jews, even though it was competition from larger financial enterprises that most threatened their livelihood. The Nazis' anti-Semitic rhetoric and policies appealed to this lower-middle-class group, "for it legitimated hostility toward the hated Jewish competitor while providing an ideological basis for community with the owners of large-scale business and the managers of large-scale government" (Rubenstein and Roth 1987:105). Voting patterns in pre-Nazi Germany support this analysis insofar as a higher proportion of the lower-middle class (in comparison to the upper, upper-middle, and working classes), voted for the Nazi Party. However, since the working class constituted the largest proportion of the voting public, it was "of equal importance in determining the result" (Hamilton 1982:46).

    A word also should be said of two other class constituencies that supported the Nazis but that are left out of both the lower-middle class and big-business interpretations of Nazism. One group includes businessmen who occupied a position between the lower-middle and big-business class, entrepreneurs who felt threatened by the "increasingly cutthroat competition for shrinking markets" (Turner 1985:344). The other group includes salaried white-collar workers in clerical, sales, and similar occupations who jealously guarded what they believed to be their superior status vis-à-vis blue-collar workers, and who were decidedly anti-Semitic, nationalist, and supportive of efforts to suppress labor unions (Speier 1986).

16. IBM had developed what at the time was an innovative computing technology, the Hollerith, a machine that processed data stored on punch cards. These machines were used by the Nazis to help organize deportations of Jews and to process them at concentration camps, including Auschwitz (Black 2001).

17. Weber's father was a bureaucrat and his mother an intensely religious woman. While Weber was not religious himself, he was an astute observer of the history of the world's faiths (Gerth and Mills 1946; Ritzer 1992).

18. Durkheim was descended from a long line of rabbis and studied to be a rabbi himself. However, by his teens he had become an agnostic, and his interest in religion turned from the theological to the academic (Ritzer 1992).

19. The Holocaust, of course, can by no means be attributed to anti-Semitism alone. Moreover, Germany was arguably not the most anti-Semitic country in Europe, and collaboration of non-Germans with the Nazis was widespread, as we will explore in more detail in later chapters (Browning 1998; Deák, Gross, and Judt 2000; Marrus 1987; Rubenstein and Roth 1987).

20. In addition to Berger (2011), Levy and Sznaider (2006), Novick (1999), Schwartz (1996), and Young (1993), see Berger (2011:207–208, note 24) for a more complete list of the expansive literature on collective memory of the Holocaust. For a review of the more general literature on social memory studies, see Olick and Robbins (1998).

21. They are part of the phenomenon that Murray Edelman (1977) referred to as "symbolic politics."

2

Why the Jews?

Why the Jews? This is the question we must address, because the Nazi antipathy toward the Jews has deep-seated roots. The Nazis drew upon a centuries-old tradition of Christian anti-Semitism rooted in religious hostility and combined it with a strident German nationalism and pseudoscientific theory of race to articulate, in Émile Durkheim's terms, a powerful collective representation of the Jew, one that endowed them with symbolic "pollution powers" to undermine all that was good in German society (see Alexander 2006; Douglas 1966). As Irving Louis Horowitz notes, paraphrasing George Mosse (1978), in Nazi Germany "racism so infected Christianity that in the end no real battle between racism and Christianity ever took place" (2002:22). Such professed Christian virtues as "cleanliness, honesty, moral earnestness, hard work, and family life" made an "unholy reliance" with racism, as these virtues "were presumed absent in the Jewish people as a 'race'" (see chapters 4 and 5).

In this chapter, we review the ancient origins of the Jewish people, as recounted in the Bible, and address the question of how they came to occupy a pariah social status in the course of world history. We then consider the emergence of Christianity and Christian anti-Semitism and the paradox of the Enlightenment's emancipation of the Jews, reserving coverage of the Church's response to and complicity in the Holocaust until later chapters of the book. Finally, we examine the emergence of biological racism and racial anti-Semitism, including the rise of the eugenics movement and the manner in which eugenics was applied by the Nazis.

Before turning to this review, it is worth noting a distinction between religion as a theological system of thought and action, and social science as a secular examination of religion as a social institution and ritualistic practice. This was indeed the task Durkheim set for himself in making religion the object of sociological analysis in his classic study *The Elementary Forms of Religious Life* ([1915] 1965). As he wrote, his

27

study rested on the "postulate that the unanimous sentiment of the believers . . . cannot be purely illusory" (p. 464).

> [W]e admit that these beliefs rest upon a specific experience whose demonstrative value is, in one sense, not one bit inferior to that of [the scientific method]. . . . It is said that science denies religion. . . . But religion exists; it is a system of given facts; in a word, it is a reality. How could science deny this reality? . . . [I]n so far as religion is action, and in so far as it is a means of making men live, science could not take its place. . . . [I]t may well seek to explain the faith, but by that very act it presupposes it. Thus there is no conflict [between religion and science] except upon one limited point, [religion's] speculative function. That which science refuses to grant to religion is not its right to exist, but its right to dogmatize upon the nature of things and the special competence which it claims for itself for knowing man and the world. (pp. 465, 478)

In other words, for Durkheim, science, including the sociology of religion, does not aim to deny the reality of religious belief but rather its claim to superior knowledge on matters of which it does not know. As such, when we draw upon biblical accounts in the following pages, we make no claims as to the truth of divine revelation. For our purposes, it is enough to note that although people may believe them to be true, it does not necessarily "follow that the reality which is its foundation, conforms objectively to the idea which believers have of it" (p. 465).

The Biblical Jews

The Jews as a distinct group in human history trace their origins to the ancient patriarch Abraham, who religious scholars think lived in southern Mesopotamia (now southeastern Iraq) somewhere between 2000 and 1900 BCE (Rubenstein and Roth 1987). According to biblical accounts, Abraham was chosen by God to "Leave your country, your people and your father's household and go to the land I will show you" (*Genesis* 12:1, cited in Gitlin and Leibovitz 2010:4). Abraham subsequently led a mass migration of tribes of different origin, who at that time were called Hebrews (and later Israelites), southward into Canaan (later Palestine and then Israel).[1]

It was not until the time of Moses, however, around 1300 BCE, that the people who became known as the Jews adopted a common faith. According to biblical sources, Moses was born during the reign of Seti I, Pharaoh of Egypt, at a time when the Hebrews were slaves. Fearful that the Hebrew population was getting too large, Seti I ordered the killing of every newborn Hebrew male. But Moses survived after his mother put him in the Nile River in a reed basket, upon which he was discovered by an Egyptian princess, who raised him, along with Moses's mother, in Pharaoh's court.

Although Moses enjoyed many of the privileges of the Egyptian nobility, he retained his Hebrew identity and sympathized with the plight of the oppressed. On one occasion, he witnessed an Egyptian soldier beating a Hebrew slave. Moses intervened and killed him, and then fled to the desert, where he lived with a tribe called the Midianites. It is there that Moses had his famous biblical encounter with the burning bush that was not consumed by its own fire, and Moses came to believe that the God called Yahweh ("The One who causes to be") directed him to return to Egypt to lead the Hebrew slaves out of bondage (Ausubel 1964; Rubenstein and Roth 1987).

The biblical story of Passover recounts the Hebrews' exodus from Egypt and Moses's receipt of the Ten Commandments from God on the top of Mount Sinai. It was at this point that the Jews and Judaism as a distinct people and theological faith came into being; and Yahweh, the God of Moses, was identified as the God of Abraham and his descendents. After years wandering in the desert, the Jews finally settled in Canaan; and after much warfare and division, the Hebrews who settled in the southern kingdom of Judea (or Judah) came to be identified as Jews (Ausubel 1964; Johnson 1987; Rubenstein and Roth 1987).

According to biblical accounts, upon receiving the Ten Commandments, the Jewish people had entered into an historic *covenant* with God, whereby they would become God's "chosen people" and be delivered to the "promised land," provided that they obeyed all of God's laws. If they failed to obey, however, God's wrath would be mighty (Gitlin and Leibovitz 2010; Rubenstein and Roth 1987).

The Emergence of Christianity

"The historic Jesus, as opposed to Jesus as the object of religious veneration," was born in Bethlehem, a small town in the province of Judea, to Mary and Joseph of Galilee (Botwinick 2001:11).[2] He lived during a time of Roman occupation of the region, and at the time of his crucifixion, under the control of the Roman military governor Pontius Pilate.

Jews of that era lived in anticipation of the arrival of a messiah, not a literal son of God but a divinely inspired human like Moses, who would bring the Kingdom of God to humankind here on earth—not in heaven, as Christians later came to believe (Ausubel 1964). By most accounts Jesus was a devout Jew, a Jewish Rabbi, which suggests he was not only a religious teacher but someone with the recognized authority to interpret Scripture (Bivin 2004). At what point he and his disciples came to believe that he was indeed the expected messiah is unclear, but his emphasis "on love of one's neighbor, on the need for repentance, [and] on liberation of the oppressed" was an appealing message (Rubenstein and Roth 1987:33). He was also critical of the Jewish leadership for exploiting the poor and allowing the Holy Temple in Jerusalem to be used as a marketplace.

Biblical accounts implicate one of his disciples, Judas Iscariot, in turning Jesus over to the Sanhedrin, the Jewish High Court, which charged him with blasphemy and false messianic claims and consigned him to the Roman authorities. Under Roman law the Sanhedrin had no jurisdiction over capital offenses, and crucifixion was a method of "punishment that was exclusively the prerogative of Roman courts of law and reserved for political prisoners" (Rubenstein and Roth 1987:33). In a biblical account that was written about a century later, Pontius Pilate is said to have been reluctant to execute Jesus and offered the Jewish crowd outside the courthouse a choice between sparing Jesus or Barabbas, a convicted murderer. As the story goes, the crowd chose Barabbas (Ausubel 1964; Botwinick 2001).

According to Richard Rubenstein and John Roth, "Neither Jesus nor his followers intended to establish a new religion, although their intentions did entail purification and reform of the Jewish faith" (1987:32). Had his disciples not come to "believe—and were able to convince others—that Jesus was resurrected from death . . . his demise would probably have given him no more than a footnote in history" (1987:33). But his followers did come to believe that he had been resurrected and then ascended to heaven; that he was literally God's chosen son (not just a holy man), born of the Virgin Mary; that he had died for the people's sins; and that he was expected to return and lead true believers to everlasting life in the heavenly kingdom. The historic Jesus had now become Jesus Christ, which translates as Jesus the Messiah, and Christians the followers of Christ, their Lord and Savior (Bloom 2005; Botwinick 2001).

The most noteworthy post-crucifixion Christian who developed and elaborated these doctrines was Saul of Tarsus, known as Paul of the New Testament, who, like Jesus during his lifetime, was an observant Jew. One of Paul's most seminal innovations was the idea that Jesus's teachings did not simply apply to Jews, but to everyone.[3] Whereas the initial efforts of Christian evangelicals had been aimed at Jews, the church would now be *catholica*, or universal. As a result of Paul's gospel, Christians came to view their parent Jewish faith as only "preparatory to Christianity," and they reinterpreted the Hebrew Bible, now called the Old Testament, as anticipating the Christian faith, as espoused in the New Testament (Botwinick 2001:13). Thus, for example, Christians no longer required believers to follow many of the proscribed religious practices of the Jews, such as circumcision and dietary laws. Christianity was not a reform of Judaism, but an entirely distinct religious faith. Years later, when the Roman emperor Constantine converted to Christianity in the early fourth century, Christianity had triumphed as the religion of the state (Bloom 2005; Friedländer 2009; Rubenstein and Roth 1987).

Christian Anti-Semitism

Anti-Semitism is a relatively modern term. Its introduction into popular usage is credited to the German racist ideologue William Marr, who used the term in his book *The Victory of Judaism over Germanism*, published in the 1870s, to refer to different language-speaking groups—Aryan (Indo-European) and Semitic (Middle Eastern)—as separate races (Rose 1990). Of the Jews Marr wrote, "I believe Judaism, because it is a racial particularity, is incompatible with our political and social life" (cited in Rose 1990:282). But before there was racial anti-Semitism, there was Christian anti-Semitism.

Once Christianity was established as a distinct religion, Judaism and Christianity became each others' "disconfirming other," whereby genuine belief in the veracity of one required belief in the falsity of the other (Rubenstein and Roth 1987:43). During the centuries that followed the death of Christ and the evangelical teachings of Paul, however, the power differentials between these disconfirming faiths was immensely unequal. As we bring our account up to the Middle Ages, Jews had by now immigrated and been dispersed throughout the Mediterranean, Europe, and Russia—living in what became known as the Diaspora (Ausubel 1964; Rubenstein and Roth 1987). In Christian-dominated countries, they were a powerless and often oppressed minority, subject to prejudice and discrimination, yet they remained committed to their Jewish faith. In doing so, they continued to represent a persistent "challenge to the certainty of Christian" belief,

31

a constant reminder that Christianity was not universally accepted (Bauman 1989:37). This recalcitrance, observes Zygmunt Bauman, was all the more disconcerting to Christians because it "could not be dismissed as . . . pagan ignorance" insofar as Jews were well schooled in the Hebrew Bible and refused to accept Christianity "in full consciousness" of its meaning (1989:37). Moreover, Christians came to believe that Jews were forestalling the Second Coming of Christ, which, according to Christian prophecy, would occur only after they were converted to Christianity (Rose 1990). Thus, according to Bauman, "Christianity could not reproduce itself . . . without guarding and reinforcing Jewish estrangement," and the Jewish challenge "could be repelled, or at least rendered less dangerous, only by explaining Jewish obstinacy by a malice aforethought, ill intentions and moral corruption" (1989:37–38).

In this context, what emerged in Christian culture and was preached by religious authorities was a set of myths and accusations, a malicious collective representation, which held Jews responsible for a host of horrific acts. In addition to holding the Jewish people almost exclusively responsible for Christ's death, Jews were accused of engaging in "blood libel" (i.e., the murdering of Christian children to use their blood in religious rituals), desecrating the body of Christ (i.e., despoiling the Christian sacraments of bread and wine), poisoning wells, and spreading plagues and famines (Botwinick 2001; Rubenstein and Roth 1987). Christian theologians came to believe that Jewish suffering was God's punishment for having rejected his Son and that God's hatred of Jews "was evident by their miserable state" (Botwinick 2001:17). In the *Book of John*, Jesus is said to have admonished Jews who refused to accept his authority:

> If God were your Father, you would love me, for I proceeded and came forth from God. . . . Why do you not understand what I say? It is because you cannot bear to hear my word. You are of your father the devil, and your will is to do your father's desires. . . . He who is of God hears the words of God; the reason why you do not hear them is that you are not of God. (John 8:42–44, 47, cited in Rubenstein and Roth 1987:43)

According to Rubenstein and Roth (1987), no greater defamation of one religious faith by another can be found in the annals of religious history.

As a discriminated minority class, Jews were often forbidden from agricultural land ownership and hence excluded from a common source of livelihood (Botwinick 2001; Hertzberg 1968). They thus sought their economic survival in areas that complemented the majority population. In a world where commerce was poorly developed, people lacked literacy skills, and usury was discouraged by Christian Scripture, Jews found a niche "as merchants, traders, artisans, physicians, and moneylenders" (Rubenstein and Roth 1987:38). However, their very success in these areas bred resentment. Importantly, Jews were perceived as unlike any other minority group, for the threat they posed did not emanate from local conditions of friction or conflict with the dominant population. Rather, the Jewish threat was ubiquitous, vague, and diffuse; and hostility toward Jews could be found in countries where Jews had not lived for centuries and among people who had little if any contact with Jews (Cohn 1967). In this way, the oppositional collective representation of the Jew was used to account for a multitude of local problems even though it was "not causally related to any" (Bauman 1989:41).

In Germany, the sixteenth-century theologian Martin Luther (1483–1546) is credited with Germanizing the Christian critique of Judaism and establishing anti-Semitism as a key element of German culture and national identity (Rose 1990; Rubenstein and Roth 1987). Luther denounced Jews as Germany's particular "misfortune," "plague," and "pestilence" (cited in Rose 1990:7). In his treatise, "On the Jews and their Lies," which Luther wrote in response to Jewish rabbis in Germany who challenged his interpretation of Scripture, Luther exhorted:

> [D]o not engage much in debate with Jews about the articles of our faith. . . . They are real liars and bloodhounds. . . . [B]e on guard against the Jews, knowing that wherever they have their synagogues, nothing is found but a den of devils in which . . . blasphemy, and defaming of God and men are practiced most maliciously. . . [T]here is no hope until they reach the point where their misery finally makes them pliable and they are forced to confess that the Messiah has come, and that he is our Jesus. . . .
> What shall we Christians do with this rejected and condemned people, the Jews? . . . First, . . . set fire to their synagogues or schools and . . . bury and cover with dirt whatever will not burn. . . . Second, I advise that their houses also be razed and destroyed. For they pursue in them the same aims as in their synagogues. . . . This is to be done in honor of our Lord and of Christendom, so that God might see that we are Christians, and do not condone or knowingly tolerate

such public lying, cursing, and blaspheming of his Son and of his Christians.... We are at fault in not slaying them (cited in Rubenstein and Roth 1987:56–59; see also Sherman and Lehman 1971).

It would be difficult for any hate monger to match the viciousness of this condemnation of a group of people. And it would also be difficult to exaggerate Luther's contribution to German anti-Semitism. As Paul Rose observes:

> The first great national prophet of Germany and the forger of the German language itself, Luther . . . shaped the overwhelmingly pejorative, indeed, demonic, significance of the word *Jude*. Through the influence of Luther's language and tracts, a hysterical and demonizing mentality entered the mainstream of German thought and discourse . . . . The Jews . . . were blocking the Germans' need to fulfill themselves in achieving both their "Christian freedom" and their political "freedom." . . . Having crucified Jesus, they were . . . intent on crucifying the German people. . . . Morally, the Jews were the worldly agents of the devil . . . . Materially, [they] were extorting money from . . . [the] German nation. . . . Germany's redemption [meant] her redemption from the Jews and Judaism. (1990:4, 7–8)

The Paradox of the Enlightenment

By the eighteenth century, the Enlightenment, or Age of Reason, opened up new possibilities for European Jews. Enlightenment philosophy promoted the belief that humanity could rely on rational thought rather than religious authority to govern its affairs. Historically the monarchal states of Europe had used one brand of Christianity or another to delineate the boundaries of national identity, even establishing "state religions" as the basis of their authority (Bell-Fialkoff 1999). But the Enlightenment, which promoted democratic ideals and the separation of religion from politics, fostered Jewish emancipation. Jews achieved greater formal political equality and moved forward on a path of assimilation. At the same time, traditionalists like church officials and royalists who favored religious-based monarchies over secular democratic governments blamed Jews for fostering unwanted social change. Modernists, on the other hand, expected Jews to relinquish their religious "superstitions" in order to become full citizens of the nation. They wanted to integrate Jews into the economy "so that no particular pursuit, not even money lending, should be the Jew's own preserve" (Hertzberg 1968:7). And they hoped to undermine the capacity of the "organized Jewish community" to advance any economic or political claims that were considered distinct from the broader national community (p. 288).

Arthur Hertzberg argues that the architects of the Enlightenment were themselves divided on the "Jewish question" and that "there was no straight line from their corporate outlook to the granting of equality for Jews" (1968:248). He suggests that modern anti-Semitism "was fashioned not as a reaction to the Enlightenment" but as part of it (p. 7). Some of the most influential Enlightenment thinkers such as Voltaire were intensely anti-Semitic. However, this prejudice was derived not from the Christian tradition but from secular notions (that can be traced to Greco-Roman pagans) that viewed Jews as "by the very nature of their own culture and even by their biological inheritance an unassimilable element," a people who were inherently deceitful, greedy, intolerant, and arrogant (p. 11). It was a racist view that predated nineteenth century biological racism.

The more sympathetic Enlightenment thinkers thought that this inferior Jewish character was due not to their nature but to their circumstances or environment. According to this view, "the faults of the Jews were created by the conditions under which they were made to live and earn a living. . . . If the Jews were given opportunity and freedom, they would change and very rapidly lose their bad habits" (Hertzberg 1968:292). In other words, if a Jew could become "enlightened" and detach himself from his cultural traditions, then he might become an acceptable member of society. In Jeffrey Alexander's (2006) terms, it was possible for a Jewish *person* to be cleansed, but the polluting *qualities* that defined Jewishness remained foreign and impure.

At the same time, many Enlightenment thinkers thought that the Jews were among "the most difficult of all peoples to enlighten and regenerate," and some considered them beyond regeneration altogether (Hertzberg 1968:286). At best the "new Jew" born of the Enlightenment was asked to "keep proving that he was worthy" of citizen status (1968:366). In practice, this often meant conversion to Christianity, for to remain un-Christian was to remain a perpetual and potentially disloyal outsider (Rubenstein and Roth 1987).

In this way, Jews remained a "lightning rod" for the social strains and discontents of modern Europe (Volkov 1989). In France, for instance, a French-Jewish army captain, Alfred Dreyfus, was arrested and tried for treason in 1894. Dreyfus was accused of passing military secrets to the German military attaché in Paris, which allegedly contributed to France's defeat in the Franco-Prussian War of 1870–1871. The case

35

became "a national obsession" as a trial that symbolized the trial of all French Jews (Rubenstein and Roth 1987:84). Church officials were among Dreyfus's most vehement critics.[4] For instance, the *Civilta Cattolica*, the official journal of the Jesuit order in Rome, opined:

> The Jew was created by God to serve as a spy wherever treason is in preparation . . . . The Jews allege an error of justice. The true error was . . . the [French Constitution] which accorded them French nationality. That law has to be revoked. . . . Not only in France, but [throughout Europe] . . . the Jews are to be excluded from the nation. Then the old harmony will be re-established and the peoples will again find their lost happiness. (cited in Rubenstein and Roth 1987:84)

Dreyfus, however, had been framed by army officials seeking a scapegoat for the military defeat. He was convicted on the basis of forged documents and sentenced to life imprisonment on Devil's Island. In 1899, he was pardoned by the president of France when the true story of the conspiracy against him finally came to light (Botwinick 2001; Rubenstein and Roth 1987; Yahil 1990).

As a "curtain raiser" for the twentieth century, the Dreyfus affair illustrates the degree to which the Jew had remained a social type "construed as compromising and defying the order of things, . . . the prototype and arch-pattern of all nonconformity, heterodoxy, anomaly and aberration" (Bauman 1989:39). It was a flexible and free-floating characterization that allowed Jews to be criticized for being both capitalists and communists, both for flaunting their wealth and social superiority and for being uncouth and miring in poverty and disease.

Racial Anti-Semitism and Eugenics

In the late nineteenth and early twentieth centuries, the historical legacy of Christian anti-Semitism was given a new foundation through anti-Semitic interpretations of modern biological and anthropological research. This transformation of anti-Semitism from a religious ideology to a "scientific" theory of race elevated the social credibility (and eventual legal legitimacy) of Nazi claims about the "Jewish problem" (Rose 1990; Volkov 1989; Yahil 1990).

The British biologist Charles Darwin (1809–1882) had postulated that life had evolved through a process of natural selection or survival of the fittest among diverse species, including humans. Social

Darwinists in both Europe and the United States applied this theory to the social realm, assuming that some races had natural qualities that made them more "fit," more adaptable members of society than others (Hofstader 1959). In addition, Sir Francis Galton (1822–1911), Darwin's cousin, had pioneered the eugenics movement. Eugenics, which means "well born" or "good genes," was a philosophy that advocated social intervention to regulate the genetic composition of the population by encouraging the breeding of parents with good genes and discouraging the breeding of parents with bad genes. The former may be characterized as "positive eugenics" and the latter as "negative eugenics" (Friedländer 2009).

In Germany the belief that there were distinctive Jewish and German characters or social types led anti-Semites to conclude that Jews were an inferior race and Germans were a superior race.[5] In Aryan racial theory, Caucasians were viewed as superior, with the so-called Nordic race (Germanic people of northern Europe, especially Scandinavians) characterized by tall stature, light hair, and blue eyes viewed as the original Caucasian stock. German eugenicists favored social policies that would promote the purity of this race.

Alfred Rosenberg (1893–1946), an early member of the Nazi Party and its chief anti-Semitic ideologue, impressed Hitler with his theory of a Jewish-Communist conspiracy that undermined "the foundations of our existence" (cited in Kochan 1990:1304). Rosenberg was one of the principal disseminators of the *Protocols of the Elders of Zion*, initially a Russian forgery, which claimed to be the minutes of a secret meeting in which Jewish leaders were plotting to achieve world domination. In his major original work, *Der Mythus des 20 Jahrhunderts* (The Myth of the Twentieth Century), which had influence comparable to Hitler's *Mein Kampf* (My Struggle), Rosenberg claimed that "race was the decisive factor determining art, science, culture, and the course of world history" and that Aryans were the "master race" who were destined to dominate Europe (cited in Kochan 1990:1305). In this world-view, "It was because of their race that [individuals] acted for good or bad and tended toward survival or extinction. When citizens were corrupted by the rule of an inferior race, government was corrupted. When they were governed by a positive and lofty race . . . they enhanced humankind, its society, and its culture" (Yahil 1990:37).

The Nazis were, of course, eugenicists *par excellence*, and they practiced both positive and negative eugenics. An example of positive eugenics was the *Lebensborn* (Spring of Life) program that was established by Heinrich Himmler (1890–1945), head of the *Schutzstaffel* (Defense Corps), or SS, in 1936.[6] Lebensborn was a home for unmarried and married mothers of "racially pure" stock who were impregnated by "racially pure" (especially SS) men to give birth to "offspring who were praised as a gift of pure life to the nation" (Rubenstein and Roth 1987:234). Later, in 1939, Himmler announced that it was the duty of women of "good blood" acting out of "profound moral seriousness" to bear the offspring of soldiers going off to battle (quoted in Spielvogel and Redles 2010:108).

Extermination was, of course, the most extreme example of negative eugenics practiced by the Nazis. But before extermination, there was compulsory sterilization, and not initially against Jews, but primarily against the physically and mentally disabled and those with hereditary diseases. In fact, Sharon Snyder and David Mitchell (2006) argue that the eugenics campaign against this population was crucial in paving the way for more radical actions later, including the extermination of the Jews. And it was the medical profession's endorsement of eugenics and participation in the forced sterilization campaign that also helped to publicly legitimize the Nazi's program of cleansing Germany of the biologically deleterious Jews as well (Gellately 2001; Koonz 1991; Proctor 1988).

In this regard, German physicians looked to their counterparts in the United States for guidance and affirmation regarding the practice of compulsory sterilization. Indeed, the United States was the first country to pass laws calling for sterilization of the disabled in the name of population purification. As early as 1923, in the pre-Nazi era, a prominent German medical director wrote to the Ministry of Interior: "[W]hat we racial hygienists promote is not all new or unheard of. In a cultured nation of the first order, in the United States of America, that which we strive toward was introduced and tested long ago" (cited in Rubenstein and Roth 1987:141).[7] Later, during the 1930s, physicians used the U.S. example to facilitate "a favorable reception for compulsory eugenic sterilization in Germany" (p. 142).

In July 1933, the Nazis passed their first eugenics legislation, the Law for the Prevention of Progeny with Hereditary Diseases (LPPHD), which was modeled after legislation in the United States. The LPPHD mandated that individuals be sterilized, "If, in the opinion of a genetic health court, they suffered from certain specified . . . 'illnesses' . . . [including] congenital feeblemindedness, schizophrenia, manic-depressive insanity, . . . epilepsy, Huntington's chorea, [hereditary] blindness, deafness, serious physical deformities, and . . . chronic alcoholism" (Fischer 1995:384). Next, the Law for the Protection of the Genetic Health of the German People, established in October 1935, required couples wishing to marry to submit themselves to a medical examination to certify that they did not have a hereditary or contagious disease. Finally, a centralized system of regional State Health Offices with Departments of Gene and Race Care were empowered to review marriage and sterilization proposals and to compile a national index of the "gene value" of all inhabitants of Germany (Bock 1983; Braddock and Parish 2001; Friedlander 2001; Snyder and Mitchell 2006).[8]

Under this legal framework, German physicians conducted sterilization experiments using various techniques such as surgical castration and exposure to X-rays, and it is estimated that 300,000 to 400,000 people were sterilized without their consent (Braddock and Parish 2001; Fisher 2001; Müller-Hill 1998; Snyder and Mitchell 2006). But in September 1939, this eugenics program took a more radical turn, when Hitler issued an order that authorized physicians "to be designated by name, to the end that patients considered incurable according to the best available human judgment of their state of health, can be granted a mercy death" (cited in Lifton 1986:63).[9]

The euthanasia project that was hence established was called the General Foundation for Welfare and Institutional Care, or T_4, because it was headquartered at Tiergartenstrasse 4 in Berlin (Friedlander 2001). The T_4 program, which included some of the most prominent physicians in Germany (including psychiatrists), and which operated six main killing centers, began in January 1940 and was responsible for the death of an estimated 200,000–275,000 innocent people (Braddock and Parish 2001; Wilhelm 1990). Staff decisions about which patients under their care were killed "were made without consulting either the victims or their families, who first learned of the fate of their loved ones by a duplicitous form letter . . . [notifying them] that the victim had died of heart attack, pneumonia, or some other fictitious ailment" (Rubenstein and Roth 1987:143). These "mercy deaths" had nothing to do with euthanasia as the practice had previously been understood: the release of "a terminally-ill patient from unbearable pain, usually with consent" (p. 143).

Initially the T_4 killers starved their patients to death, had them shot in the back of the neck, or injected them with drugs. Christian Wirth (1885–1944), a nonphysician SS officer who headed the euthanasia center at Brandenburg, was the first to experiment with gassing, which subsequently became the preferred method of inducing death. Gas chambers disguised as showers were constructed, and carbon monoxide in the form of bottled gas or from motor vehicle exhaust fumes was piped in to kill the victims. The bodies were then disposed of in crematoria (Lifton 1986; Rubenstein and Roth 1987).[10]

In early 1941, Himmler authorized the use of T_4 personnel and facilities to rid the concentration camps of physically and mentally ill prisoners. Under the code name *Aktion 14f13*, inmates were designated for "special treatment." According to Robert Jay Lifton, the 14f13 program was a crucial step in the emergence of the Final Solution, because it was the first time that the camps "became connected with a principle of medical-eugenic killing," and it was broadly construed to encompass those who held aberrant beliefs—including political prisoners, draft evaders, and Jews (1986:138).

Saul Friedländer notes that the Nazis' eugenics program aimed at the disabled and infirm, on the one hand, and the Jews, on the other hand, "followed a simultaneous and parallel development," but they had different origins and aims (2009:17). One of the rationales for compulsory sterilization and euthanasia of the disabled/infirm, he suggests, was the financial cost of maintaining these populations. The Jews, on the other hand, were perceived as "an active, formidable enemy that was . . . endangering the very survival of Germany and of the Aryan world," and the struggle against them was viewed "as a confrontation of apocalyptic dimensions" (p. 17).

Although some historians doubt whether Hitler actually believed the scientific basis of Nazi racial theory, he was nonetheless committed to translating these ideas into action, to finally and once-and-for-all doing something about the problem of the Jews (Volkov 1989; Yahil 1990). As Hitler is purported to have said, "I know perfectly well . . . that in the scientific sense there is not such a thing as race. . . . [But] I as a politician need a conception which enables the order which has hitherto existed on historic bases to be abolished and an entirely new and antihistoric order enforced and given an intellectual basis" (quoted in Yahil 1990:37).

Notes

1. See Gitlin and Leibovitz (2010) for a consideration of the question of why Abraham was chosen.
2. Jesus is a Hellenized version of Joshua, which in Hebrew means "the Lord saves."

3. Paul also developed the doctrine of grace, "the special gift whereby God reclaims sinners" (Botwinick 2001:130).
4. Dreyfus was compared to Judas Iscariot.
5. William Marr viewed the Jews as "a mixed people, of a strongly prevailing Caucasian character" (cited in Rose 1990:283).
6. The SS was initially created for the purpose of protecting Hitler and other Nazi Party leaders, but later grew to be one of the most influential organizations of Nazi Germany, with functions that included surveillance and intelligence-gathering, mobile military units that killed civilians, and the operation of the concentration camp system (see chapter 4).
7. By the 1930s, about thirty U.S. states had passed laws allowing for the involuntary sterilization of people with physical and cognitive disabilities, legislation whose constitutionality was affirmed by the U.S. Supreme Court in *Buck v. Bell* in 1927. All told, more than 63,000 people were involuntarily sterilized in the United States (Braddock and Parish 2001; Snyder and Mitchell 2006).
8. While Nazi policy allowed for abortions performed on Jewish and other "unfit" women, it prohibited abortions for Aryan women. Doctors and midwives were obliged to inform State Health Offices of all miscarriages, and only after undergoing two cesarean operations did a woman have a right to an abortion, and then only after she agreed to be sterilized (Bock 1983).
9. This order appears to have been issued in October but was backdated to coincide with the September 1939 invasion of Poland (Lifton 1986).
10. In Warthegau, a part of Western Poland annexed by the Nazis after the start of World War II, a special SS unit led by Captain Herbert Lange murdered disabled patients by piping carbon monoxide from canisters into the interior of a van. The vans had the advantage of being mobile so that the method of killing could be brought to the patients and the dead bodies delivered to a designated mass gravesite (Browning 2004; Friedlander 2001).

3

The Rise of Nazism
and the Evolution
of Anti-Jewish Policy

In November 1923, Hitler led a failed *putsch* (coup) against the government of the Weimar Republic in the city of Munich. He was tried and convicted of treason and sentenced to five years in prison, although he served little more than a year. While he was incarcerated, he wrote *Mein Kampf,* a book that reverberates with insidious epithets against the Jews. In that book Hitler discusses Germany's defeat in World War I. He had served as a dispatch runner carrying messages from "regimental headquarters to men in the trenches" while dodging barrages of artillery (Poole 1997b:xxiv). He was wounded and hospitalized after a mustard-gas attack and was awarded the Iron Cross, a high military honor. In *Mein Kampf* he wrote: "If at the beginning of the War, twelve or fifteen thousand Hebrew corrupters of the people had been held under poison gas, as happened to hundreds of thousands of our very best German workers in the field, the sacrifice of millions at the front would not have been in vain. . . . It would have been the duty of a serious government . . . to exterminate the agitators who were misleading the nation" (cited in Dawidowicz 1976:3, 211).

Lucy Dawidowicz (1976) is arguably the most well-known historian who represents what has been characterized as the *intentionalist* view of the Final Solution, which places emphasis on Hitler's anti-Semitic ideology and continuity of thinking from his experiences in World War I through his writing of *Mein Kampf* and his later ordering of the Final Solution in the last half of 1941. It emphasizes the premeditation and planning of the Nazi leadership who were following Hitler's explicit instructions, and the role of bureaucratic subordinates who carried out the orders of superiors (Browning 2000; Friedländer 1989; Marrus 1987).

Another line of historical interpretation, however, suggests that the road to the Final Solution was not as straightforward as the intentionalist view depicts. This interpretation, the *functionalist* view, emphasizes a broader range of responsibility for the genocide, focusing instead on the multiple participants and bureaucratic functionaries who often improvised and competed with each other to devise the most efficient means of removing Jews from Germany and its annexed territories. While Hitler may have set the goal of a Germany *Judenfrei* (free of Jews), he did not specify how this goal was to be accomplished. Rather, according to the functionalist view, the Final Solution emerged gradually through a process of incremental decision-making and "cumulative radicalization" (Marrus 1987:42),[1] as a bureaucratic system of interrelated but often disharmonious parts eventually coalesced into a coherent program of extermination in response to circumstances created by German territorial expansion and World War II (to be discussed later in this chapter). Thus, Hitler's advocacy of extermination takes on the appearance of a preordained, planned policy only from the vantage point of historical hindsight. As Karl Schleunes (1970) observes, the Nazis came to power expecting to solve the "Jewish problem," but at first they had not yet worked out the particulars of what that solution would entail, and the Final Solution had yet to be anticipated (Browning 2000; Friedländer 1989).

Christopher Browning (2000) notes that the once polarized nature of the intentionalist-functionalist debate has given way to a more nuanced and microscopic analysis derived from a broader array of historical documentation regarding key decision-making points in the evolution of Nazi anti-Jewish policy. In this chapter, we review this evidence, but first we must consider the rise to power of Hitler and the Nazi Party.

Hitler's Rise to Power

One value of the intentionalist perspective is its emphasis on Hitler's indisputable central role, for without him, arguably there would have been no Holocaust. Hitler (1889–1945) was born in Germany's neighboring country of Austria. At one time, Austria had been part of the German empire and thus shared many German cultural traits. (Between 1867 and 1918, Austria was merged with Hungary as Austria-Hungary.) As a boy, according to James Poole's account, Hitler grew up on "stories of heroic Germanic battles and conquests . . . [and]

was taught to admire nationalism, militarism, order, and discipline" (1997b: xix and xxi).[2]

The cultural environment of Vienna, where Hitler moved in 1908, was intensely anti-Semitic. But, according to Poole (1997b), Hitler was propelled down the road to radical anti-Semitism first through his confrontation with Marxist socialism. While working as a laborer on a construction project, "he refused to join a socialist labor union" and was beaten and "kicked off the job" (1997b:xviii). In addition to this personal experience, Hitler acquired an intellectual distaste for socialism because this ideology (and its variants, such as communism) advocated international solidarity among workers and hence rejected nationalist beliefs. Hitler also noticed that many socialist leaders were Jewish. He started reading anti-Semitic pamphlets, some quite fanatical, and was exposed to the view that Jews were not simply a religious group but an inferior race as well (Dawidowicz 1976; Fischer 1995; Shirer 1960).

Prior to World War I, Hitler had left Vienna for Munich, Germany. When the war broke out, as noted earlier, he distinguished himself as a dispatch runner. The war undoubtedly hardened Hitler and reinforced his conviction that ruthlessness and violence was necessary to get what he wanted. "In later years, when trying to convince his hesitant partners to participate in the Holocaust, he would often refer to the war saying, 'If two million of Germany's best youth were slaughtered in the war, we have the right to exterminate subhumans who breed like vermin'" (quoted in Poole 1997b:xxvi).

When Germany was defeated in 1918, Hitler was furious over the armistice terms imposed by the Allies. He blamed weak German leaders and "Jewish interests from within" for stabbing Germany in the back and selling out the country by agreeing to the terms of the Treaty of Versailles (see chapter 1). The Weimar Republic was an unstable government that never received full popular support. Economic malaise and political rebellions undermined the government's legitimacy. Hitler's road to power was to culminate in the abolition of the Republic and the eventual annihilation of European Jewry. Even before he wrote *Mein Kampf*, in an interview with journalist Josef Hell in 1922, Hitler boasted:

> Once I . . . am in power, my first and foremost task will be the annihilation of the Jews. . . . I will have gallows built in rows— at the Marienplatz in Munich, for example—as many as traffic

allows. Then the Jews will be hanged indiscriminately, and they will remain hanging until they stink. . . . As soon as they have been untied, the next batch will be strung up, and so on down the line, until the last Jew in Munich has been exterminated. Other cities will follow suit . . . until all Germany has been completely cleansed of Jews. (quoted in Poole 1997a:271–72)

According to Poole, however, by the time Hitler came to power in 1933, he had concluded that his goal of a Germany *Judenfrei* could be achieved through emigration and expulsion rather than through extermination. Richard Breitman (1998), on the other hand, suggests that Hitler may have simply become more circumspect in his public pronouncements and that he never lost his murderous impulse (see also Dawidowicz 1976). At the same time, Breitman acknowledges a point that is integral to the functionalist perspective: "[T]he scope and methods of killing" were not anticipated early on and the details "evolved substantially over time" (1998:4).

Mobilization and Legitimation of the Nazi Movement

In some respects, the Nazi movement in its early years may be analyzed as a social movement, which, like other social movements, was attempting to mobilize adherents, raise financial resources, and seek popular legitimacy for its policies (Zald and McCarthy 1987)—in this case, unburdening Germany from the yoke of the Versailles Treaty, reestablishing Germany as a European economic and military powerhouse, and taking action to solve the "Jewish problem" (Berger 2002).

In this regard, anti-Semitism was a vehicle for attracting support, for as we have seen, there was much sentiment in German culture that was congruent with Nazi claims about Jews. As Hitler observed in 1922, "I scanned the revolutionary events of history and . . . [asked] myself: against which racial element in Germany can I unleash my propaganda of hate with the greatest prospects of success? . . . I came to the conclusion that a campaign against the Jews would be as popular as it would be successful" (quoted in Rose 1990:379).

It was not always (or even usually) anti-Semitism, however, that was the Nazi's most effective theme in garnering popular support. At various times and with different audiences the appeal to German nationalism (including the complaint about the Versailles Treaty), opposition to the threat of communism, and proposed solutions to economic problems were more attractive issues. Nevertheless, the Nazi's vehement anti-Semitism was well known, and supporters were not bothered by this stance, at best (Allen 1984; Browning 1998; Gellately 2001; Kater 1984).

Richard Hamilton thinks that the Nazis' rise to power was not inevitable, not structurally determined, for "widely varying developments may occur within the same structural frameworks" (1982:443). Other political parties did not offer attractive alternatives to deal with Germany's problems, and the Nazis seized upon political opportunities that created an opening or historical contingency for change. They were able to "generate a plausible program and . . . mobilize cadres to sell it" (p. 18).

The Nazi Party

The German Workers' Party, later named the National Socialist German Workers' Party (*Nationalsozialistiche Deutsche Arbeiterpartei*), or Nazi Party, was founded in 1918. It was but one of many right-wing nationalist parties that existed in Germany in the post-World War I period (Spielvogel and Redles 2010). The Party's initial financial sponsor was the Thule Society, a secret organization that took its name from an ancient legend of a "mythological land of the north, . . . Ultima Thule, believed to be the original home of the Germanic race" (Poole 1997b:7).

> Among the group's members were lawyers, judges, university professors, police officials, aristocrats, physicians, scientists . . . [and] rich businessmen. Only those who could prove their racial purity for at least three generations were admitted. . . . [Their] motto was: "Remember that you are a German! Keep your blood pure!" . . . [They] espoused German racial superiority, anti-Semitism, and violent anti-communism . . . [and their goal] was the establishment of a pan-German state of unsurpassed power and grandeur. (Poole 1997b:7–8)

One of the Thule Society's primary strategies for accomplishing this end was "to bring the working man . . . into the nationalist camp" (p. 8).

Hitler was an early Party member (board member #7), and he provided the leadership and inspiration that transformed it from a rather inchoate group of beer brawlers to a potent political force (Fischer 1995; Shirer 1960). He gained notoriety as an exceptional orator who could mesmerize audiences with his voice. He "spoke with certainty when others equivocated . . . [and] offered simple, bold solutions with an air of absolute assurance" (Botwinick 2001:59).

A social movement's success is in large part dependent on the development of a movement culture that links members' personal identities to broader political objectives (Snow et al. 1986). Indeed, Hitler had a keen appreciation for the role of symbols and a celebratory atmosphere in creating a sense of belonging among adherents. He adopted the swastika, an ancient occult symbol that invoked the power of the sun, as the party's official insignia; and this emblem was displayed on flags and members' uniforms during rallies and parades. Hitler also introduced the *heil* salute. The word *heil* in German had "a religious-medical connotation . . . meaning 'healed' or 'saved'" and was historically reserved for dignitaries like princes (Fischer 1995:130; Spielvogel and Redles 2010).

It was in 1920 that Hitler changed the name of the German Workers' Party to the Nationalist Socialist German Workers' Party. This change was calculated to invoke positive feelings among seemingly incompatible constituencies: nationalists and socialists. According to Klaus Fischer (1995), Hitler saw "national socialism" as a symbolic slogan that could unify diverse ideological orientations under one banner. Socialism, for Hitler, did not refer "to a specific economic system but to an instinct for national self-preservation," to the promotion of "a homogenous and prosperous whole" over private interests (1995:125–26). Germans had to be "taught that they work not just for their own selfish ends but for the good of the nation; and by working for the collective, Germans [could] be secure in the knowledge that the state, in turn, works on their behalf by guaranteeing them a good livelihood, conducive working conditions, unemployment benefits, old-age pensions, free education, and other social benefits" (1995:126). German nationals living outside German territorial borders (primarily in Austria, Czechoslovakia, and Poland) were to be included in this scheme, while immigrants (especially Jews) living within German borders were not. However, William Brustein (1996) argues that it was nationalism, not anti-Semitism per se, that was the issue that attracted most new members. Anti-Semitism was such a "taken-for-granted part of [German] political discourse" that Party leaders viewed it as a weak recruiting device for distinguishing themselves from other political groups (Bernston and Ault 1998:1201).

In the early 1920s, Hitler thought that the Weimar Republic could be overthrown through armed resurrection rather than through the electoral process. Thus the Nazi Storm Troops (*Sturmabteilung*), or SA, became central to his strategy. First established under the auspices of a gymnastic and sport division of the Party, the SA became the armed force of the movement. Hitler sensed that the SA could be used not only to intimidate opponents but to draw new members as well. According to Fischer, his "immediate aim was to attract recruits with military backgrounds" (1995:123). Indeed, the early Nazi rank-and-file was composed largely of "bands of World War I veterans who were unable to give up fighting and adjust to civilian life . . . [and] young people . . . attracted to a group that offered adventure in secret meetings, parades, the painting of slogans on buildings, and fighting with opponents" (Spielvogel and Redles 2010:14, 35).

Nonetheless, by 1923, the Nazi Party (with a membership of about 55,000) attracted Germans from varying social strata. Thirty-six percent were working class, 52 percent were lower-middle class, and 12 percent were upper class (Kater 1983). In an analysis of Party membership in Munich between 1925 and 1930, Helmut Anheier and Friedhelm Neidhardt (1998) found that the party had more socioeconomic breadth than any other party of the extreme political right or left.

Raising Money from the Elite

The Nazi Party, like other social movements, required financial resources to sustain its activities. Kurt Lüdecke, an early member, describes the situation this way:

> The Nazi organization itself lived from day to day financially, with no treasury to draw on for lecture hall rentals, printing costs, or the other thousand-and-one expenses which threatened to swamp us. The only funds we could count on were membership dues, which were . . . merely a drop in the bucket. Collections at mass meetings were sometimes large, but not to be relied on. Once in [a] while, a Nazi sympathizer would make a special contribution, and in a few cases these gifts were quite substantial. But we never had enough money. . . . Instead of receiving salaries for the work we did, most of us had to give to the Party in order to carry on. Clerks and officers, except for a very few, got no pay, and the majority of members pursued their usual occupations during the day. . . . [O]nly two or three . . . who gave full time to Party work . . . had sufficient means to support themselves. The rest were chiefly recruited from the jobless men who would work for their meals. (cited in Poole 1997b:27)

The Thule Society and right-wing military organizations did contribute funds, but they gave to other nationalist groups "and there was only so much money to go around" (Poole 1997b:27). With the creation of the SA in 1921, however, paramilitary funds originally targeted for other groups were increasingly funneled to the Nazis.

Harvard graduate Ernst Hanfstaengl, who came from a wealthy family that owned an art publishing business in Munich, was the first upper-class contributor to invite Hitler into his home. Although Hanfstaengl did not share Hitler's anti-Semitic views, he found his criticisms of Jews amusing and witty. Hanfstaengl made handsome donations to the Party and used his family's connections to introduce Hitler to other high-society donors, especially well-to-do matrons (Fischer 1995; Poole 1997b).

A key Nazi Party fundraiser among businessmen and aristocrats was Max Erwin von Scheubner-Richter, who had been brought into the Party by Alfred Rosenberg (see chapter 2). Among Scheubner-Richter and Rosenberg's most important contacts were anticommunist Russian oil producers living in Germany in exile, who hoped to overthrow Joseph Stalin's regime in the Soviet Union with German help. In many cases the contributions secured from the elite "did not take the form of cash" but of valuable art objects and jewelry, which Hitler typically used as collateral to obtain loans (Poole 1997b:49). In the early years, between 1919 and 1923, Ernst von Borsig and Fritz Thyssen were the only German industrialists who gave the Nazis significant financial support. Borsig, who headed "an old Berlin firm that manufactured locomotives, boilers, and heavy industrial equipment," wielded considerable influence over the German business community as chairman of the Alliance of German Employers' Association (Fischer 1995:139). Thyssen, who at the time was the "heir-in-waiting" to the fortune built by his industrialist father, which included the largest shareholdings of United Steel Works, a gigantic steel firm that eventually contributed over a million marks to the Nazis (Wistrich 1995).

The Party also solicited money from beyond German borders. Hitler himself went on several fund-raising tours in Switzerland, Austria, and Czechoslovakia. Italian dictator Benito Mussolini had his government provide support. Through Rosenberg the party received money from wealthy British oilman Sir Henri Deterding. And there is evidence that the U.S. automobile magnate Henry Ford contributed money as well. Ford shared Hitler's anti-Semitic and anticommunist views.

In the United States he financed anti-Semitic propaganda, including the *Independent* newspaper, which had a circulation of a half million by the mid-1920s. In the early 1920s reprints of anti-Semitic articles that appeared in the *Independent* were published in a four-volume compilation called *The International Jew*, which was translated into 16 languages and published throughout the world. In *Mein Kampf* Hitler specifically praised Ford for his views and appears to have taken passages from him (Black 2009; Poole 1997b).

Another source of financial support came from Alfred Hugenberg, a German newspaper and film tycoon, who joined forces with Hitler in a 1929 campaign against the Young Plan (endorsed by the Allied powers) that would have reduced Germany's reparations imposed by the Versailles Treaty but still obligate it to make payments for another six decades. Instead, Hugenberg and his allies "called on the government to renounce the moral grounds on which reparations had been anchored . . . and to reject any further . . . payments" (Fischer 1995:212). "Every speech made by Hitler and other Nazi leaders was carried by all the newspapers in Hugenberg's chain. Millions of Germans who had hardly ever heard of Hitler before now became interested in him, since he was given such good publicity in the 'respectable' press" (Poole 1997b:49). Although the anti-Young Plan forces lost, the campaign brought considerable revenues into the Party, including contributions from the upper middle-class.

Appealing to Voters and Acquiring Power

As noted, in November 1923 Hitler led a failed *putsch* (coup) against the Weimar government in the city of Munich. The idea of a coup at that time was not novel. The Communists in Russia and Mussolini's fascists in Italy had risen to power this way in November 1917 and October 1922, respectively. And in Germany there had been other attempted takeovers, albeit unsuccessful ones (Hilberg 1992).

After the writing of *Mein Kampf* and his release from prison, Hitler faced opposition for leadership of the Party, especially from Gregor Strasser, who along with his younger brother Otto took "the socialist part of the Nazi program seriously" (Spielvogel and Redles 2010:47). Hitler, of course, triumphed, and in 1926 at the first Party congress since the failed coup, he declared himself the un-disputed leader of the group.

During this time Hitler became more interested in an electoral strategy for gaining power (Hamilton 1982). But while the Party continued to grow, this progress did not translate into votes, and it remained a "membership organization without an electorate" (Anheier, Neidhardt, and Vortkamp 1998:1265). A key turning point was the Nazis' electoral failure of May 1928 in which the Party received only 2.6 percent of the *Reichstag* (German parliament) vote. Hitler decided to reorganize the party into *Gaue* (regions) that corresponded to national election precincts. He gave the *Gaueleiter* (regional leaders) greater flexibility to plan their operations and shift strategies if necessary to respond to local conditions. In addition, the Gaue were "further divided into *Kreise* (districts), these into *Ortsgruppen* (local groups), which, in larger cities, were further subdivided into *Zellen* (cells) and *Blocks* (blocks)" (Fischer 1995:205; Spielvogel and Redles 2010).

> The entire operation . . . was held together through a steady stream of memorandums, suggestions, and guidelines coming down a chain of command, and activity reports passing up. . . . From the top came . . . [instructions] as to how issues should be handled in a given campaign, or a review of techniques that had proved useful in recent elections. . . . The activity reports let people at the top know which units were performing and which . . . were lagging. They also indicated which tactics had been used and with what success; such information in turn . . . [was] passed on to other units . . . for more general use. The higher echelons did, unquestionably, reserve an absolute right of intervention. But that was something to be used . . . [only] for a malfunctioning or insubordinate unit. The intended relationship of top to bottom was . . . one of close monitoring (as opposed to close control), of guiding, helping, encouraging. (Hamilton 1982:324)

The Party also established the Reich Propaganda Office, under the direction of Joseph Goebbels (1897–1945), and a public speakers' program, the National Socialist Speakers School, to train members in rhetorical and propaganda techniques as well as the "official party responses to standard questions" (Brustein 1998:1253; Hamilton 1982). More mass rallies were held, with speakers brought in from the outside. An emphasis was placed on making the rallies entertaining for audiences. In addition, a Christmas party might be held for children, a youth group taken on a hike or camping trip, or a soup kitchen set up for the unemployed. Loudspeaker vans, leaflets, and personal letters were used to communicate with voters. Hitler himself would travel throughout Germany "in whirlwind campaigns by car, train, and airplane" (Spielvogel and Redles 2010:60). In one tour he covered 50 cities in just 15 days.

In the countryside, the Party targeted farmers suffering from "high indebtedness and high interest rates combined with poor harvests and a general decline in land prices" who had been largely ignored by other political groups (Hamilton 1982:365). Appeals were made to restore traditional communal values shared by a common German *Volk*, and Jews were blamed for the farmers' problems, "especially when Jewish middlemen could be used as a convenient target" (1982:370). In the cities, anti-Semitism was used when it would work and "played down or abandoned" when it would not (1982:367). In an analysis of Party speeches between 1925 and 1930, Helmut Anheier, Friedhelm Neidhart, and Wolfgang Vortkamp (1998) found that anti-Semitic themes declined and were replaced by increasing references to anticommunism, economic problems, and the Young Plan. Rather than making *negative* references to certain groups (such as Jews and foreigners), the speeches were more likely to make *positive* references to the German people or nation and portray the party as the "savior" offering solutions.

At the same time, other political parties did little to effectively repel the Nazi challenge. On the left, for instance, the Communists tried to transform workers' discontents into more radical actions against the state. Workers, however, did not respond favorably when the Communists tried to turn wage strikes intended as short-term events with specific, immediate goals into protracted struggles that would keep workers off the job "for longer, indefinite periods and for goals that, at best, seemed a doubtful gamble" (Hamilton 1982:298). And workers were also turned off when the Communists attacked both fascism and democracy as if they both were forms of government that did not have the workers' interest at heart. Political parties on the right, on the other hand, became more extreme in their attacks on the Weimar Republic, making the Nazis appear more mainstream. They attempted to engage the Nazis in "a competition of toughness" that they could not win (p. 264).

As a consequence of all this, the Nazis' public standing improved, and in September 1930 the Party received 18.3 percent of the Reichstag vote, an eightfold increase from the 1928 election. Moreover, total Party membership rose to 389,000. Only the leftist Social Democrats now had more members than the Nazis in parliament. The Weimar Republic was in increasing disarray, and it became difficult to maintain stable political coalitions to run the government. Repeated elections were held, and in July 1932 the Nazis received 37.3 percent of the vote, and Party membership rose to 450,000. Although the Nazi vote declined to 33.1 in November 1932, Hitler had emerged as one of the leading political leaders in Germany (Anheier et al. 1998; Hamilton 1982; Shirer 1960; Spielvogel and Redles 2010).

At that time, perhaps the only politician of Hitler's public stature was the aging General Field Marshal Paul von Hindenburg (1847–1934).[3] Hindenburg had been president of Germany since 1925, and as president he was the chief dignitary of the country and the military commander-in-chief. He also retained the power to appoint the Reichstag chancellor to run the government. After the November 1932 election, Hindenburg selected General Kurt von Schleicher (1882–1934) to replace Franz von Papen (1879–1969) as chancellor. Previously, Schleicher had supported Papen, but now he wanted his job. In January 1933, however, Papen persuaded Hindenburg to appoint Hitler as chancellor with Papen as vice chancellor. Papen managed to convince Hindenburg that Hitler could be co-opted and his radical impulses controlled. Papen, of course, was wrong (Fischer 1995; Shirer 1960; Spielvogel and Redles 2010).

On January 30, 1933, Hitler was sworn in as chancellor of Germany. He "had come to power legally and within the system" (Spielvogel and Redles 2010:68). Politicians who thought they could use Hitler for their own purposes were out-maneuvered. Hitler proved to be more formidable than they ever imagined. The Weimar Constitution provided for the suspension of parliament and civil liberties in cases of national emergencies. Indeed, Papen had invoked this power before, and Hitler got Hindenburg to agree to disband parliament for seven weeks and hold new elections in March 1933. In that period Hitler also convinced Hindenburg to issue an emergency decree directed at the Communists that curtailed freedom of the press and outlawed "public meetings that posed a threat to the vital interests of the state" (p. 70). The Nazis monopolized the state-directed public radio, enabling them to transmit Hitler's speeches throughout the country. In March 1933 the Party received 43.9 percent of the Reichstag vote.

Hitler immediately pressed for the passage of the Enabling Act, also called the Law for the Relief of the Distress of the Nation and State, which gave him the power to issue laws without the Reichstag's approval for a period of four years "in order to solve Germany's economic and social problems, to create political stability, and to establish the new Germany" (Spielvogel and Redles 2010:73). The Enabling Act was passed on March 24 with 83 percent of the Reichstag vote. Hitler then proceeded to suppress all other opposition, eliminating trade unions and other political parties, and turning Germany into a one-party state.[4] When Hindenburg died on August 2, 1934, Hitler merged the offices of the chancellor and president and became the "Führer of the German Reich and people." In a plebiscite held on August 19, 85 percent of the people gave Hitler their approval. The country was now run by the *Führerprinzip*, the leadership principle: "One man rules the whole . . . [and] that one man empowers his subordinates . . . to accomplish the goals set for them by their overlords and so on down the . . . chain of command" (Fischer 1995:297).

Anti-Jewish Legislation

After the war, a German architect shared his thoughts about what had transpired in Nazi Germany vis-à-vis the Jews with sociologist Everett Hughes:

> Jews, were a problem. They came from the east. You should [have seen] them in Poland; the lowest class of people, full of lice, dirty and poor, running about in their Ghettos in filthy caftans. They came here, and got rich by unbelievable methods after the first war. They occupied all the good places . . . in medicine and law and government posts! . . . [What the Nazis did] of course . . . was no way to settle the problem. But there was a problem and it had to be settled some way. (Hughes 1962:5)

To be sure, a policy of extermination was not what this architect and other Germans had in mind as a solution to the "Jewish problem." But the legal disenfranchisement and eventual compulsory deportation of German Jews was an entirely different matter.

Thus the Nazis, after acquiring political power, were now in a position to develop and implement specific policy proposals regarding the Jews. As we shall see, the solutions that were adopted evolved through progressively radical (though overlapping) stages. According to Raul Hilberg (1985), only with the Final Solution were the Nazis truly inventive, for at first they employed policies that were quite ordinary in their consistency with historical precedent—for example, the laws requiring Jews to wear badges or specially marked clothing and live in compulsory ghettos, as well as the laws prohibiting Jews from holding public office, practicing law and medicine, attending institutions of higher education, and marrying or having sexual relations with Christians (Botwinick 2001; Hilberg 1961). As Hilberg observes:

> [S]uch measures had been worked out over the course of more than a thousand years by authorities of the church and by secular governments that followed in their footsteps. And the experiences gathered over that time became a reservoir that could be used, and which indeed was used to an amazing extent . . . even in detail, as if there were a memory which automatically extended to the [Nazi] period. (quoted in Lanzmann 1985:71)

Although Hitler and other Nazi officials sometimes encouraged hooliganism and random violence against Jews, they preferred a more systematic, legal approach in order to acquire and maintain public support for their policies. All told, they issued over 2,000 legal decrees against the Jews (Adam 1990). In April 1933, for instance, the Law for the Restoration of the Professional Civil Service (LRPCS) and the Law Regarding Admission to the Bar were passed. These laws dismissed persons of non-Aryan descent from the civil service and denied them admission to the bar. In April as well, the Law Against the Overcrowding of German Schools and Institutions of Higher Learning mandated that new admissions of non-Aryans not exceed the proportion of non-Aryans in the German population and that non-Aryans be prohibited from taking the final state exams for occupations requiring official certification. Such restrictions were "also introduced into the bylaws of professional organizations, societies, and clubs" (Adam 1990:53). And in September of that year, additional legislation excluded non-Aryans from cultural enterprises having to do with literature, theater, music, art, broadcasting, and the press (Yahil 1990).

Two years later, in September 1935, the Nazis' legal solution to the "Jewish problem" entered its second stage with the passage of the so-called Nuremberg Laws. These laws included the Reich Citizenship Law, which restricted German citizenship and all the rights contained thereof to persons of "German or kindred blood," and the Law for the Protection of German Blood and German Honor (LPGBGH), which prohibited marriages and sexual relations between Jews and persons of German or kindred blood, and forbade Jews from flying the German flag and from hiring German female domestic servants under the age of forty-five. The laws also prescribed penalties for violation that included hard labor and imprisonment (Fischer 1995; Fraenkel 2001; Yahil 1990).

Hitler considered the Nuremberg Laws a milestone in the anti-Jewish campaign (Yahil 1990). The Nazis had succeeded in transforming the "Jewish problem" into a technical matter amenable to legitimate legal solutions. The question remained, however, as to how to define the target population. The LRPCS, for instance, had defined "non-Aryan" as a person "descended from non-Aryan, particularly Jewish, parents or grandparents," even if only one parent or grandparent fit that category (cited in Yahil 1990:65). But bureaucrats responsible for implementing the law encountered difficulty verifying non-Aryan status on the basis of just one grandparent's background. In the event of a dispute, an opinion had to be obtained from the expert on racial research in the Ministry of Interior. Moreover, at President Hindenburg's request, the law contained an exemption for non-Aryans who had held their positions since August 1, 1914, and who had either fought at the German front during World War I or were the son or father of a soldier who had been killed in that war.

With the Nuremberg Laws, the term "Jew" replaced "non-Aryan." According to Leni Yahil (1990), a major reason for this change was the objections of non-Aryan countries (especially Japan) with whom Germany wished to curry favor. Still, at first "Jew" remained undefined, and it took a subsequent legal addendum issued in November 1935 to clarify the matter. The First Implementation Order to the Reich Citizenship Law defined a Jew as "anyone descended from at least three grandparents who were full Jews by race" (cited in Yahil 1990:72). The law also created the status of *Mischlinge* that was composed of persons of mixed background. David Bankier describes the rather complicated Mischlinge status as follows:

> Mischlinge of the first degree, or half Jews, were those who had two Jewish grandparents, did not belong to the Jewish religion, and were not married to a Jewish person as of September 15, 1935. They had the rights of regular German citizens, although these were curtailed by a series of regulations: for example, they could marry only Mischlinge of the first degree. . . . Mischlinge of the second degree, or quarter Jews, were those with one Jewish grandparent. They were subject to certain limitations in [occupations] requiring full German origins, but were drafted into the army and allowed to marry Germans. . . . In all other matters they were treated like German "Aryans." (1990b:981)

For the most part, it was Nazi policy to equate Mischlinge of the first degree with Jews and "to absorb the Mischlinge of the second degree into the German nation" (1990b:982). While many Nazis (including Hitler) remained concerned about the problem of all Mischlinge polluting German society, they did not reach consensus on this, and there was considerable variation in how officials responsible for implementing Jewish policy treated Michlinge Jews. Similarly, while the LPGBGH prohibited marriages between Germans and Jews, it did not cover already existing intermarriages, and Jews in mixed marriages were sometimes treated more benevolently than others (Ehmann 2001; Hilberg 1985; Johnson 1999).

Ian Hacking observes that particular types of persons "come into being . . . with our invention of the categories labeling them" (1986:236). Thus in an important sense the Nuremberg Laws brought the "Jew" into being as a legally inferior entity. At the same time, these laws remained a far cry from the Final Solution. Although Hitler and the Nazi elite may have envisioned them as the first step toward a Germany *Judenfrei*, the German Information Agency reported that "the German people has no objection to the Jew as long as he wishes to be a member of the Jewish people and acts accordingly, but . . . [we decline] to look on the Jew as a national of the German Nation . . . and to accord him the same rights and duties as a German" (cited in Yahil 1990:72). Consequently, the new laws could be perceived as offering German Jews the opportunity to establish themselves as a "national minority" comparable to discriminated minorities in other countries (such as African Americans in the United States at that time). Some Jews even regarded the legal solution as somewhat acceptable, viewing them, as one survivor recalls, "as a sort of guarantee, . . . a definitive legal adjustment, which would make it possible for [Jews] to remain in . . . the homeland that meant so much to [us]" (quoted in Engelmann 1986:80).

The Nuremberg Laws, however, were just a prelude to countless other decrees that followed, including those that extended the list of occupations from which Jews were completely barred; closed schools and universities to Jewish students; prevented Jews from entering certain places (such as parks, theaters, hotels), from using public transportation, and from driving cars; required Jews to wear the "Star of David" insignia, to live in designated districts, and to relinquish their valuables (such as gold, jewelry, art objects); and restricted Jewish businesses to those that dealt only with other Jews, eventually, as we shall see, requiring the complete transfer of Jewish-owned businesses to Aryan-German ownership (Botwinick 2001; Chesnoff 1999; Friedländer 2009; Hilberg 1985).

Emigration and Deportation

As early as 1919, Hitler had written of the need to physically remove Jews from Germany (Browning 1990a). But it was not until the mid-1930s that Nazi leaders turned to a policy of expulsion. This policy took place in the context of the Four-Year Plan, a directive issued by Hitler in 1936 and carried out by Hermann Göring (1893–1946), who, as *Reichsmarshall*, was Hitler's designated successor, the second most powerful man in the country.[5] The Four-Year Plan was designed to prepare the German economy for war aimed at the conquest of new living space to the East, what the Nazis called *Lebensraum*, to be colonized by Germans and appropriated for raw materials and food production. For this effort, Hitler wanted Germany to become economically self-sufficient, less dependent on foreign imports in the event of an international economic blockade; and it would entail the complete Aryanization of the economy, that is, the transfer of Jewish business assets to Germans (Bankier 1990a; Friedländer 2009).

At first, the expulsion policy took the form of "voluntary" emigration. By creating conditions that were so bad for Jews, the Nazis hoped that they would simply choose to leave. However, disincentives for emigration were created by restrictions on "the amount of currency and property Jews could take with them" (Kaplan 1998:70). The Reich Flight Tax, first put in place before the Nazi era to prevent "capital flight," was raised to prohibitive heights. Many prospective emigrants "had to sell all their belongings simply to pay this . . . tax" (p. 71). And they were not allowed to directly transfer their after-tax money abroad but were required to deposit it in "blocked accounts . . . [from which] they could buy foreign currency—at very unfavorable exchange rates" (p. 71). In 1935, the exchange rate was only half the market value of the German mark, and it became progressively lower, falling to just 4 percent by 1939. Moreover, obtaining the necessary documents "took months of running a bureaucratic gauntlet," and German officials often demanded bribes and some demanded sexual favors from Jewish women (p. 130). Another significant barrier was the absence for most Jews of "relatives or friends abroad who could sponsor admission into a country of refuge" (p. 72). In addition, the Nazis issued "passports for emigration only," thus forbidding exploratory trips intended to assess opportunities elsewhere (p. 72).

At times initiatives were developed to circumvent some of these restrictions to make emigration easier. The *Ha'avarah* (transfer) Agreement, for instance, allowed the transfer of German-Jewish capital in the form of German goods into British-controlled Palestine, thus facilitating the emigration of those Jews whose capital was transferred. According to Yehuda Bauer:

> The details were rather complicated, but the general idea was that Jews with capital at their disposal would be permitted to buy German industrial goods, mainly tools of production—irrigation, pipes, cement mixers, machinery—that were in demand in Palestine. . . . The goods were shipped to Palestine, and when the German Jewish investors arrived there, they received their money back in pounds sterling. (1994:10)

With this policy, the Nazis also hoped to expand Germany's export market in the Middle East and to undermine an anti-German economic and diplomatic boycott that had been started by several (mostly U.S.) Jewish organizations. This agreement was in effect until the outbreak of World War II (Friedländer 2009).

In March 1938, German troops marched into neighboring Austria and took over the nation.[6] The *Anschluss* (annexation) of Austria was followed by pogroms directed against Austria's Jewish population and many were "arrested, humiliated, tortured, and sent to the Dachau concentration camp" (Yahil 1990:105). Adolf Eichmann (1906–62), who was serving in the Jewish Section of the *Sicherheitsdienst* (Security Service), or SD, and who had emerged as a leading expert on Jewish affairs, was sent to Vienna "to organize the emigration of the Jews and introduce a new system" of compulsory deportations (Yahil 1990:105). This system involved the confiscation of Jewish property that left Jews with "only the sum required to enter their proposed countries" of destination, if such destinations could indeed be found (Yahil 1990:105). It was here that Eichmann introduced the methods that were later used to expel Jews from other areas: concentrate Jews in a central location, fix quotas, instruct designated Jewish leaders to fill these quotas, and force wealthier Jews to finance the costs of deporting Jews "who had no means of their own" (Cochavi 1990:1733).

The events in Austria diffused the "Jewish problem" into the international arena as U.S. President Franklin Roosevelt called for a conference on Jewish refugees that was held in Evian, France, in July 1938. At the Evian Conference delegates from thirty-two countries met, but no one (including the United States) was willing to modify its existing immigration policies to accommodate more Jews (Bauer 1994; Rosen 2006; Wyman 1984).

Hitler was quick to exploit this impasse, admonishing the Evian Conference nations that they had no right to tell Germany what to do with its Jews when they did not want to accept more Jews themselves. "The world has sufficient space for [Jewish] settlements," he warned, "or sooner or later . . . [the Jews] will succumb to a crisis of inconceivable magnitude" (quoted in Bauer 1994:36). Hitler argued that settlement of the "Jewish problem" was an international responsibility upon which the peace of Europe depended, for as he said, "European questions cannot be settled until the Jewish question is cleared up" (1994:36). Failing an international agreement, Hitler told Göring: "The Jewish question is to be summed up and coordinated once and for all and solved one way or the other" (1994:36). Thus Richard Breitman and Alan Kraut (1987) believe that Hitler was in fact contemplating extermination of those Jews who could not be emigrated.

In January 1939, Hitler instructed Reinhard Heydrich (1904–42)—who at that time commanded the SD, the surveillance and intelligence-gathering component of the SS, and the Gestapo (*Geheimes Staatspolizei*), the national secret police—to establish a Central Office for Jewish Emigration to further "[t]he emigration of Jews from Germany by all possible means" (cited in Bauer 1994:38).[7] In essence, this office was designed to expand and coordinate the methods of deportation previously used by Eichmann in Vienna. Still, the Nazis were concerned that it might take eight to ten years to accomplish full emigration of German Jews (Cochavi 1990; Yahil 1990).

The Aryanization of the Economy

Our earlier discussion of Karl Marx should remind us that economic self-interest is a central component of much human action (see chapter 1). Indeed, the Nazi campaign against the Jews, though driven by racial ideology, was marked by myriad opportunities for self-enrichment in the name of broader national goals by plundering Jewish assets in Germany and throughout Nazi-occupied Europe.[8] *Arisierung*, or Aryanization, was the term that was used to denote policies aimed at transferring Jewish-owned businesses to "Aryan" (i.e., German) ownership (Barkai 1989). In the early years, from 1933 to 1938, Aryanization took the form of unsystematic "voluntary" sales of Jewish property. The Nazis organized boycotts of

Jewish businesses and harassed and intimated merchants, sometimes violently. They tried to make conditions so bad for Jews that they would simply choose to sell their property and emigrate. For Jews who decided to leave, however, the prices they received were far below market value, and many Germans prospered from the bargains (Botwinick 2001; Chesnoff 1999; Kaplan 1998).

Although "few of the approximately 100,000 Jewish businesses in Germany were of sufficient size or importance to attract the avarice of the nation's major firms," in 1934 the *Frankfurter Zeitung* reported that there were twenty-one transfers of multimillion dollar Jewish companies (Hayes 1998:198; Simpson 1993). In his research, Peter Hayes found that at first the larger German firms tended to offer Jews a better price than the smaller ones, but this was not always the case, and by 1938 many of the largest German companies "plunged into the scramble for the spoils" (1998:205). All told, corporate participation in Aryanization "was a crucial link in the cumulative radicalization" of a discriminatory process that excluded Jews from German society and ultimately led to the Final Solution (James 2001:4; see also Feldman and Seibel 2005).

The banking industry was at the forefront of the feeding frenzy, with the Dresdner Bank setting "the standard for rapacity" (Hayes 1998:203). Some German bankers contended that failure to take advantage of Aryanization would make them uncompetitive and leave them open to charges of failing to protect their stockholders' and depositors' interests. In early 1938, Deutsche Bank headquarters urged its regional offices that "it is very important that the new business possibilities arising in connection with the changeover of non-Aryan firms be exploited" (cited in Hayes 1998:206). To be sure, there were risks involved in taking over Jewish enterprises that were unprofitable or laden with debt. Nevertheless, the banking industry (especially the Dresdner Bank) played "an active role in brokering deals, finding buyers and sellers, and [providing] the financing for purchases and acquisitions" (James 2001:43 see also Feldman and Seibel 2005; Hayes 1998). In addition, the banks began trading Aryanized securities around the world—in New York, London, Zurich, and other financial centers (Simpson 1993).

As early as 1935, German Minister of Economics Hjalmar Schacht realized that the government was losing out on the profits of Aryanization, so he initiated a variety of taxes and transfer charges to ensure that more of the capital gain would go directly to the state

(Simpson 1993). And after the infamous *Kristallnacht* pogrom of November 1938, Aryanization moved into its second stage.

Kristallnacht, which is typically translated as Crystal Night or Night of the Broken Glass, was precipitated by an edict that had been issued the previous month to deport all Polish-born Jews living in Germany back into Poland. When Herschel Grynzpan, a young Jewish man living in Paris, learned that his parents had been deported, he retaliated by shooting (and killing) an official at the German embassy in Paris. Goebbels, with Hitler's approval, instructed the Nazi cadre to attack Jewish businesses, homes, and synagogues. Amidst the looting and massive destruction that ensued, "thousands of windows were smashed and the broken shards glittered the streets like crystal" (Botwinick 2001:129). About a hundred Jews were killed, countless others injured, and some 26,000 arrested and herded into concentration camps (Bauer 1994; Fischer 1995; Gilbert 2006).

While most of the Nazi leadership was pleased with Kristallnacht, Göring was concerned that too much property the Nazis could have otherwise seized was destroyed (Barkai 1989; Chesnoff 1999). To make the pogrom more profitable, he ordered an "atonement tax" to be paid by every Jew who owned assets of over 5,000 marks, an amount that yielded 1.25 billion marks. In addition, 250 million marks of insurance payments that were due to the Jews who lost their property during the pogrom were confiscated. Göring also ordered the compulsory Aryanization of the economy, requiring the closure of all Jewish businesses and the "sale" of Jewish property and valuable possessions (through government-appointed fiduciaries) at a fraction of their market value. In essence, businesses, homes, securities, jewelry, gold and other precious metals, artworks, rare books, coin and stamp collections, antiques—anything of value was virtually confiscated with little or no compensation, for after the taxes levied by the Nazis, the Jews who emigrated were left with only a small fraction of their assets (Chesnoff 1999; Friedländer 2009; Simpson 1993).

As the Nazis conquered other countries, the same pattern emerged. But what had taken years in Germany to accomplish was elsewhere carried out in months. Even before the Austrian Anschluss, for example, Deutsche Bank director Hermann Abs was informed of the impending invasion. Abs "quickly assembled a team of the bank's foreign trade specialists to identify Austria's choicest Jewish-owned business and real estate for acquisition" (Simpson 1993:70). Although the corporate (and especially the banking) sector profited from the plunder,

Hayes (1998) estimates that about 60–80 percent of the profits went into government coffers. In the year before the start of World War II, such proceeds constituted about 5 percent of the German national budget and were critical to the financing of military rearmament. Nazi officials, of course, personally profited as well.[9] Later, during the war years and after the Final Solution was underway, gold from the teeth and jewelry (especially wedding rings) that were taken by the SS from concentration camp victims was shipped to the *Reichsbank* (German state bank) in Berlin. The Reichsbank credited the SS in marks and melted the stolen gold into ingots and mixed it with its other holdings.

It took more than the Reichsbank, however, to help the Nazis convert the stolen property (gold and other items) into usable currency. Here, foreign art dealers, diamond traders, and bankers literally fenced or laundered stolen goods for the Nazis (Chesnoff 1999; Petropoulos 1997). Among all the nations of the world, Switzerland's banking industry arguably had "the deepest and most crucial economic relationship with Nazi Germany" (Bower 1997:337). Although Switzerland claimed to be a "neutral" country during the war, its business and political leaders "were convinced of Germany's ultimate victory and were untroubled by the Allied perception that [its banks were] acting as a partner to the Nazis" (p. 53). Swiss banks accepted over three-quarters of the gold transferred abroad by the Reichsbank and in exchange provided Germany with the foreign currency it needed to purchase materials on the international market for its war machinery.[10] The Swiss National Bank in particular also laundered gold into other neutral nations such as Portugal, Spain, Sweden, and Turkey, which provided foreign currency to Germany. Thus between 1939 and 1943 Switzerland's national gold reserves increased from $503 to $1,040 million. The reserves in other neutral countries increased dramatically as well.[11]

The Emergence of the Final Solution

As noted earlier, the functionalist view posits that the Final Solution emerged only gradually through a process of incremental decision-making and cumulative radicalization, as German territorial expansion made emigration/deportation less viable as an overall solution to the "Jewish problem." World War II, which began with the German invasion of Poland in September 1939, was a crucial turning point in this regard. In the months before, Hitler had made it clear that the conquest of Poland would mark the beginning of a new set of expectations regarding the Jews, especially because Poland contained Europe's largest Jewish population. Following the invasion, plans took shape in discussions between Hitler and a small "coterie of faithful followers" (Yahil 1990:128)—including Heydrich and Heinreich Himmler, head of the SS and the entire German policing system—for a "sweeping demographic reorganization of Poland" (Browning 2000:3).[12] Jews, Gypsies, and Poles were to be resettled into areas of German-occupied Poland further east, creating space in the western regions for the establishment of "pure German provinces" (Browning 2000:4). Heydrich was to coordinate the eastern resettlements, while Himmler was charged with the resettlement of ethnic Germans and the elimination of "harmful" indigenous elements in the west. To this latter end, a division of the SS, the *Einsatzgruppen* (Operational or Special Action Squads), were employed. The Einsatzgruppen, which were first introduced during the Anschluss, followed the German *Wehrmacht* (army) into occupied areas. The Wehrmacht secured the area militarily, and the Einsatzgruppen performed non-military operations against the civilian population. During the Polish invasion, the Einsatzgruppen murdered "thousands of prominent Poles and Jews" (Breitman 1991:146; Browning 1990c; Rhodes 2002; Spector 1990a).[13]

Concentration of Jews into urban ghettos or reservations was the first step toward their eventual resettlement, and various proposals were circulated as to how this was to be done (Browning 2000). Prior to the invasion of Poland, Hitler had signed a secret pact with Soviet leader Joseph Stalin in which the two powers had agreed to divide and occupy Poland, and plans for ghettoization were temporarily derailed when the need to resettle Germans from Soviet-occupied Poland took precedence, trains for transportation were in limited supply, and Polish workers were needed for the war effort. Göring, whose first priority was the war, insisted that, "all evacuation measures are to be directed in such a way that useful manpower does not disappear" (cited in Browning 2000:12). Himmler was among those most disappointed with the curtailment of the deportation program.

As a result of the Polish invasion, Great Britain and France declared war on Germany. But by May 1940 prospects of a German victory in France emboldened Himmler to try to persuade Hitler to step up the deportations. He drafted a memorandum entitled "Some Thoughts on the Treatment of Alien Populations in the East" that he submitted to Hitler. Himmler proposed "completely to erase the concept of Jews through the possibility of a great emigration of all Jews to a colony in Africa or elsewhere" (cited in Browning 2000:14). The colony Himmler was referring to was Madagascar, an island off the coast of southeastern Africa that was controlled by the French. For decades anti-Semites had contemplated Madagascar as a place to send Jews, and it had been mentioned frequently in Nazi policy circles since 1938. Himmler's memo indicates that as of May 1940 the Nazis had not yet decided upon extermination as an overall solution to the "Jewish problem." Himmler wrote, "However cruel and tragic each individual case may be, this method is still the mildest and best, if one rejects the Bolshevik method of physical extermination of a people out of inner conviction as un-German and impossible" (cited in Browning 2000:14). On the other hand, Breitman (1991) suggests that Himmler's mention of extermination in this memo indicates that this method had in fact crossed his mind and that his reservations about it may have been reserved for (non-Jewish) Poles. Breitman thinks that by this time the Nazis had come to view compulsory emigration and murder of Jews as complementary rather than as alternative policies (Breitman and Kraut 1987).

Hitler read the memo and found the ideas, in Himmler's words, "very good and correct" (cited in Browning 2000:14). Himmler obtained Hitler's authorization to distribute the memo to other Nazi leaders, including Göring, along with the message that the Führer had "recognized and confirmed" the plan (cited in Browning 2000:14). Franz Rademacher, the newly appointed Jewish expert in the German Foreign Office, proposed that Jews in German-occupied Western Europe be sent to Madagascar as well, a suggestion that was quickly expanded by others to include all European Jews. In June, Heydrich referred to the Madagascar Plan as a "territorial final solution" (cited in Browning 1990b:491).

Nazi leaders anticipated that the Madagascar plan could be implemented at the end of the war, which they thought was imminent. They had quickly defeated France and expected to conquer Great Britain. The defeat of France and England "promised both the colonial territory and the merchant fleet necessary" for the realization of the plan (Browning 2000:17). By September, however, it was clear that a timely defeat of Great Britain was not possible, and the Madagascar plan was aborted. Nevertheless, the need to find a comprehensive solution to the "Jewish problem" was now on the table. "[T]he Nazi were . . . committed to a way of thinking . . . that precluded any solution that was less than . . . 'final' and trans-European" (Browning 1990b:491).

In violation of the Hitler-Stalin pact, planning for Operation Barbarossa, an invasion of the Soviet Union that took place in June 1941, constituted the next major radicalization of the anti-Jewish policy. According to a January 1941 memorandum written by Eichmann's close associate, Theodore Dannecker, Heydrich had "already received orders from the Führer . . . [to bring] about a final solution to the Jewish question within European territories ruled or controlled by Germany" (cited in Browning 2000:20). This solution would involve "the wholesale deportation of Jews as well as . . . the planning to the last detail of a settlement action in the territory yet to be determined." "Territory yet to be determined," it turns out, was a code phrase for the Soviet Union.

In the months before the invasion, Himmler and Heydrich reached agreements with the Wehrmacht to allow both the Einsatsgruppen and Order Police to engage in "pacification" measures to eliminate the "Bolshevist-Jewish intelligentsia" (Breitman 1991, 1998). Many army officers were receptive to this plan because they "equated Jews with Bolshevik agitators, guerrillas, and saboteurs" (Browning 2000:22). In addition to these killing operations, which in fact had no military objective, Nazi leaders made plans for the expropriation of local food supplies (to feed the German army and to export to Germany) and for the massive resettlement of Jews further to the east, which they knew would result in starvation for millions of people.

Christopher Browning argues that Operation Barbarossa "*implied* nothing less than the genocide of Soviet Jewry. . . . Now mass executions, mass expulsions, and mass starvation were being planned . . . on a scale that would dwarf what had happened in Poland" (2000:25). However, Browning adds, the implied genocide was still a vague and unspecified policy that "commingled the fates of Jewish and non-Jewish victims" (p. 25). It did not yet entail a plan to exterminate all European Jews, or even all Soviet Jews, "down to the last man, woman, and child" (p. 30).

It was not until after the Soviet invasion that a second decision was made to target all European Jews for extermination. Most historians believe that this decision was made by Hitler in consultation with Himmler and Heydrich during the euphoria of the initial success of the Barbarossa campaign (Bauer 1991; Browning 2000).

On July 31, Heydrich presented Göring with a written order that he had prepared for Göring's signature. This order, which brought Göring on board, authorized Heydrich to make "all necessary preparations with regard to organizational, practical and financial aspects for an overall solution of the Jewish question in the German sphere of influence in Europe" and to submit "to me promptly an overall plan of the preliminary . . . measures for the execution of the intended final solution" (cited in Bauer 1991:144).

By the fall, the outlines of the plan began to emerge. Himmler ordered the end to all Jewish emigration, "experimental" gassing of Jews at Auschwitz was undertaken, and construction of death camps at Bełzec and Chelmno was begun. At this point, according to Browning's account, "a widening circle of initiates . . . were aware that the ultimate goal or vision of Nazi Jewish policy was now the systematic destruction and no longer the decimation and expulsion of all European Jews," but much of what happened over the course of the next few months took place "on local or regional initiative. . . . [W]hen such initiatives dovetailed with the vision of the Nazi leadership, they were seized upon with alacrity precisely because they met perceived needs. Those initiatives that did not were rejected or ignored." The central Nazi leadership "was not passive but interacted in a goal-directed manner with local authorities in the surge of killing actions and preparation for killing actions that characterized" that period (2000:39). Later, in January 1942, Heydrich convened the Wannsee Conference, at which point the decision to proceed with the Final Solution was officially transmitted to a group of high-ranking Nazi bureaucrats. Although most of those in attendance were aware of the killing operations, only now were they informed of the full scope of the plan. By May 1942, the Final Solution to the "Jewish problem" was underway with full force (Browning 1990b, 2000).[14]

Notes

1. The concept of cumulative radicalization is attributed to Hans Mommsen (1986), but as used here does not imply acceptance of the entirety of Mommsen's position. For a critique of that position, see Friedländer (1989).

2. Hitler's ancestry remains somewhat of a mystery since his father, who was apparently a cruel man who beat his wife and children, was born out of wedlock and thus the religious background of Hitler's grandfather is unknown. This has led to some speculation that Hitler had doubts about the purity of his own racial make-up. For biographical accounts and psychological interpretations of Hitler, see Botwinick (2001), Kershaw (1998, 2000),

Rosenbaum (1998), and Shirer (1960). For representations of Hitler in popular culture, see Rosenfeld (1985).

3. In March 1932, Hitler had run against Hindenburg for the presidency. Hitler received only 30 percent of the vote, but in a multi-candidate field, Hindenberg did not gain a majority. Hindenburg won in a run-off election, while Hitler got 37 percent of the vote (Shirer 1960; Spielvogel and Redles 2010).

4. To appease the German military, which was concerned about the SA, Hitler decided to overthrow the SA leadership. In June 1934, a number of SA leaders, most notably Ernst Roehm, were arrested and killed in what has been called the "Night of the Long Knives." Subsequently, the SA's function was increasingly confined to ceremonial duties. The SS, originally established in 1925 as an elite core of the SA whose purpose was to protect Hitler and top Nazi leaders, became independent of the SA and took on expanded functions (Fischer 1995; Rubenstein and Roth 1987; Shirer 1960; Spielvogel and Redles 2010; see chapter 2, note 6).

5. Göring was also Commander-in-Chief of the *Luftwaffe*, the German air force.

6. Prior to that time, the German army had moved into the Rhineland in 1936, the demilitarized zone which bordered France, and it had taken control of Czechoslovakia in 1938, neither of which provoked serious opposition from Great Britain or France.

7. Although Heydrich administered the SD and Gestapo, these organizations were under Heinrich Himmler's command (see chapter 2). Later that year the SD and Gestapo (as well as other organizations) were combined into the RSHA (*Reichssicherheitshauptamt*), or Reich Security Main Office, which Heydrich also headed. After being appointed acting governor of the Protectorate of Bohemia and Moravia in late 1941, Heydrich was shot and killed by a group of Czech anti-Nazi resistance fighters near Prague in June 1942 (Aronson and Longerich 2001).

8. We will consider German corporate profiteering from slave labor in the next chapter.

9. It was not just Jewish property that was plundered, for the Nazis also confiscated the gold reserves of the other nations it occupied. Tom Bower (1997) estimates that Germany's gold reserves increased to about $120 million by 1939, while the Simon Wiesenthal Center puts the figure at $180 million in 1939 and $800 million by the end of the war (Cooper 1996/1997).

10. Supposedly neutral countries not only offered financial services, but also produced armaments or provided needed raw materials that aided Germany's war effort. Additionally, there was a general reluctance to accept Jewish refugees and in the case of Switzerland many were turned back at the border (Cooper 1998; Petropoulos 1997).

11. In addition, an international bank—the Bank for International Settlements (BIS)—located in Basel, Switzerland, played an important role during the Nazi period (Higham 1983; Simpson 1993). The BIS, founded in 1930, was the joint creation of the world's largest central banks, including the Federal Reserve Bank of New York, the Bank of England, and the Bank of France. Bankers throughout the world desired "an institution that would retain channels of communication and [collaboration] . . . even in the event of an

international conflict" (Higham 1983:2). According to BIS bylaws, votes on the board of directors were allocated on the basis of financial contributions. During the war years, the bank took in so much stolen Nazi gold that it was dominated by German representatives such as Walter Funk of the Reichsbank and Hermann Schmitz of IG Farben, even though an American, Thomas Harrington McKittrick, became its president in 1940.

12. In 1943 Himmler also became Minister of the Interior (Wistrich 1995).

13. The Wehrmacht was also implicated in the civilian killings (see chapter 4).

14. According to Gerhard Weinberg, by November Hitler had "made it clear that the project of killing Jews was by no means confined to Europe. As he explained to the Grand Mufti of Jerusalem," Hitler's hopes of military victory in Africa and the Middle East would bring about the destruction of Jews in the Arab world (1998:484).

4

The Social Structure of the Genocidal Regime

As we have seen, the ultimate decision that led to this systematic killing of Jews in Nazi extermination camps was the gradual outcome of incremental (but increasingly radical) decision-making. I believe that the intentionalist view is correct in suggesting that Adolf Hitler was the driving force behind the policies that led to the Final Solution, although Nazi elites like Heinrich Himmler, Reinhard Heydrich, and Adolf Eichmann shared his fanatical vision and were crucial in helping him turn his dream into a reality (Breitman 1991, 1998). On the other hand, the functionalist view is also right in pointing to a broader range of responsibility. Indeed, the Final Solution involved nothing less than the coordination of "German society as a whole" (Hilberg 1985:264). Countless individuals in various official and unofficial capacities engaged in the work that was necessary to formulate and implement the Final Solution to the "Jewish problem" (Berger 2002). In this chapter, we will examine the organizational settings and processes that enabled the Nazis to implement their anti-Jewish policy and the Final Solution.

Constructing Nazi Culture

After acquiring state power, the Nazis embarked on a systematic media campaign to build a new moral order or cultural fabric that, in Émile Durkheim's terms, would penetrate and socialize individual consciences and create a new "collective conscience" (see chapter 1). In March 1933, Hitler established the Reich Ministry for Public Enlightenment and Propaganda that was headed by Joseph Goebbels. As Goebbels remarked, "It is not enough to reconcile people more or less to our regime, to move them towards a position of neutrality. . . . [W]e would rather work on people until they are addicted to us . . . [and] the ideal of the national revolution"

71

(quoted in Welch 1993:24). Later that year, Goebbels was put in charge of a new Reich Chamber of Culture that consisted of seven divisions: radio broadcasting, the press, literature, film, theater, music, and the visual arts. In order to work in any of these areas, Germans had to become a member of the division that represented their group. People could be denied membership if they lacked "reliability or suitability," that is, if they were Jews or insufficiently pro-Nazi (Spielvogel and Redles 2010:148). Numerous other organizations were also established to regulate cultural content in these fields, enabling the Nazis to control everything from the news to the entertainment that Germans were allowed to receive. Among the films produced under Goebbels's direction was *The Eternal Jew*, which has an infamous sequence in which swarms of rats are shown scurrying through cellars and sewers, in rapid alteration with hordes of Jews moving from Palestine to remote corners of the globe. The accompanying narration says: "Where rats turn up, they spread diseases and carry extermination into the land. They are cunning, cowardly and cruel; they mostly move in large packs, exactly as the Jews among the people" (quoted in Friedländer 2009:189).[1]

The Nazis intervened in educational settings as well. The National Socialist Teachers Association "assumed responsibility for the ideological indoctrination of teachers," and the Reich Ministry of Education exercised control over the curriculum (Spielvogel and Redles 2010:163). For example:

> Instruction in German . . . inculcate[d] racial ideology or "German awareness" and utilized literary works stressing the idea of folk, blood and soil, and national and military values. . . . History classes focused on the Nazi revolution and Hitler's role in it. The whole of history was reinterpreted in light of racial principles . . . [and] the significance . . . of the Aryan race. Biology . . . centered on the laws of heredity, racial breeding, and the need for racial purity. Children learned to measure skulls and to classify racial types accordingly. Biology classes underscored the necessity of cultivating racial health by the correct choice of Aryan spouses and the bearing of large families. . . . [The teaching] of geography . . . justified [territorial] expansion and the need for *Lebenscraum* (living space). (2010:164)

In addition, the Nazis created a number of elite schools for boys who were trained to become the future political and military leaders of Nazi Germany. The objective of these schools was to create a cadre of committed National Socialists who were ready to fight and die for their country.

The *Hitler Jugend*, or Hitler Youth, founded in 1926, was another means of indoctrinating boys into Nazi ideology. By 1936 the Hitler Youth attracted two-thirds of ten- to eighteen-year-olds, and in 1939 membership was made mandatory. All Hitler Youth were required to swear allegiance to the Führer: "I swear to devote all my energies and my strength to the savior of our country, Adolf Hitler. I am willing and ready to give up my life for him, so help me God" (quoted in Spielvogel and Redles 2010:160). Although Hitler Youth participated in activities such as model-plane building, sports, hiking, and camping, the organization was modeled on military values and included constant drilling, the exaltation of German military heroes, the honoring of war dead, and weapons training. Boys were encouraged to cultivate a fighting spirit, to become hardnosed and ruthless in their pursuit of Nazi ideals (Koch 2000; Rempel 1989).

The female counterpart of the Hitler Youth was the *Bund Deutscher Mädel*, or League of German Girls (Spielvogel and Redles 2010). Girls were taught to serve the state by becoming dutiful wives and mothers and by bearing as many children as possible to propagate the Aryan race. Indeed, the Nazis envisioned a culture of gender roles based on presumed biological traits that was hypertraditional in delegating women to the private sphere of childrearing and housework, dependent upon men for support but also providing men with the nurturance that sustained them in their quest for economic, bureaucratic, and military power (Koonz 1987).

Finally, the Nazis tried to exert control over the religious sphere of German culture. The vast majority of Germans were baptized Christians, with Lutherans comprising the largest denomination (Rubenstein and Roth 1987). German Lutheranism, as noted in chapter 2, was characterized by its antipathy toward Jews and by its highly nationalist sentiments. Since early 1933, Lutheran and other Protestant denominations had been moving toward a unified Evangelical Church; and by July, Ludwig Müller, Hitler's envoy to the Evangelical community, was elected as the first bishop of the Evangelical Reich Church. Müller was the leader of the pro-Nazi "German Christian movement," the radical right-wing of German Lutheranism. Although relatively small in number (about 600,000), German Christians came to occupy key positions "within theological faculties, in regional bishops' seats, and on local church councils" (Bergen 1998:567). German Christians saw no contradiction between worshiping Hitler and worshiping Christ. They viewed Hitler as "God's man for Germany, the savior himself," and his program of racial purity a "holy crusade" (Rubenstein and Roth 1987:203). Of the Jews, Müller wrote that once it was believed that "if a Jew was baptized, he was then a Christian. Today we know that you can baptize a Jew ten times, he still remains a Jew and a person whose nature is alien to us" (cited in Bergen 1998:568).

The Economic Context: State and Corporate Enterprise

The German economy under Nazism consisted of both state-owned enterprises and private corporations, with some involving both government and corporate ownership. Hitler was well aware that he needed the support of big business for reviving the economy and for building and maintaining his war machinery. Initially, corporate leaders were not enthusiastic about the Nazis rise to power, and they were concerned about the state's interference with the market economy. Nevertheless, they understood that their profits depended upon their willingness to cooperate with the regime (Hayes 1987, 1998; James 2001; Spielvogel and Redles 2010; see chapter 1).

With the advent of the Four-Year Plan aimed at German economic self-sufficiency (see chapter 3), Göring was given virtual dictatorial control over the economy and "alternately cajoled and bullied big business into expanding factories . . . [that produced] synthetic rubber, textiles, fuel, and other scarce products" (Fischer 1995:377). He placed restrictions on imports and exports, initiated wage and price controls, and demanded that profits be limited and used for a firm's expansion and for buying government bonds to help finance the military build-up. In 1937, after industrialists found it unprofitable to invest in the conversion of low-grade iron ore to steel, Göring established the *Reichswerke Hermann Göring*, or Göring Reichs Works (GRW). GRW was primarily a state-owned enterprise, with the government financing 70 percent of its operations (with help from Dresdner Bank loans) and the private sector financing the rest. It soon became a huge industrial complex, employing some 700,000 workers, nearly 60 percent of whom were slave laborers. In the process, Göring acquired a large personal fortune (Simpson 1993; Taylor and Shaw 1987; Wistrich 1995).

We will discuss the Nazi concentration camp system in more detail later in this chapter. But it is worth noting here the government and corporate profiteering from inmate slave labor. The SS *Wirtschafts-Verwaltunghauptamt* (WVHA), or Economic-Administrative Main Office, was a division that ran a vast array of SS business enterprises that exploited such labor. These businesses included companies involved in armaments, building materials, furniture, textiles, leather, fishing, forestry, shale oil, printing, foodstuffs, soft-drinks, and mineral water (Pingel 1990; Poole 1997a; Taylor and Shaw 1987). Relying on slave labor, the expropriation of valuables taken from extermination camp victims, and generous low-interest loans from Dresdner Bank and the Reichsbank (German state bank), the WVHA amassed huge profits. SS leader Heinrich Himmler and Oswald Pohl, who headed the WVHA, were the principal shareholders of most of the SS-owned companies. It was Himmler's intention to make the SS profitable enough to become a financially independent empire, and although he and Pohl held their shares as representatives of the SS, they had extensive access to the funds and used them as they saw fit (Breitman 1991; Poole 1997a; Taylor and Shaw 1987).

Himmler also personally profited from the leasing of inmate labor to private corporations. He had been trying to attract corporate interest in this idea since 1935, when a contingent of industrialists visited Dachau (Hayes 1987). Although corporate officials were at first reluctant to do this, the war depleted the available labor pool and thus made Himmler's offer more attractive. As Auschwitz commandant Rudolf Höss (1900–1947) recalled:

> Prisoners were sent to enterprises only after the enterprises had made a request. . . . In their letters of request the enterprises had to state in detail which measures had been taken by them, even before the arrival of the prisoners, to guard them, to quarter them, etc. I visited officially many such establishments to verify such statements. . . . The enterprises did not have to submit reports on causes of death. . . . I was constantly told by executives . . . that they want more prisoners. (cited in Poole 1997a:326)

As more and more firms pursued this labor policy, the competition for inmates intensified. By mid-1942 the SS had become a major provider of slave labor for virtually every important sector of the economy. As time went on, the treatment of these workers became more ruthless, and many were either worked to death or sent to a concentration camp to be gassed.[2]

Arguably the most notable collaboration between the SS and private industry involved IG Farben, a huge chemical conglomerate whose subsidiaries included Bayer and Degesch (see chapter 1). IG Farben, the largest corporation in Europe and the biggest chemical firm in the world, produced products such as synthetic oil and gasoline, synthetic rubber, explosives, plasticizers, dyestuffs, and even the Zyklon B gas that was used in gas chambers.[3] Carl Krauch, a senior executive in the corporation, also served as Göring's Plenipotentiary General for Chemical Production. In this latter capacity, Krauch was charged with procuring Germany's chemical needs, a sphere that included fuel, explosives, and light metals. Eventually, IG Farben became the government's main supplier of these materials, especially during the war years, and operated more than 330 plants and mines across German and Nazi-occupied Europe. Nearly 40 percent of its workforce consisted of slave laborers (Hayes 1987; Rubenstein and Roth 1987; Simpson 1993; Taylor and Shaw 1987).

IG Farben's most infamous operation was the synthetic oil and rubber plant that the SS contracted to run at the Monowitz subsidiary of the Auschwitz concentration camp complex (we will discuss the Auschwitz camp system further later in this chapter).[4] IG Farben officials had been attracted to this location because of its ample coal and water supply and convenient access to highway and rail facilities. There was of course a ready-made supply of concentration camp laborers. Peter Hayes (1987) argues that the company had decided on this location before the Final Solution and its interest in the site "contributed mightily to [Auschwitz's] expansion and . . . eventual evolution into a manufacturer of death" (1987:351). As SS demands for wartime production increased, IG Farben "partook more and more of the brutal madness that ruled its setting" (1987:356). In addition, the Degesch company, an IG Farben subsidiary, supplied Zyklon B to the Auschwitz-Birkenau and Majdanek concentration camps. Although the chemical was initially developed for use as a disinfectant and insecticide, Degesch officials were hardly unaware that their company was now manufacturing a product designed to induce death, for the "SS ordered that the special odor, required by German law as a warning, be removed. This odor was intended to alert humans to the lethal presence of the gas. Ordering its removal was a clear indication of the purpose it was to serve" (Gutman 1990e:1750; Hayes 1998; Pressac and van Pelt 2006; Rubenstein and Roth 1987).

But Degesch was not the only German corporation to provide Zyklon B or to aid in the extermination program in some other way. For instance, J.A. Topf und Söhne, a manufacturer of ovens and incinerators, was contracted by the SS to help design and construct larger gas chambers and crematoria at Birkenau. Topf provided the special multiple-muffle ovens that could accommodate more bodies. And

AEG, a major electrical equipment company, helped design and install the electrical system that was used in the new buildings (Hilberg 1992; Pressac and van Pelt 2006; Public Broadcasting Corporation 1995).

Finally, it is worth noting the Allianz insurance company, which the SS contracted to insure the buildings and contents of the concentration camps, including Auschwitz (Bower 1997). Allianz officials regularly visited the camps and regarded them as good risks. As one inspector remarked during a visit to Auschwitz, "Thanks to constant military supervision, impeccable order and cleanliness prevails" (p. 335).

The Bureaucracy of Destruction

In the tradition of Max Weber, as noted in chapter 1, many scholars consider the bureaucratic administration of the Final Solution to be central to the entire process (Browning 2000; Hilberg 1961, 1985). The German government under the Nazi regime consisted of a myriad of organizations that often had overlapping functions and jurisdictions that changed over time. Himmler and Heydrich in particular oversaw a complex terror apparatus that "struck fear into the hearts" of those who opposed it or were the targets of its actions (Spielvogel and Redles 2010:102).

In 1929, Himmler was selected to head the SS and given the title *Reichsführer-SS* (Breitman 1991; Wistrich 1995). At that time, the SS was a relatively small organization that had been formed from a select group of SA storm troopers for the purpose of protecting Hitler and other Nazi Party leaders. Under Himmler's leadership the SS grew and became one of the most influential Nazi organizations, with Himmler eventually rivaling Göring as the second most powerful man in Germany. SS members wore black uniforms, which distinguished them from the brown-shirted SA, and were sometimes referred to as Blackshirts, the Black Corps, or the Black Order. As the SS expanded, it took on multiple functions that were administered by various sub-units. In 1931, for example, the SD became the surveillance and intelligence-gathering division of the SS (see chapter 3). Himmler appointed Heydrich as its head. The Einsatzgruppen, first deployed during the invasion of Austria, was a division of the SD and hence came under Heydrich's control (Botwinick 2001; Koehl 1983).

In 1936, when the German policing system was reorganized to create a centralized national police force, Himmler was given the additional position of Chief of the German Police. With this reorganization, the secret state police called the Gestapo was established as a national organization that handled political offenses, including Jewish matters.[5] Again, Himmler placed Heydrich in charge. In 1939, when several SS institutions (including the SD and Gestapo) were combined into the Reich Security Main Office, Heydrich became its head (Aronson and Longerich 2001; Taylor and Shaw 1987).[6]

It was not just Nazi organizations, however, that operated to implement anti-Jewish policy and the Final Solution. Although these organizations were of course central, many of the government bureaucracies that implemented the anti-Jewish campaign, including the Final Solution, were not the creation of the Nazis (Hilberg 1992). To be sure, new offices were created and specialists in Jewish affairs placed into influential positions. But the Nazis "never had to restructure or permeate extensively" (Rubenstein and Roth 1987:237) the existing bureaucratic apparatus whose occupants tended to favor the "racial dissimilation" of Jews and who often acted as if they were engaged in the most ordinary of operations, following orders and performing routine tasks (Mommsen 1998:220).

Many of the bureaucrats of the Nazi regime were bright, ambitious university (especially law) graduates who sought successful administrative careers and who "understood that power and influence were at stake in managing well the Jewish affairs that fell to them" (Rubenstein and Roth 1987:237). They played an indispensable role in drafting legal decrees, maintaining files on Jews, investigating disputes about individuals' Jewish status, prosecuting and convicting Jews in stacked courts of law, expropriating Jewish property, segregating the Jewish population, deporting Jews to concentration (including extermination) camps, and even killing innocent people. They helped direct unsystematic Nazi violence into legal channels, hence sanitizing and legitimating anti-Jewish actions (Gellately 2001; Hilberg 1961; Miller 1991; Spielvogel and Redles 2010).

These bureaucrats competed with each other to expand their organizational domains and sought their superiors' favor by pursuing and attempting to anticipate their wishes (Feldman and Seibel 2005). Initially working without a blueprint for the Final Solution, they often improvised policies to operationalize rather vague Nazi goals (Browning 2000; Mommsen 1998). Practically speaking, Raul Hilberg observes, the Final Solution could not have been accomplished "if everyone . . . had to wait for instructions," and it was this bureaucratic initiative that "eventually brought about the existence of experts accustomed to dealing with Jewish matters" (1989:127–128).

Finally, as Hilberg notes, the Final Solution was a European-wide operation, and "a multiplicity of measures were taken by non-German authorities" in other countries to disenfranchise, segregate, and deport the Jews (1992:75). To be sure, as recent research strives to document more fully, officials in different localities throughout Nazi-occupied Europe differed in their degree of enthusiasm for the Nazis' anti-Jewish program, but sufficient numbers were willing to contribute to (and benefit from) this effort (Bloxham 2009; Horowitz 2009; Polonsky and Michlic 2004). They tried to carefully maneuver between drawing maximum benefit from an alliance with Germany and preserving "a modicum of independence as an assurance for the future" in the event that Germany would lose the war, which at first seemed unlikely (Deák 2000a:8; Deák, Gross, and Judt 2000; Vago 1987). Jan Gross (2000) suggests that we understand the motivation for collaboration not as something that was imposed by the Nazis, but as endogenous to the social and political milieu of the collaborating localities (see also chapter 6 and 7). In his study of the massacre that took place in Jedwabne, Poland, in July 1941, for example, Gross reports that about half the Gentile residents of this small town (some 1,600 people) rose up and killed the other half, who were Jews, with the approval but without the participation of the handful of Germans who occupied the area (Gross 2002; Polonksy and Michlic 2004).[7]

Also, take the case of the Vichy government in France, which was among the most notable of the collaborating governments. After its military defeat, France was divided into an occupied zone that covered its western coast and northern region, and an unoccupied zone in the southeast, with Vichy as its capital.[8] Under the leadership of Marshall Philippe Pétain, the Vichy government was permitted complete autonomy by the Nazis; and between October 1940 and December 1941, it initiated over 100 anti-Jewish edicts and had the "distinction of being the only nation to have voluntarily turned over Jews to the Nazis" for deportation to concentration camps "from outside areas of German military occupation" (Chesnoff 1999:135; Marrus and Paxton 1981, 1987; Weinberg 2001).

At the same time, as Mark Biondich's (1999) research has shown, the Ustaša regime in anti-Semitic Croatia had the distinction of killing "more of its own Jews than it deported to the Nazi-operated death camps" (Horowitz 2009:499). "[A]lthough Croatia was a satellite state under the direct rule of the German and Italian fascists, . . . the Croatian authorities quickly realized that they, rather than their masters, could reap significant economic benefits by confiscating monies and property—and they did so in the name of solving the so-called Jewish Question" (p. 499).

The Role of the German Citizenry

With the Nuremberg Laws and its amendments, a "Jew" had been officially defined, and the Nazis required those who met this definition to register with the authorities and otherwise identify themselves with special cards and insignias on their clothing (Hilberg 1985). Ordinary German citizens, however, also played a key role in identifying Jews who were allegedly in violation of anti-Jewish laws. By providing authorities with voluntary denunciations of others, they helped socially isolate the Jews and target them for official action (Gellately 2001; Johnson 1999). As Heydrich told Göring at a meeting in 1938, "the German population . . . [will] force the Jew to behave himself. The control of the Jew through the watchful eye of the whole population is better than having . . . a control of his daily life through uniformed agents" (quoted in Hilberg 1985:50).

In many respects, anti-Jewish law enforcement operated much like contemporary, conventional law enforcement, where the majority of police interventions occur in response to citizen initiatives (Reiss 1971). During the Nazi period, the Gestapo was the policing agency empowered to "investigate and suppress all anti-State tendencies," especially violations of anti-Jewish laws (Gellately 1988:654). Although the Gestapo was undoubtedly a brutal, repressive organization, it lacked the personnel resources to exercise effective surveillance over the population. Eric Johnson (1999) estimates that in the cities there averaged only about one Gestapo officer for every 10,000 to 15,000 citizens; and in the countryside there were next to none. Thus "the perceived omnipresence of the Gestapo was not due to large numbers of Gestapo officials" but to the omnipresent eyes of the citizenry (Gellately 1997:187). As one Gestapo official remarked, the "officers let things come to them" (quoted in Johnson 1999:5).

Indeed, studies of Gestapo case files indicate a high degree of unsolicited informing against Jews, especially for alleged violations of laws that restricted Aryan-Jewish contact (such as the Nuremberg prohibitions on sexual relationships between Germans and Jews). Robert Gellately (2001) reports, for instance, that 59 percent of "racial mixing" or "race defilement" cases from the Lower Franconia region of Bavaria, including simply being friendly to Jews, involved denunciations by citizens. If one adds the 12 percent of cases that indicate no source of the denunciation but include phrases like "This office has been informed" or "It has been discovered," and are thus likely to have come from ordinary citizens, the total is even higher (Gellately 1997:189). Similarly, Johnson (1999) found that 41 percent of Gestapo case files from Krefeld were initiated by citizen denunciations. (Johnson's study includes a broader range of offenses, such as alleged business/property violations associated with Jews' attempts to secure their assets in preparation for emigration.) If one adds the 27 percent of cases in which the source was unknown, the proportion of citizen-initiated denunciations in Johnson's study rises to the level found by Gellately. Gellately (2001) also studied Gestapo case files on reports of German citizens accused of violating the prohibition against listening to foreign radio broadcasts and found that fully 73 percent were initiated by citizens, with an additional 10 percent of the sources unknown.

Often the motivation for informing was quite banal. For example, a resident would denounce a neighbor with whom they had quarreled, a businessman would denounce an economic competitor or an employee he wanted to fire, a disgruntled employee would denounce an employer or coworker he didn't like, or a spouse would denounce a partner from whom he or she wanted a divorce. At times the Gestapo was so flooded with false accusations that government officials issued warnings not to misuse denunciations for personal gain. Ironically, even Hitler complained that "we are living at present in a sea of denunciations and human meanness" (quoted in Gellately 1988:679). In 1937, an article in the *Frankfurter Zeitung* offered "a reward of up to one hundred marks (the monthly wage of an unskilled worker) for anyone who could provide correct information about false informers" (Johnson 1999:153).

Johnson (1999) cautions against overstating the number of German citizens who provided denunciations to the Gestapo. He estimates that only one to two percent of the population were denouncers. At the same time, he notes, "considerable numbers of ordinary citizens used the repressive political means afforded by the Nazi dictatorship ... to their own advantage" (1999:16). Gellately adds that the "Nazi system of party and state was certainly repressive and highly invasive, but it was almost immediately 'normalized' by many people as they began to accept it as part of the structure of everyday life" (1997:203).

To be sure, the Nazis, as we have seen, exercised considerable control over the social institutions that they used for propaganda and indoctrination purposes and that helped build broad popular support for their policies. And of course the regime dealt ruthlessly with those who opposed it in any meaningful way. Nevertheless, outside of Germany's defeat in the war, many Germans subjectively experienced the Nazi period as "liberating, ecstatic, and empowering" (Patterson 1991:404). As one citizen recalled, "To be honest . . . I wasn't really against the Nazis at that particular time. I often found their methods appalling . . . [but the] truth is, all that business about the 'unity of the German people' and the 'national rebirth,' really impressed me" (quoted in Engelmann 1986:15). Another person remembered the 1930s this way: "Of course later on we found out that mistakes had been made, that certain things happened that shouldn't have. But [Hitler] . . . really did accomplish the impossible! Millions of desperate people found new happiness, got decent jobs, and could face the future once more without fear" (1986:189).

Thus after the war many Germans interpreted the Final Solution not as an abomination for which they should be held responsible, but as a "mistake" made by a few bad Nazis (Marcuse 2001). In his study of public opinion, David Bankier concludes "that on the whole the population consented to attacks on Jews as long as these neither damaged non-Jews nor harmed the interests of the country, particularly its reputation abroad" (1992:73–74). It is arguably true that the average German citizen never expected things to go as far as they did, but after all, "the Jews . . . were a problem . . . [that] had to be settled some way" (quoted in Hughes 1962:5).

Ghetto Management

The concentration of Jews into specially designated districts, or ghettos, was at first viewed by Nazi leaders as a transitional measure designed to facilitate deportation elsewhere (Browning 2000; Hilberg 1985). Before the Final Solution was articulated, deportation meant emigration, primarily to the east. After the Final Solution, it meant deportation to a concentration camp.

There is no record of a general order that was ever given for the creation of Jewish ghetto communities. Hitler and his inner circle did discuss ghettoization as a strategy as early as the mid-1930s, but the policy appears to have evolved as a decentralized process, with initiatives taken by local German officials at various times. In smaller

Jewish communities an entire town might be ghettoized. In larger ones a Jewish district would be partitioned off (with barbed wire, wooden fences, or brick walls) from the rest of the city. *Judenrate*, or Jewish councils, were used to manage the Jewish population and administer Nazi demands. The councils were generally headed by a group of twelve to twenty-four Jews who were already respected as community leaders. They administered a ghetto bureaucracy that in some cases was quite elaborate, for they essentially performed all the administrative functions of a city government. They dealt with the food, housing, and medical needs of the population. They set up schools and a police force and supported cultural events. At the Nazis' request, they arranged for the confiscation of Jewish valuables and selected people for forced labor and even transports to extermination camps (Corni 2003; Gutman 1990a; Hilberg 1985; Rubenstein and Roth 1987).

Although the councils relieved the Germans of the burden of administering the day-to-day operations of the ghettos, the Nazis of course remained in charge. Recall Franz Grassler, the deputy commissioner of the Warsaw Jewish ghetto, who said that his job "was to maintain the ghetto and try to preserve the Jews as a work force. . . . [The] goal was very different from the one that later led to extermination" (quoted in Lanzmann 1985:79; see chapter 1). But Grassler and others like him were not given the resources to do their jobs without incurring mass starvation, disease, and death. There was inadequate food, coal, soap, and medicine; and sewage and garbage littered the streets. To be sure, there were some Nazis for whom the exploitation of Jewish labor was more important than Jewish deaths; and there were periods, even after the Final Solution was announced, that proponents of the "productive use of Jewish labor were permitted brief and precarious opportunities to pursue their goals" (Browning 2000:59). After the Final Solution, however, the prevailing Nazi policy was for Jewish workers to receive only a temporary reprieve from their ultimate fate. They were to be literally "worked to death" or gassed in a camp.

Didn't Grassler realize he was in fact a manager of death? Perhaps, for he admits that "people were dying in the streets. There were bodies everywhere. . . . [N]aturally with those inadequate rations and the overcrowding, a high, even excessive death rate was inevitable" (quoted in Lanzmann 1985:183–84). But he does not want to accept responsibility for what happened: "I had no power. . . . [Don't] overestimate my role. . . . [Don't] overestimate the authority of . . . a lawyer who got his degree at [age] twenty-seven" (1985:192–93). Nevertheless, overall, ghettoization and general privation overseen by ghetto bureaucrats like Grassler accounted for about 16 percent of Jewish deaths in the Holocaust (Hilberg 1985).

The Railways

The majority of Jews who died in the Holocaust (59 percent) perished in concentration camps (Hilberg 1985). And most of these Jews were delivered to these camps by rail. Thus the Reichsbahn, the German State Railways, was key to the annihilation process. The Reichsbahn was a large administrative unit housed in the Ministry of Transportation that employed about 1.4 million personnel who serviced both civilian and military transportation needs. All told, the Reichsbahn used about 2,000 trains to transport Jews to death camps and other locations where they were killed (Mierzejewski 2001; Spector 1990b).

Bureaucrats in the Reichsbahn performed important func-tions that facilitated the movement of trains (Hilberg 1989; Mierzejewski 2001). They constructed and published timetables, col-lected fares, and allocated cars and locomotives. In sending Jews to their death, they did not deviate much from the routine procedures they used to process ordinary train traffic. Recall Walter Stier, the bureaucrat who booked Jews on transports to the Treblinka extermi-nation camp (see chapter 1). "The work," he said, was "barely different from . . . [any other] work" (quoted in Lanzmann 1985:133). As Hilberg explains, the Reichsbahn was willing to ship Jews as if they were like any other cargo as long as it was paid for its services "by the track kilometer, . . . [w]ith children under ten going half-fare and children under four going free" (quoted in 1985:142). While the guards on the train required a round-trip fare, the Jews only had to be paid for one way. The party responsible for payment was the Gestapo, which had no separate budget for its transportation needs. However, the proceeds from the Jews' confiscated property was usually enough to cover the costs if the Gestapo received group rates.

> The Jews were . . . shipped in much the same way [as] any excursion group. . . granted a special fare if there were enough people traveling. The minimum was four hundred. . . . So even if there were fewer . . . it would pay to say there were four hundred . . . [to] get the half-fare. . . . [I]f there [was] exceptional filth in the cars . . . [or] damage to the equipment, which might be the case because the transports took so long and because five to ten percent of the prisoners died en

route, there might be an additional bill for that damage. (quoted in 1985:142–43)

Although Stier denies that he knew Treblinka was a death camp, he admits that, "without me these trains couldn't reach their destination" (quoted in Lanzmann 1985:135). For him, Treblinka was nothing but a destination, a place where people were "put up" (quoted in 1985:136). "I never went to Treblinka. I stayed in Krakow, in Warsaw, glued to my desk.... I was strictly a bureaucrat!" (quoted in 1985:135). Indeed, as Hilberg observes, Stier and others like him did their job as "a matter of course," as if it was "the most normal thing to do" (quoted in 1985:143). But it was not really a "normal job," for Jews were in fact crammed into freight and cattle cars, without ventilation or protection from the cold in winter and heat in summer, filling every inch until "there was no room to sit down" (Botwinick 2001:171). They were given no food or water and just a single pail in the corner that "soon overflowed with human waste." And upon arrival to their destination, most of them were killed.

The Killing Apparatus

As noted, about 16 percent of Jewish deaths were due to the general privation of ghetto living conditions. The rest of the Jews were either killed in open-air shootings (25 percent) or concentration camps (59 percent) (Hilberg 1985). We now turn to a consideration of these latter two methods of annihilating the European Jews.

Open-Air Shootings

The SS Einsatzgruppen, as noted in chapter 3, were the first troops deployed for the mass murder of civilian populations. However, they were substantially assisted by the Wehrmacht, the German army (Breitman 1991; Browning 2000; Förster 1986). The Wehrmacht not only permitted the Einsatzgruppen to operate in the eastern territories under its control, but it also engaged in mass killings themselves. In fact, Omer Bartov argues that Wehrmacht troops were directly "involved in widespread crimes against enemy soldiers and the civilian population, acting both on orders by their superiors and in many instances also on their own initiative" (1997a:169). Thus, according to Bartov, the military campaign on the eastern front was not simply a war of territorial expansion but "a war of annihilation" (see also Bartov 1992).

The Order Police were also involved in the mass killing of Jews (see chapter 1). This organization was established in 1936 when the entire policing system (including the Gestapo) was reorganized on a national basis under Himmler's control as Chief of the German Police. Under the command of Kurt Daluege, who had risen through the ranks of the SS, the Order Police consisted of both stationary and mobile formations that were initially intended to carry out more-or-less ordinary, civilian police functions. They were organized into battalions and reserve units, much like the U.S. National Guard, and those who enlisted in it were exempt from military conscription. The Order Police grew from about 131,000 troops on the eve of World War II to about 310,000 by 1943 (Browning 1992; Goldhagen 1996).

Whereas the Einsatsgruppen was a select group of Nazis who received special training for deployment in the killing of civilians, what is noteworthy about the Order Police is that they consisted of men who "were not particularly Nazified in any significant sense save that they were, loosely speaking, representative of the Nazified German society" (Goldhagen 1996:182; Spector 1990a). While Daluege was a dedicated SS man, only a fifth of the Order Police officers were SS, and a third were not even Nazi Party members. Among the rank-and-file, only a fourth were Nazi Party members and none were SS. The rank-and-file were older than the average military recruit (especially the reserves, who constituted about 42 percent of the troops), and many were thus socialized in the pre-Nazi era. They "were men who had known political standards and moral norms other than those of the Nazis . . . [and] would not seem to have been a very promising group from which to recruit mass murderers on behalf of the Nazi vision of a racial utopia free of Jews" (Browning 1992:48).

Some Order Police had participated in the civilian killings that began with the Polish invasion, but they were used to a greater extent during the Soviet campaign (Breitman 1998). Himmler in particular was aware that the execution of civilians would be difficult for these men. Thus at first the men were told they were eliminating anti-German resisters, saboteurs, and looters; and the victims were limited to male Jews between the ages of seventeen and forty-five. However, Himmler reasoned that "[o]nce they carried out mass murder in response to an alleged crime or provocation, it would be easier to get them to follow broader killing orders" and later kill men, women, and children of all ages (p. 48).

Himmler was right, for few men refused to participate. There is no evidence of significant dissent among the troops or of significant punishment for those few who were unwilling or unable to kill

(Breitman 1998; Browning 1992; Goldhagen 1996). Nevertheless, as Himmler had expected, many of the men had difficulty coping with their task. They were instructed to position their rifles on the victim's backbone just above the shoulder blade in order to make a "clean" shot. But they did not always shoot their victims properly; and blood, bone, and tissue were splattered all over the ground and on the men's faces and clothes. Killing people one to one, face to face, can indeed be a messy business. Alcohol was passed out to dull the men's anxiety. Most of the men who quit shooting appear to have done so more because they were physically repulsed and less because they thought what they were doing was wrong. One participant described the range of reactions this way: "When I am asked about the mood of [my] comrades, . . . I must say that I . . . observed nothing special, that is the mood was not especially bad. Many said that they never again wanted to experience something like that in their entire lives, while . . . others were content with saying an order is an order. With that the matter was settled for them" (quoted in Browning 2000:123). Some even developed astonishingly odd justifications. As one man admitted: "I made the effort . . . to shoot only children. It so happened that the mothers led the children by the hand. My [comrade] then shot the mother and I shot the child that belonged to her, because I reasoned . . . that after all without its mother the child could not live any longer. It was . . . soothing to my conscience to release children unable to live without their mothers" (quoted in Browning 1992:73).

Other shooters were more enthusiastic about their work. One man observed that "with few exceptions, [they were] quite happy to take part in shootings of Jews. They had a ball!" (quoted in Goldhagen 1996:396). Some inflicted special humiliations, for instance, making the Jews run a gauntlet and beating them before they were killed, or making the Jews strip naked and crawl to the mass graves that awaited them. Some police took souvenir photos that they sent home to their wives and girlfriends. One officer, an SS man, even invited his new bride to watch a massacre (Browning 1992). At night the men would celebrate and make jokes about their actions or keep scores on the number of kill. When "Jew hunts," or *Judenjagd* as they were called, were organized to track down Jews who had fled into the forest, more men volunteered than was necessary for the job. Indeed, in German the term *Judenjagd* has a positive valence insofar as *jagd* suggests "a pleasurable pursuit, rich in adventure, involving no danger to the hunter, . . . its reward . . . a record of animals slain" (Goldhagen 1996:238).

To relieve the Order Police of its more gruesome duties, the Nazis increasingly relied on SS-trained, Ukrainian, Latvian, and Lithuanian prisoners of war to do the actual killing. These men were screened for "their anti-Communist (and hence almost invariably anti-Semitic) sentiments, offered an escape from probable starvation, and promised that they would not be used in combat against the Soviet army" (Browning 1992:52). This enabled the Order Police to be deployed mostly as "ghetto clearers" who rounded up Jews for deportation or delivered Jews to others who did the killing. After their earlier experiences, this type of work seemed relatively innocuous to the men.

The Role of the Medical Profession

In chapter 2 we noted the participation of the German medical profession in the Eugenics campaign that involved compulsory sterilization and euthanasia. We discussed the T_4 program that operated six killing centers, where Christian Wirth, a nonphysician SS officer began experimenting with gas chambers as a means of inducing death. We also noted Himmler's authorization of the use of T_4 personnel and facilities to rid the concentration camps of physically and mentally ill prisoners, which was a crucial step in the emergence of the Final Solution because it was the first time that the camps "became connected with a principle of medical-eugenic killing" (Lifton 1986:138).

As previously noted, Himmler was aware of the psychological strain imposed on Germans involved in the open-air shooting of Jews. In August 1941, he had attended the execution of some 100 Jews by an Einsatsgruppen unit and was deeply disturbed himself, according to one eyewitness account, "Almost fainting, pale, limbs quivering" (quoted in Adam 1989:139). Himmler was also concerned that his men remain internally "correct," that "despite the difficulty of the task," they did not become brutes (quoted in Adam 1989:139).[9] Moreover, it took too long to kill large numbers of people this way, and too many dead bodies were left without efficient means of disposal (prior to the use of crematoria, the bodies were buried in mass graves or burned in open air fires).

Chelmno was the first of six Polish camps that were specifically intended for extermination, and killing by gas began there in December 1941.[10] Fifty or more people were crowded into each of three vans, which looked like furniture delivery trucks.[11] A hose was attached to the exhaust pipe of each van, filling the vehicles with carbon monoxide. The vans were driven around for about

15 minutes, stopped near a pit, and emptied of their dead occupants. The executioners soon realized that this was an inefficient method of mass killing. The victims would bang on the doors, screaming and pleading with the drivers, who experienced much distress. It sometimes took longer than 15 minutes to kill everyone, and gasoline to run the vans was in short supply. Clearly, another method for increasing "output" had to be found (Adam 1989; Botwinick 2001; Krakowski 1990a).

Wirth, who regarded the Chelmno operation as amateurish, was soon brought in to revamp the killing process. He was named commandant of the Bełzec death camp and by February was supervising carbon-monoxide executions in gas chambers modeled after those he used in the T_4 program. Wirth also oversaw the construction of gas chambers at the Sobibór and Treblinka extermination camps. Eventually about 100 T_4 personnel were transferred to Bełzec, Sobibór, and Treblinka (Adam 1989; Friedlander 1998; Rubenstein and Roth 1987).

Beginning with *Aktion 14f13*, Nazi physicians were also put in charge of the "selections," the process by which concentration camp inmates deemed capable of work were separated from those deemed incapable (Lifton 1986). Nazi leaders hoped that doctors' involvement in these decisions would lend a veneer of credibility to the killings by making it appear that the selections had been made for medical reasons, as one doctor explained, "with precise medical judgment" (quoted in Lifton 1986:173).

In addition, during the war years Nazi physicians conducted horrendous medical-research experiments on an estimated 7,000 persons in hospitals and concentration camps. At least seventy projects of this kind were undertaken. Some experiments were designed to test human endurance under severe conditions. In conjunction with the German air force, for example, high-altitude experiments tested the maximum height at which an individual could survive without oxygen equipment. Inmates were subjected to freezing cold temperatures to the point of unconsciousness to study methods of reviving them. Some were made to drink ocean seawater to examine its dehydration effects. Wounds were inflicted with the intent of causing severe infections in order to test remedies. Bones were intentionally fractured and even severed from inmates to develop transplantation techniques, and some people's limbs were amputated. Prisoners were injected with the typhus virus and other contagious diseases to experiment with immunization vaccines. Most of these inmates of course died (Cohen 1990; Fisher 2001; Lengyel 1947).

Joseph Mengele (1911–79) was arguably the most notorious Nazi doctor. He ordered the deaths of prisoners with physical anomalies (such as dwarfs and hunchbacks) so he could dissect and study them. He is perhaps most well known for the experiments he conducted on some 1,500 sets of twin children—subjecting them to X-rays and various chemicals, ultimately killing them so he could examine their internal organs—in the hopes of learning about the causes of twin births (Lifton 1986; Rubenstein and Roth 1987).

The Concentration Camp System

The Nazi concentration camp system consisted of hundreds of camps across Europe (Gutman and Saf 1984; Pingel 1990). "Concentration camp" is a term that designates a variety of facilities with different (though sometimes overlapping) functions—for instance, incarceration, forced labor, or extermination. Some camps, like Auschwitz, consisted of numerous sub-camps. The camp system was run by the SS and guarded by a special unit known as the *Totenkopfverbande*, or Death's Head Units, named after the skull and crossbones insignia worn by members' on their black caps. In 1942 the camps were incorporated into the SS-run WVHA, or Economic-Administrative Main Office, which, as noted earlier, ran a vast array of SS business enterprises that exploited slave labor (Pingel 1990; Poole 1997a; Taylor and Shaw 1987).

Initially the Nazis used the concentration camps to incarcerate their political adversaries within Germany (such as Communists, leftists, trade unionists, and oppositional church leaders). Next they sent so-called "asocial elements" (such as vagrants, beggars, and criminals with prior convictions). After the Kristallnacht pogrom in November 1938, the camps were increasingly used to deal with the "Jewish problem." Dachau and Buchenwald, established in 1933 and 1937, respectively, are among the most well known of the early camps operated within German borders (Gellately 2001; Marcuse 2001; Pingel 1990; Rubenstein and Roth 1987).

Elsewhere, in the Nazi-occupied territories, concentration camps were opened at Mauthausen in Austria (1938) and Auschwitz in Poland (1940). The Auschwitz camp, which after expansion became known as Auschwitz I, was constructed on the site of a converted prewar compound that initially had been used to house seasonal migrant workers and later as a Polish military barracks; and before expansion by the Nazis, it had consisted of twenty-two brick buildings (Buszko 1990; Dwork and van Pelt 2002; Steinbacher 2005).

Theresienstadt, established in Czechoslovakia in November 1941, was set up in a former military fortress as a ghetto-style camp, with a Jewish council that ran its internal affairs. Heydrich envisioned it as a "model" Jewish settlement, designed, in Eichmann's words, "to preserve appearances to the outside," to reassure foreign governments that conditions in the camps were not so bad after all (quoted in Browning 2000:55). In reality it was only a transit camp, a temporary holding place for Jews who were eventually sent to Auschwitz or Treblinka (Bondy 2001; Dov Kulka 1990; Friedländer 2009).

Experimental gassings were first conducted on about 900 inmates (mostly Soviet prisoners of war) in Auschwitz I in September 1941. A gas chamber and crematorium were installed, and prussic acid (hydrogen cyanide)—which had been used in the camp as a disinfectant and pesticide—was used to gas the inmates. Crystalline pellets of the chemical, whose commercial name was Zyklon B, were dropped through small holes in the roof. The pellets vaporized upon contact with the air and heat, killing the inmates. The corpses were then burned in the crematorium. The use of Zyklon B to gas inmates was apparently the brainchild of Auschwitz Deputy Commandant Karl Fritsch, who had been responsible for procuring the chemical for disinfectant/pesticide purposes. Rudolf Höss, the Auschwitz commandant, was pleased with the results and discussed them with Eichmann (Adam 1989; Breitman 1991; Dwork and van Pelt 2002; Friedrich 1994).

When Himmler had visited Auschwitz I in May 1941, he ordered the construction of an additional camp outside the main camp to be used for prisoners of war. Construction at Birkenau, a site about two kilometers away, began in October. However, its original mission changed, for by May 1942 the new Auschwitz-Birkenau camp was receiving all types of prisoners, including Jews. Gas chambers with large holding capacities were added, and special crematoria ovens with two to three muffles were built, enabling the killing and disposal of more bodies in less time (Dwork and van Pelt 2002; Piper 2006; Public Broadcasting Corporation 1995). Birkenau became the largest killing center in the camp system. According to Höss's calculation, when the gas chambers/crematoria were running at maximum capacity, it was possible to process as many as 9,000 bodies a day. From

1.1 to 1.5 million people, about 80 percent of whom were Jews, died at Birkenau (Adam 1989; Buszko 1990; Friedrich 1994; Greif 2001). In addition, in November 1942, a third Auschwitz camp was constructed a few miles away at Monowitz, where IG Farben, as noted earlier, was contracted by the SS to operate a synthetic oil and rubber plant. Given the food rations and hard labor at that camp, most of the prisoners at Auschwitz-Monowitz lasted no more than about three months before they were sent to Birkenau to be gassed. At the same time, a prisoner had a better chance of surviving Monowitz than Birkenau, provided he could find extra provisions, a matter we will take up in the next chapter (Berger 2011; Hayes 1987; Levi [1960] 1993; Rubenstein and Roth 1987).

Notes

1. See also Kreimeier (1996) and Spielvogel and Redles (2010) for accounts of the German film industry's complicity with the Nazi regime.
2. The list of companies that used slave labor reads like a "who's who" of German business and includes corporations such as BMW, Daimler Benz, and Volkswagen (Simpson 1993).
3. The name "Zyklon B" comes from the first letters of the German names for cyanide, chlorine, and nitrogen (Friedrich 1994).
4. This camp is sometimes called Buna or Buna-Monowitz, Buna referring to the synthetic rubber plant that was constructed but which never went into operation. Neither was much synthetic oil actually produced (Rubenstein and Roth 1987).
5. Gestapo is an acronym of *Geheime Staatspoizei*.
6. See chapter 3, note 7.
7. For a consideration of postwar Polish violence against Jews, see Browning (2010), Gross (2006), and Polonsky and Michlic (2004).
8. Although more than half of the Jews killed in the Holocaust were from Poland, and about a fifth were from the Soviet Union, an additional fifth were from Western Europe (Gutman and Rozett 1990). But whereas the Nazis thought that the non-Jewish people of Eastern Europe were racially inferior, subject to colonization and use as slave laborers, they did not think that of the non-Jewish people of the West. Although many non-Jews in the East were killed, they were not targeted for extermination; and at times Nazi actions were inconsistent in their treatment of them. For instance, the Slavic-speaking people of Slovakia, Croatia, and Bulgaria were treated as "honorable allies," and many were even admitted into the *Waffen SS* (SS army) (Deák 2000a).
9. In a speech to a group of SS leaders, Himmler said: "Most of you know what it means to see a hundred corpses lying together, five hundred, or a thousand. To have stuck it out and at the same time—apart from exceptions caused by human weakness—to have remained decent fellows, that is what has made us hard . . . [and] is a page of glory in our history which . . . shall never be written" (quoted in Wistrich 1995:114).

10.   The other Polish extermination camps were at Auschwitz-Birkenau, Bełzec, Sobibor, Treblinka, and Majdanek. There was also an extermination camp at Maly Trostinets in Minsk in German-occupied Belorussia. In addition, camps not initially intended for extermination, such as Mauthausen in Austria and Dachau and Ravensbruck (a women's camp) in Germany, were later used for this purpose (Adam 1989; Gilbert 2000).

The camps at Bełzec, Sobibor, and Treblinka were part of *Aktion Reinhard,* named after Heydrich, who had been assassinated (see chapter 3, note 7), which was aimed at killing the 2,284,000 Jews who were living in the General Government for the Occupied Areas of Poland. The General Government, which had been established after the invasion of Poland, was the German occupying government in the part of interior Poland that had not been annexed by Germany per se for German ethnics (Arad 1987).

11.   Gas vans had also been used to kill disabled patients (see chapter 2, note 10).

5

Jewish Responses
to the Holocaust

During the war, Abba Kovner (1918–88), a young Jewish poet and writer was a leader of the first Jewish resistance organization to emerge in the ghettos of Eastern Europe—in Vilna, a city in Lithuania. Vilna had been captured by the Germans in June 1941 and scourged by squads of Einsatzgruppen. Six months later, after the Nazis continued to kill Jews throughout Lithuania, Kovner and about 150 of his compatriots founded a Jewish combat organization, *Fareinikte Partizaner Organizatsie* (United Partisan Organization). Adopting a biblical image from *Psalms* (44:11), Kovner insisted, "We will not be led like sheep to the slaughter!" (Gutman 1990b; Rubenstein and Roth 1987).

At the time of the final liquidation of Jews from Vilna in September 1943, Kovner led members of his group into the forest to escape. Kovner survived the war, but he lived to regret how his admonition about "sheep to the slaughter" was misused to blame Jews for their own victimization (Rubenstein and Roth 1987). As we shall see, however, it is simply a "failure of imagination to expect" a largely untrained and unarmed population (that included children and the elderly) to engage in meaningful acts of physical resistance against armed German soldiers who had been ordered to kill them and who engaged in the practice of collective reprisal, punishing innocent people for the actions of others (Clendinnen 1999:58).

At the same time, there was in fact resistance, which belies the stereotype of Jewish passivity. Some of this resistance took place at the individual level. As survivor and psychiatrist Viktor Frankl suggests, a person had to make an "inner decision" to persevere and be on the constant lookout for opportunities to ameliorate their plight (1959:87). But some of this resistance was organized as well, and constituted a "countermovement" to the Nazi social movement aimed at killing the Jews (see Zald and Useem 1987).

Irving Louis Horowitz (2009) reports that by now there are some 3,500 first-person books and monographs, published in English alone, written by witnesses to the Holocaust, often by victims and survivors of the death camps. Currently as well, there are numerous video archive projects, most notably at the Fortunoff Video Archive for Holocaust Testimonies at Yale University and the Shoah Visual History Foundation, founded by Steven Spielberg, at the University of Southern California, which have recorded countless videotaped testimonies of Jewish survivors (Berger 2011; Kraft 2002; Langer 1991). "Each of these accounts," Horowitz observes, "is unique, and many provide moving insights in their own right, as a whole and as a collectivity" (2009:494). Shamai Davidson, the Israeli psychiatrist who worked extensively with Holocaust survivors, suggests that the accumulation of these testimonies may make possible an analysis of their experience that was even "denied some individual survivors as they were preoccupied by the bitter drama of their own battle for survival" (1992:24).

It is to this analysis that we now turn, as we address the Jewish response to the Holocaust: how they accommodated themselves to and attempted to resist the Final Solution, how they perished and how they survived. We begin with some general observations about the phenomenon of survival and then consider the dilemmas of both Jewish accommodation, as in the case of the Jewish councils, and of resistance to the Nazi death machine.

The Question of Survival

The question of survival has been a long-standing preoccupation of literature and popular culture, whether it is the story of Robinson Crusoe castaway on a remote tropical island or the artificially constructed competition of the "reality" TV show *Survivor*. In his book *Deep Survival: Who Lives, Who Dies, and Why*, Laurence Gonzales purports to describe "the art and science of survival, . . . whether in the wilderness or in meeting any of life's great challenges" (2003:back cover). According to Gonzales, "every survival situation is the same in its essence"—it is one in which the individual is "annealed in the fires of peril, . . . looking death in the face" (2003:13, 24). More recently, in *The Survivors Club: The Secrets and Science that Could Save Your Life*, Ben Sherwood defines a survivor as "anyone who faces and overcomes adversity, hardship, illness, or physical or emotional trauma," including "the friends and family who stand beside them," noting that "everyone is a survivor" (2009:15–16).

It is surely a stretch, to say nothing of lacking in analytical rigor, to say that "every survival situation is the same in its essence" and that "everyone is a survivor." Is the experience of Auschwitz really the same as being stranded in the wilderness? It is one thing to portray genuine victims of terror as "survivors" (such as survivors of rape, domestic violence, and childhood sexual abuse, or even survivors of life-threatening illnesses), but it is quite another to portray the crises and challenges of everyday life (such as surviving a divorce, surviving college, getting a job, or keeping a job) as akin to surviving the Holocaust. Nevertheless, popular culture is replete with such injudicious comparison.[1] Clearly, if we are going to consider survival of the Holocaust as an object of serious scholarly inquiry, the concept requires more rigor. As far as I can tell, outside of some early studies of human behavior in the concentration camp, which treated the prisoners more as passive *victims* than as survivors (Bettelheim 1960; Bloch 1947; Cohen 1953), as well as the genre of the Holocaust memoir itself, of which Elie Wiesel's *Night* (1958) and Primo Levi's *Survival in Auschwitz* (1960) stand out as classics, Robert Jay Lifton (1967) was perhaps the first scholar to bring the concept of survival into the social and behavioral sciences, beginning with his work on the survivors of Hiroshima. Later in his essay "The Concept of Survivor," Lifton aimed to delineate "common psychological responses of survivors" without implying that the events themselves—Hiroshima, Auschwitz, or a devastating flood—could be equated (1980:113–14). His focus was the *"total disaster*: the physical, social, and spiritual obliteration of a human community," and he defined the survivor in this context as "one who has encountered, been exposed to, or witnessed death, and has himself or herself remained alive" (pp. 113, 117).

During the period in which Lifton was working on this topic, Terrence Des Pres (1976) published his important treatise *The Survivor: An Anatomy of Life in the Death Camps*. Des Pres defined the *context* of survival as a "condition of extremity" that persists beyond one's "ability to alter or end" and where "there is no escape, no place to go except the grave" (p. 7). The survivor, according to Des Pres, is one who sustains unimaginable physical and psychic damage and yet "manages to stay alive in body *and* in spirit, enduring dread and hopelessness without the loss of will to carry on in human ways" (p. 6). He is not a hero but "a protagonist in the classic [literary] sense, for by staying alive he becomes an effective agent in the fight against evil and injustice" (pp. 7–8).

According to data compiled by Israel Gutman and Robert Rozett (1990), the Holocaust took the lives of about 5.6 million to 5.9 million Jews, out of an initial population of about 9.8 million European Jews, leaving about 4 million prewar Jews who remained alive after World War II, a figure that includes about 2 million Jews from the Soviet Union alone (see chapter 1, note 1). Some of the survivors managed to emigrate before the war. For example, in the years between the Nazis' rise to power in 1933 and the start of World War II, many German Jews did manage to leave Germany. We have already noted the disincentives to emigrate caused by restrictions on the economic assets Jews were allowed to take with them and the lack of places to go (see chapter 2). Nevertheless, over 70 percent of German Jewry was able to leave before the gates of emigration were closed (Rubenstein 1997). In addition, nearly 70 percent of Austrian Jews emigrated in the twenty-one months between the German invasion of their country and World War II, and over 20 percent of Czech Jews left in the five months between the annexation of Czechoslovakia and the war. To be sure, if the Allies' immigration policies had been more generous, more Jews might have found safe havens elsewhere (Breitman and Kraut 1987; Tilles 2008; Wyman 1984). We will consider this issue in chapter 6.

During the war, some Jews tried to escape or otherwise hide from their Nazi antagonists, but this was a feat that could not be accomplished without substantial help and risk-taking from the non-Jewish population, which we will also discuss in more detail in chapter 6, and this kind of help was rarely forthcoming. As for those who did not escape but who managed to survive, was their survival random? Survivors themselves suggest so when they have commonly attributed their own survival to luck, chance, or miracles—a matter of being in the right place or the wrong place at the right or wrong time (Browning 2010; Helmreich 1992; Kraft 2002; Rothchild 1981). Holocaust scholar Lawrence Langer suggests this as well when he observes that the situation of the Jews during this period indicates "what it meant (and means) in our time to exist *without* a sense of human agency," without the ability to exercise control over one's life (1991:199). In fact, Gerald Markle and colleagues (1992), sociologists no less, believe that generalizations about survival should be resisted because this would deny "the singular humanity of each survivor. . . . [E]ach stands alone, . . . paints its own picture" (pp. 180, 200).

To follow Markle et al.'s advice, however, would only mean another missed opportunity for sociological analysis of the Holocaust. Raul Hilberg points out, for example, that "[s]urvival was not altogether random," especially insofar as there were prewar differences among survivors that maximized or minimized their chances, as the case might be (1992:188).[2] "Although the German destruction process was a massive leveler, it did not obliterate" all prewar differences (p. 159). These differences, however, acquired new meaning during the Nazi period. They were no longer a measure of high or low status but of more or less vulnerability. Age, for instance, was among the key factors, for survivors were more likely to be relatively young (between their teens and thirties) and in good health at the start of their ordeal, a characteristic that maximized their ability to endure hardship and withstand disease. Additionally, those with particular occupational skills—such as physicians, carpenters, shoemakers, and tailors—also fared better, because they remained useful to others who might want to keep them alive (Berger 2011).

Prewar knowledge of non-Jewish cultural schemas, including language and religion, was also crucial to Jewish survival, particularly outside of the camps, where, in Erving Goffman's (1959) terms, impression management skills were necessary to maintain a "front" or orchestrate a "performance" as someone who was not Jewish. One's physical appearance was among the factors that could make it more difficult to pass as a non-Jew, as in the case of Orthodox Jewish men who grew long beards and sideburns that curled down to their shoulders, and who wore black hats and long black or gray caftans. If one had lived in relative isolation from non-Jews, they also would have had more difficulty interacting with them as one of them. In prewar Poland, more than half the Jewish children attended special Jewish schools, which inhibited their mastery of the Polish language; during the war years, these characteristics limited their ability to pass as Gentile Poles (Berger 2011; Paldiel 1996; Tec 1986).

The experience of my uncle, Sol Berger, is illustrative here. Sol survived the war, in part, by passing as a Catholic among Catholic Poles. Prior to the emergence of the Final Solution and his escape from his hometown of Krosno, Poland, Sol had been arrested for trading illegal currencies on the black market. He spent several months in jail incarcerated with a Polish Catholic Priest who conducted religious services three times a day. Sol paid close attention and learned about religious rituals and customs that later helped him pass as a Catholic and attend church with other Poles. However, as he said, "I never dared go to confession because I did not know what to do" (quoted in Berger 2011:82).

Hilberg also suggests that there was a psychological profile, a set of personality traits, that maximized Jewish survival, which he describes as "realism, rapid decision making, and tenacious holding on to life" (1992:188). Similarly, William Helmreich (1992) attributes survival to inner qualities such as assertiveness, tenacity, courage, willingness to take risks, flexibility, optimism, and intelligence; and Christopher Browning (2010) to ingenuity, resourcefulness, adaptability, perseverance, and endurance. Michal Unger (1986) highlights the role of internal defense mechanisms, which enabled individuals to block out the horror and focus on their survival needs; while Gerhard Botz (1991) describes survivors in terms of their capacity for voluntary action, sociability, and readiness to offer and receive support. Mary Gallant and Jay Cross (1992) characterize survivors as individuals who acquired a "challenged identity" after an initial period of disorientation, which gave them the will to go on by observing others' courageous responses to their common ordeal.

Indeed, these characterizations of Jewish survival are a far cry from earlier portrayals of Jews that emphasized their passive or predatory responses. In an influential early appraisal of concentration camp behavior, for example, Bruno Bettelheim (1960) described prisoners as regressing to a childish dependency on the SS guards, experiencing deindividuation, abandoning previously inculcated norms and values, and eventually identifying completely with their oppressors. Others noted the physical deprivation and psychological degradation that ground down prisoners into a state of profound apathy and lack of affect, as was the case with the *Muselmänner*, those skeleton-like prisoners or "walking corpses" who were on the verge of death but not yet of it. [The term *Muselmänn* (singular) or *Muselmänner* (plural) is apparently derived from the German word for Muslim and was based on the fallacious belief that Muslims were fatalistic and indifferent to their environment (Lifton 1980; Marrus 1987).] Other prisoners were described as descending into a primal state of self-preservation, an "all against all" atmosphere that bred corrupt and predatory behavior (Bloch 1947; Cohen 1953; Des Pres 1976; Marrus 1987).

Des Pres (1976) was one of the first to observe that these formulations were derived from limited observations and were misleading as generalizations. Bettelheim, for one, developed his thesis on the basis of camp conditions in the 1930s, at a time when prisoners who held positions of power (trustees) were not political prisoners or Jews but those who had been convicted of predatory crimes, including murder. Increasingly analysts adopted a more nuanced view of the variety and complexity of the Jewish response and turned their attention to the constructive, indeed agentive, strategies that emerged during the Nazi period. Considerable testimony and scholarly research indicates that Jews who survived the war often emerged from an initial period of shock, despair, and disbelief able to realistically appraise their situation and take strategic courses of action through calculated risk-taking and disobedience. Moreover, many were also able to do so without complete abandonment of prewar norms of human reciprocity and systems of morality.

Lawrence Langer (1991), in his study of Fortunoff Archive testimonials, makes a distinction between acts that were "selfish" and acts that were "self-ish."

> The selfish act ignores the needs of others through choice when the agent is in a position to help without injuring one's self in any appreciable way. Selfishness is motivated by greed, indifference, [or] malice. . . . [In the] self-ish act, however, . . . [one] is vividly aware of the needs of others but because of the nature of the situation is unable to choose freely the generous impulse that a more compassionate nature yearns to express. (1991:124)

But more than that, survivors' accounts regularly include reports of people maintaining hope, holding onto their humanity, and offering and receiving help from others. Davidson notes that even in the camps, individuals bonded and provided each other with mutual aid that helped them maintain hope and preserve "a sense of self despite the dehumanization and amorality" (1992:121). Anna Pawełczynska points out that those "who made no revisions" in preexisting humanitarian impulses perished if they "applied them in an absolute way," but there were always those who united "together in the practice of the basic norm, 'Do not harm your neighbor and, if possible, save him'" (1979:144). In his recent study of the Wierzbnik-Starachowice slave-labor camp system in Central Poland, Browning reports that prisoners "created a moral system . . . based on a hierarchy of moral obligation rather than either an impossible universality or a total annulment of moral obligation. What they expected and accepted of one another was first of all loyalty to one's own remaining family members. Second, one had obligations to one's friends and neighbors, third to one's townspeople, and fourth to Jews vis-à-vis other non-Jewish prisoners" (2010:298).[3]

Psychologists Patricia Benner, Ethel Roskies, and Richard Lazarus (1980) have applied a general model of stress and coping behavior to describe the internal and external structure of the survival process. They characterize stress as a relational concept that reflects "reciprocity between *external* demands, constraints, and resources" and "*internal* resources to manage them" (p. 219, emphasis mine). They do not view survivors as helpless victims or passive responders to circumstances but as persons who attempted to manipulate the stress experience to achieve some degree of control over "those small segments of reality that could be managed . . . [and contained] possibilities for direct action" (pp. 236, 238). Coping proceeded through cognitive appraisal of the stress situation and evaluation of available resources and options. Actions were then taken on the basis of this appraisal. "Any cessation of appraisal, as in the case of individuals who withdrew into . . . [a] state of apathy, . . . was a signal of impending death" (pp. 235–36).[4]

At the same time, all these observations about survival require mention of an important point: survival was a *collective* accomplishment. In the concentration camps, it required an ability to "organize," to use the camp lexicon, that is, to acquire additional life-sustaining resources through unauthorized means; and successful organizing was a matter of collective action and derived from a person's position in the functional hierarchy of the camps and the network of social relationships among prisoners (Berger 2011; Des Pres 1976; Pawełczynska 1979). Outside the camps, as mentioned earlier, Jews' ability to pass as Christians was invariably dependent on the support they received from the non-Jewish population (see chapter 6).

The Jewish Councils

The Jewish councils in the ghettos of Nazi-occupied Europe, which were set up by the Nazis to issue their edicts and manage the remnants of the Jewish community in various localities, arguably comprised the central organizing framework of the Jewish response to the Holocaust (see chapter 3). Perhaps for this reason, they have been subject to criticism, most notably from Hannah Arendt (1963) and Raul Hilberg (1985), for being overly compliant with the Nazis and for collaborating, however unwittingly, in the destruction of their own people. Browning notes that these "councils, at least in the first generation of membership, were usually composed of traditional community leaders, though often they were those who had held only second-echelon positions before the war, as the most prominent leaders often had successfully fled" (2010:35).

The councils were faced with a difficult and untenable task, what Langer (1991) describes as a series of "choiceless choices." Some council members genuinely believed that if they did not cooperate with the Nazis—even to the point of helping to register and round up Jews for deportation to the camps—the Jewish community would be even worse off. They tried to ameliorate conditions in the ghettos by negotiating (usually unsuccessfully) with the Germans for more resources and by helping to maintain the religious, educational, and cultural life of the community and provide social-welfare assistance (when available) for those who were in the most need. They pursued a strategy of "rescue through work," hoping that by making Jews economically useful to the Nazis, they might maximize the number of people who could hold on until the Allies won the war. The unfortunate irony was that the "crowded disease-ridden ghetto as such had become the promise of a haven, and the imposition of forced labor a lifeline to survival" (Hilberg 1992:114; see also Bauer 2001; Braham 1989; Friedländer 2009).

In chapter 2 we noted that social movements provide members with a frame or scheme of interpretation to make sense of events. Movement frames allow certain lines of action to be defined as "morally imperative in spite of associated risks" (Snow et al. 1986:466). In the case of the Jewish councils, their task was to convince their local Jewish communities that the circumstances called for compromise and accommodation to Nazi policies. Other Jewish groups, however, insisted upon engaging in armed resistance. Some councils tried to undermine these efforts, fearing they would provoke Nazi reprisal. They often withheld knowledge of the Final Solution from the rest of the population, denied rumors of atrocities, maintained false hope that things were going to get better, and tried to suppress internal resistance.

It is also true that the council system of ghetto government entailed a distribution of privileges. At least for the time prior to deportation to a concentration camp, council members themselves were spared some of the "intense deprivations of crowding, cold, and gnawing hunger" (Hilberg 1992:160–61). The tasks needed for the administration of the ghettos also created a layer of bureaucratic functionaries who fared better. These positions included a Jewish police force, which was used by the Nazis to enforce their edicts, including roundups for deportation to death camps. And people with more prewar financial means were able to live better than those without such means. In the long run, few were spared, but some were more likely than others to be deported later in the process. In that sense, their chances of survival were enhanced.

Mordechai Chaim Rumkowski (1877–1944), perhaps more than any other Jewish council leader, has "attracted the attention of historians and writers, and opinions about him, his behavior, and his accomplishments range from one extreme to the other" (Krakowski 1990b:1314). Rumkowski headed the Jewish council in Łódz, and he "displayed great zeal and organizational ability in running the factories and the internal life of the ghetto," trying to insure that Jewish labor remained valuable to his Nazi overseers (p. 1313). But Rumkowski's duties also included organizing the deportation of ghetto Jews to death camps, and the "few who dared to speak up against [him] or organize resistance to him ran the risk of his taking revenge, which in some extreme instances meant being included in the lists of candidates for deportation" (p. 1314). From as early as the end of 1941, after the Chelmno extermination camp had been in place (see chapter 4), and even as the final liquidation of the Łódz ghetto was underway in the spring of 1944, Rumkowski complied with Nazi deportation orders while trying to maintain a saving remnant.

Although Rumkowski's critics brand him as a "traitor and collaborator," others acknowledge that he "helped extend the life span of the Łódz ghetto, which remained in existence when all the other ghettos in Poland had been liquidated. Those who hold the latter opinion point out that the [5,000 to 7,000] survivors of the Łódz ghetto constituted, in relative terms, the largest among all the groups of Holocaust survivors in Poland" (p. 1314).

Jewish Resistance

To a large extent, Jews' historical adaptation to persecution had imbued Jewish culture with the notion that accommodation, rather than resistance, was the most effective strategy of survival (Hilberg 1985). During the war, only when all hope was lost, when knowledge of certain death was undeniable, was armed resistance perceived as the preferred option by some elements of the Jewish community. In the ghettos, the impetus for such a counter-movement generally came from members of Zionist youth movements (Einwohner 2003, 2009; Gutman 1990c,d). Zionism was a European-Jewish social movement that emerged in the last half of the nineteenth century to create a national Jewish state in Palestine (now Israel).[5] Theodor Herzl (1860–1904) was arguably the most notable proponent of Zionism. Herzl was a Jewish journalist from Vienna who covered the trial of Alfred Dreyfus in Paris in 1894 (see chapter 2). The conspiracy against Dreyfus, an assimilated French Jew, led Herzl to conclude that emigration to Palestine was the only viable solution for the plight of the European Jews. Subsequently, he published a book, *Der Judenstaat* (The Jewish State), and in 1897 became the first president of the World Zionist Organization. According to Herzl:

> The Jewish Question still exists. It would be foolish to deny it. It exists wherever Jews live in perceptible numbers. Where it does not yet exist, it will be brought by Jews in the course of their migrations. We naturally move to those places where we are not persecuted, and there our presence soon produces persecution. . . . We are one people—our enemies have made us one. . . . Distress binds us together, and thus united, we suddenly discover our strength. Yes, we are strong enough to form a state. . . . We possess all human and material resources necessary for the purpose. . . . Palestine is our ever-memorable historic home. . . . We shall live at last, as free men, on our own soil, and die peacefully in our own home. (cited in Mendes-Flohr and Reinharz 1995:534, 537)

The Zionist movement gave birth to a number of youth organizations of both the political left and right. In Poland, the country with the largest Jewish population in Europe, these youth movements were characterized by their rejection of traditional Jewish culture and what they perceived as the general passivity of adult Jewish society. During the German occupation they more quickly abandoned the "illusions still held by their elders" and clearly recognized "the threat to their existence" (Bauer 1989b:239; Gutman 1990c).

Wartime Zionist youth groups built upon preexisting organizational ties to establish armed resistance groups in the ghettos and forests of Poland. However, a basic requirement of effective armed resistance was the acquisition of weapons that Jews locked in the ghettos had difficulty obtaining. In addition, those on the outside of the ghettos often encountered hostility from the local Polish population, including, anti-Nazi Polish partisan (armed resistance) units. Sol Berger, for example, who joined an anti-Semitic Polish partisan group in the forests of eastern Poland, had to conceal his Jewish identity not just from the Nazis but also from his Polish comrades: "I never told them I was Jewish because I was fearful of what they would do to me. They often talked about the Jews—that the one good thing that Hitler was doing was killing the Jews" (quoted in Berger 2011:84).[6] Moreover, while the Allies parachuted arms to Polish partisan groups, they withheld similar assistance from Jews, "ostensibly because Jews were not a clearly defined national group" (Rubenstein and Roth 1987:175; see also Marrus 1987).

Arguably the most famous Jewish resistance effort took place in the Warsaw ghetto, the largest Jewish ghetto in Europe. By November 1940, the Jewish population of about 500,000, which now included refugees from other communities, was sealed in a 3½ square mile area surrounded by an 11½ foot brick wall topped by barbed wire. Mass deportations to the Treblinka extermination camp began in July 1942, and the Warsaw Jewish council complied with Nazi directives to deliver 6,000 to 7,000 Jews a day. This predicament spawned the *Zydowska Organizacja Bojowa* (ZOB), the Jewish Combat Organization, a resistance group of less than a thousand members under the leadership of a young, left-wing Zionist, Mordekhai Anielewicz (1919–43). Anielewicz and his followers understood the implication of the deportations. Whereas the Jewish council "acted as though the ghetto had a future," the ZOB realized that it did not (Rubenstein and Roth 1987:166). They believed that it was better to die with honor than passively accept their fate (Botwinick 2001; Einwohner 2003; Gutman 1990b).

In January 1943, with only about 65,000 Jews left in the ghetto, Anielewicz led a small ZOB contingent armed with only a few pistols and hand grenades against the Nazi troops who were trying to deport a large group of Jews. The revolt temporarily saved about 90 percent of the intended deportees and gave the Warsaw Jews an unaccustomed thrill of seeing the Germans retreat (Gutman 1990b; Lubetkin 1981).

For a while the Warsaw deportations were halted, but in April Heinrich Himmler ordered the total dissolution of the ghetto in three days. The Jewish resisters, vastly outnumbered by Nazi troops and local police who had far greater fire power (including armored vehicles and tanks), held out for four weeks. In the end, however, the ghetto lay in ruins and most of the Jews were killed (Botwinick 2001; Gutman 1990b).

The ghetto resisters were fully aware that they would eventually lose, and their slogan was "Let everyone be ready to die like a human being!" (cited in Mendes-Flohr and Reinharz 1995:674). Before the final defeat, Anielewicz took his own life rather than fall into Nazi hands. He left the following message:

> Only a few will be able to hold out. The remainder will die sooner or later. Their fate is decided. . . . [But] what we dared to do is of great, enormous importance. . . . [We will be] remembered beyond the Ghetto walls. . . . The dream of my life has risen to become fact. . . . Jewish armed resistance and revenge are facts. I have been a witness to the magnificent heroic fighting of Jewish men and women of battle. (cited in Mendes-Flohr and Reinharz 1995:675)

In the last analysis, however, it is evident that neither the Jewish councils nor Jewish resistance groups were able to thwart the Final Solution and save large numbers of Jews (Rubenstein and Roth 1987). To be sure, every saved life mattered, and Jews fought valiantly within both Jewish and non-Jewish partisan units throughout Nazi-occupied Europe, defying the stereotype of Jewish passivity. One group of Jewish guerrilla fighters, which operated out of the forests of Belorussia, was led by Tuvia Bielski (1906–87), who made protection of Jews a primary objective and provided shelter for more than 1,200 women, children, and elderly Jews (Duffy 2003; Tec 1993). There were also uprisings in the concentration camps, most notably at Treblinka, Sobibór, and Auschwitz-Birkenau. Richard Glazer, a survivor of the August 1943 revolt at Treblinka, observed that no one could have escaped that camp if it were not for inmates who had already "lost their wives and children" and who were willing to stay and fight it out with the guards in order "to give the others a chance" to escape (quoted in Clendinnen 1999:59). Still, only about a dozen of the 150 to 200 prisoners who escaped actually survived the war. Most were either killed in the minefield that had been planted around the camp, were caught in a dragnet and shot in the forest, or were discovered while in hiding and killed, mostly by hostile local Poles. Later, in October 1943, a Jewish-Soviet prisoner of war, Lt. Aleksandr Pechersky, led an escape from Sobibór. Eleven SS and several hundred Ukrainian guards were killed, but only 40–50 of the 300–400 escapees survived. That same month, *Sonderkommando* (special detail) prisoners who worked in the crematoria at Auschwitz-Birkenau got word that some of them were to be liquidated. They attacked the guards and set one of the buildings on fire. Three SS guards and 250 prisoners were killed during the uprising (Arad 1987; Botwinick 2001; Hilberg 2001; Maher 2010).

Perhaps my own father, Michael Berger, who was a survivor of several concentration camps, including Auschwitz-Birkenau and Auschwitz-Monowitz, expressed the sentiments of the average inmate who understood resistance "realistically, not romantically," since the opportunities to escape or in others ways resist beyond becoming an organizer were quite limited (Rubenstein and Roth 1987:187).[7] I will quote from my father at length here, because his observations are instructive.

> We did sympathize with the more skilled and experienced prisoners who were planning organized escapes or sabotage efforts that were more likely to be successful, but most of us were not privy to these schemes. They were very secretive, and I was never in a position to join them. But I don't think I would have joined them if I could have because I felt that my chances of survival . . . were greater if I didn't risk being executed for something I could choose to avoid. Others, however, may have felt that they would be killed anyway, which could have happened without notice at any time. (quoted in Berger 2011:114)

At the same time, my father's survival was dependent upon his ability to appraise his situation in order to take actions that would maximize his opportunities, an ability that was derived in part from accumulated experience. By the time he arrived in Auschwitz-Birkenau in November 1943, he had already been interned in two other camps for over a year, and he was somewhat familiar with the camp experience. Unger observes that prisoners "who had lived in a more or less normal environment immediately before arriving" at Auschwitz had a more difficult time overcoming their initial shock and trauma, especially if this was the first time they had to cope with the sudden loss of family (1986:287). Others, like my father, had been more gradually acclimated to camp life, to the extent that was possible, and continued to "ponder ways of ameliorating their situation (1986:290). As my father recalled, upon arriving at Auschwitz-Birkenau:

> We were surrounded by SS soldiers and ordered to line up in formation four deep. Then the . . . selection process began. Women and children were separated from the men. A couple of officers

went through the lines and pointed a finger at each prisoner and ordered, "Step left, step right, left, right." . . . I quickly surmised that one group was probably going to be killed and the other group saved for slave labor. I closely observed which group appeared to have a better chance of survival and assumed that the group with the stronger and taller people would be picked for work and that the group with the weaker people would be killed. I was standing next to a middle-aged man who had an obviously crippled leg. When he was ordered to the left, I went right! The whole selection process . . . occurred with such speed that the guards did not notice that I had disobeyed the order and switched groups. I assume that others did the same thing, but I didn't see it myself. You had to have nerve to do what I did, but I didn't hesitate. I could have been shot on the spot, but if I hadn't done what I did, I would have been killed anyway. (quoted in Berger 2011:95–96)

After toiling for a month at hard labor at Birkenau, my father was fortunate enough to be transferred to the Auschwitz camp at Monowitz. His first impression of Monowitz was:

[S]urvival was possible here. I could see that while some inmates looked emaciated, others seemed well fed. I assumed that some inmates were managing to get additional resources, and I knew that I would have to find out where these resources came from if I was to survive. . . . [I soon] learned that there were two classes of inmates in the camp: those who existed only on food rations allocated to them by the camp authorities, and those who managed to supplement their rations with extra contraband food. These inmates were referred to as "organizers." An organizer was a person who was successful at finding ways of acquiring additional provisions. On the other hand, those who were unable to organize continued to deteriorate, and those who lost a lot of weight and became emaciated . . . either died . . . of malnutrition or beatings, because [they] couldn't work, or [they were] sent back to Birkenau . . . to be gassed. (quoted in Berger 2011:105)

At Monowitz, my father was able to become part of an organizing scheme by providing tailoring services for the Kapo (work-group leader) who was in charge of his work detail at the IG Farben plant.

At great risk of getting caught and beaten . . . there were many ways an enterprising or opportunistic inmate could organize in the camps. . . . [S]ome inmates were able to get extra rations by performing personal services, like tailoring, for prominent inmates like *Blockälteste* [barracks leaders], Kapos, or kitchen personnel. Some of

> the younger ones performed sexual favors. . . . [I]t was a known fact that many Blockälteste had their favorite boy, whom they sheltered, fed, and protected. . . . And some [inmates], especially Kapos, were in a position to barter with the civilian employees who worked at the IG Farben plant. These civilians were interested in the various commodities that were being stored in the warehouses but that were not available on the open market—a loaf of bread, a pound of salami or pork meat, or some butter. Since the inmate then had plenty to eat, he was no longer dependent on his camp rations and could give them to anyone he favored. A Kapo in this position would share the food with his favorite underlings. In this way a prisoner who was successful at organizing, or who established a good relationship with a Kapo or other organizer, could acquire enough food to sustain himself. (quoted in Berger 2011:106)

In his own small way, my father's account, too, belies the stereotype of the Jew who passively accepted his fate, for he was constantly appraising his circumstances to capitalize on even the smallest opportunity to maximize his chances. To be sure, there were many times along the way that he was on the verge of death. He recalled an occasion at Monowitz where he was selected by the SS doctor to be sent along with other prisoners back to Birkenau to be gassed. But before the transport was underway, the SS doctor allowed a Polish doctor, a prisoner who worked in the camp hospital, to review the selections. The Pole was accompanied by a Jewish orderly, and the two of them picked out a few of the younger people, my father included, and substituted some of the elderly and sick hospital patients for them. Apparently, the doctor was permitted to fulfill the Nazi death quota in this way, "thus living up to an unwritten code of saving the younger people," my father said (quoted in Berger 2011:109). The Polish doctor, as others like him, operated on the basis of a utilitarian ethic, recognizing that although individual lives would end, they hoped that some would have the strength to persevere, hence maximizing the survival of the group (Gallant and Cross 1992; Pawełczynska 1979).

Nevertheless, it is also true that the saving remnant of Jewish survivors remains a "fragmentary achievement" in light of the masses of people who were killed (Langer 1991:157). Moreover, if the Allies had not won the war, all of the Jews of Europe would have inevitably perished, for as we noted in chapter 1, World War II was not only a military war of German territorial conquest but "a war against Judaism in the bowels of Europe" (Horowitz 2009:495). It is at the same time true that the specter of unpredictability and randomness that survivors characterize as luck does not necessarily mitigate a more sociological interpretation of their experience. As Frankl observed, of prisoners in the camps, "Even if we could not expect any sensational military events in the next few days, who knew better than we, with our experience of camps, how great chances sometimes opened up, quite suddenly, at least for the individual. . . . For this was the kind of thing which constituted the 'luck' of the prisoner" (1959:103–04). And this was the kind of thing that gave them hope, as Filip Müller (1979), a survivor of the Auschwitz-Birkenau Sonderkommando, said:

> The "special detail" lived in a crisis situation. Every day we saw thousands and thousands of innocent people disappear up the chimney. With our own eyes, we could truly fathom what it means to be a human being. There they came, men, women, children, all innocent. They suddenly vanished, and the world said nothing! We felt abandoned. By the world, by humanity. But the situation taught us fully what the possibility of survival meant. For we could gauge the infinite value of human life. And we were convinced that hope lingers in man as long as he lives. . . . That's why we struggled through our lives of hardship, day after day, week after week, month after month, year after year, hoping against hope to survive, to escape that hell. (quoted in Lanzmann 1985:145–46)

Notes

1. Cultural critic Christopher Lasch (1994) was among the first to make this observation, which includes use of the Holocaust, Nazism, and Nazi concentration camps as metaphors to describe such diverse phenomena as the condition of women in society, abortion, the AIDS epidemic, the Israeli-Palestinian conflict, the experience of adult children of alcoholics, and the exploitation of animals (Berger 2011; Novick 1999; Rosenfeld 1997).
2. Des Pres also noted that "survival is an experience with a definite structure" (1976:v).
3. See also Bartrop (2000), Berger (2011), Des Pres (1976), Dimsdale (1980), Kraft (2002), Pingel (1991), and Unger (1986).
4. Elsewhere I have interpreted these processes in terms of both life-course and agency-structure theory (Berger 2011).
5. For a history of the Zionist movement, see Laqueur ([1972] 2003).
6. Of his group's activity, Sol noted, "Occasionally we attacked German military installations or transports, but mostly we were on the run," waiting to meet up with the advancing Soviet army. "We thought more of survival than of fighting" (quoted in Berger 2011:83).
   Unlike Berger's experience with the Poles, Western European resistance groups more readily accepted Jews as members. There was also a Polish group, the *Zegota* (code name for Council for Aid to Jews), that was explicitly involved in the rescue of Jews (Bauer 1989a,b; Botwinick 2001;

Prekerowa 1990). But see Gross (2000, 2006) and Redlich (2002) for accounts of Polish anti-Semitism during the war, which we will discuss further in chapter 7.

7. There was also the German practice of collective punishment to consider; if a prisoner decided to attack a German and thus risk his own death, he would have been a party to the execution of other people as well (Berger 2011; Tec 1986). For discussions of the special problems facing women, such as pregnancy, childbirth, and rape, see Browning (2010), Offer and Weitzman (1998), and Rittner and Roth (1993).

6

Bystanders and Third-Party Resistance

We have thus far focused on the role of the German perpetrators and the ways in which Jews responded to the Holocaust. In this chapter we raise the question of the bystanders, both individuals and nations, those who stood by and did nothing to help. We also consider non-Jewish resistance, including the actions of ordinary people who risked their lives to save Jews. Samuel Oliner and Pearl Oliner (1988) estimate that less than one-half of one percent of the non-Jewish population under Nazi occupation tried to defy the Final Solution by lending assistance to Jews. These individuals are often called "righteous Gentiles" or "righteous Christians."[1] Paul Levine refers to them as "third-party protagonists who attempted, at least on some occasions, to stop the Germans from killing" (1998:520).

German Resistance

Although the Nazis dealt ruthlessly with their enemies, they remained concerned about maintaining legitimacy in the eyes of the German public (Breitman 1998; Johnson 1999). To some degree they realized that knowledge of the Final Solution threatened to undermine this legitimacy. They understood that many Germans would not view extermination as acceptable, however much they were concerned about the "Jewish problem" and however much they favored or at least tolerated other anti-Jewish measures. Hence the Nazis tried to keep the Final Solution a secret, as much as this was possible. Heinrich Himmler even informed his SS troops that the course they had embarked upon was "a page of glory in our history which . . . shall never be written" (quoted in Wistrich 1995:114).

The Nazis used euphemisms such as "resettlement" or "special treatment" to rhetorically obscure what they were doing to the Jews (Hilberg 1985). The Final Solution itself was an obvious euphemism.

But the policy of secrecy was somewhat of a pretense, for it was an illusion to think that a crime of this magnitude could be kept secret for very long. Too many people were involved in the killings. Military troops, Order Police, and others wrote letters back home, or returned home themselves, telling people what they had witnessed. Photos were taken. A sizeable portion of the population listened to foreign radio broadcasts, especially the BBC (British Broadcasting Corporation). The Allies dropped leaflets informing the German people about what was occurring. Some people lived in the vicinity of the concentration camps. Besides, everyone had heard Hitler's ominous pronouncements about what was in store for the Jews. They had witnessed the discrimination and segregation of Jews, the violence of Kristallnacht, and the deportations of their former neighbors. However, few chose to speak of this "terrible secret," few chose to openly break the silence (Breitman 1998; Gellately 2001; Johnson 1999; Marcuse 2001).

According to Eric Johnson, "The only open demonstration against the deportations of German Jews . . . was carried out by Aryan wives of Jewish husbands" (1999:423). As noted in chapter 3, Nazi policy regarding Mischlinge (Jews with mixed ancestry) and Jews in mixed marriages was somewhat ambiguous, and there was much variation in how local Nazi officials treated these people. On February 27, 1943, during the Nazis' final roundup of the remaining Jews in Germany, about 200 German women "gathered outside of the administrative offices of Berlin's Jewish community . . . to inquire about the fate of their husbands, who had been arrested that same day" and began shouting, "Give us back our husbands! Give us back our husbands!" (1999:423). During the next week the protest grew in size and intensity, and the crowd of more than 1,000 refused to disperse in the face of repeated warnings from SS and Gestapo officers brandishing their weapons. On March 6, Joseph Goebbels, concerned with the adverse publicity that the protest was causing, called for the release of some 1,700 Jews. "The decision to deport intermarried spouses . . . [was] blamed on 'over-zealous subordinates' . . . and Jewish spouses elsewhere in Germany were spared, since their deportation would have become too public, perhaps too unpopular," and might have caused more critical scrutiny of the killing program (Breitman 1998:162).

Johnson thinks that "many more Jewish lives might have been saved" had similar protests been made earlier and more often by a broader segment of the German population (1999:423). To be sure, the German citizenry was not slavishly obedient to the Nazi regime.

A majority listened to foreign radio broadcasts, which was against the law to do. People told political jokes that criticized Hitler and the Nazis. The young listened to swing music, which celebrated what the Nazis despised as "Jewish- and Negro-inspired American music" (p. 278). More significantly, Communists, trade unionists, and church officials were sent to concentration camps and even killed for their opposition to the regime. Still, Johnson believes that "there is no escaping the fact that Germans mounted next to no meaningful protest against" the mass murder of Jews (p. 379).

One resistance group, which called itself the White Rose, involved a small cadre of students at the University of Munich, who passed out a series of six leaflets calling for nonviolent resistance and who used black tar paint to write anti-Nazi phrases like "Down with Hitler," "Freedom," and "Hitler mass murderer" on public buildings. But the protests were mounted late—between June 1942 and February 1943 and at a time when the tide of the war was already turning against Germany—and had little impact on the course of events (Johnson 1999; Moll 1994). Of more potential significance was the attempted assassination of Hitler on July 20, 1944, by Claus Schenk Count von Stauffenberg. This "attempt was part of a broader conspiracy against Hitler organized by nationalist conservative leaders . . . [with] ties to some leading figures in the military, counterintelligence service, and aristocracy," as well as to some in the clergy and trade union movement (Johnson 1999:305–6). It was aimed primarily at minimizing Germany's losses and negotiating a favorable settlement with the Allies. Even Himmler seems to have had a general (though not detailed) knowledge of the plot and did nothing to stop it (Bauer 1994).

The Role of the Christian Churches

David Gushee, a professor of Christian ethics, believes that the Christian churches deserve special mention in understanding German resistance, or lack therefore, because in both "its historical antecedents and in its wartime course, the annihilation of the European Jews was inextricably related to Christianity and the behavior of Christian people. . . . [E]very church official at every level who had the opportunity to help Jews faced a test of Christian moral leadership, while every Christian with similar opportunity faced a test of Christian moral character" (1994:13, 15). Regrettably, during the Nazi period the vast majority of Germans who were in fact baptized Christians were not up to this test, and they instead did their best to stay clear of controversy (Rubenstein and Roth 1987).

In response to the establishment of the pro-Nazi Evangelical Reich Church in 1933 (see chapter 4), an oppositional group of clergy formed the anti-Nazi "Confessing Church." The Confessing Church, which had the support of about one-third of the Protestant clergy, "rejected any belief that God's revelation" could be found through Hitler and the Nazi state (Gushee 1994:129). In the Barmen Declaration of 1934, leaders of the Confessing Church condemned "the false doctrine that the State, over and above its special commission, should and could become the single and totalitarian order of human life" (cited in Rubenstein and Roth 1987:204). They asserted that Christianity and Nazism were inherently irreconcilable and that Christian followers of Hitler had abandoned their true faith. But this declaration was not so much a repudiation of Hitler as a statement of the limits of secular authority. Even within the Confessing Church, there was mixed opinion regarding the legitimacy of the regime, and not all of its leaders were thoroughly opposed to it.

Dietrich Bonhoeffer (1906–45) was among the most notable leaders of the Confessing Church movement. Although he wrote in 1933 that the "church of Christ has never lost sight of the thought that the 'chosen people,' who nailed the redeemer of the world to the cross, must bear the curse for its action through a long history of suffering," he nonetheless warned his followers that Nazi attacks against the Jews perverted the spirit of Christianity, and he encouraged them to aid the victims of Nazi repression (cited in Rubenstein and Roth 1987:208). Bonhoeffer himself plotted to assassinate Hitler and was involved in efforts to help Jews escape from Germany. He believed that "[t]hose who take upon themselves the mantle of Christian leadership must be prepared to suffer and die in the service of Christian moral fidelity" (Gushee 1994:173–74). In 1943, he was arrested and sent to a concentration camp, where he was executed in 1945.

Unlike Protestants, Catholics (who comprised about a third of the German population) had an organizational center with autonomous ruling authority outside of Germany in the Pope and the Vatican City in Rome. In 1933, however, the Vatican secretary of state Eugenio Cardinal Pacelli, a former papal diplomat to Berlin, signed a concordant with Hitler on behalf of Pope Pius XI that guaranteed religious freedom for Catholics. In return Pius XI agreed to recognize the legitimacy of the Nazi regime, to refrain from criticizing it, and to confine the church's activity to purely religious matters (Botwinick 2001; Cornwell 1999; Deák 2000b). Pacelli, who became Pope Pius XII after the death of Pius XI in 1939, wrote Hitler a letter just four days after becoming Pope, which read:

> To the Illustrious Herr Adolf Hitler, Führer and Chancellor of the German Reich! Here at the beginning of Our Pontificate We wish to assure you that We remain devoted to the spiritual welfare of the German people entrusted to your leadership. During the many years We spent in Germany, We did all in Our power to establish harmonious relations between Church and State. Now that the responsibilities of Our pastoral function have increased Our opportunities, how much more ardently do We pray to reach that goal. May the prosperity of the German people and their progress in every domain, come, with God's help to fruition! (cited in Hitchens 2007:239–40)

For the most part, therefore, German Catholic bishops admonished their followers to be obedient to the Nazi regime (Braham 1999). They increasingly adopted a nationalist stance and were supportive of German military expansionism. Some even spoke out vehemently against the Jews, associating them with communism and reminding the faithful that Jews were Christ killers who were "harmful to the German people . . . [and who] in their boundless hatred of Christianity were still . . . seeking to destroy the Church" (Zahn 1962:279).

Nevertheless, Hitler was not satisfied with Catholic cooperation and attempted to further erode the Church's influence by closing Catholic schools, prohibiting publication of Catholic literature, and dissolving Catholic associations such as the Catholic Youth League. Thus in 1937 Pope Pius XI issued an encyclical entitled "With Burning Anxiety" that was read in Catholic Churches, which condemned the Nazis' racial ideology and usurpation of religious authority. Still, for the most part both Pope Pius XI and Pope Pius XII "counseled prudence not boldness . . . [and] urged that a lack of restraint would invite further evils" (Rubenstein and Roth 1987:215). They arguably feared Communism as much or more than Nazism and were inheritors of a religious tradition that viewed Jews as the carriers of modern ideas that threatened established Church doctrine (see chapter 2). John Pawlikowski notes that Pius XII had a "high regard for the German church" and to some extent may have been relieved that "the Jewish community's 'subversive' influence on the traditional social order was being removed" (1998:564; see also Braham 1999; Cornwell 1999; Deák 2000b; Goldhagen 2004).

117

While Pius XII's commitment to the "traditional social order" seems to have waned as the war went on, the Vatican was concerned about losing the allegiance of Catholics in Germany and elsewhere, and it used private diplomacy rather than public protest in its efforts to ameliorate the plight of Jews under Nazi control. Papal diplomats tried to persuade neutral countries such as Spain and Portugal to accept more Jewish emigrants, and when emigration was no longer an option, they tried to get Nazi-occupied governments such as Hungary and Slovakia to resist Nazi orders to deport Jews to the death camps. The possibilities for influence differed from country to country, however, and we will consider these variations later (Deák 2000b; Pawlikowski 1998).

To be sure, many Catholic and Protestant clergy did speak out against the Nazi regime and some tried to help Jews escape (Johnson 1999; Phayer 2000; Zuccotti 2002). Few other Gentile groups in Nazi Germany were put under as much surveillance by the Gestapo and had as many cases lodged against them. Most of the protests, however, took the form of critical sermons, and relatively few clergy were actually sentenced to lengthy prison terms or sent to concentration camps for making them. Church leaders spoke most loudly when the Nazis invaded church prerogatives and persecuted Jewish converts to Christianity. Their protests were effective in curtailing the euthanasia program that was carried out against German citizens (see chapter 2).[2] But according to Richard Rubenstein and John Roth, rarely did they speak out or act "on behalf of Jews as Jews," never did they rally "their congregations to make a unified, principled protest against the Nazis' fundamental Jew-hatred" (1987:207, 213).

In Germany only the Jehovah's Witnesses, a small Christian minority, refused to make any compromises with the regime, and they continued to meet, organize, and proselytize even after they were banned in 1933 (Johnson 1999; Reynaud and Graffard 2001). They refused to join any Nazi organizations, attend political rallies, give the Hitler salute, or serve in the armed forces. They even passed out "literature that pointed out specific instances of Nazi atrocities, cited Gestapo, police, and Nazi Party torturers by name, and called on the German people to turn away from the false prophet Hitler and to place their faith in the true savior, Jesus Christ" (Johnson 1999:239). Although estimates vary, about a third of their 25,000–30,000 members were imprisoned or sent to concentration camps, and some 1,200 were killed.

The Question of Altruism

As noted above, third-party protagonists who helped Jews are often called "righteous Gentiles" or "righteous Christians." Here I also refer to them as helpers and rescuers (H/Rs). According to Oliner and Oliner's (1988) research, the majority of these individuals lent assistance to more than five people and were involved in some form of helping or rescue activity for at least two years. They stored personal possessions for Jews and provided food, shelter, medical assistance, and critical information about Nazi activity, useful contacts, escape routes, and so forth. They helped Jews find sources of livelihood and, in some cases, ran businesses for them, diverting profits to their former Jewish owners. They smuggled arms, bribed officials, and provided false identification papers and food ration cards. They hid Jews (for the short- and long-term) and helped them escape to safe havens (Berger, Green, and Krieser 1998; Fogelman 1994; Paldiel 1996; Tec 1986).

In the scholarly literature, the subject of Holocaust helping/ rescue (H/R) activity has often been framed as a question of "altruism," which may be defined as voluntary behavior directed toward increasing another's welfare without the expectation of external reward (Berger et al. 1998; Oliner et al. 1992).[3] Postwar interviews with Holocaust H/Rs and non-H/Rs suggest that some individuals were more predisposed than others to engage in such conduct. They had acquired a commitment to helping the needy before the war and continued this commitment in the postwar years (Oliner and Oliner 1988; Tec 1986).

Altruism research has also found that certain socialization experiences are associated with the development of both *cognitive altruism* based on cultural values regarding what is "right" and "wrong" as well as *affective altruism* based on sympathy, empathy, or an emotional concern for another's well-being (Oliner et al. 1992; Piliavin and Charng 1990). Interviews with Holocaust H/Rs indicate that they were more likely than non-H/Rs to come from homes where parental–child interaction was close, nurturant, and affectionate. Their parents were less likely to rely on physical punishment and authoritarian disciplinary styles and more likely to rely on reasoning or cognitive discipline that socialized children to consider questions of right and wrong and the consequences of their actions on others. Parents also modeled altruism, as H/Rs reported seeing their parents behaving kindly toward others.

119

Tolerance as a general moral value and toward Jews in particular was stressed in their homes, as was an orientation that emphasized treating individuals as equals regardless of social status and that promoted a feeling of obligation, hospitality, and generosity toward people in need. Before the war, H/Rs were more likely to have had Jewish friends as well as friends from different class backgrounds. In addition, parents taught H/Rs to be independent, self-reliant, and self-confident, which enabled them to act even in the face of disapproval from others and grave risks to their own safety (Berger et al. 1998; Oliner and Oliner 1988; Tec 1986).

Nechama Tec (1986) observes that altruism may be *autonomous*, that is, without social support, or *normative*, that is, reinforced or supported by one's group or society. During the war, normative altruism was more likely in countries that had a national culture or general cultural environment that was more hospitable toward Jews. Historical data indicate that, all other things being equal, the degree of prewar anti-Semitism had an impact on the number of Jewish deaths during the Holocaust.[4] Countries with a tradition of religious tolerance and civil equality were more likely to "engender sympathy for Jews that sometimes found expression in efforts to save them" (Baron 1988:17). Belgium, Bulgaria, Denmark, Holland, and Italy are often cited on this score. In these countries "Jewish acculturation and socioeconomic integration often created strong business or personal relationships with non-Jews" (1988:17). While the mere absence of anti-Semitism was insufficient to instigate third-party resistance, it created a broad consensus that made accommodation or collaboration with the Nazis less likely. Moreover, during the war, these sentiments facilitated the emergence of collective networks that considered aid to Jews a part of their opposition to Nazism (Baron 1992; Berger et al. 1998; Fein 1979).

Collective Networks and Resource Mobilization

In her research on helping/rescue behavior, Eva Fogelman (1994) found that about one-fifth of H/Rs participated in collective rescue networks, while Tec (1986) found that about one-third were involved in both individual and collective forms of assistance. The Oliners (1988) found that 44 percent of their sample participated in formal resistance or rescue groups, and nearly all cooperated at least informally with other H/Rs, including family, friends, and neighbors. One Polish H/R estimated that it took the support of at least ten people to save one

Jew. Michael Gross, whose study uncovered few instances of solo rescue, argues that third-party resistance was not "simply the cumulative effect of . . . high-minded individuals collaborating to oppose an unjust regime" but of collective efforts of coordinated action that could not be undertaken by individuals on their own (1994:464, 468).

We have previously noted the role of social movements in mobilizing resources to advance proponents' political agenda (see chapter 3). Following Gross's (1994) suggestion, the question of altruism can be recast in terms of a countermovement theory of resource mobilization (see Zald and Useem 1987), that is, an account of how rescue groups mobilized resources to resist the Final Solution. More specifically, these movements utilized *leadership*, *ideological*, and *organizational resources* to mobilize third-party resistance on behalf of Jews.

Leadership Resources

Direct invocations from civic and religious leaders who had established legitimate authority before the war were often important in mobilizing potential H/Rs to action (Baron 1992; Gross 1994). In Nieuwlande, Holland, for example, a number of H/Rs cited the persuasive appeals of Johannes Post, a highly regarded councilman, as the main reason for their involvement. In Bulgaria, vigorous condemnation of "anti-Semitic laws by the Bulgarian Orthodox clergy, various professional organizations, and prominent politicians contributed to the government's lax enforcement of these laws and eventual refusal to deport native Jews" (Baron 1988:18–19; Gilbert 2000; Todorov 2001a). In France, Catholic congregants were at times ordered by church authorities to assist in rescue activity; and in Poland, Catholic nuns engaged in third-party resistance at the behest of their convent superiors (Gushee 1994; Kurek-Lesik 1992). In October 1943, Pope Pius XII finally encouraged the Vatican clergy in Rome to provide sanctuary for "non-Aryans" who faced German deportations to the death camps, thus saving the lives of over 5,600 Jews (Gilbert 2000).[5]

The village of Le Chambon-sur-Lignon in southern France, where over 3,000 Jewish adults and children were given sanctuary, helped to find hiding places, or smuggled to safety in Switzerland, is often cited as the classic example of collective rescue (Baron 1988; Gilbert 2000; Gross 1994). In that village Pastor André Trocmé drew upon a tradition of Protestant leadership that had evolved through the community's historical experience of religious persecution. The collective memory of the state-sponsored persecution of their Huguenot ancestors predisposed the community to favor its local religious leadership over secular governmental authority.[6] This historical legacy was "foundational for the community's persistent practice of hospitality to the needy" (Gushee 1994:127). For centuries Le Chambon had been a safe haven for Protestant refugees. In the 1930s, for instance, the village sheltered refugees from the Spanish civil war, and during World War II, it was only natural to identify with the plight of the Jews and unite around their pastors in defiance of anti-Jewish policies.

Ideological Resources

Social movement theory notes that movements provide frames or schemes of interpretation to help members interpret events (Gamson 1992; Snow et al. 1986). As was the case in Le Chambon, religious or political sentiments could be used as ideological resources that mobilized third-party resistance. While Holocaust H/Rs were more likely than non-H/Rs to describe themselves as very religious, only a minority attributed their actions to their religious beliefs or sense of religious duty per se (Oliner and Oliner 1988; Tec 1986). This apparent anomaly is perhaps explained by the fact that some even helped Jews when this was opposed by church officials. According to Kristen Monroe, religious altruists shared "something that may bear superficial resemblance to but differs critically from what we would commonly think of as organized religion or even religious belief" (1996:129). They were following their own feelings of concern and compassion for human suffering, or their own interpretations of what God wanted them to do, rather than specific instructions or teachings of the church (Fogelman 1994; Gushee 1994; Koffler and Koffler 1995).

Gushee (1994) observes that religious-based H/Rs came disproportionately from reformed Protestant denominations rooted in Calvinist teachings that expressed a special religious kinship with the Jewish people. John Calvin, a sixteenth-century French Protestant who settled in Switzerland, advanced a Christian ideology that differed from both Catholicism and Lutheranism in its respect for "Old Testament moral law and its continuing validity for Christians" (p. 122). Calvin encouraged his fellow Christians "to appreciate rather than to deride continuing Jewish fidelity" to the Old Testament, while other Christian faiths "juxtaposed Old Testament 'law' with New Testament 'grace,' denigrating and deemphasizing the former" (p. 123). In countries like

Denmark and Holland, prewar Calvinist ideology proffered pro-Jewish sentiments that made citizens less inclined to support Nazi policies against Jews.

Often, however, Jewish rescue activities simply went hand-in-hand with a more general anti-Nazi orientation. As Gushee suggests:

> Some Gentiles rescued Jews because they hated the Nazis and simply wanted to thwart them at every opportunity. . . . Those acting on this basis were more likely to have been involved in general underground resistance activities [sabotage, gun-running, armed actions, etc.] . . . and rescued Jews as one part of their underground work. . . . [Others] saw the rescue of Jews . . . as a defense of their fellow citizens and national values. . . . This response was more likely to occur where Jews had won full and unequivocal citizenship rights before the war and where there existed little or no political sentiment in favor of [Jewish] disenfranchisement. (1994:110)

Similarly, socialists and communists often cited general antifascist sentiments as their motivation for helping Jews (Oliner and Oliner 1988; Tec 1986). Although most H/Rs described themselves as apolitical, individuals committed to leftist politics or a belief in democratic pluralism were more likely than those with other political orientations to engage in rescue efforts. At the same time, not all anti-Nazi resistance groups included protection of Jews as part of their activities. In Poland, for example, aid to Jews was an issue that divided the underground, and many Polish partisans agreed with Hitler's anti-Jewish campaign and even killed Jews who escaped into the forests.[7] In France, on the other hand, Jews comprised about 20 percent of some resistance groups. Thousands of Jews were also active in the Soviet partisan movement led by escaped Soviet prisoners of war (Baron 1988; Berger et al. 1998; Fogelman 1994; Gilbert 2000).

Organizational Resources

It is axiomatic that organizations are a resource for collective action that individuals cannot engage in on their own. During the war, organizational resources were necessary for the acquisition of valuable information and the procurement of food ration cards, false ID's, places of hiding, and so forth. Officials often had to be bribed and persons who transported and sheltered Jews had to be paid for their expenses. Even in as pro-Jewish setting as Denmark, fishermen smuggling Jews to safety in neutral Sweden demanded substantial fees, which they reduced only after the Danish underground insisted they do so (Fogelman 1994; Yahil 1990).

Although several studies have found that the diffusion of responsibility in larger groups may increase the passivity of bystanders, other research shows that willingness to help in risky situations increases with group size (Crader and Wentworth 1984). In larger groups the capacity to overcome initial fear is augmented by a sense of social support, the risk of being exposed is reduced, and altruistic impulses are reinforced rather than discouraged.

At times, prewar organizations could be adapted for rescue activities. The Le Chambonese H/Rs, for instance, were able to draw upon a national network of like-minded Protestant educators to aid in the hiding of Jewish children. In Poland, over 60 percent of the nunneries were engaged in Jewish rescue. When Pope Pius XII ordered the sheltering of Jews, over a hundred monasteries, convents, and other church organizations were available to provide sanctuary (Gilbert 2000; Gross 1994; Kurek-Lesik 1992).[8]

In other cases, wartime organizations not initially intended for Jews could be transmuted for such efforts. In Holland, for example, a network established to aid Gentiles fleeing Nazi conscription for forced labor was later used for Jews. In Denmark, several anti-Nazi resistance groups were eventually coordinated into one larger group, the Freedom Council, that organized a "fishing armada" that transported about 7,900 Jews, half-Jews, and Christians married to Jews to safety in Sweden (Fogelman 1994; Gilbert 2000; Gross 1994).

Situational Contingencies

The ability of individuals or groups to engage in third-party resistance on behalf of Jews was contingent on various situational factors, the most important of which was the degree of Nazi control, that is, the extent of Nazi military occupation, their use of terror, and their direct involvement in the administration of anti-Jewish policies (Berger et al. 1998; Marrus 1987). In Eastern Europe, this control was greatest in Poland, and in Western Europe it was greatest in Holland and Norway. This helps explain the high percentage of deaths among Dutch Jews (over 70 percent) in spite of "Holland's long tradition of religious tolerance and civic equality" (Baron 1992:307; Yahil 1990).

In Italy, most of the population and "[e]ven some Italian Fascists openly voiced support for and solidarity with Jews" (Carpi 2001:334). Government officials, including policemen and soldiers, often tried to delay compliance with German requests for Jews while maintaining plausible pretexts to justify inaction, what Florette Koffler and Richard Koffler characterize as "willed inefficiency in the face of an inhumane order" (1995:xxviii). In the latter part of 1943, however, the Italians surrendered to the Allies who occupied the southern part of the country. Germany, in turn, took control over the central and northern regions, the home of most of Italy's Jews. At this point the fate of Italian Jews took a dramatic turn for the worse.

In France, the Germans left significant elements of control in the hands of the Vichy government (see chapter 4). Although the Vichy regime is known for its cooperation with the Nazis, it was reluctant to deport native French Jews. According to Leni Yahil, the Vichy government's "attitude toward the Jews vacillated between xenophobic anti-Semitism and a democratic tradition that stood for offering refuge to the persecuted" (1990:590). French authorities maintained a sense of loyalty to French citizens but were also greedy for Jewish property. They capitulated to the Nazis but also desired a degree of independence. These fluctuating tendencies led to both the persecution of Jews and to occasional opportunities for escape. Moreover, in the later years of the war "French cooperation with the Nazis and indifference toward Jewish persecution decreased as the strains of German occupation and prospects of Germany's ultimate defeat became greater" (Baron 1988:39).

Indeed, the changing tide of the war provided a new context in which resistance to the Final Solution became more feasible. By early 1943, the Nazis had suffered a series of military defeats against Allied forces in North Africa and on the Eastern front. Under these circumstances, foreign leaders and church authorities in German-aligned and neutral countries became more willing to either resist Nazi edicts to deport Jews or to help Jews find refuge in safe havens. In some cases, as in Italy and Hungary, the Nazis had to exert more control over the deportations to the death camps when local cooperation was not forthcoming (Koffler and Koffler 1995; Weinberg 1998; Yahil 1990).

Geographical location was also an important contingency that affected third-party resistance. In Eastern Europe hiding places for Jews were quite primitive, "with people hiding in holes underground, beneath rooms, or in fields or forests" (Paldiel 1996:14). In Western Europe, however, a small, secluded side room, a section of a room, or a corner of an attic were more likely to be available. In cities it was easier for Jews to blend in with their surroundings and "flee and mingle with the crowd at a moment's notice" (1996:24). But in the countryside there was less anonymity and greater precaution was required to guard against betrayal by informers. In addition, certain types of terrain made concealment of fugitives, escape across borders, or guerrilla maneuvers more feasible. As Lawrence Baron observes:

> The sparsely populated and rugged wilderness of eastern Norway, the extensive and thick forest of Belorussia, and the mountainous regions of southern France, Greece, and Yugoslavia served as natural arenas for these kinds of activities. . . . Denmark's proximity to neutral Sweden . . . allowed the Danes to relocate most of their Jews. . . . Access to [neutral] Spain [and] Switzerland, territories under Italian control, and Mediterranean sea routes to Palestine favored Jewish escape from Vichy France and the countries of the Balkan Peninsula. (1988:21)

Conditions confronting Holland, on the other hand, were more difficult to support, as it was bordered by waters heavily patrolled by the Nazis and surrounded by other occupied countries and Germany itself (Baron 1992).

The United States, the Allies, and Neutral Countries

The Statue of Liberty, standing tall in New York Harbor since 1886, was at the time of the Holocaust an international symbol of freedom and hospitality for immigrants seeking a better life in the United States. A poem by Emma Lazarus inscribed on a bronze plaque in the interior wall of the monument reads:

> Give me your tired, your poor,
> Your huddled masses yearning to breathe free,
> The wretched refuse of your teeming shore.
> Send these, the homeless, tempest-tost to me.
> I lift my lamp beside the golden door!

The sentiment expressed in this poem, however, was not generally consistent with U.S. immigration policy. As Richard Breitman and Alan Kraut note, "Before 1933 the United States was far more the aloof isolationist seeking to insulate itself from the world's troubles than it was the defender of universal 'human rights'" (1987:248). Thus even if Jews could have managed to escape Nazi-occupied Europe, where were they to go? Ultimately, third-party resistance to the Final Solution not only required the mobilization of countermovements under optimal situational contingencies but also the mobilization of resources available only to governmental nation-states.

Donileen Loseke observes that governments have limited "carrying capacities," that is, there are countless issues that might benefit from its actions but only a limited number that can be effectively addressed (1999:113). Thus third-party resisters had a formidable task trying to convince U.S. policymakers that the "Jewish problem" warranted their attention.

U.S. Immigration Policy

Practically speaking, no nation can be expected to take in all the people who may wish to enter it; and in the 1920s, U.S. immigration law had established specific limits on the number of people who would be allowed to immigrant in any given year from any given country. The quotas for different countries were "set at a small percentage of those resident in America, but born in that foreign country, in 1890" (Rubenstein 1997:33). The year 1890 was chosen because it occurred prior to the large influx of eastern and southern Europeans (mainly Italians, Poles, and Russian Jews) and was designed to favor those of Anglo-Saxon descent. This approach reflected a view that the Immigration Restriction League (IRL) had been lobbying for since 1894. It was the IRL's view, now represented in U.S. policy, that the government needed to safeguard the racial and ethnic purity of the population. Thus one country alone, Great Britain, received 43 percent of the 153,774 annual quota slots, although Germany received 17 percent, the second highest allotment of any country in the world (Breitman and Kraut 1987; Diner 2004).[9]

In 1930, in the midst of a devastating economic depression, President Herbert Hoover issued an executive order to further restrict immigration by more narrowly interpreting existing immigration law that already denied visas to all persons who were "likely to become a public charge" (LPC), that is, who were unable to financially support themselves. Although the LPC stipulation "was originally aimed at persons who lacked physical or mental skills required for constructive employment," it was now construed to include "anyone unlikely to obtain a job under current market conditions" (Breitman and Kraut 1987:7–8).[10] Throughout the 1930s and the war years, the annual immigration quota was never filled beyond 54 percent, and this was not due to a lack of demand, especially from Jews.

Even before the Final Solution emerged, Nazis emigration policy had diffused the "Jewish problem" cross-nationally and created a dilemma for other countries that did not wish to modify their immigration policies to accommodate more Jews (see chapter 3). When Franklin Roosevelt assumed the presidency in 1933, government officials and citizen advocates debated the country's immigration policy, which was framed in terms of *humanitarian* versus *nationalist* claims about what the United States should do.

According to Loseke (1999), a humanitarian frame consists of the view that appropriate moral action requires efforts to eliminate pain and suffering, while a nationalist frame insists that the greater moral good lies in advancing the interests of the country. U.S. protagonists in the debate about the refugee problem engaged in what Loseke describes as a "reality-definition contest" about which morality should receive priority as they used these two frames to mobilize political support for various policies (p. 57).

Frances Perkins, Roosevelt's Secretary of Labor and the first female cabinet member in U.S. history, favored reversal of the Hoover order and a liberalization of immigration quotas to accommodate "visa applicants seeking to avoid racial or religious persecution" in Germany (Breitman and Kraut 1987:13). While the Immigration and Naturalization Service (INS) was under the auspices of the Labor Department, the State Department had jurisdiction over the issuance of visas by U.S. consuls abroad. Perkins had learned that since 1930, State Department officials had been instructing their "consuls in Germany to reduce the number of visas issued to 10 percent of the quota levels," which in her view ran contrary to the American humanitarian tradition of offering refuge to those fleeing persecution (p. 15).

On the other hand, career bureaucrats and Roosevelt appointees in the State Department, who were typically upper-class elites who were insensitive if not hostile to non-Anglo-Saxon immigrants, were among the staunchest opponents of reversal. They took the position that the State Department's primary responsibility was to protect the national interest and that this interest was best served by neutrality on the question of Germany's treatment of its own citizens. State Department officials also believed that the economy simply could not absorb more people and that liberalizing immigration policy would provoke an anti-immigration backlash among the U.S. population that might induce Congress to pass legislation that would reduce quotas even further (Breitman and Kraut 1987; Tilles 2008; Wyman 1984).

For the most part, prominent Jews in the United States weighed in on the side of immigration reform. Roosevelt had never hesitated to include Jews among his advisors or to appoint them to public positions. Among them were Secretary of Treasury Henry Morgenthau, Jr. and U.S. Supreme Court Judge Felix Frankfurter, who tried to persuade the president to modify his restrictionist stance.[11] Representatives of influential Jewish organizations, such as Rabbi Stephen Wise of the American Jewish Congress, had access to Roosevelt as well. Although the president tactfully listened to these men, his openness to Jewish appeals was largely symbolic, aimed at mollifying them "without making any promises," and generally he sided with the restrictionists (Breitman and Kraut 1987:226; Hamerow 2008; Rosen 2006; Tilles 2008).

Roosevelt had little to gain politically, and much to lose, by a policy that favored increased immigration of Jews. Public opinion polls conducted in the late 1930s and early 1940s revealed less than hospitable attitudes towards immigrants in general and Jews in particular, with 67–83 percent of U.S. respondents opposing the liberalization of immigration quotas to help refugees, and about two-thirds wanting to keep refugees out altogether, even objecting to a one-time exception that would have allowed 10,000 children to enter outside the quota limits. While a poll taken after the November 1938 Kristallnacht pogrom found that 94 percent disapproved of Nazi treatment of German Jews, another poll indicated that nearly one-half thought that the persecution of Jews was partly their own fault. In addition, various polls found that 35–40 percent said they would actively support or sympathize with policies that were unfavorable to Jews, 15–24 percent thought that Jews were a menace to the United States, over one-half considered Jews greedy and dishonest, and one-third to one-half believed that Jews had too much power in business, politics, and government (a figure that rose to 56 percent during the war years), with one-fifth wanting to drive Jews out of the country altogether to reduce their power (Breitman and Kraut 1987; Wyman 1984).

Nevertheless, there were times when the contingent events of the Nazi period created a political opportunity for advocates of change. As long as the INS remained in the Labor Department, Perkins had some leverage over immigration policy, and the State Department was willing to make some modest accommodations if Roosevelt approved of them.[12] The Nazis program of legalized discrimination against Jews that culminated in the 1935 Nuremberg Laws did not go unnoticed, and at least one U.S. consul in Germany reported that his office had been "inundated with visa inquiries and applications" (Breitman and Kraut 1987:48).

Up to this time advocates of immigration reform had been proposing various remedies. Perhaps children, spouses, and parents of current U.S. residents could be treated more leniently. Or U.S. relatives or friends could be allowed to post a bond to "guarantee that a potential immigrant would not become a public charge" (Breitman and Kraut 1987:18). Also, some of the red tape required of applicants who had to submit copies of documents (such as birth certificates, military records, and police dossiers) that the German government made difficult to obtain could be waived.

The Nuremberg laws provided a new political context that gave reform advocates some additional moral leverage. Roosevelt felt compelled to make some symbolic gesture of concern, for instance, by making public statements that condemned what the Nazis were doing. He "spoke out on the need to rebuild Palestine, the Jews' ancient homeland," and urged the British who controlled Palestine to keep this area open for Jewish immigration (Breitman and Kraut 1987:227). He also made it known that he would appreciate some leniency from the State Department on immigration policy. The State Department agreed to instruct consuls abroad that they were to use their discretion to deny visa requests only if they thought applicants would "probably" become a public charge, but not if they thought applicants would "possibly" become a public charge. As a result, refugees began "experiencing an unusual easing of consular requirements, especially on matters of documentation and proof of support" (p. 227). After the German invasion of Austria in March 1938, Roosevelt also ordered the combining of the German and Austrian quotas, enabling the unused portion of the German quota (which was considerably larger than Austria's) to be used for Austrian refugees. And following Kristallnacht, he instructed "the Labor Department to extend the visitors' visas of over 12,000 German Jewish refugees in the United States for another six months" (p. 230).

William Rubenstein (1997) believes that the U.S. response to the Jewish refugee problem in the latter half of the 1930s was better than many critics of U.S. immigration policy suggest. For example, the annual number of Jews allowed into the United States increased from 6,252 in fiscal year 1935 to 43,450 in fiscal year 1938, and Jews were the largest single group of immigrants allowed into the country in that period. Still, by June 1939 there was a backlog of over 300,000 Jews from Germany, Austria, and Czechoslovakia who had applied for immigration visas but who were not allowed into the country (Breitman and Kraut 1987).

Critics argue that the United States could have done more before the Nazis stopped all emigration and began implementing the Final Solution in the latter part of 1941. Indeed, Secretary of Labor Perkins favored legislation that would have allowed children to enter the country outside of the quota limits. But the Wagner-Rogers Bill that was introduced in February 1939 by Senator Robert Wagner of New York and Representative Edith Nourse Rogers of Massachusetts, which would have allowed 20,000 German children to come into the United States over a two-year period, died in Congress for lack of support. Similarly, a 1940 bill that would have relaxed quota limits and allowed refugees to go to Alaska floundered as well (Breitman and Kraut 1987).

The plight of the passenger ship the *St. Louis* is often used to illustrate the critics' point. In May 1939, the *St. Louis* left Hamburg, Germany, for Havana, Cuba, with 933 passengers who were mostly Jewish refugees. More than seven hundred of the passengers had applied for U.S. visas and had secured affidavits of support. They expected to qualify for entry into the United States in a matter of months and hoped to wait their turn in Cuba rather than in Germany. Before their arrival, however, the Cuban government changed the policy that had previously allowed immigrants to seek temporary refuge in Cuba, and only twenty-two of the *St. Louis* passengers were given approval to land. The captain of the ship then headed for Florida but was denied permission to dock. A U.S. Coast Guard cutter was dispatched "to prevent anyone from trying to swim ashore" as a telegram from the ships' passengers to the president went unanswered (Breitman and Kraut 1987:71). The *St. Louis* cruised for a month on its way back to Hamburg before Great Britain, France, Holland, and Belgium finally agreed to accept the passengers. Seventy percent of them were killed in the ensuing Holocaust (Gilbert 2000; Rosen 2006; Rubenstein and Roth 1987).

Internationalizing the Refugee Problem

Roosevelt sought to relieve the burden that the refugee problem posed to the United States by diffusing it into the international arena. Recall that in 1938 he promoted the Evian Conference that was attended by delegates from thirty-two countries (see chapter 3). By demonstrating leadership on this issue, Roosevelt hoped to symbolically cast himself and the United States as upholding humanitarian principles. But neither he nor the other nations in attendance wanted to commit themselves to a serious solution. According to Breitman and Kraut, it was clear that the other countries were gauging their own response to that of a "reluctant United States" (1987:97).

In the Balfour Declaration of 1917, the British had promised to establish a Jewish national homeland in Palestine. However, in May 1939, they issued the so-called White Paper that reversed this position. The White Paper outlined "plans for a Palestinian state with a permanent Arab majority" that would put an end to Jewish immigration in 1944 after 75,000 Jews (15,000 per year) were admitted, unless the Arabs agreed otherwise, which was most unlikely (Rubenstein and Roth 1987:124). As a consequence of this policy, critics contend, European Jews lost a place of refuge at precisely the time they needed it the most (Rosen 2006; Tilles 2008).

The new British policy was a response to increased Arab resistance to Jewish immigration, which was encouraged by Germany, and to Britain's concern about its ability to contain an Arab uprising and hence to maintain itself as a colonial power in the region (Breitman 1998; Rosen 2006; Tilles 2008). Moreover, once World War II was underway, the British planned to rely substantially on troops from India, two-thirds of whom were Muslim, to defend "the southern approach to Palestine through Egypt" (Weinberg 1998:485). Gerhard Weinberg thinks that these troops were unlikely to fight if they thought they were being asked to defend Jews. In addition, at the time it was not a forgone conclusion that the Allies would stop the Germans from taking over the Middle East. Indeed, in November 1941, Hitler informed the Grand Mufti Haj Amin El Husseini of Jerusalem at a meeting in Berlin that he intended to kill every Jew living in the Arab world, including those in Palestine as well as in "Syria, Iraq, Iran, the Arabian peninsula, Egypt, and French Northwest Africa" (1998:484). Thus more Jewish immigration to Palestine, Weinberg argues, could have jeopardized the survival of the Jews.

As for Britain's policy regarding immigration into its own country, Rubenstein (1997) sees the response in a more favorable light than most critics. He argues that after Kristallnacht, until the outbreak of the war, emigration visas to Great Britain were granted "virtually without limit" (1997:27–28). Weinberg points out, however, that

Britain's relaxed immigration policy "was at the time intended for, and restricted to, those who had prospects of leaving Great Britain for the United States or another country after what was expected to be a short time" (1998:481).

Given the British position on Palestine, Roosevelt began to consider alternative plans for a Jewish homeland and the possibility of raising private funds to purchase land, in Asia or Africa, for instance (Breitman and Kraut 1987). But the outbreak of World War II dramatically changed the president's priorities and those of the nation. Now, fear of foreign subversives, especially from Germany and the Soviet Union, who "might be planted among the refugees by the warring powers . . . nourished the restrictionism that long predated it" (pp. 112, 232).[13] Roosevelt signaled the State Department that he favored tighter immigration regulations, and the subsequent decline in the issuance of visas was dramatic, with the number of German and Austrians (or former citizens of these nations) who were given immigration visas falling from 27,370 in fiscal year 1939 to 4,883 by 1942.

Breitman and Kraut (1987) found little evidence that refugees were a source of internal subversion in the United States. In fact, they note, after the United States entered the war in December 1941 "hundreds of thousands of these refugees served in the armed forces and in defense-related industries" (1987:124–25). Nevertheless, "State Department officials stiffened their resolve not to allow a misplaced humanitarianism to interfere with their duty" to defend the country's interests (1987:125). Military victory was now the nation's top priority, and "Americans might recoil at the sacrifices" they were being asked to make if they thought the United States had gone to war to protect Jews (1987:138). And like the British, the State Department was concerned that alienating the Arabs might endanger U.S. troops that were being deployed in North Africa. Roosevelt hastened to reassure Saudi Arabia that no action would be taken that altered the status quo in Palestine without consulting them fully (Rosen 2006; Tilles 2008).

Responding to the Final Solution

Neither the humanitarian nor nationalist framings of the refugee problem were sufficient to characterize what was occurring in Europe as a "genocide" or "Holocaust." These latter frames, which might have established a greater moral imperative to act, were for the most part postwar constructions of the events.[14] But how much did the Allies really know about what the Nazis were doing to the Jews?

As early as spring of 1940, British intelligence operatives were receiving and decoding German radio messages on a regular basis (Breitman 1998). Consequently, they were aware of the atrocities the Nazis committed during the invasion of the Soviet Union in the summer of 1941. They had reports of staggering numbers of Jews who were killed, although they had not yet understood the full implications of what had transpired, nor had the Nazis quite yet arrived at the Final Solution, which emerged in the ensuing months. Knowledge of the killings, however, did not provoke official reaction, other than efforts to prevent such information from being made public. Any public confirmation of Jewish casualties, the British believed, would be contrary to their nation's interest, for it would narrow the anti-Nazi cause and reinforce Nazi claims that "the Allies were fighting a war on behalf of Jews" (1998:105). There is no evidence that the British shared this information with the United States, but in the fall of 1941, a U.S. official in Berlin reported that he had learned that "SS units were killing Jews in many occupied localities in Russia" (1998:124). The U.S. response was the same as the British: suppress public exposure to the information (Tilles 2008).

By the summer of 1942 reports from the Polish underground army were beginning to confirm what was happening. In November, the Poles informed the British government that tens of thousands, mostly Jews and Soviet prisoners of war, had arrived at Auschwitz-Birkenau "for the sole purpose of their immediate extermination in gas chambers" (cited in Breitman 1998:116). This information reinforced evidence that the British had obtained from decoded messages from Himmler's minions. Later, in the spring of 1944, four escaped prisoners from Auschwitz, most notably Rudolf Vrba and Alfred Wetzler, provided more detailed (and more widely disseminated) information on the operation of the gas chambers and crematoria (Tilles 2008).

It is understandable that people would be skeptical of such reports. The Final Solution was unprecedented and unimaginable; and reports from Jewish sources were held in particular suspicion, since Jews, some thought, had reason to exaggerate their plight. In August 1942, Dr. Gerhart Riegner, the Swiss representative of the World Jewish Congress (WJC), went to the U.S. and British consulates in Geneva hoping to pass a cable to Rabbi Wise and to Sidney Silverman, a British parliament member who was the WJC representative in London. The cable included the following message:

Received alarming report that in Fuehrer's headquarters a plan has been discussed and [is] under consideration according to which [the] total of Jews in countries occupied [or] controlled by Germany numbering three and one-half to four million should after deportation and concentration in east be at one blow exterminated. . . . Informer is reported to have close connections with highest German authorities and his reports to be generally reliable. (cited in Hilberg 1992:238–39).

The informant was German industrialist Eduard Schulte. While traveling in Switzerland, Schulte had contacted a Jewish journalist who conveyed the information to Riegner (Bauer 2001; Browning 1996; Rosen 2006; Tilles 2008).

The Riegner cable was first forwarded to the U.S. State Department and the British Foreign Office. The State Department, which did not want to make the report public, did not pass it on to Wise. The British Foreign Office, on the other hand, felt compelled to inform Silverman because he was a government official. Silverman, at Riegner's request, sent the cable to Wise. Wise contacted the State Department, which asked him not to make the cable public until the information could be verified.[15] Wise did not inform the press, but he did contact a number of high-ranking governmental officials outside of the State Department, including Treasury Secretary Morgenthau, the only Jew in the Roosevelt cabinet and one of the staunchest advocates of intervention. Finally, in November, the State Department confirmed the report and gave Wise the go-ahead to make the information public. Wise held a press conference that was carried by the national media and that generated more publicity about the Final Solution than anything previously (Breitman 1998; Breitman and Kraut 1987; Rosen 2006; Tilles 2008).

The Riegner cable and the publicity around it dramatically altered the context of America's response to the plight of the Jews. Although the news was unwelcome "for those who wanted the [Allies] to focus solely on military goals," it gave those lobbying for action more credibility (Breitman 1998:141). Moreover, as the Allies' prospects for a military victory improved the next year, proponents of rescue gained momentum, receiving more backing from the media and some public officials, including Eleanor Roosevelt, the president's wife (Wyman 1984). One of the most frequent proposals that was advanced called "for the Allies to facilitate the escape of Jews into neutral countries and to . . . [resettle] refugees already in neutral lands" (Breitman 1998:168). The record of neutral countries like Switzerland

and Spain had up to that time been rather mixed: while thousands of refugees had been let in, thousands of others who had reached neutral borders were denied entry and were turned back to face their deaths. The Swiss government even requested that a "J" be put on German passports to make it easier to identify Jews and bar them from entering the country (Cooper 1998; Yahil 1990).

In April 1943, the United States and Great Britain held a conference in Bermuda to discuss what could be done. Both sides were reluctant to acknowledge the specifically Jewish character of the problem, preferring to frame it as a more general refugee issue affecting a number of different groups. The conference delegates seemed more bent on creating the illusion of action than on doing anything concretely. They agreed to take steps to encourage neutral countries to accept more refugees temporarily, to find other temporary havens (such as North Africa), and to provide financial assistance for these efforts. The British agreed "in principle to admit 29,000 Jews to Palestine, the number remaining under the White Paper limit" (Breitman and Kraut 1987:179). Only children, however, with some accompanying adults, would be allowed to immigrate. Otherwise, neither Britain nor the United States were willing to assume ultimate responsibility for the refugees after the war (Breitman 1998; Rosen 2006; Tilles 2008; Wyman 1984).[16]

Nevertheless, several events in the next few months compelled Roosevelt to take further action. In July 1943, the president met with Jan Karski, a lieutenant in the Polish underground army who had firsthand knowledge of what was occurring in Poland. Karski tried to persuade Roosevelt that the Nazis' treatment of Jews was fundamentally different from their treatment of other groups, and that if the Allies did not intervene, Polish Jewry would be annihilated (Breitman 1998; Breitman and Kraut 1987; Rosen 2006; Tilles 2008).

In the meantime, Jewish activists in the United States staged public protests, and organizations such as the WJC proposed that they be allowed to deposit funds in blocked bank accounts to help finance relief and evacuation efforts.[17] WJC representative Riegner, for example, submitted a request that would have permitted the WJC to finance efforts to relocate Jews from Romania and southern France.[18] The proposal was approved by the Treasury Department but opposed by the State Department (as well as the British Foreign Office). In January 1944, after months of delay, Treasury Secretary Morgenthau met with Roosevelt and advised him of the need to take action in order to avoid a public scandal over the State Department's obstructionist stance. He asked the president to sign an executive order that would create an independent agency to handle rescue operations (Breitman 1998; Breitman and Kraut 1987; Tilles 2008; Wyman 1984).

Roosevelt finally felt compelled to act. On January 22, 1944, he signed the order that established the War Refugee Board (WRB), charging it with the responsibility "to take all measures within its power to rescue the victims of enemy oppression who are in imminent danger of death and otherwise afford such victims all possible relief and assistance consistent with the successful prosecution of the war" (cited in Yahil 1990:609). The Departments of Treasury, State, and War were instructed to provide the WRB, which operated with a small staff of about thirty people in Washington, DC, with information and assistance and to execute the measures the WRB deemed necessary. The WRB was also permitted to accept contributions, financial and otherwise, from private individuals and groups. Ultimately, 85 percent of its money came from Jewish sources (Breitman and Kraut 1987; Rosen 2006; Tilles 2008; Wyman 1984).

Under the leadership of its executive director John Pehle, an official in the Treasury Department, the WRB abandoned the Allies' policy of downplaying the Nazis' targeting of Jews. For the first time the doomed Jews of Europe had a special agency of an Allied government committed to thwarting the Final Solution. WRB activities focused on three areas: (1) issuing threats to prosecute Nazis and collaborating officials for war crimes, (2) aiding people trying to escape Nazi-controlled Europe and find refuge in safe havens, and (3) providing relief supplies to those who could not be evacuated but were lingering in ghettos and concentration camps.

David Wyman (1984) credits the WRB with helping to save about 200,000 Jewish lives. The WRB was created at a time when European governments were already reconsidering their policies in light of the turnabout in the war. Definitive U.S. expressions of concern and threats to punish Nazi collaborators helped persuade German-aligned governments in Romania, Bulgaria, and Hungary to think twice about complying with Nazi requests to deport Jews to extermination camps. Neutral nations became more willing to offer temporary havens and to provide transit visas to Jews who managed to escape from German-controlled territories. The International Red Cross modified its previous neutral stance that had prevented it from providing relief to the ghettos and camps.[19] And Jewish organizations such as the WJC and the American Jewish Joint Distribution Committee (AJJDC) were given more support to pursue various rescue schemes of their own (Breitman and Kraut 1987; Rosen 2006; Tilles 2008; Yahil 1990).

Negotiating for Jewish Lives

One of the biggest problems facing the WRB and others engaged in rescue efforts was the Nazis' unwillingness to release Jews. Rubenstein (1997) points out that with the emergence of the Final Solution the Jews under German control were no longer refugees—they were prisoners. Hitler, Himmler, and others were fanatical in their resolve to continue with the extermination program even as Germany's prospects of winning the war were turning bleak. As we shall see, however, there is evidence that some Nazi officials were willing to consider the release of some Jews in exchange for substantial concessions and that this willingness increased with the certainty that they would lose the war (Bauer 1994; Hindley 1996; Tilles 2008).

According to Levine (1998), German-aligned and neutral countries that maintained diplomatic ties with Germany had the best chance of negotiating for Jewish lives. He offers neutral Sweden as a case in point. Insofar as the Nazis relied on Sweden for iron ore, ball bearings, and ball-bearing parts, they had an interest in placating Swedish demands. When the Nazis began implementing the Final Solution in neighboring Norway, the Swedish government asked that Swedish Jews residing in Norway be allowed to return to their homeland. Germany acceded to this request, as it did to a subsequent Swedish demand to allow all Jews in Norway to emigrate to Sweden.

It was at this point that Sweden developed the tactic of offering to naturalize and issue "protective passports" to Jews who under normal conditions would have had no claims to Swedish citizenship. As long as these Jews possessed the appropriate documents that verified their right to Swedish protection, German Foreign Service bureaucrats were at times willing to respect normal diplomatic protocols and release Jews to their home country or at least temporarily exempt them from deportation to extermination camps. The leverage that Swedish diplomats had to pursue this strategy increased with the changing tide of the war as German bureaucrats "began to seek alibis for future eventualities" (Levine 1998:528). Levine argues that Sweden's response to the Final Solution (which included its acceptance of some

7,900 Danish Jews) illustrates how "determined intervention by an officially recognized third party [could] be decisive" (p. 531).

Levine (1998) adds that the highly regarded rescue efforts of Swedish diplomat Raoul Wallenberg in Budapest, Hungary, in 1944 must be understood in this context. Prior to his arrival in Budapest, Wallenberg had been introduced to Iver Olsen, the WRB representative in Sweden. The Swedish Foreign Office agreed to dispatch Wallenberg to Budapest to negotiate with the German-aligned Hungarian government to try to exempt Jews from deportation to death camps. Wallenberg essentially became the WRB representative in Hungary and was given WRB financial backing with money that came mostly from the AJJDC (Rubenstein 1997; Wyman 1984).

Even before Wallenberg's arrival, the Swedish foreign minister in Budapest had issued protective passports to several hundred Hungarian Jews who had family or business ties with Sweden, delaying the deportations that Adolf Eichmann began organizing in March 1944 after the initial German occupation of Hungary (Yahil 1990). Before that time "Hungarian killing and deportation of Jews [had] occurred only sporadically," and the 800,000 Jews in Hungary represented the largest concentration of Jews remaining alive in Europe (Breitman and Kraut 1987:210). Within two months over half the Hungarian Jews were deported, and most of them were killed at Birkenau (Bauer 1994; Breitman 1998).

In response to the Hungarian deportations, King Gustav V of Sweden, Pope Pius XII, and Max Huber, the president of the International Red Cross, had appealed to Hungarian regent Admiral Miklos Horthy to stop any further deportations of Jews. In addition, Roosevelt had warned that "Hungary's fate will not be like that of any other civilized nation . . . unless the deportations are stopped" (cited in Breitman and Kraut 1987:213). In July the United States had also bombed Budapest (for military not humanitarian reasons), and the Soviet army was advancing toward the Hungarian border. All these factors combined to persuade Horthy to try to cooperate with the Allies and temporarily halt the deportation of the 250,000 Jews who remained in Budapest. He submitted the so-called "Horthy Offer" to high-ranking German officials, requesting that particular categories of Jews be allowed to emigrate. Historical accounts differ on the specifics of the proposal, but they place the number at about 400–450 Jews who held Swedish passports and about 7,000 who held immigration certificates to Palestine (Bauer 1994; Breitman 1998; Yahil 1990). Some accounts also indicate that the proposal included a request to send an additional 10,000–20,000 children to Palestine. The offer was apparently relayed to Hitler through the German ambassador in Hungary and the German Minister of Foreign Affairs. Hitler is reported to have approved the release of some Jews provided that Horthy agreed to immediately resume the deportations of the remaining Hungarian Jews. According to Yehuda Bauer (1994), the Nazis were willing to consider the release of about 7,000 Jews to Palestine, 87 to Sweden, and a handful to other neutral countries.

It is not at all clear that the Nazis ever intended to abide by the agreement. They may simply have been trying to get Horthy to resume the deportations or to embarrass the Allies, whom they doubted really wanted to accept the Jews. Indeed, it took the Allies about a month to assure Horthy that they would in fact be willing to arrange for the transportation and temporary resettlement of the released Jews, and they made no commitment to allowing Jews permanent residence in Palestine. There is evidence that Himmler opposed sending the Jews to Palestine and that Eichmann intended to get German emigration officials "to procrastinate in granting transit permits," assuming that once the deportations began, "all the Jews would be included . . . [and] would disappear . . . before anyone realized it" (Bauer 1994:213; Yahil 1990).

Nevertheless, the negotiations helped extend the moratorium on deportations and gave Wallenberg and other neutral diplomats (from Switzerland, Spain, Portugal, San Salvador, and the Vatican) more time to issue additional protective passports to Jews. By the end of August over 17,000 Jews had received such papers. The actions of these diplomats also provided cover for Jewish activists in the Budapest Zionist youth movement who distributed thousands of additional forged documents as well—not just protective passports but food coupons, work passes, military papers, and the like (Bauer 1994; Rubenstein 1997).

In October, a Nazi-backed Hungarian military coup by the more staunchly fascist and anti-Semitic Arrow Cross Party forced Horthy's ouster, and the deportations to Auschwitz were resumed. Although the passports that had been issued by the neutral governments were not always honored, the Jews holding them were often released before or even during the deportations. Wallenberg in particular is credited with heroically pursuing transports that had already left Budapest and with managing to secure Jews' release before they crossed the Hungarian border. He also tried to use his diplomatic leverage and the sheer force of his personality to save Jews who had not yet received protective documents (Bauer 1994; Tilles 2008; Wyman 1984).

In November, as the deportations continued, a coalition of neutral diplomats issued a formal communication to the Arrow Cross government protesting the deportations and the government's failure to honor the protective documents. The Arrow Cross agreed to establish an "international ghetto"—a safe haven apart from Budapest's main ghetto—that held over 30,000 people who were crammed into rented quarters without adequate resources to meet food, heating, health, and sanitation needs (Yahil 1990).

When the Soviet army liberated Budapest in January 1945, over 100,000 Hungarian Jews were still alive. Nonetheless, Bauer (1994) notes that Wallenberg's singular role in saving these Jews has often been exaggerated, for Swiss diplomat Charles Lutz actually arranged for more protective passports than he did. Rubenstein (1997) adds that the WRB's role in saving Hungarian Jews has been overestimated as well, since both Wallenberg and Lutz's influence derived not from their association with the WRB but, as Levine (1998) suggests, from their status as neutral diplomats.[20]

At its inception, the WRB was limited in the official mandate that required its actions to be "consistent with the successful prosecution of the war." This mandate was thus constrained by a previous agreement reached by the United States, Great Britain, and the Soviet Union at the Tripartite Conference in November 1943, where the three nations committed themselves to demanding unconditional surrender from Germany. They also agreed not to enter into any separate negotiations with Germany, and if Germany solicited such negotiations they were obligated to inform each other immediately. Thus the Tripartite agreement imposed strict limits on the negotiations that could take place between the WRB and the Nazis with respect to the release of Jews (Hindley 1996; Weinberg 1998).

Bauer (1994) notes that as early as December 1942, Himmler had approached Hitler with the idea of ransoming a limited number of Jews for appreciable quantities of foreign currency and that Hitler appears to have approved the idea as long as the money was substantial and the Final Solution would continue unabated. At the same time, both men doubted that the Western Allies would in fact be willing to accept more refugees and that their refusal to do so could be used as propaganda to counter Allied criticism about Nazi treatment of Jews. Moreover, if the Allies did agree to pay ransom money for Jews, this might stimulate anti-Semitic reaction abroad and thus help Germany's cause. Later, in April 1944, Eichmann contacted Joel Brand, a Zionist member of the Budapest Relief and Rescue Committee (RRC), to broker a deal with the Western Allies. Eichmann offered to exchange one million Jews for 10,000 trucks, 800 tons of coffee, 200 tons of cocoa, 200 tons of sugar, and 2 million bars of soap. The Jews would be allowed to emigrate to any Allied-aligned country with the exception of Palestine. The proposal appears to have originated with Himmler for the purpose of sowing dissension among the Allies and opening up negotiations with the West for a separate peace agreement that would isolate the Soviet Union. Eichmann agreed that the trucks would be used only for civilian purposes or on the eastern front (Bauer 1994; Teveth 1996; Tilles 2008; Yahil 1990).

In May, Brand was sent to neutral Turkey to bring the offer to the United States and Great Britain. Although it was extremely unlikely that the United States and Great Britain would violate the Tripartite agreement, Allied proponents of rescue—including WRB director Pehle, Treasury Secretary Morgenthau, and leaders of influential Jewish organizations—hoped to string out negotiations to delay the deportations. Once the Russians were informed, however, the scheme was quickly abandoned. Nevertheless, while Brand was on his mission to Turkey, Budapest RRC member Rezsö (Rudolf) Kasztner took over negotiations with Eichmann and succeeded in securing the release of about 20,000 Hungarian Jews in exchange for ransom money provided by the AJJDC (under the auspices of the formally neutral Swiss Funds for Aid to Refugees) and the Hungarian Jews themselves.[21] Although these Jews managed to avoid deportation to Auschwitz, they were not released outright but were sent to work and transit camps in Germany, Austria, and Czechoslovakia. Ultimately about 13,700 of them survived the war (Bauer 1994; Teveth 1996; Yahil 1990).

Bauer (1994) and Levine (1998) remind us that the Final Solution evolved gradually through a process of cumulative radicalization. They suggest that this radicalization could be reversed as the wartime context that facilitated its emergence changed. Nazi concessions on Jewish policy that allowed for the emigration of Jews may have been a retreat from the Final Solution but were nonetheless consistent with the more modest goal of achieving a greater Germany *Judenfrei*. Some Jewish lives could be spared if it was in Germany's interests. Moreover, Himmler's anti-Semitism led him to hold an exaggerated view of the power of international Jewry to influence Allied policy. The reality was that Jews were never in a position to deliver what Himmler ultimately wanted: a separate peace with the Allies that would preserve the Nazi regime at the expense of the Soviet Union (Hindley 1996; Teveth 1996; Yahil 1990).

Nevertheless, Wyman (1984) believes that the WRB could have played a greater role in rescue efforts if it had been established earlier and given more support. These efforts, however, were constrained not only by the Tripartite agreement but by the Allies' firm belief that the military defeat of Germany was their primary—if not only—concern. Only "[v]ictory would end the killing, and anything that might delay victory would only hurt, not help, those whom the Germans had marked out as victims" (Weinberg 1998:489). Williamson Murray (2000) adds that from the hindsight of history Allied victory sometimes seems inevitable. At the time, however, victory was very much in doubt.

The Bombing of Auschwitz Controversy

One of the proposals considered by the WRB in June 1944 was the bombing of Auschwitz-Birkenau and the railway lines leading to the camp. After some investigation, however, the WRB concluded that the bombing would have little effect, because "even if the infrastructure was successfully destroyed, it could quickly be rebuilt" (Tilles 2008:94). Moreover, as German minister of armaments Albert Speer (1905–81) noted in a postwar interview, if the Birkenau gas chambers had been destroyed, "Hitler would have hit the roof . . . [and] ordered the return to mass shooting . . . as a matter of top priority" (quoted in Rosen 2006:473). Importantly, the military was opposed to the plan. Assistant Secretary of War John McCloy asserted that "such an operation could be executed only by the diversion of considerable air support essential to the success of our forces now engaged in decisive operations elsewhere and would in any case be of such doubtful efficacy that it would not warrant the use of our resources" (cited in Wyman 1984:296).

It is arguably true that at this stage of the war Allied aircraft could have reached Birkenau, since they had in fact bombed the IG Farben industrial facility (four times) at the nearby Monowitz camp. However, these tactical attacks on Monowitz, which were aimed at curtailing synthetic oil and rubber production that could aid the German war effect, caused little damage due to the inaccuracy of the strikes. Even if an attack on the Birkenau gas chambers had been attempted, the bombs may have missed their mark, and in any case, would have likely killed more prisoners than they would have saved. As for the bombing of railway lines, these strikes would have been even more difficult and would have required daily attacks "to keep them out of service for any length of time" (Rosen 2006:474; see also Neufeld and Berenbaum 2000; Rubenstein 1997; Tilles 2008).

Deborah Lipstadt (2000) characterizes the bombing controversy as a largely symbolic issue that pertains to "a relatively late stage of the destruction process" that is often "substituted for anger about the whole [of] the United States' apathetic response to Jewish suffering" (2000:229). More generally, considering the broader range of Allied inaction both before and during the war, Walter Laqueur (2000) is among those who thinks that it would have been possible for the Allies to save more Jews if that had been a priority when, in fact, it was not. Weinberg adds that "[e]very single life counts . . . and each person saved could have lived out a decent life" (1998:490).[22] On the other hand, he cautions against shifting the blame for the Holocaust from the killers to the bystanders. While the question of whether enough was done to help the Jews will continue to tarnish the legacy of the Allies' response to the Holocaust, governmental and public "indifference to suffering in faraway lands and unwillingness to take responsibility for persons" who need our aid are still very much with us today (Breitman and Kraut 1987:10).

Notes

1. In 1953, Israel established Yad Vashem, "The Memorial Authority for the Martyrs and Heroes of the Holocaust," which has as one of its missions the recognition and remembrance of "the Righteous among the Nations" who risked their lives to save Jews (Spector 1990c; see chapter 8). This category excludes those who saved Jews primarily for monetary gain, a group that includes anti-Semitic individuals (Fogelman 1994; Tec 1986).
2. The Church's protests led Hitler to "officially" terminate the program in August 1941, but children continued to be killed in T_4 centers throughout the war, as were prisoners of concentration camps (Friedlander 2001; Hilberg 1992; Rubenstein and Roth 1987).
3. Study of altruism is an interdisciplinary field that focuses on a wide range of areas, including blood and organ donation, bystander intervention, disaster research, philanthropy, and volunteerism, among others. Some analysts believe that self-interest or egoism ultimately underlies altruistic conduct. C. Daniel Batson (1991) describes three variations of this point of view. According to the "empathy-specific reward" hypothesis, individuals learn through socialization that rewards follow the helping of others. The "empathy-specific" hypothesis postulates that individuals expect that punishment in the form of guilt, shame, or censure will

follow failure to help. The "aversive-arousal reduction" hypothesis suggests that concern for others evokes internal distress that is relieved by helping others. However, other analysts believe that genuinely altruistic behavior does in fact exist (Berger et al. 1998; Piliavin and Charng 1990; Simmons 1991).

4.   But "all other things," as we shall see, were not necessarily equal.

5.   Some researchers suggest that there is little evidence that the Pope ever gave a direct order to the Italian clergy to help Jews, although "local archbishops, bishops, priests, and nuns . . . [often] worked out their own methods" for lending assistance (Deák 2000b:48; Zuccotti 2002).

6.   The Huguenots were French followers of Calvinism.

7.   See chapter 5, note 8.

8.   See chapter 6, note 4.

9.   Alexander (2006) notes that nineteenth-century German Americans were the first non-Anglo-Saxon group to be accepted as a legitimate member of the mainstream core group of American society.

10.   The State Department had already been using this interpretation to limit immigration from Mexico.

11.   Frankfurter was appointed to the Court in 1939 and served until 1962.

12.   When the INS was transferred from the Labor Department to the Department of Justice in 1940, the State Department tightened its regulations again.

13.   The United States, as is well known, interned Japanese Americans in camps, although it never did this to German Americans and Italian Americans.

14.   In August 1941, British Prime Minister Winston Churchill observed that "in the face of Nazi atrocities in Eastern Europe . . . the world was faced with 'a crime without a name'" (Ignatieff 2001:26). It was Raphael Lemkin, an American Jewish refugee from Poland, who first advanced the term "genocide" to refer to the Nazi assault on the Jews in his book *Axis Rule in Occupied Europe* that was published in 1944. After the war, Lemkin drafted and lobbied for the passage of the United Nations Convention on the Prevention and Punishment of Genocide. For further discussion of Lemkin and this issue, see chapter 9.

15.   Although Riegner's cable contained some errors of detail, Browning considers it "an astonishingly accurate piece of wartime intelligence" (1996:3).

16.   Roosevelt did agree to allow one thousand refugees from Italy to receive temporary asylum in a camp at Oswego in northern New York.

17.   One of the most vocal activists was Peter Bergson, a Zionist who led the Bergson Group. Bergson was critical of Jewish-American leaders' inaction and of what he considered to be their obsequious behavior (Rosen 2006; Wyman 1984).

18.   In late 1942 and early 1943, Romanian authorities had informed the Jewish Agency for Palestine that it was prepared to release 70,000 Jews for 200,000 lei per person. The Jewish leadership "was well aware that the Allies would not allow the transfer" of so many people to Palestine, and the proposal was in fact scuttled by both the U.S. State Department and the British Ministry of Economic Warfare (Friedländer 2009:390).

19.   After some international pressure, Adolf Eichmann did consent to allow the International Red Cross to inspect the Theresienstadt camp in June 1944,

but only after he had time to prepare the camp to look presentable as a "model" Jewish settlement, and after the Red Cross agreed to not also visit Auschwitz, the place to which Theresienstadt "residents" were deported. After the inspection, Red Cross delegate Maurice Rossel reported: "The voyage to Prague will remain an excellent memory for us and it pleases us to assure you, once again, that the report about our visit to Theresienstadt will be reassuring for many, as the living conditions are satisfactory" (quoted in Friedländer 2009:388). On the role of the International Red Cross, see Favev (1990).

20. Charles Fenyvesi (2001) notes that Wallenberg not only worked for the WRB but for the Office of Strategic Services, the wartime precursor to the Central Intelligence Agency, and that his influence was due in part to this association. In January 1945, he met with Soviet military officials who controlled the area at the time and was subsequently imprisoned. The Soviets claim that he died in 1947, but others believe he was alive as late as 1989.

21. See Bauer (1994) for the details of the rather complex rescue schemes involving Kasztner, and chapter 8 for a discussion of the postwar accounts of his efforts.

22. Novick (1999) estimates that a more aggressive Allied rescue policy could have saved about one to two percent of the Jewish deaths, a sizeable number of people. There is also the matter of potential descendents who were not born because Jews were killed (see chapter 1, note 2).

7

European Collective Memories: Germany and Poland

In chapter 1 I indicated that this book is not only concerned with the Holocaust itself, but also its aftermath, that is, the social and political ramifications of varying postwar collective memories of the genocide. I introduced the concept of collective memory, developed by Maurice Halbwachs, in anticipation of an examination of postwar mnemonic disputes in different nation-states. Recall we noted that varying collective agents of memory often compete with each other in both national and international arenas to establish particular narratives of the past as the "master frame" that foregrounds certain elements and backgrounds or erases others. These memories are constructed in light of present concerns and interests and, as such, often become embroiled in political disputes as they are strategically manipulated by social actors to alter the balance of power between groups.

There are, on the other hand, commonalities to these narratives insofar as they rely upon a general cultural rhetoric of victimization that emerged in the twentieth century that is concerned with the question of "who suffers what at whose hands," which Joseph Amato characterizes as "the major moral axis" of contemporary public discourse that structures claims and counterclaims about the past (1990:xxv).[1] In this context, as we shall see, an accused group may respond to accusations about its culpability in the victimization of others by deploying counterrhetorical strategies that deny or in other ways deflect responsibility for such actions. It is important to note that this rhetoric is not simply a contest of words, but a persuasive communicative strategy, a form of what Murray Edelman described as "symbolic politics," intended to induce others to make preferred judgments and political decisions (Berger 2002).

147

In chapter 9 we will consider Jewish collective memories in Israel and the United States. In this chapter we look at two European nations: Germany and Poland. Germany is arguably the most important place to start, because this was the country that perpetrated the genocide of the Jews. But Poland merits further examination, too, insofar as it was the home of the largest prewar Jewish population of Europe, some 3.3 million Jews, about 90 percent of whom were killed, the largest Jewish death toll of any nation in the war (Gutman and Rozett 1990).

The Federal Republic of Germany

Immediately after the war, in June 1945, the major Allied powers— the United States, Great Britain, France, and the Soviet Union— divided a devastated Germany into four zones of military occupation (Marrus 1997). The experience of being occupied was not pleasant for Germans. Residents surrounding the liberated concentration camps were forced to view the horrors of the remains, and some were recruited to help with burial and clean-up responsibilities. Germans were exposed to an Allied media campaign that confronted them with film footage of the camps and accusations regarding their "collective guilt." Intended by the Allies as "educational," these experiences engendered feelings of bitterness and humiliation among Germans, whose most common reaction was not to reflect on their own complicity but to say "we did not know" and to "deny having anything to do with the atrocities" (Marcuse 2001:57). Rather than expressing penance for the misery their nation had wrought, they made counterrhetorical claims about their own victimization.

The International Military Tribunal

Among the important tasks that lay before the Allies was the postwar adjudication of Nazi war criminals. Previously, in the Moscow Declaration of November 1943, the United States, Great Britain, and the Soviet Union had agreed to undertake joint prosecution of "the major criminals whose offences have no particular geographical location" (cited in Marrus 1997:21). Other prosecutions, it was decided, would take place independently in "the countries in which [the] abominable deeds were done in order that they may be judged and punished according to the laws of these liberated countries and of the Free Governments which will be erected therein" (1997:21). All told, the number of trials undertaken in the aftermath of World

War II was historically unprecedented (Deák, Gross, and Judt 2000; Marcuse 2001).[2]

The International Military Tribunal (IMT) that conducted proceedings in Nuremberg, Germany, between October 1945 and October 1946 is the most well known of the many postwar trials. The IMT was presided over by judges from the four occupying Allied powers. Nuremberg was chosen for its symbolic importance as the place where the infamous Nuremberg laws were passed (see chapter 3). The term "Nuremberg trials" is often used to refer to several different criminal proceedings, but it is most commonly associated with the trial of twenty-four defendants who were chosen because they were "the most important surviving principal[s] in [their] domain of responsibilities and activities" (Rosenbaum 1993:19).[3] Reichsmarschall Hermann Göring was arguably the most infamous luminary on the list of defendants. Adolf Hitler and Heinrich Himmler would have been among the most notable Nazis to be prosecuted if they had not committed suicide before they could be apprehended. After his capture Joseph Goebbels committed suicide as well.

There was some initial disagreement among the Allies as to the purpose of the trials. The British wanted to summarily execute the defendants, while the Soviets wanted to use the trial solely to establish the appropriate punishments though not to determine questions of guilt or innocence. In contrast, U.S. Supreme Court Justice Robert Jackson, who was appointed to head the U.S. prosecution team, believed that the trial should be more than a showcase for the victors to engage in collective acts of retribution. For the IMT to have moral legitimacy, he argued, it must obey the "ultimate principle" that no man should be prosecuted unless "you are willing to see him free if not proved guilty. . . . The world yields no respect to courts that are merely organized to convict" (cited in Rosenbaum 1993:21). Thus there were in fact three acquittals in the IMT proceedings; and two other cases were dropped, one because the defendant was too ill to stand trial and the other because he committed suicide. The remaining nineteen defendants were convicted and twelve were sentenced to death (Mushkat 1990).[4]

The IMT prosecuted individuals under three broad areas of international law: *crimes against peace*, *war crimes*, and *crimes against humanity*. Crimes against peace included "the planning, preparation, initiation, and waging of wars of aggression, or a war in violation of existing treaties, agreements, and assurances" (cited in

Marrus 1997:122).[5] War crimes included violations of "the laws and customs of war," including murder, enslavement, and ill-treatment of war prisoners or civilians in occupied territories (1997:149). Crimes against humanity included "murder, extermination, enslavement, deportation, and other inhumane acts committed against any civilian population . . . or persecutions on political, racial or religious grounds . . . whether or not in violation of the domestic law of the country where perpetrated" (1997:187–88). Importantly, it was with crimes against humanity that the Nuremberg trials really broke new ground, because it was the first time a country was held "internationally responsible for what it did to its own people . . . no matter what its own national laws . . . allowed" (Rosenbaum 1993:34; Simpson 1993).

While the particularity of Jewish victimization was acknowledged at the IMT, it was subsumed under the broader categories of war crimes and crimes against humanity and soon half forgotten (Hilberg 1991; Osiel 1997). Except for the defendants, Germans did not participate in the proceedings, leaving an impression of separation between Nazis and other Germans, as if Germany had been occupied by a foreign element that had imposed its will on a reluctant population. Thus the guilt of a select few absolved the many of their responsibility and allowed them to put the war behind them. Mark Osiel (1997) notes that criminal trials quite naturally focus on the intentions and motivations of defendants, and in the case of Nuremberg, contributed to the focus in Holocaust historiography on the Nazi elite. He also suggests that prosecutors' arguments at Nuremberg framed the crimes not as a rupture from the past but as in violation of "longstanding doctrines in the law of war" (p. 117). Moreover, no representative of German industry was included among the high-profile IMT defendants. Although some businessmen were convicted and imprisoned in other proceedings, they were released after a few years (Domansky 1997; Judt 2000; Miller 1990; Rubenstein and Roth 1987).

Most of the defendants in the postwar trials pleaded not guilty to the charges against them and made appeals to defeasibility.

> They had known a little about what was happening but not too much; it was too dangerous to know more. They had only been following orders and had served their country faithfully. Besides, the conditions in the camps weren't always that bad. And they had tried their best to save as many as they could. Without them more would have been killed. Why should they be singled out? If they were guilty, who in fact was innocent?

In such claims the myth of the "good Nazi" was born. Decent men who had done their best during difficult times now claimed to be victims of postwar injustice (Deák 2000a; Johnson 1999; Marcuse 2001).

Denazification and the Cold War

The Allies did not rest with criminal prosecutions, and they also instituted a policy of German "denazification" in an attempt to cleanse Germany of its disreputable elements. Denazification was first articulated by the United States, Great Britain, and the Soviet Union at the Yalta Conference six months before the end of the war. The conference generated a joint statement whereby the countries agreed "to wipe out the Nazi Party, Nazi laws, organizations, and institutions, remove all Nazi and militarist influences from public office and from the cultural and economic life of the German people, and take such other agreed measures in Germany as may be necessary for the future peace and safety of the world" (cited in Ruckerl 1990a:359). At the war's end, about 240,000 Germans were placed under mandatory arrest and interned in camps. Some Germans complained that the conditions in these camps were worse than the camps Germany had operated during the war, and that the denazification program was "an attempt to exterminate National Socialists as people with differing political opinions" (quoted in Marcuse 2001:102).

In 1946, the Allies drew up denazification guidelines that identified the "offices and positions from which former Nazis were barred" (Ruckerl 1990a:361).[6] The designees were distributed into varying categories based on their perceived degree of culpability, and different punishments were specified that included imprisonment, loss of employment, confiscation of property, loss of pension rights, special deductions from income taxes, and restrictions on voting rights. "Had these guidelines been observed, the denazification measures would have been much harsher than they were in practice" (1990a:361). In actuality, however, the program resulted in "an ever-increasing number of 'Germans'" being included on the side of the innocent and "an ever-decreasing number of 'Nazis'" being included on the side of the guilty (Domansky 1997:246; Marcuse 2001; Simpson 1993).

At the same time, the emerging Cold War between the Western Allies and the Soviet Union dramatically changed the postwar political context, and the initial postwar focus on the past quickly gave way to present concerns. The United States, Great Britain, and France, of course, favored a capitalist-style democracy for Germany, while the

Soviet Union favored a Communist-style regime. Consequently, the three Western nations combined forces and consolidated their control over their zones of occupation, while the Soviet Union entrenched its position in the East. In 1949, Germany was officially divided into two nations: the Federal Republic of Germany (FRG), also known as West Germany, and the German Democratic Republic (GDR), also known as East Germany. This division lasted until the end of the Cold War, when East Germany became part of the FRG in 1990 (Marcuse 2001; Ruckerl 1990a; Simpson 1993).

The Soviets were the first to abandon denazification. They viewed Nazism and fascism as logical outcomes of Western capitalism and credited German Communists with spearheading the anti-fascist resistance that had occurred during the Nazi era. East Germany was now seen as a bulwark against the resurgence of Nazism in Germany, and in the East German collective memory that was subsequently constructed, the memory of the Jewish genocide was buried under the rhetoric of communist ideology, as the legacy of World War II was framed in terms of the suffering the Nazis had inflicted upon the Soviet Union and the ongoing Communist struggle against international capitalism and the imperialist powers of the West (especially the United States), which were equated with Hitlerism and other forms of fascism (Domansky 1997; Herf 1997; Huener 2003; Judt 2000).[7]

In West Germany, the Cold War also took precedence over further attempts to denazify Germany. Up to that point, U.S. Secretary of Treasury Henry Morgenthau had been a leading proponent of dismantling the German corporate structure that had supported the Nazis and been complicit in the Final Solution. Secretary of State George Marshall, on the other hand, placed priority on reintegrating the FRG into the postwar global capitalist economy, and it was this view that prevailed. The West needed German industrialists with financial resources and technical and administrative expertise, whatever their Nazi past, to help rebuild the West German economy. In addition, the North Atlantic Treaty Organization (NATO), the military alliance of Western nations that was established in 1949, needed to count on West Germany to oppose the bloc of Eastern European nations that were controlled by the Soviet Union. Thus there was little interest in implicating the German military in the crimes it had committed in the eastern territories of Nazi-occupied Europe (Bartov 1997a; Simpson 1993; see chapter 4).

Moreover, the U.S. government even helped hundreds of Nazi war criminals avoid prosecution and escape to safe havens. Nazis from Germany and other collaborating governments who claimed expertise about the Soviet Union were recruited as intelligence agents. German scientists from the wartime armaments program that had utilized slave labor were given false identity papers and brought to the United States to work in the U.S. rocket program. Vatican officials, who were fervently anticommunist, assisted in these efforts, providing Nazis temporary refuge in Italy and helping them emigrate to South America. Adolf Eichmann was among them, and it was not until 1960 that Israeli intelligence agents brought him to Israel to stand trial for his crimes (Rosenbaum 1993; Simpson 1988, 1993; see chapter 8).

In the early postwar years, the Allies supervised West Germany's political and economic reconstruction and provided millions of dollars in U.S. aid. With the 1949 election of Chancellor Konrad Adenauer (1876–1967), leader of the Christian Democratic Union (CDU), the new Germany began to distinguish itself from its Nazi past and demonstrate its commitment to Western values and democratic institutions. Importantly, Adenauer was willing to express public regret over what had transpired during the war and to pay restitution on behalf of the Jewish victims of the war to the newly formed state of Israel, which was established in 1948 (see chapter 8). In a speech before the German *Bundestag* (parliament) in 1951, Adenauer announced the reparations agreement he had worked out with Israel by noting that "unspeakable crimes have been committed in the name of the German people" and calling for "moral and material indemnity, both with regard to the individual harm done to the Jews and with regard to the Jewish property for which no legitimate individual claimants still exist" (quoted in Segev 1993:202; see also Wolffsohn 1993).[8]

The Legacy of Resistance and Critique from the Left

A 1952 public opinion poll taken in West Germany found that only 20 percent of the respondents believed that Hitler's opponents should have resisted during the war, 34 percent thought that the resisters should have waited until after the war was over, and 15 percent felt there should have been no resistance at all (Large 1994). Survivors of the German wartime resistance complained that they had not been accorded the same degree of influence in political parties and in government as those who had "wintered over" during the Nazi years. Although Adenauer was included in the latter group, he had not been a Nazi supporter and understood that political capital could be gained from identifying himself with the resistance legacy. At the tenth anniversary of the 1944 assassination attempt on Hitler (see chapter 6), Adenauer took the opportunity to enter West Germany into the international competition for postwar victimhood and martyrdom. In a speech at the newly constituted German Foreign Office (FO), he declared that former FO resisters had "given their lives . . . so that the unjustifiable condemnation [of the FO] at home and abroad might be reversed" (quoted in Large 1994:246–47). He also made note of FO officials who "had urged the Western powers to stand up to Hitler" and not appease him at Munich. This counterrhetorical appeal to defeasibility attempted to share or shift the blame for the "other [Nazi] Germany" on to the Allies. President Eugen Gerstenmaier added, in a speech on the same occasion, "The blood of the martyred resisters has cleansed our German name of the shame which Hitler cast upon us" (quoted in Large 1994:247).

At the same time, the Cold War climate significantly skewed political characterizations of the resistance movement. Domestically, CDU leaders downplayed the significant resistance efforts of the political left, especially the Communists, and exaggerated the degree to which conservative institutions, like the FO and ecumenical organizations, represented the anti-Nazi resistance. The left, in turn, proclaimed its right to carry the banner of heroism and lead Germany in its quest for a positive postwar national identity. According to Kurt Schumacher, leader of the Social Democratic Party until his death in 1952, "We Socialists would have been the resisters even if the Americans and the British had become fascists" (quoted in Large 1994:250).[9]

Christopher Simpson (1993) adds that the German left actually played a greater role in the postwar denazification of Germany than any other domestic group. After the war, left-wing antifascist groups "organized local unions known as *Betriebsrats* (work councils) that took over management of hundreds of companies, particularly larger factories," driving out Nazi-era boards of directors and personnel managers, Nazi activists, and Gestapo informers (p. 247). However, the radical politics of the work councils disturbed the occupying Western governments, which quickly moved to suppress them.

In the 1960s, a countervailing trend in German memory construction emerged with the left-wing student protest movement that had developed in West Germany as well as other Western nations. The

West German student left challenged what they perceived as their elders' silence regarding the country's Nazi past, and they called into question the older generation's commitment to democratic institutions. Employing "fascism" as a general rhetorical motif, the left claimed that the West German government was still run by "fascists," a charge that was also leveled by protesters in other Western countries against their governments, including the United States.[10] Taking a cue from the Communist left, including the Soviet Union and other Eastern bloc nations, the protesters claimed that the "fascism" of the postwar democracies was comparable to the fascism of the 1930s, though perhaps more subtle and technologically sophisticated. Similarly, the genocide of World War II was comparable to more recent military campaigns such as the United States' involvement in the Vietnam War. Thus Germans had to remain constantly on guard against future "holocausts," especially a nuclear one that was a possible consequence of U.S. imperialism (Brunner 1997; Marcuse 2001; Markovits 1990; Miller 1990).

In another counterrhetorical move, the German left aligned itself with Israel's Arab opposition by turning the politics of victimization back against the Jews, especially after Israel's victory against its Arab adversaries in the 1967 Six Day War and subsequent occupation of Palestinian territory (Krondorfer 1995; Marcuse 2001). As I will explain more fully in chapter 8, the United Nations had voted in November 1947 to partition Palestine, which had been controlled by the British, into a Jewish state (Israel) and an Arab state (Palestine). In the face of Arab opposition, Israel was victorious in a War of Independence against the indigenous Palestinian Arabs and the neighboring Arab states. Later, in 1967, when Egypt began amassing troops on the Israeli border, Israel launched a preemptive air strike and emerged victorious in just six days, occupying territory the UN had designated for the Palestinians. In the rhetoric of the left, however, the Israelis were dubbed the "new 'Nazis'" and the Palestinians the "new 'Jews'" (Markovits 1990:271). Perhaps Zionism was a "fascist" political formation comparable to National Socialism. Thus the left (in West Germany and elsewhere) not only questioned Israel's policies but the very legitimacy of its existence (Roiphe 1988).

The Politics of Historiography

The political climate of the 1960s helped break the silence of West German academic historiography regarding the Nazi period. Prior to that time, West German historians generally viewed Nazism as an historical accident that was disharmonious with the general thrust of German history. Gradually a younger generation of historians initiated a scholarly inquiry into the structural and ideological dimensions of Nazism, including the role of the bureaucracy, although controversial topics such as the complicity of the German army, the professional and medical class, and the citizenry at large did not receive close attention until the late 1970s. Significantly, the younger historians, who identified with the liberal/social-democratic wing that dominated West German politics for a time, began to contextualize the Nazi period in terms of the evolution of German nationalism and its militaristic and anti-democratic traditions (Evans 1989; Friedländer 1993; Marcuse 2001; Miller 1990; see chapter 1).

In 1983, West Germans commemorated the fiftieth anniversary of the Nazis' seizure of power with a plethora of media coverage, exhibitions, and conferences. But the unprecedented negative significance given to this historical event raised doubts among conservatives about the wisdom of confronting the country's past in this way, for rarely does a nation call upon itself to acknowledge its villainous side. Five years earlier, historian Hellmut Diwald had published his *Geschichte der Deutschen* (History of the Germans), which advanced a competing claim of victimhood by arguing that Germany's past had been unjustifiably "morally disqualified" (cited in Evans 1989:15). Diwald sought to restore a popular history of Germany that celebrated the national glory of its pre-Nazi past and that devoted little more than two pages to the atrocities committed by the Nazi regime, especially against the Jews.

Diwald's book was not well received when it was first published, but the ascendancy of Chancellor Helmut Kohl's conservative (center-right) coalition in 1982 marked a change in West Germany's political climate. According to Kohl, West Germany had paid its debt to the Jews and to the international community. It was now time for Germans "to stand up and take their rightful place in the struggle for Western freedom and democratic values" (Miller 1990:45). Public opinion polls indicated that Germans at that time were less proud of being German, for example, than Americans were of being American. Michael Stürmer, a professor of history who advised Kohl on historical matters, wrote a series of newspaper articles arguing that the German people needed a positive sense of their historical past to provide cohesiveness to the country, and that those who wished to undermine Germans' national self-confidence were collaborating with the Eastern bloc (Evans 1989, 1991).

In 1984, Western leaders met to celebrate the fortieth anniversary of the landing at Normandy, France, the site of the Allied invasion of Europe that marked the beginning of the last campaign of World War II (Hilberg 1986). Chancellor Kohl, who was not invited, was compensated with an invitation from French President Francois Mitterand to participate in a ceremonial observance of World War I at a Verdun battlefield cemetery in France. Kohl, however, sought to redeem Germany not merely for its role in World War I but for World War II as well. For this purpose he invited Ronald Reagan, president of the United States, to a ceremony at a German military cemetery in Bitburg in May 1985. Reagan agreed to participate because he wanted to support his Cold War ally, especially since Kohl had incurred criticism in his country for "allowing NATO to station Cruise missiles and Pershing II rockets on West German soil" (Marcuse 2001:360).

When the White House announced the intended visit to Bitburg "in a spirit of reconciliation, in a spirit of forty years of peace, in a spirit of economic and military compatibility" with West Germany, it failed to anticipate the forthcoming barrage of criticism, most vocally from the Jewish community but also from U.S. veterans and Congressional representatives (quoted in Miller 1990:47). Bitburg, it turned out, was the site not only of some two thousand buried German soldiers but about fifty SS men as well (Hartman 1986; Marcuse 2001; Schmitt 1989).

Reagan had initially conferred with Kohl about also visiting the Dachau concentration camp, but he decided not to go there because he didn't want, in his words, to "reawaken the memories . . . and the passions of the time" (quoted in Hilberg 1986:19). After the public outcry about Bitburg, however, he did visit the Bergen-Belsen camp to pay respect to the victims. Still, Reagan only antagonized protesters further when he claimed that the men buried at Bitburg "were victims, just as surely as the victims in the concentration camps" (quoted in Hartman 1986:xiv). Reagan described World War II as a "war against one man's totalitarian dictatorship" and asserted that the German people had an "unnecessary . . . guilt feeling that's been imposed upon them" (quoted in Hartman 1986:xiii, 258). Thus Reagan lent his support to a counterrhetorical construction of the past based on notions of universal victimhood and military martyrdom.

As Geoffrey Hartman observes, it was as if Reagan wished "to recall nothing of the past except common sacrifices and a shared code of military honor," as if the behavior of the German military during the war was no different than that of any other armed forces that were fighting for the security of their nation (1986:5). But the behavior of the German military was in fact different. German troops, as we have noted, were not simply defending the country against a hostile enemy; they helped carry out the Final Solution, turning Jews over to the SS and engaging in mass killings themselves. And even when the troops were not directly involved in the killings, it was the army's conquest of the eastern territories that made the Final Solution possible in the first place (Bartov 1997a; Brunner 1997).

Nonetheless, Chancellor Kohl could not have been more pleased with Reagan's rendition of the past. In a rather brilliant rhetorical sleight of hand, Kohl used the bodies of the dead soldiers at Bitburg to both bury a guilty past and to exalt a noble future for Germany. As he said: "[T]he President of the United States . . . and I paid homage . . . to the dead buried there and thus to all victims of war and tyranny, to the dead and persecuted of all nations. . . . Our visit to the soldiers' graves . . . [is] a reaffirmation and widely visible and widely felt gesture of reconciliation . . . [and] deep friendship . . . between our peoples" (quoted in Hartman 1986:256).

In Germany, Kohl and Reagan's "Bitburg history" did not go unchallenged. Three days later, on the fortieth anniversary of the war's end, the more moderate West German president Richard von Weizacker countered with a speech before the Bundestag that urged Germans to take a more honest look at their past.

> We need to have the strength to look truth straight in the eye—without embellishment and without distortion. . . . Who could [have remained] unsuspecting after the burning of the synagogues, the plundering, the stigmatization of the Star of David, the deprivation of rights, the ceaseless violation of human dignity? Whoever opened his eyes and ears and sought information could not fail to notice Jews were being deported. The nature and scope of the destruction may have exceeded human imagination, but in reality there was . . . the attempt . . . not to take note of what was happening. There were many ways of not burdening one's conscience, of shunning responsibility, looking away, keeping mum. When the unspeakable truth of the Holocaust then became known at the end of the war, all too many of us claimed that we had not known anything about it or even suspected anything. (quoted in Hartman 1986:262, 265)

Following the Bitburg affair, and in spite of von Weizacker's rebuttal, conservative West German historians increasingly lent their voices in the popular print media to the call for a positive national identity. One rhetorical strategy was to normalize or relativize the Nazi period and hence make the Nazis' crimes less reprehensible by equating their actions to those that occurred in other nations as well. Philosopher-historian Ernst Nolte, for instance, whose *Three Faces of Fascism* (1965) gained him an international reputation, argued that every powerful nation had "its own Hitler era, with its monstrosities and sacrifices," and that the experience of Jews under Nazism was comparable to the experience of persecuted minorities elsewhere (cited in Maier 1988:28). Moreover, Nolte argued that the Soviet Union, not Nazi Germany, was the prototype terror state, and that Hitler had been driven primarily by his resolve to prevent the spread of Communism (see also Mayer 1989). Nolte also claimed that Hitler's actions against the Jews in the German-occupied territories, however misguided or excessive, were taken in response to Jewish support of the Allied war effort and the threat of Jewish partisan activity behind German lines (Baldwin 1990; Brunner 1997; Evans 1989; Olick and Levy 1997).

Nolte's critics countered that the problem with his view was not that historical comparisons are illegitimate, but that Nolte undertook them to gloss over differences that painted German national identity in a negative light (Evans 1989, 1991). Thus when Stürmer, among others, argued that the absence of an integrating national identity had precipitated the rise of Nazism by undermining prewar Germany, Jürgen Habermas, Germany's most distinguished contemporary philosopher, sounded an alarm about conservatives' revision of history. According to Habermas, "The only patriotism that does not alienate us from the West is a patriotism of commitment to constitutionalism. . . . Whoever wants to suppress the blush of shame . . . and summon the Germans back to a conventional form of . . . national identity, destroys the only reliable basis of our Western loyalty" (cited in Maier 1988:45). Expressing implicit agreement with some of the German left's views on fascism, Habermas argued that the legacy of the Nazi era still bound the German people because they shared a common heritage that had made the Holocaust possible and that could make it possible (in other forms) again.

Thus the *Historikerstreit* (historians' dispute), as this controversy was called, emerged full bloom (Baldwin 1990; Brunner 1997; Evans 1989). Although most German historians agreed that many of the conservatives' claims lacked empirical support, the latter had "succeeded in giving some respectability to arguments previously thought beyond the pale" (Evans 1991:13). In a 1988 address that was supposed to commemorate the fiftieth anniversary of Kristallnacht, for example, Bundestag president Phillip Jenninger reinforced the claim of German victimhood by saying:

> [A]s for the Jews: Hadn't they in the past presumed a role—as was said back then—that they weren't entitled to? Shouldn't they have finally had to accept restrictions? Didn't they perhaps even deserve to be put in their place? And especially: Didn't the propaganda—aside from a few wild exaggerations that couldn't be taken seriously—correspond in the main points with their own suspicions and convictions? (cited in Marcuse 2001:367)

Jeffrey Olick and Daniel Levy suggest that "the delivery of the speech made it difficult to determine whether Jenninger was simply portraying how the situation might have seemed reasonable to average Germans at the time, or whether in fact he was saying that it was reasonable" (1997:931). Harold Marcuse, on the other hand, thinks the remarks "contained too much Nazi vocabulary and diction . . . [and] was completely inappropriate for the occasion" (2001:367). In either case, many left-wing members of the Bundestag walked out in protest and two days later Jenninger was forced to resign.

With the end of the Cold War and the reunification of the FRG, German claims and counterclaims about the past continue to mark the nation's collective memory. In October 1990, at the first parliamentary meeting of the reunited country, Chancellor Kohl called for a moment of silence to remember all the victims of Nazism, Communism, and his formerly divided nation. According to James Young, "By uniting memory of its own martyrs with those it once victimized," Kohl placed universal victimhood at the center of the unified FRG's "first nationally shared memorial moment" (1993:25–26). But without a divided Germany "as a punitive reminder," Young wonders, will the future Germany eventually recall only its own martyrs and its own triumphs?

There are arguably reasons to expect that such historical amnesia will be next to impossible, and Habermas, once again, was willing to do his part to make sure that Germans never forget their country's ominous past. The occasion was a 1997 award ceremony for an American Holocaust scholar, Daniel Goldhagen, at which Habermas had been invited to make some laudatory remarks as Goldhagen received the

Blatter für Deutsche and Internationale Politik (Journal for German and International Politics) prestigious Democracy Prize.

Goldhagen had first made his mark in the United States with the publication of his *Hitler's Willing Executioners: Ordinary Germans and the Holocaust* in 1996, which became a national best seller. In that book, Goldhagen follows Christopher Browning, whose *Ordinary Men: Reserve Police Battalion 101 and the Final Solution in Poland* was published in 1992 with much less fanfare and attention from the lay public, in documenting the role of the Order Police in the Nazi killing machine (see chapter 4).

Goldhagen's thesis that ordinary Germans participated in the Holocaust stands on solid ground, but less so is his claim that the German people had been adherents to a uniquely virulent and "eliminationist" form of anti-Semitism that predates the rise of Nazism. Many historians dispute his contention that Germans were more anti-Semitic than the peoples of other European countries, noting that a variety of anti-Semitisms existed in Germany and that the "eliminationist" strain was not typical of most Germans (Augstein 1998; Browning 1998; Deák et al. 2000).

When *Hitler's Willing Executioners* was released in Germany, the Historikerstreit had barely subsided, and the book reignited "discussion of painful problems that [were] far from having been conclusively resolved" (Wehler 1998:94). The press seemed to react defensively, perceiving Goldhagen as "really writing about Germany today, or about the 'eternal German', and not specifically about the very different Germans who had set out to destroy the Jews of Europe" decades earlier (Riemer 1998:177). Some of the attacks got rather personal. It was pointed out that Goldhagen was Jewish, son of a Holocaust survivor no less. Who was he to indict Germans with such dribble? Was this "yet another act of Jewish aggression against the German people?" (Markovits 1998:123). The message seemed to be: Don't even bother to read the book (Joffe 1998).

But Germans did read the book, in droves, and those on the left-wing side of the historians' debate accused Goldhagen's opposition of being "in the camp of the normalizers or even the deniers, at least [on the side] of those denying that ordinary Germans participated" in the Holocaust (Shandley 1998:22). Goldhagen, they said, should be celebrated as a friend of postwar Germany, reminding Germans that they should look to the Western democracies, not to their predemocratic past, to construct a positive national identity. Thus, during his speech,

Habermas praised Goldhagen for having shook Germans' "naïve trust in our own tradition" (1998:265).

> On the present occasion we are evaluating the contribution that an American, a Jewish historian, has made toward Germans' search for the proper way to come to terms with a criminal period of their history. . . . [I]n an ethical-political discourse, the question is not primarily the guilt or innocence of the forefathers but, rather, the critical self-assurance of their descendants . . . . [Those who] were born later, who cannot know how they themselves would have acted, are trying to [reach] some clarity about the cultural matrix of a burdened inheritance . . . to decide what is to be continued, and what revised, from those traditions that had earlier formed such a disastrous motivational background. . . . Goldhagen's work . . . refers to very specific traditions and mentalities, to ways of thinking and perceiving that belong to a particular cultural context—not something unalterable to which we have been consigned by fate but factors that can be transformed through a change of consciousness and that in the meantime have actually been transformed through political enlightenment. (1998:267, 271–72)

Indeed, upon accepting the award, Goldhagen acknowledged that Germany had in fact become an "internationally responsible" democratic nation and that this had been due in large part to Germans' ability to develop a "remarkably self-critical national history," responsive to critiques from abroad and outsiders such as himself (1998:277): "That I am being . . . [honored] in Germany for writing a book with the unsettling and painful content that mine has is the strongest testimony to . . . the character and democratic promise of contemporary Germany, and to the fact that it is really all the people in Germany, responsible for making the Federal Republic the democratic country that it has become, who deserve the prize" (p. 285).

Be that as it may, Marcuse (2001) observes that younger Germans are generally more interested than their elders in learning about Germans as perpetrators and less tolerant about claims of German victimhood. The older cohort's often "strident insistence on a right to ignorance is giving way to the willingness . . . to confront the question of . . . [German] responsibility" (2001:382). Moreover, in 1990, the teaching of the Nazi period (including the anti-Jewish campaign) became required in German schools. This compulsory curriculum is intended to encourage students to understand "the dangers for their own society of those things that made the Nazi regime and the Holocaust possible" (Fox 2001:308).

Nowadays, it can hardly be said that Germany is bereft of memorials and museums that commemorate the Holocaust and history of the Jews. In some ways, however, this engagement with the past suggests the disappearance of Jews as an integral part of contemporary German society. In the post-Cold War era, the Jewish population has grown from about 40,000 in the early 1990s to about 118,000 in the mid-2000s, but much of this increase has been due to the immigration of Soviet Jews (Jewish Virtual Library 2006). Jews living in Germany still occupy a social status as the "other," and they perceive themselves more as "Jews in Germany" than as "German Jews" (Brumlik 1996:1; see also Bodemann 1996; Gilman and Remmler 1994; Rapaport 1997).

Poland

The foregoing account of German collective memory is but one indication of the "dejudification" of the Holocaust that occurred in Europe during the postwar years. This dilution and even erasure of Jewish memory was particularly acute in the Soviet Union and Soviet-bloc nations like the GDR (Dawidowicz 1981; Herf 1997; Hoffman 1992). Communist-controlled Poland, the site of the largest prewar Jewish population, where 90 percent of the three million Jews who once lived there were killed, is a case in point (Gebert 2008; Huener 2003; Krajewski 2005; Zubrzycki 2006).

Non-Jewish Poles, of course, suffered immensely under German occupation. The political, intellectual, and religious leadership was decimated, and an estimated three million people were killed, which Richard Lukas (1986) calls the "forgotten Holocaust." As the majority population, the proportion of deaths among non-Jews was much lower (about 10 percent) than the proportion of deaths among Jews, but it was significant nonetheless. In the initial postwar years, however, Polish commemoration of the tragedy downplayed the Final Solution and the specifically Jewish causalities and focused instead on a more general Polish martyrdom, with an emphasis on the patriotic Polish resisters who tried to defend the Polish nation against Nazi aggression. This was the initial narrative, for instance, that was constructed at the State Museum that was established at the site of the Auschwitz concentration camp in the immediate postwar years (Dawidowicz 1981; Huener 2003; Polonsky and Michlic 2004; Zubrzycki 2006).

By the end of the 1940s, however, the Polish Communist Party, subservient to Joseph Stalin and the Soviet Union, was already asserting greater control over postwar Polish memory with a narrative that focused on the Communist struggle against Western imperialism and fascism. At the Auschwitz museum the initial nationalist theme was supplanted by a narrative that emphasized the implications of wartime resistance for the ongoing struggle against the West. According to this narrative, as Jonathan Huener explains, "American 'imperialists' were the successors and postwar patrons of German criminals, and concentration camps were not simply sites of senseless suffering and death, but arenas of antifascist struggle for the progressive and internationalist resistance forces" (2003:102).

Contested Memory at Auschwitz

In the 1950s, especially after Stalin's death in 1953, Polish nationalists redoubled their efforts to impose a nationalist frame on Polish memory. By now as well, Auschwitz was emerging as an international symbol of the Holocaust, and international groups began inserting themselves into the politics of memory construction at the Auschwitz site, pressuring Polish agents of memory to represent more of the Jewish experience.

In the 1970s, the Roman Catholic Church began asserting greater resistance to atheistic Communist authority and involving itself, too, in disputes about collective memory at Auschwitz, hoping to increase the Church's visibility, underscore its relevance for Polish nationalism, and lend a "redemptive meaning to Auschwitz" (Huener 2003:217). In October 1972, for example, the Church organized a holy mass in honor of Father Maksymilian Kolbe on the grounds of Birkenau, which was attended by a large gathering of people. Kolbe had suffered a martyred death in Auschwitz in 1941, after offering to take the place of another man who had been sentenced to death by starvation as punishment for the escape of another prisoner. Before the war, however, Kolbe had been a prominent anti-Semite, an editor of an anti-Semitic newspaper, so his choice as an iconic symbol of the Holocaust evoked controversy internationally, especially among Jews. This event, however, only foreshadowed additional conflicts to come (Zubrzycki 2006).

When Polish Cardinal Karol Wojtyła was elected as John Paul II in 1978 and began speaking out on behalf of religious freedom and human rights, the Polish people were emboldened to assert themselves against Communist domination through expressions of religious faith that were conflated with nationalism. During his papacy, Pope John Paul II also engaged in acts of reconciliation between Catholics and

Jews, including the historic opening of diplomatic ties between the Vatican and Israel in 1994. His imprint on Holocaust memory, however, was not without controversy (Huener 2003; Zubrzycki 2006).

Early in his papacy, in June of 1979, Pope John Paul II made an historic nine-day visit to Poland, giving sermons at various historical sites, Auschwitz-Birkenau among them, where he gave a speech on a raised alter adorned with a tall cross before tens of thousands of faithful and described the camp as "the Golgotha of our age" (quoted in Huener 2003:217). To invoke Golgotha, the place of Christ's crucifixion, was an explicit invocation of a master narrative of Auschwitz as a site of Christian suffering, a point that was brought home further when he also invoked Father Kolbe's martyrdom, as well as the martyrdom of Carmelite Sister Bendicta of the Cross, better known as Edith Stein, who also died at the camp.[11] Stein had been a well-known philosopher, but she also had been a Jew who had converted to Catholicism. For the Pope to have invoked Stein's memory "was perhaps only natural and may also have been intended as a gesture of inclusivity and reconciliation between Catholics and Jews," but in light of his Golgatha comparison, many Jews worldwide regarded it as a misconstrued effort to bring the Holocaust under the banner of a Christian narrative of suffering and redemption (Huener 2003:217; Zubrzycki 2006).[12]

Later, in 1984, a group of Carmelite Catholic nuns moved into and renovated a building that was adjacent to the first Auschwitz camp for use as a convent. During the war, the building had been used to store Zyklon B and the stripped belongings of camp prisoners. Many Jews were offended by this infringement of "symbolic territoriality," to use Marvin Prosono's (1994) phrase, especially when Father Werenfried van Straaten, a Dutch Dominican priest, began a fund-raising drive for the convent that would help it become, in his words, "a spiritual fortress and a guarantee of the conversion of strayed brothers from our countries," a not-too-veiled call to convert Jews to Catholicism (quoted in Prosono 1994:178). As pressure mounted from both Jewish and Catholic circles to relocate the convent as a gesture of respect and sympathy for world Jewry, a number of religious leaders met at an interfaith gathering in Geneva in 1986 and signed an accord declaring that there would be "no permanent Catholic place of worship on the site of the Auschwitz and Birkenau camps," and agreeing to relocate the convent within two years nearby but clearly outside the immediate vicinity as part of a center for "information, education, meeting and prayer" (quoted in Huener 2003:236).

By the summer of 1989, when construction on the relocated convent had not yet begun, the conflict escalated. New York Rabbi Avraham Weiss led a small group of demonstrators who climbed over the gate surrounding the convent and knocked on the convent door, wanting to confront the nuns about their occupation of what Weiss called "the world's largest Jewish cemetery" (quoted in Prosono 1994:179). The protesters were greeted instead by Polish workmen who threw buckets of water mixed with paint (and purportedly urine) on them and who beat and kicked them while the nuns and Polish police looked on. A few weeks later, Cardinal Józef Glemp, the head of the Polish Catholic Church, delivered an inflammatory speech before tens of thousands of followers at Czestochowa, the holiest Christian shrine in Poland, accusing the Jewish protesters of trying to assault the nuns and destroy convent property. He also chastised world Jewry for using their clout in the media to spread anti-Polish sentiments (Huener 2003; Zubrzycki 2006).

The War of the Crosses

The Carmelite convent was eventually relocated in 1993, when Pope John Paul II finally intervened, but that was not the end of the dispute. During the convent controversy, a local Catholic priest and some Catholic Auschwitz survivors had placed the cross that had been used at the Pope's Birkenau visit on the grounds of the convent. The "papal cross," as it was called, had been dismantled and stored in the basement of a local church and was now reconstructed at the site without any public fanfare or ritual. According to Geneviève Zubrzycki's account:

> the planting of crosses to sacralize a site, to give it sacred immunity, had been a common practice under Communism. Most frequently, the tactic was used to defend church property, but the symbol was also used as a "protective weapon" against the Communist state during protests and rallies. In this case, the erection of the papal cross in the yard of the Carmelite convent was clearly such a tactic as well as a form of protest against the planned relocation of the Carmelite nuns. (2006:7)

After the nuns vacated the convent, the cross remained, against the well-publicized objections of world Jewry. In the spring of 1998, during the annual "March of the Living" program, which brings Jewish students from all over the world to Poland, Catholic protesters raised banners and posters with slogans such as "Defend the Cross" and "Keep Jesus at Auschwitz," turning the issue into a full-blown controversy.[13] Kazimierz Switon, a former anticommunist activist and official of the right-wing Confederation for an Independent Poland, initiated a hunger strike at the site of the cross, demanding that the Roman Catholic Church make a firm commitment to keeping the cross in place. After failing to secure this commitment, Switon then "appealed to his fellow Poles to plant 152 crosses on the grounds . . . both to commemorate the (documented) deaths of 152 ethnic Poles executed at that specific site by the Nazis in 1941 and to 'protect and defend the papal cross.'" (Zubrzycki 2006:10). Switon's appeal was successful, and the site was

> transformed into the epicenter of the War of the Crosses, as individuals, civic organizations, and religious groups from every corner of Poland (and as far away as Canada, the United States, and Australia) answered Switon's call to create a "valley of crosses" . . . During that summer, the site became the stage for prayer vigils, Masses, demonstrations and general nationalist agitation. It was the destination of choice for pilgrims, journalists, and tourists in search of a sacred cause, a good story, or a free show. Religious . . . as well as secular symbols such as red-and-white Polish flags and national coats of arms featuring a crowned white eagle [a symbol of Polish sovereignty] . . . adorned the crosses and added to their symbolic weight and complexity. (Zubrzycki 2006:7)

The War of the Crosses lasted for fourteen months and became an international controversy, as U.S. Congressional representatives and Israeli officials demanded their removal. In the end, the Polish government and Catholic Church arranged for all but the initial papal cross to be relocated elsewhere. This "compromise" essentially left Switon and his followers victorious, since the maintenance of the papal cross was their objective all along.

Importantly, the War of the Crosses conflict over symbolic territoriality was not simply a dispute about the significance of Auschwitz. As Zubrzycki observes, the conflict was also, if not primarily, about the nature of Polish identity in post-Communist Poland. During the Communist era, the cross was in many respects a progressive symbol of opposition to the State. But with the fall of Communism, especially as it had been appropriated by right-wing nationalists, it has become a narrow symbol of Polish exclusivity, a declaration of Polish citizenship and Catholicism as being one and the same. Jews or Jewishness are invoked as symbols of anyone, Jews and non-Jews alike, who oppose a "strictly exclusive ethno-Catholic vision of Poland" (Zubrzycki 2006:209). Even Catholic officials who advocate a more inclusive conception of Polish identity are accused of being "crypto-Jews," as are those who favor the entrance of Poland into a more cosmopolitan European Union. As Stanisław Krajewski observes, "It is not so much that Jews are blamed as enemies [of Poland] but that enemies are labeled as Jewish" (2005:217). To label someone or a set of ideas as "Jewish" is to invoke a general cultural epithet that expresses disapproval, even over matters that have nothing to do with Jews or Jewishness (Gebert 2008; Judt 2000; Polonsky and Michlic 2004). It represents a way of narrowly delineating the accepted qualities of Polish citizenship, marginalizing minority groups who are unwelcome in the civil sphere of solidarity as defined by the majority (Alexander 2006; see chapter 1). Be that as it may, in Poland "there remains only a vestigial Jewish community" in the cities of Warsaw, Kraków, and Lublin consisting mostly of elderly Jews, with a smaller group of younger people, most of whom are intermarried, and a larger group of "closet" Jews who are unaware of or are only recently coming to discover their Jewish roots in the post-Communist era (Caplan 1993:224; see also Gebert 2008; Krajewski 2005).

The Jedwabne Massacre Controversy

In 2000, Polish–Jewish historian Jan Gross published a book about a massacre that took place in the small Polish town of Jedwabne in the summer of 1941. The English translation was published as *Neighbors: The Destruction of the Jewish Community in Jedwabne, Poland*, the next year. In that book, Gross reports that about half the Gentile residents of this town of about 1,600 residents rose up and killed the other half, who were Jews, with the approval but without the participation of the handful of Germans who occupied the area (see chapter 4). That a historian should bring such a "dark past" of Poland's history to the forefront would inevitably provoke controversy because it was at variance with the Polish martyrdom theme that had been integral to the Auschwitz convent and War of Crosses controversies. One critic dismissed Gross's book as a "lie aiming to slander the good name of Poland" (cited in Polonsky and Michlic 2004:37).

But others, perhaps smaller in number, did welcome Gross's contribution to the dialogue about Poland's past, reminding Poles that after the war, in the city of Kielce on July 1, 1946, a mob of Poles had attacked and killed forty-two Jews and wounded about fifty others (Gross 2006;

Leichter 1990; Polonsky and Michlic 2004). Of that slaughter, Polish sociologist Stanisław Ossowski had written:

> A more far-sighted, cynical or wily person, or someone with a greater historical knowledge, might have recalled that sympathy is not the only reaction to the misfortune of others; that those whom the gods have singled out for extinction easily become repugnant to others and are even removed from inter-human relations. He might also recall that if one person's tragedy gives someone else an advantage, it often happens that people want to convince themselves and others that the tragedy was morally justified. Such persons as the owners of former Jewish shops or those who harass their Jewish competitors can be included in this group. (cited in Polonsky 1990:205–06)

What Ossowski pointed to was also true of Jedwebne and other wartime violence against Jews perpetrated by Poles, who confiscated Jewish businesses and other property for their own keeping.

Gross's book also reminded Poles that resistance to acknowledging this "dark past" had long been present in Polish society. In 1987, Władysław Siła-Nowicki, a prominent anticommunist attorney and wartime resistance fighter had said:

> I am proud of my nation's stance in every respect during the period of occupation, and in this I include the attitude toward the tragedy of the Jewish nation. Obviously, attitudes toward the Jews during that period do not give us a particular reason to be proud, but neither are there any grounds for shame, and even less for ignominy. Simply, we could have done relatively little more than we actually did. . . . Let no-one talk to us, our people, our nation, who fought at the time of the German occupation, about our supposedly unfulfilled moral obligations ([1987] 1990:62, 68).[14]

Of this resistance to critical self-appraisal, the Polish–Jewish sociologist Zygmunt Bauman had replied:

> . . . the issue is not whether the Poles should feel ashamed or whether they should feel proud of themselves. The issue is that only the liberating feeling of shame—the recovery of the moral significance of the joint historical experience—may once and for all exorcise the specter of the Holocaust, which continues to haunt not only Polish–Jewish relations, but also the ethnic self-identity of the Poles and Jews alike, to this very day. The choice is not between shame and pride. The choice is between the pride of morally purifying shame, and the shame of morally devastating pride. (1988:298)

In terms of the broader context of Holocaust historiography, the Jedwabne massacre is also a reminder, as Antony Polonsky and Joanna Michlic point out, of the veritable "wave of anti-Jewish violence that accompanied the first weeks of the Nazi invasion of the Soviet Union" in the summer of 1941 (2004:26). Recent research on massacres that occurred in the Ukraine and Lithuania documents thousands of Jewish deaths at the hands of non-Germans. In Kaunas, Lithuania, as many as 10,000 Jews were killed, with pogroms erupting in at least forty other Lithuanian towns. In western Ukraine, pogroms occurred in as many as thirty-five localities, resulting in 28,000–35,000 deaths. In addition to Jedwabne, research has documented the involvement of ethnic Poles in the killing of Jews in eight other towns.[15] Polonsky and Michlic conclude that Gross's *Neighbors* challenges the widely accepted view that during the Holocaust the Poles were, at worst, mostly hostile bystanders, unwilling or unable to assist their Jewish neighbors and profiting materially from their destruction: Gross provides a concrete case of active Polish involvement in the process of mass murder" (p. 31). That this makes some Poles uncomfortable, as perhaps it should, is explained by Polish psychologist Krystyna Skarzyska:

> It is understandable that we feel psychological discomfort when our own community is blamed for serious sins. The inclusion of cruelty toward others in national collective memory is completely at odds with our self-image. Its acceptance is almost impossible for people who are convinced that they have usually been victims and solely victims.... What is urgently required is a debate about our collective memory and social identity and an attempt to deconstruct our past self image. (cited in Polonsky and Michlic 2004:34)

That debate will necessarily entail engagement with the question of Poland's future national identity: Will it be a nation marked by ethnic exclusivity, marginalizing the memory of the "other" and seeking "a vision of the past that stresses Polish suffering and the wrongs done to the Poles" (p. 41); or will it be a nation of ethnic pluralism, inclusive of the memory of the "other" and acknowledging "the wrongs done to them" (p. 41)?

Notes

1.   Amato (1990) traces the historical construction of this sentiment through Christianity, utilitarianism, romanticism, and the rise of modern democratic states. For a general discussion of the rhetoric of victimization discourse, see also Berger (2002), Holstein and Miller (1990), and Ibarra and Kitsuse (1993).

2. According to one estimate, the Allied tribunals alone convicted some 60,000 German and Austrian war criminals (Ruckerl 1990b).

3. Nuremberg was also the site of twelve other trials involving 177 defendants, including Nazi Party officials, business executives, judges, and doctors (Jones 1990).

4. Göring managed to commit suicide the night before he was to be executed.

5. For a review of historical precedents, see Marrus (1997).

6. Under the denazification program, adult Germans were classified as "major offenders," "offenders," "lesser offenders," "followers," or "exonerated." Some 12,753,000 people were processed in the U.S. zone alone (Marcuse 2001).

7. Eastern-bloc collective memory also ignored the Hitler–Stalin pact that preceded the German and Soviet occupation of Poland, as well as the atrocities (including rapes) committed by Russians against civilians during its westward advance and military occupation. The hypocrisy of ignoring these actions during the postwar trials did not go unnoticed by many Germans (Deák 2000a; Judt 2000).

8. See Segev (1993) for a consideration of the negotiations between Adenauer and Israeli officials over the precise wording of Adenauer's speech announcing the reparations agreement; and see Wolffsohn (1993) for a consideration of West German opposition to the agreement, and Segev (1993) for Israeli opposition. In contrast to West Germany, East Germany "felt no obligation to make restitution to Jewish survivors living abroad or to refrain from Soviet-bloc attacks on Israel" (Herf 1994:287).

9. Schumacher had been imprisoned for ten years in the Dachau concentration camp (Marcuse 2001).

10. A study of West German politicians in 1956 found that about a quarter of them had been active Nazi supporters (Marcuse 2001).

11. The Carmelites, or Order of the Brothers of Our Lady of Mount Carmel, was founded in the twelfth century on Mount Carmel in ancient Palestine. Catholics believe that the order is under special protection of the Blessed Virgin Mary.

12. For a critique of these issues from a liberal Catholic American, see Wills (2000).

13. For an analysis of the March of the Living program and the Jewish identity-tourism business, see Aviv and Shneer (2007).

14. Siła-Nowicki had written his essay in response to an article published by the Polish literary critic Jan Błonski ([1987] 1990).

15. Polonsky and Michlic also cite massacres committed by Romanians.

8

Jewish Collective Memories: Israel and the United States

In many ways, Hitler and the Nazis accomplished their goal of a Europe that is relatively *Judenfrei*, ensuring that Jews would have to look elsewhere for their continued survival as a distinct people. Currently, Israel and the United States stand out in this regard, as each of these nations is the home to approximately 5.3 million Jews, collectively comprising more than 80 percent of the world's total Jewish population (Jewish Virtual Library 2006).

As one would expect, the nature of Holocaust collective memory among Jews in Israel and the United States was constructed in a significantly different manner than in Europe. In Israel in particular, the Holocaust became a civil religion of sorts, a principal source of Jewish identity and cohesion, although it also has been the object of considerable domestic and international contention (Young 1993). The United States, on the other hand, would seem to have little stake in mnemonic disputes about the Holocaust were it not for its Jewish population, which constitutes a small but vocal fraction of the U.S. population as a whole. But indeed the United States has moved to center stage, leading to what some analysis have referred to as the "Americanization of the Holocaust"—the popularization of the Holocaust through films and museums that have made the genocide "far more accessible . . . to increasingly larger audiences" (Rabinbach 1997:230; see also Berenbaum 1987; Levy and Sznaider 2006; Rosenfeld 1997). Of course, Jewish Americans have played a central role in developing American Holocaust memory, and like their Israeli counterparts, have been embroiled in disputes about its uses and meaning. In this chapter, we continue our inquiry into the aftermath of the Holocaust by focusing on collective memories that have emerged in these two nations.

Israel

Establishing a Jewish Nation-State

Recall that long before the Second World War, Jewish Zionists in Europe had called for the creation of a Jewish state in their ancient homeland in Palestine (see chapters 2 and 5). Zionists in prewar Palestine viewed the rise of Nazism in Germany as confirming their historical prognosis that the only solution to the plight of the Jewish people was an independent nation. David Ben-Gurion (1886–1973) was at that time the acknowledged leader of *Mapai*,[1] the largest socialist-labor Zionist party and the dominant political party in Palestine. He expected that Nazism would provide moral capital or, in his words, "a fertile force" for the Zionist movement (quoted in Segev 1993:8; see also Shapira 1995; Teveth 1996).

During the 1930s, Ben-Gurion and Mapai favored negotiations with Nazi officials over emigration of German Jewry and the transfer of their financial assets to Palestine. The Nazis were receptive because they wanted to rid themselves of Jews, and they hoped that cooperation with the Zionists would ward off an anti-German economic and diplomatic boycott that had been initiated by several (mostly American) Jewish organizations (Bauer 1994; Segev 1993).

In prewar Palestine, Zeev Jabotinsky's Union of Zionist Revisionists, Mapai's principle opposition party to the right, was at first adamant in its rejection of any contact with Nazi Germany. The Revisionists supported the boycott as a means of ending Nazi persecution of German Jews. Mapai, on the other hand, viewed the Ha'avarah (transfer) Agreement that was worked out with the Nazi government as a means of settling German Jews in Palestine (see chapter 3).[2] Ben-Gurion viewed the debate between ha'avarah and boycott as a debate between Zionism and assimilation. According to Ben-Gurion, "The assimilationists have always declared war on anti-Semitism. . . . Now some Zionists have joined the chorus of the assimilationists. . . . But we must give a Zionist response to the catastrophe faced by German Jewry—to turn this disaster into an opportunity to develop our country, to save the lives and property of the Jews of Germany for the sake of Zion" (quoted in Segev 1993:27).

Ben-Gurion's opponents countered that his reference to assimilation was "the height of demagoguery" (quoted in Segev 1993:27). They claimed that Mapai was victimizing the Jewish people by playing politics with Jewish lives: "All this enthusiasm [for ha'avarah] from the left would not have been were institutions affiliated with Mapai not benefiting" (quoted in Segev 1993:27). Jabotinsky began calling for the evacuation of all European Jews to Palestine and criticized the Mapai-dominated Jewish Agency for Palestine for selectively distributing immigration certificates. Indeed, the labor Zionists envisioned themselves as creating a society of self-reliant "new men" achieving mastery of their environment by returning to the land and agricultural labor. In their view, urban life, as characterized by Jewish life in the Diaspora (including the United States), bred social and moral degeneration. Mapai immigration policies therefore gave preference to younger Zionists, particularly those with agricultural training or a willingness to work the land, who seemed best suited for their nation-building program. Those who wanted to come only because they had no other place to go were viewed with condescension. Jabotinsky forces claimed that their followers, who were primarily from the urban lower-middle class, were the chief victims of this policy. After the war, as we shall see, *Herut*,[3] the offspring of the Revisionist movement, charged Mapai with sabotaging rescue efforts (Davidson 1992; Shapira 1995, 1997; Teveth 1996).

The establishment of the state of Israel in 1948 did not come about as a direct consequence of the Holocaust. Great Britain was resolutely opposed to relinquishing control of Palestine, and after the war it became clear that the White Paper of 1939 that had limited Jewish emigration was not just a temporary measure implemented in the wake of World War II (see chapter 6). Rather, it was part of a broader pro-Arab turn in British policy in the Middle East. Furthermore, the war had devastated the British economy and had made the nation even more dependent on Middle-Eastern oil. The British had no desire to antagonize Arab interests in the region (Gilbert 1998; Johnson 1987; Reinharz and Friesel 1997).

Although the Palestinian Jews had been aligned with the Allies' war effort in Europe, they had opposed Great Britain in the Middle East. As Ben-Gurion had said, "We must fight Hitler as though there were no White Paper, and fight the White Paper as if there were no Hitler" (quoted in Johnson 1987:520). After the war, Jews responded to the need to relocate some 250,000 Jews in European displaced person (DP) camps by organizing illegal immigration transports to Palestine. They also engaged in armed resistance against the British administration in Palestine. Jewish rebels clashed with British soldiers, buildings and railways were blown up, and many people were killed.

Britain eventually acquiesced and in February 1947 turned to the United Nations (UN), which had substantial Arab representation, for a resolution of the problem (Gilbert 1998; Reinharz and Friesel 1997).

The UN, established in October 1945, had as its official mission the goal of saving "succeeding generations from the scourge of war" and reaffirming "faith in fundamental human rights, in the dignity and worth of the human person, in the equal rights of men and women and of nations large and small" (cited in Art 1993:52). A special committee, the United Nations Special Committee on Palestine (UNSCOP), was created to investigate the Palestine problem and recommend a solution. UNSCOP members visited the DP camps in Europe and spoke with spokespersons on all sides of the conflict. In August 1947, a report was published that recommended the partition of Palestine into a Jewish state and an Arab state. While the Arabs, who were strongly represented in the UN, opposed this resolution, Jewish Zionists accepted partition as the most practical solution (Gilbert 1998; Johnson 1987; Reinharz and Friesel 1997).

At the time, U.S. policy in the Middle East "was not very different from the British one . . . although [it was] not as sharply crystallized and certainly less self-assured" (Reinharz and Friesel 1997:104). According to Paul Johnson's account, President Franklin Roosevelt had been unsympathetic to the Zionist cause, but his successor Harry Truman had a more emotional and pragmatic view of Zionism, feeling sorry for Jewish refugees and viewing "the Jews in Palestine as underdogs. He was also much less sure of the Jewish vote than Roosevelt . . . [and] needed the endorsement of [influential] Jewish organizations in such swing-states as New York, Pennsylvania and Illinois . . . [in] the coming 1948 election" (1987:525). In addition, the Soviet Union had no particular objections to a Jewish state, savored the prospects of declining British influence in the Middle East, and viewed Israel as a potential socialist state (Gitlin and Leibovitz 2010; Novick 1999).

In November 1947, the UN General Assembly voted by a small margin to approve the partition plan. The Arabs were outraged. Azzam Pasha, Secretary-General of the Arab League, announced the Arabs' intention to resist the partition: "This will be a war of extermination and a momentous massacre" (quoted in Johnson 1987:526). Between December 1947 and May 1948, Israeli forces fought a War of Independence against Palestinian Arabs, and between May 1948 and July 1949 Arab troops from Egypt, Syria, Iraq, Lebanon, and Jordan entered the fray. By the time the fighting stopped, the Israelis were victorious and had gained control of about half the land planned for the Palestinian Arab state in the initial UN resolution. About 150,000 resentful Arabs were now under Israeli control and an additional 700,000 who had fled or were driven out of Palestine became refugees in neighboring Arab countries (Morris 2008; Penslar 1995; Shapira 1995; Teveth 1996). The Palestine problem now became the "Palestinian problem," and the construction of a Palestinian national identity, as distinct from a broader Arab or pan-Arab identity, became evermore crystallized (Litvak 1994; Taraki 1990).[4]

According to Anita Shapira (1997), during this initial period the Holocaust did not figure predominantly in Israelis' understanding of the events that led to the emergence of their nation. Rather, the state of Israel was perceived primarily "as the outcome of immanent processes precipitated by the heroic struggle against the British" and the Arab nations (1997:77). Israeli collective memory had not yet been infused with the Holocaust, and nationalist sentiments focused on the heroic fighters who had served so valiantly in the War of Independence to establish the Israeli state. The Holocaust was not yet viewed as an appropriate memory for the advancement of Jewish national identity, in part, because the perceived passivity and defenselessness of the European Jews stood in marked contrast to the image of the self-reliant "new men" fighting for their country. "The only Holocaust story that seemed fit to tell was that of the Warsaw Ghetto uprising" (1997:76; see chapter 5). Immigrant survivors who had been involved in armed resistance were sought after, treated as heroes, and urged to relate their experiences. Survivors who had not responded in this way, on the other hand, were often viewed as deficient and were even disdained (Cole 1999; Davidson 1992; Novick 1999).

Yad Vashem

The Jews are a people for whom memory has always been important. In his study of Holocaust memorials, James Young writes:

> Memory of historical events and the narratives delivering this memory have always been central to Jewish faith, tradition, and identity. . . . Throughout Torah, the Jews are enjoined not only to remember their history but to observe the rituals of faith through remembrance: "Remember the days of old, consider the years of ages past" (Deut. 32: 7). . . . "Remember this day, on which you went free from Egypt, the house of bondage, how the Lord freed you from it with a mighty hand" (Ex. 13:3). (cited in Young 1993:209–10)

Thus it was easy for Israelis to view the foundation of their new state as religiously ordained, as redeeming the Diaspora Jews from a life in exile. The Jewish people, "despite spatial dispersion and temporal ruptures had preserved its common identity" and after years of suffering—most recently in the Holocaust—had finally returned home to its birth place in the Land of Israel (Ram 1995:92; Shapira 1995, 1997).

At the same time, it was Zionism not Judaism that constrained the way in which the Holocaust was incorporated into Israeli collective memory. Nowhere is this more true than with *Yad Vashem* (everlasting name), "The Memorial Authority for the Martyrs and Heroes of the Holocaust." As early as 1942, board members of the international Jewish National Fund considered the creation of Yad Vashem, which would link the genocide of the Jews to the goals of the Zionist movement. These agents of memory therefore felt that a memorial of this nature should not be entirely negative, but should also promote the forward-looking optimism of the Zionist movement (Segev 1993).

After the war, in 1953, the Israeli *Knesset* (parliament) unanimously passed the Yad Vashem Law, which established Yad Vashem with a mandate to explicitly link the memory of Jewish victimization with the memory of Jewish heroism. In Shmuel Spector's words, Yad Vashem was designed to "commemorate the six million Jews murdered by the Nazis and their helpers; the Jewish communities and their institutions that had been liquidated and destroyed; the valor and heroism of the soldiers, the fighters of the underground, and the prisoners in the ghettos; the sons and daughters of the Jewish people who had struggled for their human dignity; and the 'Righteous among the Nations' who had risked their lives in order to save Jews" (1990c:1683). The law also assigned Yad Vashem the task of creating memorial projects, collecting and publishing testimonies of the Holocaust and the heroism of that period, granting commemorative citizenship to the victims, and representing Israel in international projects regarding Holocaust memory. Since the 1960s Israeli officials have taken important guests of state on a mandatory visit to the memorial; and conscripts in the Israeli army and Israeli school children are regularly taken as well (Cole 1999; Novick 1999; Shapira 1995).

However, an important subtext of this martyrdom-heroism interpretive motif was the implicit contrast between the Diaspora Jews, who had known only helplessness and destruction, and the Israeli Jews, who had fought for their independence and self-preservation. The victims of the Holocaust were to be remembered because they demonstrated the need for fighters, while the fighters were to be remembered for having secured the Jewish state that had redeemed the Jewish people (Segev 1993; Young 1993).

The Kasztner and Eichmann Trials

Two postwar trials in Israel marked the next significant events in the postwar construction of Israeli Holocaust memory. The Kasztner trial had primarily domestic repercussions, while the Eichmann trial had both domestic and international implications.

The Kasztner trial involved a libel suit initiated by Rezsö Kasztner, the director of the Israeli Department of Public Relations in the Ministry of Trade and Industry. In 1952, Malkiel Gruenwald, a Hungarian Holocaust survivor, published a pamphlet charging Kasztner with collaborating with the Nazis when he served as head of the Jewish Rescue Committee in Hungary during the war (see chapter 6). Gruenwald accused Kasztner of negotiating a deal with the Nazis for the release of Hungarian Jews in exchange for ransom money. Gruenwald claimed that Kasztner, who had ties with the Mapai Party during the war, used his influence to save only those Jews he favored: those who were affiliated with Mapai, those who could pay their own way, and his own relatives. He also accused Kasztner of pocketing some of the money (Bauer 1994; Gouri 1994; Segev 1993; Weitz 1994).

The Herut Party seized upon the accusation to resurrect prewar resentments over Mapai's selective immigration policies and failure to rescue European Jews. Kasztner was advised by officials of the Mapai government either to agree to enter a libel suit or resign. Kasztner reluctantly agreed to the suit. At the trial, Gruenwald's attorney, Shmuel Tamir, an ultra-conservative lawyer, took the opportunity not only to defend his client but to attack Mapai's actions during the war. Tamir accused the Mapai leadership of having withheld the truth of the Nazi's extermination program from the Jewish people, and hence of encouraging Jewish passivity and forestalling resistance efforts. In his view, Mapai, like the Jewish councils of Nazi Europe, had not done enough to save Jews and had passively complied if not actively collaborated with the enemy (see chapter 5).

Gruenwald received a favorable ruling from the judge in the libel case, who concluded that "Kasztner [had] sold his soul to Satan" (quoted in Weitz 1994:351). Although this decision was later overturned by the Israeli Supreme Court, the whole affair was the first major blow to the Mapai leadership, and according to one Mapai official, "the first time that a large number of Israelis lost confidence in the establishment" (quoted in Segev 1993:280).[5] In the next election campaign, Herut proclaimed that Mapai constituted an enemy from within: "When you vote Mapai, you vote for a Jew who turned Jews over to the Gestapo" (quoted in Segev 1993:287).

Self-righteous politicians proffering competing rhetorics of victimization were in no short supply on either side of the Israeli political spectrum. They increasingly contested the memory of the Holocaust to prove to voters that the opposition political party was the real villain of the Nazi era. However, while some criticized Mapai (and the Jewish councils) for discouraging resistance during the war, others asked whether the Jewish partisans who had advocated resistance had not also sent Jews to their deaths. According to Tom Segev, "Many Israelis took it on themselves to judge the Jews of the Holocaust as if it were within their abilities and as if it were their right to do so. These are the heroes, these are the cowards, these are worthy of glory, these of disgrace. . . . This was a debate over the value of rebellion as a symbol to be handed down to future generations" (1993:290, 297).

Following the Kasztner affair, the 1961 trial of Adolf Eichmann was an opportunity for Mapai to reassert domestic political control over the legacy of the Holocaust (Osiel 1997; Segev 1993). Internationally, it was an opportunity to remind the world of the particularity of Jewish victimization, which had at times been obscured at the Nuremberg trials, and to build international support for Israel. Thus it was Ben-Gurion's view that the purpose of the trial was not simply to punish Eichmann but to bring the entire Holocaust before the court. It was an occasion for building national pride and for highlighting not only Jewish suffering but, more importantly, Jewish resistance. According to Attorney General Gideon Hausner, the prosecutor in the Eichmann case, "Here was an opportunity to bring before the entire world the hundreds and thousands of heroic deeds that were not generally known" (quoted in Segev 1993:353). Both Jews and non-Jews would be reminded that Israel was the only country in the world that could guarantee Jewish security, that it was a nation of people who were ready and able to defend themselves, and that Jews would never again be led like "sheep to the slaughter" (see chapter 5).

When Nahum Goldmann, President of the World Zionist Organization, came out in support of trying Eichmann in an international rather than Israeli court, Ben-Gurion was enraged. Goldmann argued that "since Eichmann and the Nazis exterminated not only Jews, it would be worthwhile to invite those countries, many of whose citizens were also killed by him, to send their own judges" (quoted in Segev 1993:329). Ben-Gurion retorted:

> The Holocaust . . . is not like other atrocities . . . [of] the Nazis . . . but a unique episode that has no equal, an attempt to totally destroy the Jewish people. . . . It is the particular duty of the State of Israel, the Jewish people's only sovereign entity, to recount this episode in its full magnitude and horror, without ignoring the Nazi regime's other crimes against humanity—but not as one of these crimes, rather as the only crime that has no parallel in human history. (quoted in Segev 1993:329–30)

War and Conflict in the Middle East

Throughout Israel's history, most of the Arab community has rejected the legitimacy of its existence. In 1954, for example, the king of Saudi Arabia declared: "Israel to the Arab world is like a cancer to the human body, and the only remedy is to uproot it, just like a cancer" (quoted in Dershowitz 1991:214). In 1956, in response to attacks from Palestinian commandos aided and financed by Egypt, Israel invaded and occupied Egyptian territory to its west in the Sinai Peninsula and the Gaza Strip. Politicians of both the Israeli left and right were united in their opposition to Egyptian president Gamal Abdel Nasser, whom they rhetorically described with "fascist" and "Nazi" motifs. In response to international condemnation for their military actions, Israeli politicians countered with memories of the Holocaust: "A million and a half young people and children were slaughtered in broad daylight, and the world's conscience was not moved. But now that the Jews are gathered in to the State of Israel, the outside world cannot give its consent" (quoted in Segev 1993:297). Israel acquiesced, however, when both the United States and the Soviet Union pressured it to withdraw from the occupied territories (Johnson 1987; Segev 1993; Wolffsohn 1993).

Tensions in the Middle East soared again in 1967, as Arab spokesmen once again promised to "wipe Israel off the map" and "drive the Jews into the sea" (quoted in Novick 1999:148). When Nasser began amassing Egyptian troops in the Sinai region, Israel launched a preemptive air strike. Syria and Jordan, which had signed defense pacts with Egypt, then attacked Israel. Israel emerged victorious in a war that lasted just six days, and it reoccupied the Sinai Peninsula and Gaza

Strip and took control of territory in the Golan Heights (from Syria) and the West Bank (from Jordan) to the east. In Israel this Six Day War has often been compared to the six days of creation, and the Israeli soldiers' fighting spirit that led to their decisive victory attributed to their memory of the Holocaust (Segev 1993).

In 1973, full-scale war broke out again when Egyptian and Syrian troops attacked Israeli positions in the occupied territories on Yom Kippur, the holiest day in the Jewish calendar. Although Israel won the Yom Kippur War, "the victory came only after serious and terrifying early reverses and after substantial Israeli casualties" (Novick 1999:151; Sachar 1992). Escape from disaster was due in large measure to a massive U.S. resupply operation that provided Israel with crucial weaponry. Thus Israel was left feeling vulnerable and, with the important exception of the United States, increasingly isolated in the international community. On November 10, 1975, the United Nations, whose membership was now dominated by "non-European countries recently liberated from European" colonialism, passed a resolution proclaiming that Zionism was a form of "racism" (Novick 1999:154). The November 10 date of the resolution was particularly offensive to Israelis, since November 10, 1938, was the date of the infamous Kristallnacht pogrom (Roiphe 1988).

This is not to say that there haven't been positive developments in Israeli-Arab relations over the years. A 1979 peace treaty between Israel and Egypt, for instance, which was negotiated with the help of U.S. President Jimmy Carter, ended the conflict between these two nations and led to Israel's withdrawal from the Sinai.[6] At the same time, the vivid experience of genuine threats to Israel's security opened the door to greater use of the Holocaust as a rhetorical motif in Israel (Marrus 1991). Menacham Begin, for instance, who helped build the Likud Party,[7] the center-right coalition that carried him to power as prime minister in 1977, often referred to Israel's pre-1967 borders as "Auschwitz lines." He compared Palestine Liberation Organization (PLO) leader Yasir Arafat to Hitler and the PLO's Palestinian National Covenant to *Mein Kampf:* "Never in the history of mankind has there been an armed organization so loathsome and contemptible, with the exception of the Nazis" (quoted in Segev 1993:399).[8] Just prior to Israel's controversial 1982 invasion of Lebanon, which Israel undertook in response to Palestinian terrorist attacks, Begin rhetorically characterized his view of his country's predicament in terms of Holocaust memory: "There is no way other than to fight selflessly. . . .

[T]he alternative is Treblinka, and . . . there will be no more Treblinkas. . . . No one, anywhere in the world, can preach morality to our people" (quoted in Segev 1993:399).[9]

Ironically, the Holocaust has also become a rhetorical resource for Israel's adversaries, as Arab spokespersons and their allies have tried to turn the memory of the genocide back against the Jews. One PLO writer asserted, for example, that the Holocaust is Zionist propaganda that is used to "legitimize the new [Israeli] Nazism" and that "Nazi camps were more 'civilized' than Israeli prisons" (cited in Anti-Defamation League 1993:60). According to Anne Roiphe, such counterrhetorical claims aim to take away from Jews the moral justification of their new nation because the Jews have now "demonstrated that they are not victims but brutes" (1988:166).

The 1992 election that brought Labor Party leader Yitzhak Rabin to power as prime minister, and the subsequent 1993 Israeli–Palestinian peace accord, whereby Israel and the PLO agreed for the first time on a framework for future negotiations on "final status issues," did not lessen the use of Holocaust memory in Israeli political discourse.[10] At speeches during the White House peace accord ceremony and before the Israeli Knesset, Rabin summarized the basic outlook of Israeli collective memory:

> It is certainly not easy for the families of the victims of the wars, violence, terror whose pain will never heal; for the many thousands who defended our lives with their own and have even sacrificed their lives for our own. For them, this ceremony has come too late. . . . In 100 years of settlement, this Land [of Israel] has known great suffering—and blood. We, who returned home after 2,000 years of exile—after the Holocaust that sent the best of the Jewish people to the ovens; we who searched for calm after the storm, a place to rest our heads, we extended a hand to our neighbors—and it was rejected time after time. And our soul did not tire of seeking peace. (quoted in Roth 1993:79–80)

Up to this point in the ongoing Israeli–Palestinian dispute, however, every movement toward peace has been accompanied by a return to violence on both sides. In addition, younger left-wing historians in Israel have launched a challenge to the traditional state-sponsored view, which claims that Palestinian intransigence and terrorism are the main obstacles to lasting peace (Arad 1995; Podeh 2000). These so-called "new historians" have characterized Israel as a colonial power that has forced its will, often brutally, on an oppressed Palestinian people, whom they depict "as passive victims of Zionist aggression and manipulation" (Brunner 1997:291). They have tried "to efface the impact of the Holocaust on Israeli identity" and have called for a return to pre-1967 borders (Shapira 1995:19), noting that the Israeli–Palestinian "controversy concerns a national conflict whose violence does not belong only to the past, but also to the present and, unfortunately, . . . its future as well" (Brunner 1997:290).[11]

The United States

Increasingly, as noted earlier, the United States has moved to center stage in the construction of postwar memories of the Holocaust, a phenomenon some have referred to as the Americanization of the Holocaust. We begin by considering the symbolic importance of three American films—*The Diary of Anne Frank* (1959), the *Holocaust* (1978) television miniseries, and *Schindler's List* (1993)—which collectively represent, according to Yosefa Loshitsky, "the 'colonization' of the Holocaust by American culture" (1997:4). We then address the rise of Holocaust consciousness among Jewish Americans and the controversies that ensued as they advanced their own politics of victimization. Finally, we examine the question of Jewish continuity in the United States, which some Jews believe is in jeopardy.

American Film Memory

To a large extent, the Americanization of the Holocaust has occurred through the "Hollywoodization" of the Holocaust, for what is popularly known about this event has been significantly shaped by what has been shown on television and the theater screen. In the postwar period, as just noted, three films merit particular examination.

Representing Anne Frank

The first film to make an impact on Holocaust memory was *The Diary of Anne Frank* (1959), which evolved "from a European document of World War II into an Americanized representation" (Doneson 1987a:149). Anne Frank (1929–44) wrote her diary, which became the most widely read book of World War II, while hiding from the Nazis with her family in an attic above the business owned by her father in Amsterdam, Holland (Rosenfeld 1991).[12] First published in Dutch in 1947 under the title *Het Achterhuis* (The Annex), the diary had an inauspicious beginning, with an initial print run of just 1,500 copies.[13] Nevertheless, the early reviews were uniformly favorable, describing the book as "a moral testament," "a human document of great clarity and honesty," and an account that "transcends the misery" it records (cited in Rosenfeld 1991:248).

The first English translation was published in the United States and Great Britain in 1952, and in 1955 a popular play based on the diary that was written by Frances Goodrich and Albert Hackett, a Hollywood wife–husband screenwriting team, opened on Broadway. It was a box-office smash that won a Pulitzer Prize, Tony Award, New York Drama Critics Circle Award, and Antoinette Perry Award. The 1959 film version based on the Goodrich–Hackett script, which was nominated for an Academy Award, proved to be equally popular and was followed by several television adaptations (Doneson 1987a; Novick 1999; Rosenfeld 1991).

Many analysts attribute the success of *The Diary of Anne Frank* to the storyline that downplays Anne's Jewishness and turns her into a universal figure representing all martyred innocents (Doneson 1987b). Anne's longer mediations on Jewish persecution and anti-Semitism are not included, and instead remarks are substituted that do not even appear in the original diary: "We're not the only people that've had to suffer. There've always been people that've had to . . . sometimes one race . . . sometimes another" (quoted in Rosenfeld 1991:257). Thus one reviewer wrote that *The Diary of Anne Frank* was "not in any important sense a Jewish play" (cited in Rosenfeld 1991:254). Edward Alexander (1994), on the other hand, notes a passage from the diary that offers a different impression:

> Who has inflicted this upon us? Who has made us Jews different from all other people? Who has allowed us to suffer so terribly up 'til now? It is God that has made us as we are, but it will be God, too, who will raise us up again. If we bear all this suffering and if there are still Jews left, when it is over, then Jews, instead of being doomed, will be held up as an example. Who knows, it might even be our religion from which the world and all peoples learn good, and for that reason only do we have to suffer now. We can never become just Netherlanders, or just English, or representatives of any country for that matter, we will always remain Jews, but we want to, too. (Frank [1952] 1958:186–87)

Others note that the mass appeal of *The Diary of Anne Frank* is also due to the limited circumstance of the attic, which allows audiences a safe entry into the Holocaust by shielding them from the horrors of the ghettos, concentration camps, and mass killings (Rosenfeld 1991).[14] In addition, the script emphasizes the uplifting elements of the Holocaust insofar as the Frank family was aided by altruistic "Good Samaritan" Christians who risked their lives to help people in need (Doneson 1987a; see chapter 6). And it highlights the portions of the diary that reveal Anne as a buoyant and optimistic girl who is resolved to maintain her ideals and offering hope for the future: "In spite of everything, I still believe that people are really good at heart" (Frank [1952] 1958:237). As Garson Kanin, the play's first director, remarked at the time of the play's opening: "I have never looked on it as a sad play. I certainly have no wish to inflict depression on an audience; I don't consider that a legitimate theatrical end. I never thought the original material depressing. . . . Looking back, Anne Frank's death doesn't seem to me a wasteful death, because she left us a legacy that has meaning and value to us" (quoted in Rosenfeld 1991:253).

Thus the audience viewing the play is not subjected to that portion of the diary that would convey a different message:

> I don't believe that the big men, the politicians and the capitalists alone, are guilty of the war. Oh no, the little man is just as guilty, otherwise the people of the world would have risen in revolt long ago! There's in people simply an urge to destroy, an urge to kill, to murder and rage, and until all mankind, without exception, undergoes a great change, wars will be waged, everything that has been built up, cultivated, and grown will be destroyed and disfigured, after which mankind will have to begin all over again. (Frank [1952] 1958:201)

Importantly, *The Diary of Anne Frank* became an American export, as the European story, now Americanized to create broad appeal, was diffused back into Europe (Doneson 1987a; Marcuse 2001). Germans were especially receptive to this somewhat sanitized version of the Holocaust. As one German reviewer wrote, "the persecution and murder of Jews seems to be merely a peculiar external circumstance—secondary in importance to the personal tragedy of the heroine" (cited in Rosenfeld 1991:266). Another observed, "We see in Anne Frank's fate our own fate—the tragedy of human existence per se."

Anne Frank died in the concentration camp at Bergen-Belsen, where she was sent after her family had been discovered in the attic by the Dutch police. While her legacy endures, just what that legacy entails remains a matter of dispute. Some analysts believe that Anne is a questionable Jewish symbol since the Franks were assimilated Jews for whom religious observance was inconsequential (Novick 1999).

Others appropriate her as a Zionist symbol, even though she did not express a desire to go to Palestine herself. As one writer noted, in the aftermath of the 1967 Six Day War: "Hitler killed [Anne] and six million others. But the events recorded in her diary became part of the national memory that built the State of Israel—and the spirit behind its six-day war last June. No longer would Jews try only to survive. There would be no more martyrs. Dead heroes, if need be, but no more Anne Franks. That is her living legacy" (cited in Rosenfeld 1991:276).

Above all, however, Anne Frank remains a very American symbol, for she is faithful to the spirit of optimism that is celebrated in American culture (Doneson 1987b). In 1979, years after the opening of the Broadway play, director Kanin compared Anne to Peter Pan, writing that she "remains forever an adolescent. . . . She reminds us that the length of a life does not necessarily reflect its quality. . . . Anne lives on" (cited in Rosenfeld 1991:253).

The Holocaust Miniseries

Peter Novick points to the 1978 airing of the Emmy Award winning miniseries *Holocaust*, written by Gerald Green, as "the most important moment in the entry of the Holocaust into general American consciousness" (1999:209). This nine-and-a-half hour docudrama was shown over four nights as part of NBC's *The Big Event*, "the network's regularly scheduled series of movies, concerts, and other special broadcasts" (Shandler 1997:154). It was preceded by much advance publicity, the publication of a paperback novelization of Green's screenplay, and the distribution of educational viewing guides; and it was seen in part or in whole by an estimated 120 million viewers in the United States alone. Through the story of two fictional families—one of assimilated German Jews and the other of a highly-placed SS official—most of the principal historical landmarks were covered, including the Nuremberg Laws, Kristallnacht, the Wannsee Conference, the Warsaw ghetto uprising, and Auschwitz. The miniseries was in many respects a "mini-survey course" on the Holocaust, and more information was imparted to more people in just these four nights than over all of the preceding postwar years. When it was shown in Germany the following year, *Holocaust* prompted an unprecedented engagement with the subject that, in the words of one German journalist, "has shaken up post-Hitler Germany in a way that German intellectuals have been unable to do" (cited in Novick 1999:213; see also Cole 1999; Levy and Sznaider 2006).[15]

Many critics decried the crass commercialization of the miniseries, however. In an article in *The New York Times*, Elie Wiesel complained that the film turned the Holocaust into a "cheap . . . soap-opera."

> [It is] an insult to those who perished and to those who survived. . . . [It] treats the Holocaust as if it were just another event. . . . [But] Auschwitz cannot be explained nor can it be visualized. . . . The Holocaust transcends history. . . . The dead are in possession of a secret that we, the living, are neither worthy of nor capable of recovering. . . . The Holocaust [is] the ultimate mystery, never to be comprehended or transmitted. (quoted Novick 1999:211)

Media critic Molly Haskell added that "the Holocaust is simply too vast, . . . too incomprehensible, to fit into . . . the reductive context of the small screen" (cited in Shandler 1997:158). And others found the interruption of commercials for products such as air deodorizers and panty shields especially offensive. Media critic John O'Conner questioned whether a "story that includes victims being told that the gas chambers are only disinfecting areas" should be used to promote Lysol for "killing germs" (cited in Shandler 1997:158).

Spielberg's Holocaust

The *Holocaust* miniseries was followed by many other (mostly television) films that in the aggregate (supplemented by imported foreign films) "served to firmly affix the Holocaust on the American cultural map" (Novick 1999:214; see also Doneson 1987b; Insdorf 2003).[16] Arguably the culmination of these cinematic events was Steven Spielberg's *Schindler's List*, based on the novel by Thomas Keneally ([1982] 1993), which was released in 1993, the same year as the opening of the United States Holocaust Memorial Museum (USHMM) in Washington, DC (to be discussed later). The film has been described as the "definitive" Holocaust film that may have done "more to educate vast numbers of people about the . . . Holocaust than all the academic books on the subject combined" (Rosenfeld 1997:139–40). But Omer Bartov notes a drawback to this popularity as well, because the film transforms a relatively minor event into a matter of extraordinary significance as if it was "a representative segment" of the Holocaust when in fact it was not (1997b:46).

The chief protagonist in the film, Oskar Schindler (1908–74), is credited with saving about 1,100 Jews from certain death.

A flamboyant, hard-drinking womanizer, gambler, and black marketer, Schindler would appear to have been an unlikely hero of the war. He served as a Nazi military intelligence officer and became a wealthy factory owner, coming to Kraków, Poland, in late 1939, where he operated an enamel kitchenware factory that exploited Jewish slave labor provided by the Nazis. Nevertheless, Schindler treated his workers humanely and successfully lobbied with Nazi officials to prevent hundreds of them from being sent to death camps.

Schindler's List is indisputably a finely-acted and well-crafted film, and it fulfills what Bartov thinks are the two major ingredients necessary to satisfy the American public's "taste for representations of the past": (1) "the quest for authenticity, for a story that 'actually' happened, though retold according to accepted [Hollywood] conventions"; and (2) "the demand for a 'human' story of will and determination, decency and courage, and final triumph over the forces of evil" (1997b:46).

Several elements of *Schindler's List* make it appear authentic and give it a documentary character (Avisar 1997). Spielberg used black-and-white photography and shot much of the film in Kraków, the area where most of the events actually took place. The historical narrative covers many of the important stages of the genocide, portraying the ghetto, deportations, labor camps, selections, and death camps.

The central dramatic confrontation in the film takes place between Schindler, played by Liam Neeson, and Anon Goeth, the commander of the Plaszow labor camp, played by Ralph Fiennes. According to Ilan Avisar, Goeth is one of "the most vicious villain(s) ever to appear on the screen. He kills people for breakfast, practices shooting on living targets, murders 25 prisoners in cold blood after an attempted escape, and exercises the terror of a menacing maniac in his treatment of a helpless [Jewish] maid" (1997:51). While the beginning of the film shows Schindler's negative traits, as the film progresses this side abates as he outmaneuvers Goeth in a heroic struggle between "the good guy and the bad guy" (Bartov 1997b:54). Finally, *Schindler's List* has a positive ending, and thus allows us to enter the dark world of the Holocaust without feeling there is no escape; like the theme of *The Diary of Anne Frank*, it ends "on a note of redemptive promise" (Rosenfeld 1997:143).

In the film, the fate of "Schindler's Jews" hangs in the balance. But in elevating Schindler to the level of a saint, the Jews are diminished, for they remain passive beneficiaries of his charitable good deeds. According to Judith Doneson, this theme, which also informs

The Diary of Anne Frank, resonates with Christian audiences whose religion has historically viewed the "Jews as condemned eternally for rejecting Jesus as the Messiah but whose continuing existence is necessary . . . to test the qualities of mercy and goodness incumbent upon good Christians" (1997:140). At the end of the film this theme is brought home as "the camera pans lovingly over the crosses in Jerusalem's Latin Cemetery, coming to rest on the gravesite where Schindler himself is buried" (Avisar 1997:142). Thus what many regard as the definitive Hollywood Holocaust film is in many respects less about Jews and more about a Christian man who saved Jews.

Like both *The Diary of Anne Frank* and the *Holocaust* miniseries, *Schindler's List* was an American export. In Germany, the plot that pitted a good German against a bad German on balance mitigated what might have otherwise been a hostile reception to the film (Avisar 1997). This helps explain the generally favorable reaction in spite of German complaints about American cultural imperialism (Loshitsky 1997). As Liliane Weissberg observes, Spielberg's Holocaust "does not show what 'Germans' did but what *individual* Germans did, offering hope that one of them—Schindler—would become the many" (1997:178).

Some analysts have commented on a parallel between Spielberg's own development as a filmmaker and that of Schindler's character. Spielberg, the man who made Hollywood millions with fantasy films, invested $42 million of the profits he earned from *Jurassic Park* in order to move himself up to the next level and become a "serious" filmmaker (Avisar 1997; Bresheeth 1997). Previously he had had little interest in his Jewish heritage and had even tried to deny or forget about it (Weissberg 1997). Spielberg says that his involvement in *Schindler's List* caused him to take religious instruction and "reconvert" to Judaism. Thus, in film critic Janet Maslin's words, Spielberg had succeeded in making "sure that neither he nor the Holocaust would ever be thought of in the same way again" (cited in Avisar 1997:55). His contribution to Holocaust memory was further solidified by his creation of the Shoah Visual History Foundation, which has recorded over 50,000 videotape testimonies, making it the largest of such collections in the world (see www.vhf.org).

In Israel, the release of *Schindler's List* (along with the opening of the USHMM that same year) signified that Israelis had lost their preeminent hold on this element of Jewish collective memory.[17] Indeed, the Diaspora Jews in America were confronting the

Holocaust on their own terms, constructing their own representation of the past, and diffusing this representation to the rest of the world (Bresheeth 1997).

Jewish Americans, Memorialization, and the Politics of Victimization

Historically, Jews in the United States had been the victims of anti-Semitism and discriminatory treatment from employers, universities, and exclusionary neighborhood covenants, but by the latter half of the twentieth century this situation had changed. Jeffrey Alexander (2006) attributes this change in large part to the cultural trauma of the Holocaust, as if Americans were saying, "This country is not like Germany."[18] During the war, he observes, Americans' repulsion of Nazism had little explicit connection with the Jewish genocide, but after the war a different mentality took hold. Although the particularity of the Jewish tragedy was at first downplayed, it was not transparent, and good-willed Americans came to believe that being "against the Nazis" meant "being with the Jews" and valuing the Jewish contribution to their common "Judeo-Christian" heritage (2006:523).[19] Moreover, a large majority of non-Jewish Americans came to view Jews as a warm, friendly, and unusually hardworking people who had a deep faith in God (Bershtel and Graubard 1992). This view may be a stereotype, but it is not derogatory.

It was in this context that Jews became one of the most economically successful immigrant groups in the country and among the most affluent Jews in the world.[20] At the same time, rates of interfaith marriage rose, and involvement in organized Judaism declined, leading to a diminution of ethnic cohesion and group identity. Currently, only about one-half of Jewish Americans marry someone else of the Jewish faith, and only about one-half remain affiliated with a Jewish organization or synagogue (Bershtel and Graubard 1992; Freedman 2000; Lipset and Raab 1995). In many respects, the state of Jewish ethnicity parallels that of other white groups (such as the Irish, Italians, and Poles) for whom ethnicity has become a rather shallow and amorphous experience, what Herbert Gans (1979) calls "symbolic ethnicity," tied more to nostalgic sentiments about family and family lineage than to active membership in a larger social network.[21]

Prior to the 1960s, Jews in the United States had tried to downplay their ethnicity and present themselves as assimilated Americans, as part of the proverbial American "melting pot" (Novick 1999).[22] But the sociopolitical conflicts of the 1960s, particularly over civil rights and the Vietnam War, began to undermine Americans' sense of collective identity and feelings of social solidarity and connection to a common moral community. The "melting pot" vision of a universal American culture that would assimilate disparate ethnic groups and particularistic identities was challenged by a multicultural vision of ethnic pluralism that would preserve and celebrate diversity (Alexander 2006).

Among socially disadvantaged nonwhite groups, multiculturalism was also infused with a shared sense of victimization, or "victim identity," which was used to mobilize efforts to redress social grievances and gain access to resources such as affirmative action (Amato 1990; Holstein and Miller 1990; Novick 1999). Historically, Jewish Americans had shied away from identity politics based on victimization. Whereas victim status is nowadays appropriated as a political resource, in the past it evoked a mixture of pity and contempt.[23] According to Peter Novick, few Jewish Americans "wanted to think of themselves as victims . . . [or] be thought of that way by others . . . [and most] regarded the victimhood symbolized by the Holocaust as a feature of the Old World" they wanted to leave behind (1999:121). However, the vulnerability that Jews felt worldwide after the Six Day War and Yom Kippur War helped change this aversion to victim identity.[24]

For some Jews thinking about Israel's situation in the Middle East in terms of the Holocaust was "spontaneous and unstudied" (Novick 1999:165). But others saw the Holocaust as an ideological resource that could be used to mobilize support for Israel by imbuing complex contemporary disputes "with the moral clarity of the Nazi period" (1999:165). The newly heightened status of victims brought about by the victim-identity movements helped remove inhibitions that had previously led Jewish Americans to shun the victim label. Jewish-American leaders discovered that the Holocaust drew more Jews to public events than any other subject and was capable of appealing to Jews who had only marginal religious affiliations. They also recognized that the Holocaust could be used as a fund-raising resource for Jewish causes, particularly for support of Israel and for Holocaust-related organizations and activities themselves (Finkelstein 2000; Freedman 2000).

Some Jews hoped that "Holocaust consciousness" would become a vehicle for Jewish Americans to rediscover the religious core of Judaism. Instead, it became a civil religion of sorts, much like what had occurred in Israel (Freedman 2000; Prosono and Brock 1996; Vital 1991). It was the Holocaust, not Judaism per se, that gave Jews their sense of ethnic identity. Now all could be united in their common "knowledge that but for the immigration of near or distant ancestors, they would have shared the fate of European Jewry" (Novick 1999:190). In doing so they advanced a claim about the Holocaust's uniqueness that, as we shall see, led to hostile reactions from other ethnic groups with whom Jews have engaged in competitions of victimhood (Linenthal 1995; Rosenbaum 2009; Rosenfeld 1999). At the same time, Jewish Americans constructed a collective memory of the Holocaust that would speak to their concerns and not just to the concerns of Israelis. Israelis in turn became anxious that the Diaspora Jews were no longer accepting the primacy of an Israel-centered Holocaust memory, of the exclusive right of Israelis to speak for the Jewish dead, or for that matter, the Jewish people of the world (Bresheeth 1997; Rabinbach 1997).[25]

The United States Holocaust Memorial Museum

In many respects, the USHMM, which opened in April 1993, represents the ultimate American usurpation of Holocaust memory. Located adjacent to the Washington Mall in Washington, DC, the "ceremonial center" that holds the country's other national monuments, the USHMM places the Holocaust squarely within the official memory of the United States (Linenthal 1995:2). According to Edward Linenthal's account, the museum was the outcome of years of deliberation and planning that began in 1978, when President Jimmy Carter established the President's Commission on the Holocaust (PCH). Carter's decision to create the commission took place amid the attention given to the *Holocaust* miniseries and was motivated by a desire to appease Jewish concerns about the president's apparent pro-Arab tilt in the Middle East, particularly his linkage of aircraft sales previously promised to Israel to aircraft sales to Egypt and Saudi Arabia, as well as his willingness to include the PLO in peace talks that recognized the legitimate rights of the Palestinian people.

Carter's Chief of Domestic Policy, Stuart Eizenstat, who himself had numerous relatives who were killed in the Holocaust, helped persuade the president that the creation of a memorial would send an important symbolic message, on the occasion of Israel's thirtieth anniversary, that the administration remained a staunch supporter of the Israeli state. In an executive order, Carter empowered the PCH to make "recommendations with respect to the establishment and maintenance of an appropriate memorial to those who perished in the Holocaust" (cited in Linenthal 1995:23).

Holocaust survivor Elie Wiesel was appointed to head the commission. Wiesel was characterized by various Carter advisors as an "undisputed expert on the Holocaust period," a "non-political appointment [who would be] virtually free of attack from most sources," and the "one candidate who would be undisputed by the Jewish community" (cited in Linenthal 1995: 21).[26] Wiesel's rise to prominence reflects not only his own accomplishments as a prolific author and Nobel Peace Prize winner, but the elevated status of survivors more generally. Once the Holocaust was embraced, however belatedly, the designation "survivor" evoked not just sympathy but honor and admiration, even awe.[27] Wiesel was especially revered, acquiring what some have seen as a saint-like (even Christ-like) status, as a man who returned from the citadel of death and whose suffering carried with it a prophetic obligation to remind people of what had occurred and warn them of what might happen again if the Holocaust were to be forgotten (Novick 1999; Sachar 1992).[28]

While President Carter would have been satisfied with a monument to the Holocaust, Wiesel and other members of the PCH wanted it to be a "living memorial" that would include a museum, archive, and educational/research institute. Some discussion took place as to whether the memorial should be located in New York City or Washington, DC. One member, historian Lucy Dawidowicz, spoke in favor of New York, arguing that it was the "center of the Jewish population in the United States and the cultural crossroads of the modern world. A site facing or near the United Nations would be particularly suitable" (quoted in Linenthal 1995:58). According to Linenthal, however, others felt that a "museum built in New York, even if national in intent, would . . . be perceived as a Jewish museum built in the heart of the Jewish community in America. Memory of the Holocaust would [thus] remain the province of American Jews" (p. 59). Locating the memorial in Washington, DC, on the other hand, would more clearly situate the Holocaust within the national collective memory.[29]

The U.S. government's decision to sponsor a Holocaust memorial, especially one by the Washington Mall, understandably bewildered and raised the ire of other victimized groups. Why privilege the Holocaust, which was largely a European tragedy, when African Americans or Native Americans, for example, had no such national memorial of their own? Therefore the argument had to be made as to why the

Holocaust was an event central to American memory, why it offered valuable "lessons" for Americans themselves. According to commission member Michael Berenbaum, "we see in [the Holocaust] a violation of every essential American value, . . . [of] inalienable rights of all people, equal rights under the law, restraint on the power of government, and respect for that which our Creator has given and which the human community should not take away" (1993:2–3). Thus the Holocaust "clarified the importance of adhering to democratic values, and offered a stark historical example of what happened when such values failed" (Linenthal 1995:67).

But there was another side to Holocaust memory that provided lessons for Americans as well: the indifference to human suffering near and afar. Although the USHMM celebrates the United States' role in defeating Nazism and liberating victims from the death camps, it is also highly critical of the nation's indifference and the government's failure to act in ways that could have saved more Jews (see chapter 6). This "bystander narrative," as it has been called, depicts political officials as failing to respond with timely interventions to ameliorate the Jews' plight and avert more deaths (Berger 2003). Sybil Milton, a historian who served as a consultant to the museum, argued that the bystander narrative underscores by way of negative example the contemporary "commitment of the United States to an active participatory role in the world" (cited in Rabinbach 1997:241). And President Bill Clinton, in his dedication speech at the museum's April 1993 opening, opined: "[T]he evil represented in this museum is contestable. But as we are its witness, so must we remain its adversary in the world" (quoted in Public Broadcasting Corporation 1999).

At the same time, as Anson Rabinbach observes, the lesson of the bystander narrative is "morally ambiguous" because it does not help the visitor evaluate the circumstances that might compel a nation to act, or the conditions that would make such actions productive, futile, or even harmful (1997:241). Instead, the museum offers an apparently "universal principle of intervention . . . to be followed in all circumstances where crimes against humanity occur, when in effect it presents only the most extreme case of inhumanity as the criterion for action" (1997:241–42). Peter Novick (1999) and Samantha Power (2002) wonder whether this lesson will be interpreted as justifying humanitarian intervention *only* when contemporary atrocities parallel the Holocaust. Has the Holocaust set the "bar for concern so high that we [are] able to tell ourselves that contemporary genocides" simply don't measure up? (Power 2002:503). Commenting on the U.S. government's continued indifference to genocide, former Carter national security advisor Zbigniew Brzezinski asked readers of *The New York Times* to ponder whether Holocaust remembrance was a "proclamation of a moral imperative" or a "pompous declaration of hypocrisy" (cited in Linenthal 1995:266).

The Politics of Uniqueness

A common axiom advanced by Jews, Jewish scholars, and the institutions of Holocaust memorialization is the view that the Jewish genocide is unique and that attempts to compare it with other events constitute, in Deborah Lipstadt's words, "immoral equivalencies" (1993:212).[30] Controversy over the so-called uniqueness doctrine emerged early in the deliberations of the PCH. President Carter favored a broad definition of the Holocaust that included both six million Jews and millions of non-Jews such as Gypsies, Poles, and Soviet POWs who were also killed. Wiesel, on the other hand, was among those who were adamant about maintaining the Jewish core of the museum. Any attempt to extend the boundary of this core, he thought, would diminish, trivialize, and efface the memory of the Jewish dead. Other groups could be included, but they had to be kept at the periphery "in a carefully managed hierarchy of victims" (Linenthal 1995:113; Novick 1999).

Berenbaum tried to broker a compromise in the PCH by arguing that there was "no conflict between describing the uniqueness of the Jewish experience and the inclusion of other victims of Nazism" (cited in Linenthal 1995:228). In fact, he argued, "the examination of all victims is not only politically desirable but pedagogically mandatory if we are to demonstrate the claim of uniqueness" (1995:228). In the end, however, Wiesel's position prevailed, as the "other victims" of the Holocaust received "little more than perfunctory mention in the museum's permanent exhibition," although it was agreed that more flexibility would be allowed in "temporary" museum displays and in the museum's other educational and research activities (Novick 1999:220; see also Linenthal 1995).

The uniqueness controversy was also prominent in PCH deliberations over questions of how (or if) the museum would portray historical precedents to the Holocaust, particularly the 1915 Turkish genocide of 1 to 1.5 million Armenians, a Christian minority in Muslim Turkey (see Horowitz 2002; Mazian 1990; Rosenbaum 2009). Berenbaum was among those who favored a substantial Armenian presence, wanting to present the Armenian genocide as a "prelude" to the Holocaust while at the same time showing that "unlike the Turkish clash with the Armenians during which Armenians living in Constantinople and other cities were safe—and only those living in the East were at risk—all Jews in Europe were targeted" (cited in Linenthal 1995:236–37). In this way, Berenbaum argued, the comparison would still portray the Holocaust "as a unique, hitherto unprecedented event."

Nonetheless, resistance on the PCH to this sort of inclusion remained strong. And when the Turkish government (which to this day has refused to acknowledge that a "genocide" rather than "wartime casualties" took place) stepped into the fray, the political pressure to marginalize the Armenians grew (Novick 1999). One member of the PCH was even warned by the Turkish ambassador to the United States that "the well-being of Jews [in the Middle East] might be threatened were Armenians included in a federal Holocaust museum" (Linenthal 1995:232). Israeli officials also lobbied PCH members to exclude the Armenians, noting that Turkey was a NATO ally and "served as an escape route for Jews from Iran" (1995:239). In the end, Berenbaum succeeded in salvaging only one reference to the Armenians for inclusion in the permanent exhibit, and this was an oft-quoted remark of Hitler who said: "I have issued the command . . . that our war aim does not consist in reaching certain lines, but in the physical destruction of the enemy. . . . Only thus shall we gain the living space which we need. Who, after all, speaks today of the annihilation of the Armenians?" (cited in Berenbaum 1993:62).

Troubled by the PCH decision and the political lobbying that influenced it, Berenbaum told the members that such constraints on the boundaries of memory would evince "the politicization of our mission" and diminish "our ability to reach out and to include groups who naturally can see in the Holocaust a sensitive metaphor to their own experience" (cited in Linenthal 1995:235). Unlike other PCH members, Berenbaum was quite comfortable with an Americanization of the Holocaust that would expand the boundaries of memory and thus appeal to a broader audience.

Gavriel Rosenfeld (1999) notes that Jewish advocacy of the uniqueness doctrine emerged in the late 1970s and was in part a defensive reaction to the initial postwar indifference to Jewish survivors, to attempts to relativize the Holocaust with unwarranted comparisons (including those made by Israel's Arab adversaries), and to outright

Holocaust denial.[31] Edward Alexander, for instance, complained that the world had initially reacted as if "the enormity of the Holocaust could be recognized . . . only if it were universalized, [only] if its victims were recast, as we have seen [with] Anne Frank, . . . as 'human beings' rather than as Jews" (1994:195).

It was quite natural, however, that Jewish claims of uniqueness and the growing public interest in the Holocaust would provoke envy if not hostility from other ethnic groups who were competing for media attention and political and economic resources to address their own concerns. Armenians and Gypsies were offended by being relegated to the periphery of the USHMM; and African Americans, Native Americans, and other ethnic groups felt that it was just as important—if not more important—to remember their tragic histories (Linenthal 1995; Novick 1999). In advancing a claim that the Holocaust was unique and unsurpassed by all other atrocities, were not Jews trivializing or discounting the experiences of other groups? And were not Jews in fact one of the most privileged ethnic groups in the United States? Who were they to claim that their suffering has been (or is) worse than all others'? Perhaps claims about the Holocaust's uniqueness have supplied the United States with a convenient pretext for ignoring its own murderous past. Perhaps it is propaganda intended to divert attention from the ongoing Israeli genocide of the Palestinians. These are some of the charges that were levied by critics of the museum (Finkelstein 2000; Rosenbaum 2009; Rosenfeld 1999).

Arguably one of the most publicized ethnic-group conflicts over the Holocaust has taken place between Jewish Americans and African Americans (Novick 1999).[32] African Americans' objections to Jewish claims to preeminent victim status were explained by the critically-acclaimed writer James Baldwin in 1967:

> One does not wish . . . to be told by an American Jew that his suffering is as great as the American Negro's suffering. It isn't, and one knows that it isn't from the very tone in which he assures you that it is. . . . The Jew's suffering is recognized as part of the moral history of the world and the Jew is recognized as a contributor to the world's history: this is not true for blacks. . . . The Jew is a white man, and when white men rise up against oppression, they are heroes: when black men rise, they have reverted to their native savagery. . . . [I]t is not here, and not now, that the Jew is being slaughtered, and he is never despised, here, as the Negro is, because he is an American. The Jewish travail occurred across the sea and America rescued him from

the house of bondage. But America is the house of bondage for the Negro, and no country can rescue him. ([1967] 1994:34–35, 37).

Two decades later, in 1987, Nai'm Akbar, who served as president of the National Association of Black Psychologists, expressed a similar sentiment: "[It is a] simplistic notion of slavery which makes it easy for people to compare their holocaust to our holocaust. They don't understand that going to the ovens knowing who you are, is damn well better than walking around for 100 years not knowing who you are. . . . Our holocaust in America is worse than the holocaust in Europe" (quoted in Amato 1990:159–60). Then, in 1993, Khalid Abdul Muhammad, who at the time was Minister Louis Farrakhan's "national assistant" in the Nation of Islam, delivered a well-publicized speech at Kean College in New Jersey in which he demonized Jews as Christ killers, slaveholders, and bloodsuckers of black people—the worst of the world's exploiters, agents of the devil, who "everywhere they go . . . undermined the very fabric of society" (quoted in Berman 1994:2). It was the kind of speech that might have been given in the Middle Ages. Farrakhan himself, who has a popular following among some segments of the African American community, and whom mainstream African American leaders are reluctant to criticize, added heat to the fire by (falsely) claiming that "75 percent of the black slaves in the Old South were owned by . . . Jews!" (cited in Berman 1994:3), when, in fact, a more accurate figure is probably closer to three-tenths of one percent (Lipset and Raab 1995).

A few months later, in an attempt to promote reconciliation, then New Jersey Governor Christie Todd Whitman proposed showing *Schindler's List* at a forum on racism at Trenton College in which Muhammad was a keynote speaker. Upon seeing the film Muhammad remarked: "That was a Holocaust but African Americans pay a hell of a cost" (cited in Loshitsky 1997:6). Sometime later he referred to the film as "swindler's list." Such remarks not only illustrate the depths of resentment that some African Americans may hold toward Jews—a resentment that may be returned in kind by some Jews as well—but also the precarious nature of trying to use one group's oppression to gain insight into the oppression of another (Berman 1994; Lipset and Raab 1995; Loshitsky 1997).

In the middle of the Muhammad controversy, in January 1994, another widely-reported incident made the news. A well-intentioned teacher in Oakland, California, had arranged for a group of black and Latino high school students to attend a screening of *Schindler's List* on Martin Luther King Day. The teacher had hoped to expose the "students to the Holocaust as a paradigmatic lesson of the evils of racism on a national holiday honoring one of America's champions of civil rights and racial harmony" (Shandler 1997:163). However, when the students disrupted the showing by responding to some of the most violent scenes with raucous laughter and "in a manner reminiscent of audience participation in Rambo-style films," they had to be asked to leave the theatre (Bartov 1997b:49).

The Simon Wiesenthal Center's Museum of Tolerance (MOT) in Los Angeles, which opened two months before the USHMM, represents one of the most ambitious efforts to bridge the ethnic-oppression divide.[33] The MOT boasts an annual visitation of more than 250,000 people, including 130,000 youths who are regularly bussed in for school field trips. Its website notes that "many major corporations, educators, police agencies, and professionals from throughout the region have experienced the MOT's specialized programs," and that it is "a 'must-see' attraction in Southern California" (www.museumoftolerance.com).

The theme of the MOT departs significantly from the uniqueness doctrine by "challenging visitors to understand the Holocaust in both historic and contemporary contexts and confront all forms of prejudice and discrimination in the world today." In addition to its "Holocaust Section," the museum also includes several exhibits in its so-called "Tolerancenter." "The Point of View Diner" recreates "a 1950's diner, red booths and all, that 'serves' a menu of controversial topics on video jukeboxes" such as drunk driving and hate speech that are intended to convey the "message of personal responsibility." "The Millennium Machine" is a "high-tech 'time machine' . . . [that covers] a series of human rights abuses throughout the world, such as the exploitation of women and children, the threat of terrorism, and the plight of refugees and political prisoners." The section on "Ain't You Gotta Right?" presents a "16-screen video wall detailing the struggle for civil rights in America." And "In Our Time" is a film on "Bosnia, Rwanda and contemporary hate groups that pinpoints contemporary human rights violations going on throughout the world today" (www.museumoftolerance.com).

Some observers have complained about the "Disney" quality of the high-tech exhibits and the MOT's injudicious comparisons of the Holocaust with such a wide range of events (Rabinbach 1997; Rosenfeld 1997). On the other hand, there is no doubting that the Holocaust is the MOT's primary focus, and together with the Simon Wiesenthal Center, it is arguably one of the most successful institutions of Holocaust memorialization. The Center, which was founded in 1977, describes itself as "an international Jewish human rights organization dedicated to . . . confronting anti-Semitism, hate and terrorism, promoting human rights and dignity, standing with Israel defending the safety of Jews worldwide, and teaching the lesson of the Holocaust for future generations" (www.wiesenthal.com). Its mailings, like those of other Jewish organizations, regularly remind Jews of the dangers of anti-Semitism, both in the United States and abroad, and of their obligation to send money. The statements of African Americans such as Muhammad and Farrakhan have been good for the SWC's fund-raising efforts (Novick 1999).

Contemporary Compensation Claims

Earlier we noted that the Holocaust has been recognized by Jewish-American leaders as a fund-raising resource for Jewish causes. In the 1990s organizations such as the World Jewish Congress (WJC) headed by wealthy businessman Edgar Bronfman began focusing on the issue of compensation from European business interests that had capitalized on Jewish suffering during the war. The case that received the most attention involved the Swiss banking industry, which was negligent if not capricious in withholding monies due to Jewish depositors or their heirs after the war (Bower 1997; Chesnoff 1999; Finkelstein 2000; see chapter 3). In this effort Bronfman enlisted the political clout of Alphonse D'Amato, then Senator from New York and chairman of the Senate Banking Committee, as well as President Bill Clinton and Hillary Clinton, to pressure Swiss banks to agree to a $1.25 billion settlement. The Swiss controversy was also a catalyst for other settlements and ongoing litigation with corporations in various countries that exploited slave-labor during the war (including U.S. companies that did business in Germany), as well as insurance companies that failed to compensate Jews for their losses (Herman 1999; Hirsch 1999; Jelinek 2000; Petropoulos 2001).[34]

Although many (if not most) people commend the lobbying on behalf of Holocaust survivors, some feel that the demand for compensation has been excessive and even constitutes a form of "blackmail" of companies who fear losing even more if they contest the claims and subject themselves to civil lawsuits (Chesnoff 1999; Finkelstein 2000). Moreover, foreign financial institutions wishing to do business in the United States are vulnerable to political pressure from the U.S. government. As Congressman Benjamin Gilman of the House International Relations Committee remarked, "It is extremely important that the countries involved in the issue understand that their response . . . is one of several standards by which the United States assesses its bilateral relationship" (quoted in Finkelstein 2000:133–34).

Norman Finkelstein (2000) is one of the most strident critics of what he calls the "Holocaust industry," which he describes as a network of Jewish elites and organizations (and their Gentile lawyers/consultants).[35] According to Finkelstein, the problem is not that survivors are undeserving of compensation. Rather, it is that so much of the money will not in fact go to the victims of the Holocaust, but rather to high-price lawyers and Jewish organizations led by men earning lucrative six-figure salaries. Lawrence Eagleburger, for example, who served as Secretary of State under President George H. W. Bush, had enjoyed an annual salary of $300,000 as chair of the International Commission on Holocaust-Era Insurance Claims. D'Amato, no longer a senator, had earned $350-an-hour plus expenses for his work in mediating Holocaust-related lawsuits. Other lawyers earn even more.

At the same time, various Jewish leaders claim that their organizations deserve a substantial portion of the settlement monies, much of which involves heirless assets, which they intend to spend on their own Holocaust and Jewish education projects. Additionally, different religious denominations have fought over their right to use the money to promote their particular branches of Judaism. All the scrambling for the billions of dollars of proceeds has led survivor Abraham Foxman, who is also the national director of the Anti-Defamation League, to complain that the restitution controversy is "desecrating the memory of the Holocaust" (quoted in Chesnoff 1999:279).

Finkelstein (2000) also decries what he sees as the hypocrisy of the so-called Holocaust industry. He notes, for instance, that for a lecture fee of $25,000 Wiesel will talk about how the truth of the Holocaust "lies in silence," that it "defies both knowledge and description" and "cannot be explained nor visualized" (quoted on p. 45).[36] Or he disparages the Simon Wiesenthal Center for honoring Ronald Reagan with its 1988 "Humanitarian of the Year" award in spite of the earlier Bitburg debacle that so many viewed as an insult to Holocaust memory (see chapter 7). Finkelstein also wonders, along with African American Congresswoman Maxine Waters, why efforts to compensate Holocaust survivors are celebrated while those who have been seeking reparations for the descendants of slave laborers in the United States "have literally been ridiculed" (quoted on pp. 106–07).

Robert Chesnoff (1999), on the other hand, points out that the actions of organizations that Finkelstein decries have led to the declassification of countless invaluable documents and to investigations in many countries that have contributed greatly to our knowledge of the "whereabouts of stolen Nazi booty" and of the complicity of international businesses during the war (1999:272). And although the battles over the money at times appear unseemly, he reminds us that it is not the Jews but the perpetrators and their collaborators who exploited the Holocaust, and it would be a greater injustice to allow these profiteers to continue to enjoy the spoils of their misdeeds.

Jewish Continuity in the United States

Before World War II, the large majority of the Jewish people of the world lived in Europe. This, as we have noted, is no longer the case, as most Jews live in either Israel or the United States. For its part, Israel, is threatened by hostile surroundings in the Middle East and by the persistence of the "Palestinian problem," which is arguably inflamed by those in Israel who want to further expand Israeli settlements into the Palestinian territories and create a more expansive "Greater Israel" that undermines the intent of the United Nations partition plan that was laid out in 1947 and that makes it more difficult to achieve a two-state solution that can accommodate the interests of both groups (Burg 2008; Klug 2007). Such actions have been aided and abetted by an alliance between political neoconservatives and right-wing evangelical Christians in the United States—the former seeking to broaden the territorial reach of a political and military ally in the Middle East, the latter seeking to secure the ancient Holy Land for the Second Coming of Christ (Blumenthal 2009 Mitchell 2002; Phillips 2006). This is of course not to say that the Palestinians and their allies are not also at fault in derailing the peace process. There is plenty of blame to go around (Khalidi 2006, 2008; Morris 2009).

In the United States, the survival of Jews poses a different question. Here, in the land that so many immigrant Jews chose as a practical alternative to Israeli Zionism, a "New Jewry," to quote Avraham Burg (2008), was born. Burg, a former speaker of the Israeli parliament and a contemporary critic of aggressive Israeli policies vis-à-vis the Palestinians, describes the difference between the two countries this way:

> Being Jewish could be achieved in two different ways. As Israelis were developing collective separatism, American Jews wove themselves into the fabric of the general public. . . . Israeli ideology was tough and head-on—"You can not conquer the mountain until you dig a grave on the slope," says the tombstone of Shlomo Ben Yosef, an Israeli terrorist from the 1930s. "It is good to die for our country" is inscribed on the . . . monument to another Zionist hero, Yosef Trumpledor. The American Jewish spirit was less dramatic. Assimilate. Be American. Integrate into the spiritual and material life that America had to offer. (2008:35)

At the same time, the assimilation of Jews into American society—with their rising interfaith marriages and declining religiosity—has raised questions about the future survival of the Jewish people as a distinct social group in the United States, which some Jews characterize rather hyperbolically as a "silent Holocaust" or "Holocaust of our own making" (Freedman 2000:74).[37]

Samuel Freedman is among those who believe that without a committed community of religious adherents Jewish Americans as a distinct ethnic group will cease "to exist in any meaningful way" (2000:339). Without the signifying mark of color that restrains some groups' freedom to assimilate, Jewish Americans will continue to follow the path of other white ethnic groups (Brodkin 1998; Gans 1979). As Seymour Martin Lipset and Earl Raab observe:

> Jewish knowledge and education are, for most Jews, thin at best and becoming thinner. Some religious customs, such as attendance at an annual family Passover Seder dinner, continue to be observed by as many as three out of four Jews, but rituals are often driven more by nostalgia and family attachment than by deep religious commitment. Even those practices can be expected to diminish as older generations disappear and as intermarriage rates increase even further. (1995:46)

Still, Sara Bershtel and Allen Graubard note that it is rather remarkable how much *unaffiliated* Jewish Americans remain "concerned with questions of Judaism" (1992:29). Lipset and Raab, too, are impressed that the majority adhere to at least some "Jewish practice into the fourth generation" (1995:205). These individuals are proud of their

Jewish heritage and do not seek to avoid identification with it. They feel a sense of loss, perhaps some vague guilt connected to their inability to muster genuine religious faith. As one man observes, "I don't believe in God, so that's a problem. It is the underlying problem. To learn the blessings and light the candles and all that if one doesn't believe in God seems just like putting on a costume, nothing more" (Bershtel and Graubard 1992:21). Some secular Jews view this predicament in a benign light, attributing positive value to the fact that being Jewish is now a matter of choice, not of coercion or obligation, and that the freedom to choose one's religious and communal affiliation marks a "great moral advance" (p. 14).[38]

Freedman cautions that being Jewish is not simply a state of mind: "It demands a pattern of obligations and responsibilities, a web of mutuality that many modern American Jews find imprisoning and choose to reject" (2000:359). It is not enough to say, as does one unaffiliated Jew, "I am still not clear why I am, but I know I am a Jew" (Bershtel and Graubard 1992:85). Still, Lipset and Raab believe that it will be difficult for religious Jews to sustain Jewish continuity beyond a small remnant without finding ways to engage the larger number of "shadow Jews," as they call them, who are interested in retaining "some sense of Jewish identity or at least some knowledge of their ancestry," but who have multiple allegiances and universal commitments beyond the Jewish community and who cherish the freedom that has "so beneficently created [the] dilemma" of Jewish continuity in the United States (1995:204, 207). These Jews may be removed from the organizational structures of Judaism but are not indifferent to the cultural values and proscriptions for living that they associate with their Jewish heritage. They assert their right to construct a Jewish identity of their own making, and they resent being told by the devout that they are not "real" Jews (Bershtel and Graubard 1992; Freedman 2000).[39]

Irving Louis Horowitz, like Abba Eban (1984), assumes that at a minimum "being a Jew implies commitment to the fate and fortune of Israel and to a community of like-minded souls" (2002:279).[40] Whether that implies a commitment to Judaism is an entirely different matter, and even in Israel the trend toward secularization approximates other modernizing societies, where regular attendance at synagogue is arguably lower than Sunday morning churchgoing among Christians in the United States. Joane Nagel notes that contemporary ethnicity "is best understood as a dynamic, constantly evolving property" that consists of a portfolio of affiliations "that are more or less salient in various situations and vis-à-vis different audiences" (1994:152, 154). In this context, perhaps the greatest bond that holds Jewish Americans together is the fact they are Americans, that they live in a land where freedom of choice "requires perpetual efforts of self-definition" and the need to justify these choices to themselves and to others (Auerbach 1990:206). Hasia Diner is arguably correct when she suggests that "definitions of Jewishness may be more elastic than they have been at any time in the modern past," but that elasticity, a hallmark of the religious diversity of the United States,[41] may indeed hold the key to Jewish continuity "in a new and uncharted age" (2004:358).

Notes

1.   Mapai is an acronym for a Hebrew word that translates as Workers' Party of the Land of Israel.
2.   The Ha'avarah Agreement functioned until the middle of the war. About 20,000 Jews were assisted and about $30 million was transferred from Germany to Palestine (Segev 1993).
3.   Herut is the Hebrew word for freedom.
4.   Historical accounts lay blame on different parties for the origins and perpetuation of the "Palestinian problem" (Arad 1995; Brunner 1997; Johnson 1987; Podeh 2000). Pro-Israeli historians claim that the Palestinians were ordered, misled, or panicked into leaving by Arab radio broadcasts, hoping to return when the fighting was over. Pro-Palestinian accounts claim that they were forcefully and brutally expropriated from their land and that they fled to avoid being killed by the Israelis. Johnson (1987) adds that over 567,000 Jews living in Arab states were encouraged or forced to flee their homelands. But whereas Israel resettled these Jews, the Arab countries refused to resettle Palestinians and kept them in refugee camps.

      According to Meir Litvak's (1994) review, Palestinian historians associate the emergence of Palestinian nationalism to the rising tide of Jewish immigration in the early-twentieth century and especially to the fragmentation of Arab pan-nationalism and the dismemberment of Syria by Britain and France that occurred after World War I. He argues that "the need to refute Zionist claims of Jewish historical links to Palestine prompted a historiographical effort to prove the continuous 'Arabness' of Palestine from antiquity to the present," a view that the Israelis dispute (p. 27). Prior to 1948, he adds, the notion of a distinct Palestinian identity was a view fostered by the elite but was not widely held by the masses until they suffered the experience of rejection by the neighboring Arab states and of living as a minority within Israel.
5.   Kasztner was murdered by a Jewish-nationalist extremist in 1957 while the Supreme Court was debating his appeal.
6.   In 1981 Egyptian President Anwar Sadat was assassinated by a group of Islamic extremists for negotiating the treaty.

7. The Likud Party is heir to Herut and translates from Hebrew as "consolidation."
8. The PLO was founded in 1964.
9. In Israel the rhetorical use of the Holocaust was also omnipresent during the international crisis precipitated by Iraqi dictator Saddam Hussein's invasion of Kuwait and the subsequent Persian Gulf War of 1990–91, when Germany resurfaced as the object of Israeli indignation. Hussein, whom Israelis (and Americans) equated with Hitler, had developed about 90 percent of his chemical-weapons capability with the help of German firms (Walker 1994). The Israeli press was filled with articles and letters that compared the now-unified Germany with the Nazi regime; and a demonstration was held outside the German embassy in Tel Aviv. When Iraq attacked Israel with SCUD missiles, the Israeli civil-defense authorities distributed gas masks to the citizenry. In an article in *Yediot Aharonot*, Noah Klieger accused Germany of victimizing the Jews once again: "I did not survive the Auschwitz death camp . . . in order . . . to walk around an independent Jewish state with antigas equipment, against gas developed and manufactured by Germans" (cited in Segev 1993:506). Germany responded to Iraq's attack by sending anti-SCUD missiles, and money, to Israel. This was no mere act of sympathy, for Germany perceived Hussein's actions as a threat to its strategic interests in the Middle East (Segev 1993; Wolffsohn 1993).
10. This was the first time that Israel and the PLO had met in direct, face-to-face negotiations. The agreed upon Oslo Accords, as they are called, created the Palestinian Provisional Authority, which would have the responsibility for the administration of territory under its control. Israel also agreed to the withdrawal of its military forces from parts of the Gaza Strip and West Bank. But just as Sadat was assassinated by religious militants in his own country for negotiating the 1979 peace accord with Israel (see chapter 8, note 6), Rabin was killed by a Jewish extremist in 1995.
11. For critiques of contemporary Israeli policy, see Burg (2008), Carter (2006), and Klug (2007).
12. Alvin Rosenfeld notes that Anne "is the most famous child of the 20th century," and with the exception of Hitler himself, the most famous figure of the Nazi period (1991:244). Her father, Otto Frank, was the only member of the family to survive. He found the diary after the war. For a fascinating look into the life of Otto and the backstory to Anne's experience in hiding and the capture of her family, see Lee (2003).
13. *Het Achterhuis* means "behind" or "in back of" the "house" and is sometimes translated as "The Annex."
14. An ABC miniseries that was aired in May 2001 was the first to continue the story by taking Anne into the concentration camps at Bergen-Belsen where she and her sister Margo died (Peyser 2001).
15. Ilan Avisar (1997) notes that since the airing of the miniseries in Germany, German filmmakers have portrayed World War II as if it were like any other war (e.g., the Vietnam War), and hence they have relativised the Holocaust through counterrhetorical narratives that are either silent about Jewish victimization or that portray the German people as equal victims

of that unfortunate period. All told, these films try to come "to grips with the past" by expunging the shameful parts of it (1997:47). For discussions of pro-German films about wartime military heroics, anti-Nazi resistance, and the innocence of everyday life removed from the Holocaust, see Avisar (1997), Marcuse (2001), and Santner (1990).

16. As notable examples, Peter Novick (1999) cites *Playing for Time, Escape from Sobibor, Triumph of the Spirit*, and the *War and Remembrance* miniseries.

17. At the end of the film, Schindler's Jews are shown walking over the hills of Jerusalem as the song "Jerusalem of Gold" plays in the background. This song was made popular during the 1967 Six Day War. However, in Israel the closing soundtrack was changed to "Eli, Eli," a musical version of a poem written by Hannah Senesh in 1941. Senesh was a Jewish commando who parachuted into occupied Hungary in 1944 to aid the Jewish underground. Tim Cole (1999) thinks this change was an attempt by the Israelis to displace the heroic Gentile (Schindler) with a heroic Jew.

18. Alexander argues that America's postwar response to the Holocaust entailed a rejection of the idea that there was any similarity between German anti-Semitism and American anti-Semitism. To have acknowledged and engaged in critical self-reflection about the history of American anti-Semitism would have undermined a sacred myth about the United States being the complete antithesis of Nazi Germany.

19. The idea of a common "Judeo-Christian" tradition was initially propagated by Jews and Jewish sympathizers in response to wartime rhetoric that characterized the major thrust of Nazism as an assault on "Christian civilization" (Novick 1999:28; Silk 1984). It gained popular currency through Will Herberg's best-selling *Protestant-Catholic-Jew: An Essay in Religious Sociology*, published in 1955. Herberg argued that Americans had adopted a tripartite religious tradition that expressed a common inheritance of moral and spiritual values. During the Cold War, this view "served to bind Americans more tightly together in a confrontation with atheistic Russia, as religion, including Judaism, was mobilized in the struggle against communism" (Shapiro 1992:53). As such, non-Jews no longer considered Jews and Judaism, just 3 percent of the population at the time, "an exotic ethnic and religious minority" (p. 53).

20. The intergenerational upward mobility of Jews was also facilitated by the more general postwar economic expansion and increased accessibility and affordability of higher education in the United States, which allowed Jews to move into the professional occupational class. It was aided as well by the value placed on education and achievement that characterizes traditional Jewish culture (Lipset and Raab 1995). For further consideration of the history of Jews in the United States, see Alexander (2006), Auerbach (1990), Brodkin (1998), Diner (2004), Goldstein (2006), Sachar (1992), Sarna (2004), and Shapiro (1992).

21. The term "'ethnicity' did not come into use until after World War II, when it became the word of choice in academic and public-policy circles to describe those who had been formerly discussed as members of a less-than-white white, nation or people" (Brodkin 1998:144). While ethnicity

may be an externally-imposed category used by a majority group to oppress a minority group, it may also be self-imposed and used by members as a resource for self-understanding, social solidarity, and group advancement (Nagel 1994).

22. The term "melting pot" was first used in a play by that name written by Jewish writer Israel Zangwill, which opened before American audiences in 1908 (Alexander 2006; Goldstein 2006).

23. Prior to the Six Day War, the United States government had not been an undisputed ally of Israel. It had been concerned about some Israeli leaders' socialist leanings and had pressured Israel to return land it occupied after the 1956 military conflict with Egypt. Secretary of State John Foster Dulles urged President Dwight Eisenhower to pay more attention to the Arab states as "potential allies against the Soviet Union" (Sachar 1992:724). Nonetheless, relations between the United States and Egypt deteriorated as Egyptian president Gamel Abdel Nasser tried to expand his territorial empire, undermine pro-Western governments in the Middle East, and turn to the Soviet Union for economic aid.

During the 1960 presidential campaign, John Kennedy sought the Jewish vote in key states that helped him secure victory, and his administration introduced a more favorable tilt in U.S. foreign policy toward Israel. Although Kennedy did not support Israel on every issue, he made a point of explaining his policies to Jewish Americans and of "displaying sensitivity to their concerns" (Sachar 1992:731). Kennedy was the first U.S. president to approve the sale of weapons to Israel, providing an assurance of support that had not been forthcoming previously. Subsequently, Israel's military success in the Six Day War solidified the state's position as a capable U.S. ally and an important strategic asset in the Middle East. Jewish Americans felt increasingly self-confident in voicing political support and providing financial assistance for Israel (Miller 1990; Novick 1999).

24. In his study of Holocaust survivors in the United States, Aaron Hass (1995) found that most did not speak at any length about their experience for at least thirty years after the war, if they spoke of it at all. Until that time the world was not quite ready to listen to their stories, to say nothing of embracing them as revered figures. They were viewed as "displaced persons," "refugees," or "greenhorns," and were not yet revered as "survivors" (Berger 2011; Novick 1999).

Although survivors are portrayed in postwar psychiatric literature as suffering from a syndrome of psychopathology, this view has been derived from clinical samples and has not held up under the scrutiny of more carefully designed evaluations, which do not find survivors differing significantly from other groups in terms of psychiatric symptoms. This characterization appears to have gained a foothold in the aftermath of the war, as survivors filing German indemnification claims had to demonstrate that they suffered from symptoms unrelated to their prewar personalities or experiences. Survivors, and those evaluating them, were thus forced to emphasize their disabilities and not their positive functioning. It thus appears that most survivors did not have difficulty "reinvesting in life" and were forward-looking in their postwar orientations (Hass 1995:3;

see also Berger 2011; Davidson 1992; Harel, Kahana, and Kahana 1988; Helmreich 1992).

Psychiatric researchers have also often assumed that symptoms of pathology would inevitably be transmitted to children. According to Hass, however, "Children of survivors are extremely diverse in their personality profiles, their levels of achievement, and their life styles. Previous generalizations have often been founded on a blatant disregard for the rules of scientific inquiry" (1990:35–36). Indeed, studies that compare nonclinical populations of second-generation children with the general population find little difference in symptoms of psychopathology (Kellerman 2001; Klein-Parker 1988).

25. Horowitz (2009) reports that by now there are more than 175 separate Holocaust-related voluntary associations worldwide. He worries about the "risk in the professionalization of Holocaust studies—perhaps none greater than to convert an enormous human tragedy into a series of academic groupings debating the minutiae as if they were picking through the final leavings of a rummage sale. But such problems are a concern only for select academics that spend careers on the subject" (p. 501).

26. Although Israeli officials have welcomed financial contributions from Jewish Americans, they have cautioned their U.S. counterparts to take a backseat in Israeli affairs. As Ben-Gurion announced a few years after World War II, "I would propose that all Zionists in the Diaspora should have a voice in the affairs of the State of Israel . . . but only on the condition that they pay taxes to the State of Israel and become subject to military service" (quoted in Sachar 1992:719). Clearly the message was that only Israelis should speak for Zionism and for the Jewish people of the world.

27. In actuality, Wiesel is a more controversial figure than he was made out to be. Christopher Hitchens (2001), for instance, lambastes Wiesel for his uncritical support of Israel and apparent lack of empathy for the plight of the Palestinians in the Middle East (see also Finkelstein 2000).

28. See chapter 8, note 24.

29. For discussions of the sacralization of the Holocaust, see Bauman (2004) and Prosono and Brock (1996).

30. Cole reports that officials of the Israeli Yad Vashem memorial/museum expressed concern that "their authoritative position in exhibiting the 'Holocaust'" was being eroded (1999:146).

31. Alexander notes a profound paradox: that the very status of the Holocaust as a unique event, as a tragedy that came to be viewed as "radically different from any other evil act in modern times," would eventually compel "it to become generalized and departicularized. By providing such a standard for comparative judgment, [it] became the norm, initiating a succession of . . . evaluations that deprived it of 'uniqueness' by establishing its degree of likeness or unlikeness to other possible manifestations of evility" (2004:251–52). For an examination of the Holocaust in comparative perspective, see Rosenbaum (2009).

32. For historical accounts of the political alliances and divisions between Jewish Americans and African Americans, see Berman (1994), Brodkin (1998), Goldstein (2006), Kaufman (1994), Salzman (1992), and Sundquist (2006).

33. Simon Wiesenthal (1908–2005) was a Holocaust survivor who became known after the war for his efforts to track down Nazi war criminals. The Simon Wiesenthal Center in Los Angeles was established in honor of his life's work.

34. U.S. banks also withheld assets of Holocaust survivors (Finkelstein 2000; Jelinek 2000).

35. See Steinweis (2001) for a critique of Finkelstein's polemical excesses. More generally, Mitch Berbrier (2000) describes an "ethnicity industry" as a heterogeneous network of people and institutions involved in promoting, maintaining, and/or modifying particular constructions of ethnicity and the interests of their group. An ethnicity industry includes ethnic associations and fund-raising organizations, ethnic libraries and museums, ethnic studies programs in schools and universities, ethnic diversity and multicultural programs, ethnic festivals and rituals of ethnic commemoration, and government agencies dealing with ethnic-group issues.

36. For a less polemical and more scholarly critique of Wiesel's position, see Lentin (2004).

37. According to Samuel Freedman (2000), the phrase "Silent Holocaust" has enjoyed widespread use among Orthodox Jews. It derives from a statement by Rabbi Sol Roth, a philosophy professor at Yeshiva University who served as president of the Rabbinical Council of America, who described the high rates of interfaith marriages among Jews as a "Holocaust of our own making" that threatens the Jewish community's "very survival." Rabbi Roth also called for the elimination "from leadership roles in Jewish public life of all those who marry out of their faith and rabbis who perform marriages between Jews and non-Jews" (quoted in Alexander 2006:547, 722; and Yaffe 1980:2).

38. There is also a secular tradition of Judaism: the urban folk culture of *Yiddishkeit*. As a language, Yiddish is primarily a blend of Hebrew and German, with a smattering of other dialects; and in Europe of the late nineteenth century it "provided a common link between Jews from different villages, regions, and nations" (Brodkin 1998:106). As a secular culture, Yiddishkeit "infused Jewish life with the intellectual, political, and artistic excitement" of urban modernity and drew attention to elements of biblical Judaism that were compatible with a socialist vision of economic equality and social justice (p. 106). This tradition took hold in segregated Jewish neighborhoods in prewar United States and existed symbiotically with religious Judaism, inspiring some Jews to become involved in the politics of the American left. More generally, it meant "that part of being Jewish was being familiar with a working-class and anticapitalist outlook . . . and understanding this outlook as . . . particularly Jewish" (p. 105).

The prewar culture of Yiddishkeit did not last much longer than the initial generation that brought it to the United States, because in the postwar period the conditions for its persistence began to unravel. As Jews became upwardly mobile, Jewish interest in socialism subsided; and as they flocked to the suburbs, the close-knit communities that nourished the Yiddishkeit urban scene disbanded. Nonetheless, Yiddishkeit showed "a way to be Jewish . . . without being religious" (Freedman 2000:37), and some contemporary Jews of the political left still view their Jewish heritage as providing the raw material for their progressive values (Brodkin 1998).

39. Rabbi Emil Fackenheim is noteworthy for his contention that Jews are obligated to hold fast to their religious faith or they will grant Hitler yet another posthumous victory. In traditional Judaism, God is said to have given the Jews 613 commandments in Scripture, and Fackenheim sets forth a 614th commandment, which, he asserts, commands Jews "to survive as Jews, lest the Jewish people perish," and that forbids Jews "to deny or despair of the God of Israel lest Judaism perish" (1978:176). Michael Berenbaum thinks that Fackenheim's view is less a theological observation than an expression of "his fear of consequences"—that without their religious faith, Jews as a distinct people will cease to exist (2001:627). But even if Jews persisted in their faith, of what that faith would consist is one of the issues that continues to divide Jews today. For discussions of the most common branches of contemporary Judaism—Orthodox, Conservative, and Reform—see Bershtel and Graubard (1992), Diner (2004), Freedman (2000), Lipset and Raab (1995), Sachar (1992), and Sarna (2004).

40. "Whether being an Israeli implies, in reverse, a commitment to the fate and fortune of world Jewry" outside of Israel is a question Horowitz does not tackle (2002:27).

41. Sociologists trace this diversity to the religious individualism that was sown in colonial times, with early Protestants' emphasis on personal salvation as the key element of religious experience. In its contemporary form it allows individuals to select among an array of denominational choices the particular orientation that best suits their personal inclinations (Bellah et al. 1985; Wuthnow 1989). Historians of the Jewish-American experience attribute the relatively favorable position of Judaism (in comparison to Europe, for example) to the special character of American Protestantism, which lacks a centrally-organized structure and is composed instead of a plethora of individual denominations (Lipset and Raab 1995). The competition among these groups "enabled the Jews to fit in from the start of the republic as one religious entity out of many, rather than as the only or principal deviant group" (p. 31).

9

Genocide, Religion, and Social Solidarity

Raphael Lemkin (1900–59) grew up in a Jewish family in Eastern Poland, just fifty miles from the city of Bialystock, then part of czarist Russia. As a boy he was exposed to stories of human carnage. In 1906, about seventy Jews had been murdered and ninety gravely injured in local pogroms in the Bialystock region, and Lemkin had heard about mobs opening the stomachs of their victims and stuffing "them with feathers from pillows and comforters in grotesque mutilation rituals" (Power 2002:20). By the age of twelve, he had already read Nobel Prize winner Henryk Sinekiewciz's *Quo Vadis?*, an account of "the Roman emperor Nero's massacres of Christian converts in the first century" (2002:20). While he was studying linguistics at the University of Lvov in 1920, Lemkin also had learned of the Turkish mass murder of the Armenians, and he wondered why no one had been prosecuted for the crimes (see chapter 8). Lemkin's interests turned to law, but he never lost sight of the power of words. Perhaps the problem in the Armenian case, and later the Holocaust as well, was that we lacked the vocabulary to describe what had transpired (Cooper 2008; Elder 2005; Power 2002).

As a lawyer during the 1930s, Lemkin began working on the development of a legal framework that would address the problem of what he would later call "genocide." After the Nazis invaded Poland, he first joined the Polish Army and then escaped to Sweden, where he lectured on international law at the University of Stockholm. With the help of "a professor at Duke University with whom he had once translated the Polish criminal code into English," he received an appointment to the law faculty at Duke and was granted permission to enter the United States (Power 2002:26).

During the war, Lemkin lobbied extensively for intervention to stop the mass murder of the European Jews. In June 1942, he was hired as a consultant to the Board of Economic Warfare and the Foreign Economic Administration in Washington, DC, and in 1944 by the U.S. War Department. But much to his regret, he found that his colleagues and other government officials he spoke with were not interested in what was happening to the Jews (Cooper 2008; Elder 2005; Power 2002).

In 1944, Lemkin published *Axis Rule in Occupied Europe*, a book that aimed to provide "undeniable and objective evidence regarding the treatment of the subjugated people of Europe by the Axis powers" (p. ix). It was in this work that Lemkin coined the term genocide, which combined "the Greek derivative *geno*, meaning 'race' or 'tribe,' and the Latin derivative *cide*, from *caedere*, meaning 'killing'" (Power 2002:42). Lemkin believed that words matter—that they were capable of bringing recognition of a social reality into being. He had been looking for a word that could not be used in other contexts, finding such terms as barbarity, atrocity, and mass murder insufficient to connote "the singular motivation behind the perpetration of the crime he had in mind" (2002:41).

After the war, Lemkin helped draft and lobby for the passage of the United Nations Convention on the Prevention and Punishment of Genocide, which declared that "genocide, whether committed in time of peace or in time of war, is a crime under international law which they undertake to prevent and to punish" (cited in Ronayne 2001:1). Although the United States had taken "the lead in rallying the young United Nations behind the pledge 'never again,'" it did not actually ratify the 1948 Convention for another four decades (p. 13). Nor did its passage by the member nations, who were "shocked into action by the horror of the Holocaust," prevent future genocides from occurring (p. 7).

In this concluding chapter of the book, I trace the emergence of this new international norm against genocide and the problem of putting this norm into practice. I then aim to contextualize the norm in terms of the more general problem of social solidarity and the exclusionary social processes that deny the humanity of all too many human beings. In doing so, I also examine the ongoing dilemma of Christian-Jewish coexistence as a representative case of the challenges that confront efforts to construct inclusionary societies that are fully incorporative of social differences. Lastly,

I conclude with some final thoughts about sociology and the Holocaust (see chapter 1).

The United Nations Genocide Convention and Its Aftermath

World War II was undoubtedly a turning point in the history of the world. While the war was unprecedented in the devastation it unleashed, it also marked a step forward in the construction of an international conception of universal human rights (Todorov 2001b). The postwar human rights movement built on the groundwork that had been laid in the earlier part of the twentieth century. A clause of the Fourth Hague Convention of 1907 on land warfare articulated the idea of "laws of humanity" that would prevail among "civilized nations" and make murder of civilians during times of war an international crime (cited in Marrus 1997:185). At the Preliminary Peace Conference in 1919, France, Great Britain, and Russia denounced the Turkish genocide of the Armenians as "a crime of humanity and civilization for which all members of the Turkish government will be held responsible together with its agents implicated in the massacres" (cited in Fein 1993:2). The failure of the subsequent Versailles Treaty to follow through on this call for sanctions did not go unnoticed by Hitler who, you will recall, said, "Who after all, speaks today of the annihilation of the Armenians?" (see chapter 8).

In the late 1940s, as noted earlier, the United Nations (UN) articulated its official mission to save "succeeding generations from the scourge of war" and reaffirm "faith in fundamental human rights, in the dignity and worth of the human person, in the equal rights of men and women and of nations large and small" (see chapter 8). The postwar International Military Tribunal at Nuremberg also advanced what many consider "the central concept in the postwar moral imagination: the idea of crimes against humanity" (Ignatieff 2001:27), a notion that stood for "grave maltreatment or atrocities committed against persons who were unprotected by law because of their nationality, . . . [including] acts . . . at the hands of their own government" (Marrus 1997:185–86; see chapter 7). Additionally, the UN passed the Universal Declaration of Human Rights, which asserted "the inherent dignity and . . . equal and inalienable rights of all members of the human family [as] the foundation of freedom, justice, and peace in the world" (www.un.org).

Then came the UN Convention on the Prevention and Punishment of Genocide, often referred to as the Genocide Convention (GC), which defined genocide as:

> any of the following acts committed with intent to destroy, in whole or in part, a national, ethnical, racial or religious group, as such: (a) Killing members of the group; (b) Causing serious bodily or mental harm to members of the group; (c) Deliberately inflicting on the group conditions of life calculated to bring about its physical destruction in whole or in part; (d) Imposing measures intended to prevent births within the group; (e) Forcibly transferring children of the group to another group. (cited in Power 2002:62)

For a party to be found guilty of perpetrating this new crime, it had to carry out one of the aforementioned acts with the explicit intent of destroying all or part of one of the protected groups (Power 2002; Ronayne 2001).[1]

Notably, the GC did not protect political groups, as the Soviet Union and its Communist allies in Eastern Europe and Latin America opposed their inclusion, because they were concerned that it "would inhibit states that were attempting to suppress internal armed revolt" (Power 2002:6). Underscoring this objection, of course, was the fear that the GC would be applied to Soviet dictator Joseph Stalin's murderous regime and ongoing human rights abuses in Communist countries throughout the world (Goldhagen 2009).

The Problem of U.S. Ratification

When the GC was approved by the UN General Assembly in 1948, including the United States, "few doubted that the United States would be one of the first countries to ratify it" (Power 2002:64). As noted earlier, the United States had taken the lead in rallying the UN to the cause of preventing genocide; and Lemkin had collaborated with several State Department attorneys in preparing the first draft of the GC. President Harry Truman heartily endorsed it and called on the U.S. Senate to ratify it. But this ratification was not soon forthcoming, as the "early U.S. leadership . . . largely evaporated in the months and years that followed" (Power 2002:65; Ronayne 2001).[2]

To be sure, some of the domestic political opposition to ratification "was rooted in legitimate grievances about the text of the law. The convention's plain wording was not terribly specific about the nature of the violence that needed to occur . . . [and about] how many

216

individuals have to be killed and/or expelled from their homes . . . in order to trigger a global or national response" (Power 2002:65). But some U.S. senators also feared that the GC would be used to target the United States. Indeed, genocide scholar Leo Kuper wondered whether they feared that the United States "might be held responsible, retrospectively, for the annihilation of Indians in the United States or its role in the slave trade, or its contemporary support for tyrannical governments engaging in mass murder" (1990:423). Indeed, opponents of ratification, particularly Southern conservatives, explicitly stated their concerns that the GC would be used to invalidate Jim Crow segregation laws and be applied to anti-Black lynchings and race riots (Power 2002; Ronayne 2001).

"No doubt," Peter Ronayne argues, the GC "is a flawed document. Some ambiguous language, definition issues and omissions" mar the treaty, and its enforcement mechanisms are more clear about punishment than prevention (2001:14). Nevertheless, it does establish an evolving norm, both moral and legal, against a new crime:

> It defines a certain behavior, labels it as criminal, and declares members of the international community responsible to combat and punish the crime. This is a significant development, quite apart from issues of enforcement application. As convention champion Senator William Proxmire would term it, the convention is "a call for a high standard of human conduct. It is not a panacea for injustice." . . . Failure to ratify the [GC] put the United States in an awkward position. How could [it] profess concerns for human rights and outrage over genocide if it refused to support the single treaty dealing with that specific and horrific atrocity? (2001:14)[3]

Proponents of ratification sought to mollify domestic opposition by noting that the GC had no provisions for retroactive application, and by agreeing to attach an explicit legal "understanding" to the ratification bill clearly stating that it did not apply to "lynchings, race riots or any form of segregation" (Power 2002:68). But, as Samantha Power points out, the problem in the ensuing decades "would not be that too many states would file genocide charges against other states, but rather, too few would do so." And to the present day "no state has dared to challenge the United States by filing" formal charges against it.

Power (2002) thinks that the domestic resistance to GC ratification was driven more by xenophobia and foreign policy isolationism aimed at exempting the United States from compliance to all international legal frameworks. By way of illustration, she notes that Lemkin himself became the target of xenophobic slurs. In 1950 Senate Foreign Relations Committee member H. Alexander Smith denigrated Lemkin as the "biggest propagandist" for the GC, "a man who comes from a foreign country who . . . speaks broken English'" (quoted in Power 2002:68). Referring to Lemkin's Polish-Jewish background, Smith added that while he was "sympathetic to the Jewish people, . . . they ought not to be the ones who are propagandizing" for ratification (p. 68).[4] Thus despite having invented the concept of genocide and playing a key role in writing the GC, Lemkin was not invited to testify before the Senate subcommittee that was considering ratification.

Not until the presidency of Jimmy Carter in the late 1970s did the U.S. position begin to change. Carter, who had tried to make questions of human rights, not only national self-interest, more central to U.S. foreign policy, wrote a letter to the Senate in which he asserted that ratification would significantly enhance "the human rights commitments of this nation, demonstrating again to the world in concrete fashion our determination to advance and protect human rights" (cited in Ronayne 2001:29). And in testimony before the Senate Foreign Relations Committee, deputy secretary of state Warren Christopher stated that ratification would send a message "to the world community that the United States stands ready to develop the international law of human rights, and to make such human rights a matter of international concern" (quoted in Ronayne 2001:30).

Still, U.S. ratification of the GC was years away, and when Ronald Reagan assumed the presidency in 1981, supporters had little reason for optimism. "The Reagan foreign policy team did not view human rights as a priority, and few observers expected a conservative president to champion" a UN treaty (Ronayne 2001:32). What changed matters, however, was the Reagan administration's realization that ratification was consistent with the national interest in combating its Cold War adversary the Soviet Union. Over the years the Soviets had used the United States' refusal to ratify the GC as a way to deflect criticism of its own human rights abuses. The Reagan administration concluded that if U.S. criticism of the Soviet Union and its allied states was to carry any weight in the international community, it would need to ratify the GC. As secretary of state designate Alexander Haig said during his Senate confirmation hearing, ratification would "unquestionably be helpful in various international fora where the United States has been criticized for its failure to ratify the GC. This is ironic because the United States was a leader in the post-World War II effort to conclude the convention as an expression of revulsion to the Holocaust and as a deterrent to the recurrence of such crimes against humanity" (quoted in Ronayne 2001:36).

Politically as well, the Reagan administration also came to view support of the GC as a way to court Jewish votes, since Jewish advocacy groups were among its most staunch supporters. In 1984, during his reelection campaign, Reagan used a B'nai B'rith convention to tell the assembled:

> With a cautious view, in part due to the human rights abuses performed by some nations that have already ratified the document, our administration has conducted a long and exhaustive study of the convention. . . . [and decided to] vigorously support . . . ratification. . . . I want you to know that we intend to use the convention in our efforts to expand human freedom and fight human rights abuses around the world. Like you, I say in a forthright voice, "Never again." (quoted in Ronayne 2001:36–37)

Despite Reagan's endorsement, work remained to be done. In a resolution crafted by Republicans Richard Lugar, Jesse Helms, and Orin Hatch—the Lugar-Helms-Hatch Sovereignty Package—the senators outlined several reservations and understandings that, all told, clarified the primacy of the U.S. Constitution over the GC. Then, at the groundbreaking ceremony for the United States Holocaust Memorial Museum in 1985, Senator Bob Dole indicated his intention to bring ratification to the Senate floor: "As a nation which enshrines human dignity and freedom . . . we must correct our anomalous position on this basic rights issue" (quoted in Ronayne 2001:39). Three years later, on October 14, 1988, the full Senate finally approved the treaty, which Reagan then signed into law.

The Promise Deferred

The GC, as noted earlier, was more explicit about its mechanisms to punish genocidal offenders than to prevent genocidal victims. Regarding the latter, the GC has been honored more in the breech than in the observance. Three of the most well-known genocides of the post-World War II period—which occurred in Cambodia, Bosnia, and Rwanda—are indicative of this problem.

Cambodia

In the late 1970s, the communist Khmer Rouge (KR) led by dictator Pol Pot (1928–98) murdered 1.5 to 2 million Cambodians out of a total population of about 8 million who were perceived to be politically hostile or socially incompatible with the KR's goal of transforming Cambodia according to their "utopian" vision of a rural-based, classless society. The roots of this genocide lay in the wake of the Vietnam War which, under President Richard Nixon, expanded into Cambodia (and Laos), which borders Vietnam to the west, through relentless bombings by American B-52s and invasion by some 50,000 U.S. and South Vietnamese troops seeking to destroy communist North Vietnamese strongholds in the region (Chalk and Jonassohn 1990; Goldhagen 2009; Power 2002; Ronayne 2001).

During this time, the United States found itself supporting the anticommunist Cambodian government of Lon Nol against a feverishly oppositional KR. In 1975, following five years of civil war, the KR took control of the country and began using starvation, forced marches from the city to countryside, and outright killings to create its revolutionary society. The "radical barbarism" continued until 1979, when a now united Vietnam invaded Cambodia, toppled the despotic regime, and installed a new government (Ronayne 2001:52).

While the genocide was unfolding, the U.S. government was virtually silent. It even joined with China, which supported the KR, to allow the KR to keep its seat in the UN. At the time, U.S. officials believed that China, which had been at odds with the Soviet Union since the early 1960s, was an important bulwark against Soviet expansionism. It was best to do nothing to upset U.S.-China relations, which had been improving since Nixon had opened up diplomatic ties in 1972. All this indicates that in the UN only weaker states that are unaligned with more powerful ones are at risk of being punished for the crime of genocide (Chalk and Jonassohn 1990; Goldhagen 2009; Power 2002; Ronayne 2001).[5]

Bosnia

Another prominent genocide of the post-World War II period followed the breakup of Yugoslavia in 1991. The former nation, which was initially created out of an amalgam of different (and sometimes hostile) ethnic cultures following World War I, had enjoyed a relatively harmonious existence under the communist leadership of Josip Broz Tito (1892–1980), who came to power after World War II. Tito was known for his commitment to a multiethnic society, firmly opposing the domination of one group by another (Doubt 2007; Power 2002; Ronayne 2001; Smith 2002).

Under Tito's leadership, Yugoslavia functioned as a federal state composed of several independent republics, which were granted limited autonomy. With the end of the Cold War, the republics sought to establish themselves as separate nation-states and conflict ensued, most notably in Bosnia-Herzegovina (hitherto referred to as Bosnia). Under Communist rule, Bosnia had been the most ethnically diverse of the Yugoslavian republics, with a population that was about 44 percent Muslim, and a Christian population that was about 31 percent Serbian and 18 percent Croatian (Ronayne 2001). Although the smaller villages were relatively homogenous, the cities were marked by "considerable ethnic mixing including high rates of intermarriage" (p. 103). Now Slobodan Milosevic (1941–2006), the president of neighboring Serbia, along with Bosnian Serb leader Radovan Karadzic, sought the creation of a united "Greater Serbia" cleansed of other (particularly Muslim) groups and launched "the region into a period of brutal ethnic hostilities," civil war, and genocide that lasted from 1992 to 1995 (p. 102).[6]

During the genocidal campaign, Serbian troops "emptied Muslim villages, rounding up the inhabitants and transporting them" to concentration camps in busses or train cars, without providing them with food, water, or sanitation (Ronayne 2001:18).[7] Upon arrival to the camps, many were systematically tortured and killed, and thousands of young girls and women were raped as a matter of Serbian policy aimed at terrorizing the population. All told, more than 200,000 people were killed and as many seriously maimed; and more than 2 million became refugees (Doubt 2007; *The History Place* 1999; Power 2002; Smith 2002).

In the initial years of the conflict, inaction marked the response of the United States and international community. Policymakers were reluctant to label the situation "genocide." The administration of George H. W. Bush "willingly embraced disengagement . . . [based on the] belief that events in Yugoslavia fell outside the orbit of central or vital American interests" (Ronayne 2001:113). But as evidence mounted as to what was transpiring in Bosnia, the pressure grew from a chorus of voices in the media, nongovernmental organizations, the U.S. Congress, and the UN General Assembly to act. The only response that was forthcoming from the Bush administration, however, was not to take preventive action but to issue assurances that those responsible would be held accountable under international law (Power 2002; Smith 2002).

During the presidential campaign of 1992, Bill Clinton levied harsh criticisms of the Bush administration's policy of inaction in Bosnia. But when Clinton took office, he feared that U.S. intervention, which was arguably controversial, would weaken him politically and undermine his domestic agenda, and it was not until the summer of 1995 that Clinton finally committed the United States to leading a massive NATO bombing attack against Serbian artillery strongholds that eventually ended the Bosnian tragedy (Power 2002; Ronayne 2001; Smith 2002).[8]

Rwanda

In 1994, while the Bosnian genocide was ongoing, the Hutu majority in the African country of Rwanda waged an incredibly gruesome three-month killing campaign against the Tutsi minority that caused the deaths of some 800,000 people.[9] The roots of the Rwanda genocide can be traced to the Belgium colonization of the country following World War I, when the Belgians elevated the "Tutsis to positions of prominence in the colonial administration" (Ronayne 2001:153). "Up to that point," as Ronayne explains, "the terms 'Tutsi' and 'Hutu' did not represent strictly defined ethnic groups as they do today" (p. 153). Although ethnic boundaries had existed before, they were more permeable.

> This permeability disappeared over time as Belgian colonists and Roman Catholic missionaries viewed Rwandan society through the since discredited lens of "Hamatic" ideology. According to this worldview, any developed or "civilized" institutions in Africa . . . resulted from invasion by "Hamites," also referred to variously as "African Aryans," "white coloreds," or "black Caucasians," and seemed to represent a missing link between the races. Applied to Rwanda, this fantastic racial typography . . . rewrote the region's history and received bolstering from general physical distinctions emphasized by Western observers who explained that Tutsis were generally "taller, thinner, and more European-looking than Hutus," [creating a myth of Tutsi superiority]. (2001:153)

Eventually, this system of minority domination turned upside down as "the Hutu majority gained the upper hand in Rwandan society" and began to suppress the Tutsi minority (p. 154).

The Rwandan genocide stands out as a case where the international community had ample warning about the threat. By March 1993, UN observers had reported on more than 2,000 Tutsis who had already been killed and more than 10,000 who had been detained (Power 2002). In December 1993, UN officials working in the country had received warnings from informant army officers about a plan for mass assassinations and killings. In January 1994, the extremist Hutu-controlled Radio-Television Libres des Milles Collines (RTLMC) began calling for the extermination of the Tutsi, referring to them as "inyenzi" (cockroaches) (Ronayne 2001). That same month the U.S. Central Intelligence Agency had concluded that if "combat were to begin in Rwanda . . . it would include violence against civilians—with a worst-case scenario of the death of half a million people" (cited in Ronayne 2001:156).

On April 6, 1994, Hutu leader and Rwandan president Juvenal Hayarimana was killed when his plane was shot down and crashed over the city of Kigali. Tutsi rebels were blamed, although some think the perpetrators were actually Hutu extremists in the Rwandan army seeking to provoke a conflict. RTLMC began calling for mass murder "to avenge the death of our president" (quoted in Ronayne 2001:157). "Through its endless stream of malicious propaganda, RTLMC helped recruit and organize the *Interhamwe* militias," which had been stock-piling artillery and machetes, calling on frightened Hutu citizens to destroy their enemies, even reading lists of names of specific people to be killed, often giving their addresses or last known whereabouts (2001:157; see also Power 2002; Smith 2002).

In a short time, Interhamwe militiamen, army troops, and police began killing every Tutsi they could get their hands on. Within 100 days, 800,000 had been killed.

> Bodies polluted and clogged the Akagera River. Children and babies were slain, often smashed to death against rocks or hurled alive into pits. . . . Pregnant women were eviscerated. Victims were commonly mutilated before being killed, with penises and breasts often chopped off. To avoid such agony, people with money offered to pay their assassins to get the job done quickly with a bullet rather than suffer death by machete. (Ronayne 2001:159)

This was the Rwandan genocide, and no one did anything to stop it.[10] A month into the conflict human rights groups pleaded with the UN to send in troops to protect the people. No such response was forthcoming. The Clinton administration instructed its spokesmen not to describe the situation as genocide. To do so would have created a moral and legal obligation to act. The president and his advisors believed that Rwanda, like Bosnia, was a threat to his "legislative agenda and approval ratings at home" (Ronayne 2001:173; see also Power 2002; Smith 2002).[11]

In light of such inaction, we must therefore ask, when President Clinton opined at the opening of the U.S. Holocaust Memorial Museum in 1993—"[T]he evil represented in this museum is contestable. But as we are its witness, so must we remain its adversary in the world"—what did he really mean? It most certainly appears that Zbigniew Brzezinski was right when he asked us to ponder whether Holocaust remembrance was a "proclamation of a moral imperative" or a "pompous declaration of hypocrisy" (see chapter 8).

Nevertheless, analysts like Ronayne are not entirely grim about the prospects for strengthening the admittedly "weak norm of genocide prevention" that has been mandated by the GC (2001:189). It is true, he suggests, that the United States has failed to capitalize on its leadership position in the world to advance this norm. But it is also true that the GC and its call for the prevention of genocide "had at least enough standing and clout to compel the Clinton administration to consciously avoid using the term for fear of the pressure and criticism it might entail given their determined policy of passivity" (p. 189).[12] Words do matter, as Lemkin would be the first to remind us. The challenge remains, as the more recent genocide in Darfur attests,[13] as to how to translate these words into timely action to save lives.

Religion, Solidarity, and Difference

Andrew Bell-Fialkoff observes that it is sadly ironic that the modern impulse toward "freedom, self-determination, and representative democracy" has created a situation that pulls people apart, as particular ethnic groups seek either complete political sovereignty and independence or a distinct social identity within the boundaries of their nation's borders (1999:49). As we have seen in the case of the former Yugoslavia, for example, the end of the Cold War has been accompanied by a resurgence of ethnic conflicts in the former Soviet Union and its allied European states. For several decades after World War II, the transethnic ideology of Communism had masked and suppressed (but did not eradicate) prewar conflicts that have now come to the surface. According to Bell-Fialkoff, it was ethnic-group nationalism that helped erode "the Communist cocoon from within," but in a reconstituted Europe, this nationalism has revealed itself to have an ugly face (1999:33). In the name of democracy and representative government, different ethnic communities now demand the right to self-government in ways that solidify the political power of ethnic majorities and attempt to marginalize or even remove minorities who are perceived as the ongoing enemy from within (Gross 2000; Judt 2000).

Tony Judt notes that ethnic-group nationalism was superimposed on long-standing religious antagonisms, and of all the old prejudices that have now rushed in to fill the void left by Communism's collapse, "anti-Semitism is the most striking" (2000:312). As we noted in the case of postwar Poland (see chapter 7), it is essentially "irrelevant that there are hardly any Jews left" in the former Soviet-bloc nations, for anti-Semitism in this part of the world "has long had a central political and cultural place; it is as much a way of talking about 'them' and 'us' as it is a device for singling out Jews in particular" (2000:312). Addressing this other-creating epithet requires confrontation with the problem of Christian-Jewish coexistence in a post-Holocaust world, as well as a more general engagement with the question of social solidarity in the civil sphere, that is, the extent to which fully egalitarian membership in a society is extended to those who are marginal to the core, the extent to which the "we-ness" or connectedness that members feel toward one another is extended to all (Alexander 2006; see chapter 1).

Dilemmas of Christian-Jewish Coexistence

Earlier we saw that Christianity and Judaism were each other's disconfirming other, whereby belief in the veracity of one required belief in the falsity of the other (see chapter 2). As such, according to Zygmunt Bauman, Jews posed a problem for Christianity, which "could not reproduce itself... without guarding and reinforcing Jewish estrangement" (1989:37). Religion is itself a form of collective memory (Hervieu-Léger 2000), and in the postwar period Christianity faced a dilemma of accountability for the animosity it had long engendered against Jews as well as for its apparent acquiescence to Nazism during the prewar and war years (see chapters 2, 4, and 6). How would the organized Christian churches make amends, if at all?

Arguably the most notable postwar developments in Christian-Jewish relations have involved the Catholic Church. As the only domination with an international organization and clearly defined central leadership embodied in the Pope and the Vatican, it has the authority to issue statements that purport to speak for all Catholics in the world. An initial landmark document aimed at improving the postwar relationship between Catholics and Jews was the *Declaration on the Relationship of the Church to Non-Christian Religions*, also called the *Nostra Aetate* (In Our Age), which was issued by the Second Vatican Council under the leadership of Pope John XXIII in 1965. In this document, the Church acknowledged the common heritage of Christians and Jews, recommended that "biblical and theological studies and brotherly dialogues" be undertaken to foster mutual understanding and respect, admitted that Christ's death "cannot be blamed upon all the Jews then living . . . nor upon the Jews of today," and deplored "hatred, persecutions, and display of anti-Semitism directed against the Jews at any time and from any source" (cited in Braham 1999:223).

At the same time, this attempt at reconciliation was mitigated by two negative references to Jews, which reiterated Catholic doctrinal positions that had historically given rise to anti-Semitism. It reminded readers that Jewish leaders of biblical times did in fact press for Christ's death, and that a large number of contemporary Jews not only fail to accept Christian gospel but oppose the spread of Christianity. Many Jews as well as Christians regretted both the inclusion of these passages and the absence of an official apology for the Church's inaction during the Nazi period. Nonetheless, the document was followed by additional Vatican and other national church pronouncements that removed various anti-Jewish references from religious textbooks, liturgy, and teachings (Braham 1999).[14] In 1995, for instance, the German Catholic bishops issued a declaration "deploring the failure of Catholics to act against Nazism or speak out against the crimes committed against the Jews, and acknowledging that they consequently bore a special responsibility to fight against antisemitism" (p. 241). And in 1997 the French Catholic Church pronounced:

> It is important to admit the primary role, if not direct, then indirect, played by the constantly repeated anti-Jewish stereotypes wrongly perpetuated among Christians in the historical process that led to the Holocaust. . . . In the face of the persecution of Jews, especially the multifaceted anti-Semitic laws passed by Vichy, silence was the rule, and words in favor of the victims the exception. . . . Today we confess that silence was a mistake. We beg for the pardon of God,

and we ask the Jewish people to hear this word of repentance. (cited on p. 242)

More than any of his Vatican predecessors, the Polish-born Pope John Paul II "openly talked about—and asked forgiveness for—the sins, crimes, and errors committed in the Church's name" (Braham 1999:224). Under his leadership, a 1998 Vatican document entitled *We Remember: A Reflection of the Shoah* acknowledged the "erroneous and unjust interpretations of the New Testament regarding the Jewish people" and admitted to anti-Semitic measures that historically stemmed from "some Christian quarters" (cited on p. 225). Importantly, it noted its deep regret over the silence of Christians during the Holocaust and committed itself to preventing "the evil seeds of . . . anti-Semitism [from ever again] taking root in any human heart" (p. 225).[15]

As with the earlier *Nostra Aetate*, however, critics of *We Remember* remained unsatisfied because the document blamed followers rather than Church doctrine for anti-Semitism: It asserted that Nazi "anti-Semitism had its roots outside of Christianity" rather than emanating from it (cited in Braham 1999:226); and it postulated a difference "between anti-Semitism, based on theories contrary to the constant teaching of the church on the unity of the human race and on the equal dignity of all races and peoples, and the long-standing sentiments of mistrust and hostility that we call anti-Judaism, of which, unfortunately, Christians also have been guilty" (cited in Mitchell and Mitchell 2001:323). However, as Jules Isaac notes, "Without centuries of Christian catechism, preaching and vituperation, the Hitlerian [ideology and policies] . . . would not have been possible" (1959:508). Nor does *We Remember* admit to the failings of Church officials, including Pope Pius XI and Pope Pius XII, during the Nazi era.

These issues aside, Randolph Braham (1999) believes *We Remember* is a document that portends well for the future and has already led to more positive developments in Christian-Jewish relations. Some Christian theologians have even urged their Christian brethren to deemphasize if not repudiate the doctrine of supersession, that is, the belief that Christianity has superseded or supplanted Judaism (Berenbaum 2001). As Eva Fleischner asserts:

> Our willingness to confront the Christian past may bring us to a truer, more realistic, and humble understanding of the church: an institution divinely instituted, we believe, but rooted in human hearts

and minds, shaped by history, hence subject to all its vicissitudes; frequently denying the very love it claims to embody; yet somehow continuing to struggle to give witness to this love. I do not see how, in the face of the Holocaust, we can continue in our arrogant Christian claim to superiority. What is called for are compunction of heart and confession of our sinfulness, in knowledge that God's love and mercy are infinitely greater yet, and can indeed transform our hearts of stone into hearts of flesh. (2001:436)

John Pawlikowski adds that "the fundamental challenge of the Holocaust lies in our altered perception of the relationship between God and humanity" and of the capacity of religion to serve as the basis of morality (1997:102–3).[16]

Alice Eckardt, on the other hand, remains concerned that the Christian community is still "either largely ignorant . . . or disinterested" in the downside of its history and the challenge that history poses to Christians' claims to moral righteousness (1997:141).[17] Indeed, according to Eckardt, "some Christians are . . . incensed at any challenge to the absolute primacy of the Christian faith and its obligation to convert all other peoples. . . . [A]nti-Jewish preaching can still be heard from some clergy in all branches of the Church," and some continue to view the Holocaust as a punishment for Jews' rejection of Jesus Christ as their Lord and Savior (1997:141; Rubenstein and Roth 1987). In the United States, denominations such as the "Southern Baptist Convention, America's largest Protestant church, and the rapidly growing Assemblies of God church and other Pentecostal and charismatic groups," predict an ominous future for the Jews (Boyer 2001:5). In the prophetic doctrine of "dispensationalism" that is preached in these groups, the dawning of a divinely-inspired new age will be preceded by "an Armageddon battle between Jesus and the Antichrist" in which the persecution of Jews will be far worse than what they experienced during the Holocaust (p. 6). To be sure, religious Jews also believe in the primacy of their own teachings, although as a minority population in all nations except Israel, they are unable to use this belief as an ideological weapon to persecute others.[18]

Social Solidarity and the Humanity of Difference

E. J. Dionne observes that "[r]eligion can create community, and it can divide communities. It can lead to searing self-criticism, and it can promote a pompous self-satisfaction. It can encourage dissent and conformity, generosity and narrow-mindedness" (cited in Wolfe and Katznelson 2010:2). This truism returns us to the question of the civil sphere, and the solidarity criteria that defines who belongs and who does not belong to the group: Is it based on exclusionary or inclusionary criteria? According to Jeffrey Alexander, "The founders of [all] societies manifest distinctive racial, linguistic, religious, and geographical origins," and they establish their own "primordial qualities . . . as the highest criteria of humanity, as representing a higher competence for civil life. Only people of a certain race, who speak a certain language, who practice a certain religion, who make love in a certain manner, and who have immigrated from a certain part of the globe—only these very special persons actually possess what it takes to be members of [their] ideal society" (2006:405). At the same time, Alexander argues, in democratic societies infused with the values of the Enlightenment (see chapter 2), "members of core groups can be—and often have been—convinced that beneath these differences, and even because of them, there exists a common humanity worthy of civil respect," and under certain conditions social minorities can be incorporated into the core or mainstream of society (p. 410).[19]

Alexander identifies three modes of social incorporation— *assimilation, hyphenation,* and *multiculturalism*—and notes that even inclusionary forms of solidarity can be constructed in different ways. In assimilation, incorporation is permitted as long as marginal groups agree to "shed their polluted identities" (2006:422). This is accomplished by making a distinction between subordinate *persons* and subordinate *qualities.* The former are allowed into the civil sphere as long as the qualities that make them different are "left behind the door of private life" (p. 423). This was indeed the Enlightenment bargain offered to the Jews. Jewish persons were emancipated as long as Jewish qualities (including their religion) were abandoned, or at least kept private. It was the quality not the person that remained polluted, as we have also noted of attitudes toward Jews in the postwar Soviet-bloc nations.

In the hyphenated mode of incorporation, the outsider qualities of marginalized groups "are viewed in less one-sidedly negative ways; conceived as ethnic rather than foreign, they are more tolerated in [both] private and public life" (Alexander 2006:431). In postwar United States, for instance, we saw how the core elements of acceptable religious identity were expanded to include Jews, and the solidarity of acceptable religiosity was redefined in terms of the Judeo-Christian core.[20] Identifying oneself as Jewish American was no longer anathema. Still, like the assimilative mode of incorporation, hyphenation continues to distinguish between persons and qualities and is reluctant to redefine the core in terms of outsider qualities. One need only consider how far the United States is from incorporating Muslim Americans into the religious core of the nation to understand the limits of hyphenation.

According to Alexander, it is only with the multicultural mode of incorporation that the purification of both subordinated persons and qualities is allowed to take place. Diversity of the human condition is celebrated as the qualities that were once devalued—practicing a non-Christian religion, or being nonwhite, being gay or lesbian, being disabled, speaking a different language, and so forth—are "reinterpreted as representing [valued] variations on the sacred qualities of civility" (2006:452). Unlike assimilation and hyphenation, "multiculturalism dramatically expands the range of imagined life experience for core-group members. In doing so, it opens up the possibility not just for acceptance and toleration but for understanding and recognition" (p. 451).

Alexander understands multiculturalism as a "moral preference," (2006:451), a preference that is rejected by those who seek a more unified system of identity, most notably by religious fundamentalists (see Evans 2010). By valuing sharing and enlargement over separation and diminution, multiculturalism decenters and transforms the core. If there is a universal message to the Holocaust, as I think there must be, if we are to truly honor the memory of those who perished in this archetypal catastrophe of human history, we must look to a vision of society that accepts the common humanity in us all.[21] But along with Michael Ignatieff (2001), I understand this humanity not as a humanity of sameness but as a humanity of difference. A humanity of difference must first acknowledge, as Amartya Sen (2000) suggests, that members of socially defined groups are not a homogenous lot. Although they may share a common experience, they are themselves constituted by an internal diversity of attitudes, beliefs, and aspirations. In other words, they are unique human beings, and in that uniqueness they are like us.[22]

In this way, William Gamson (1995) also encourages us to situate the Holocaust and the phenomenon of genocide more generally in broader social context. While the particularity of the Jewish experience must never be forgotten, and we must be on guard against polemical excesses and political manipulations that trivialize and distort the memory of what happened to the European Jews, Gamson locates genocide at one end of a continuum that ranges from *active* exclusion to *indirect* exclusion.[23] To attempt to annihilate another group is of course an example of active exclusion, whereas indirect exclusion involves the indifference to others' suffering that is based on their difference and that denies them the opportunity to "make a difference" in the world. To have created a "Don't ask, don't tell" policy regarding gays and lesbians in the U.S. military, for example, is to have accepted the indirect exclusion of others by forcing them to remain silent and unseen (Belkin and Bateman 2003). Or to have failed to modify the physical structure and social organization of society to meet the needs of people with disabilities is to have excluded them from full participation in the life of a society (Wendell 1996).

Gamson does not in any way equate the experiences of active and indirect exclusion; the former is clearly worse than the latter, especially when "the agents are despots who control the repressive apparatus of the state" (1995:17). His point is that all other-creating processes share a common character based on "the creation of an 'other' who is outside" our universe of obligation to care for and about our fellow human beings (1995:17). We may adhere to the adage, "love thy neighbor as thyself," but rarely do we extend our universe of moral obligation to those who are not our neighbors. Rather we are like Cain, who when asked by God of his brother's whereabouts replied, "Am I my brother's keeper?" And we remain especially indifferent to the fate of those we perceive as different from ourselves (Fein 1979; Rubenstein and Roth 1987).

According to Ignatieff, "No other species differentiates itself in [such] individualized abundance," and it is our differences, "both fated and created," that constitute "the very basis of the consciousness of our individuality, and this consciousness, based in difference, is a constitutive element of what it is to be a human being" (2001:28). To make any one of these differences the object of active or indirect exclusion is to deny "the shared element that makes us what we are as a species." Thus Ignatieff wants us to "understand humanity, our common flesh and blood, as valuable to the degree that it allows us to elaborate the dignity and the honor that we give to our differences— and that this reality of difference . . . is our common inheritance, the shared integument that we might fight to defend whenever any of us is attacked for manifesting it."

A Final Word on Sociology and the Holocaust

In this book, I have attempted to offer a comprehensive synthesis, imbued with a sociological sensibility, of the social science literature on the Holocaust. My aim as well has been to bring the Holocaust into the disciplinary mainstream of sociology, countering the tendency to marginalize the genocide from conventional sociology courses and general concerns of sociological inquiry. Regrettably there remains, as Irving Louis Horowitz suggests, all too many sociologists who are "quite pleased to avoid confronting the issue of genocide as a critical test of the very worth of the social sciences," rather than bringing matters of life and death to the forefront of our concerns as scholars and teachers (2002:399).

The Problem of Holocaust Denial

There are a host of reasons to recommend a change in this state of affairs, not the least of which is to counter the continuing enterprise of Holocaust denial, an organized effort aimed at disputing some of the basic historical facts of the Holocaust. Holocaust deniers don the mantle of historical revisionism, claiming they are raising legitimate questions about the historical record. Revisionism entails refinement of existing knowledge about an historical event, not a denial of the event itself, which comes through an examination of new empirical evidence or a reexamination or reinterpretation of existing evidence.[24] Legitimate historical revisionism acknowledges a "certain body of irrefutable evidence" (Lipstadt 1993:21) or a "convergence of evidence" (Shermer and Grobman 2000:34) that suggests that an event—like the Black Plague, American slavery, or the Holocaust—did in fact occur.

Holocaust deniers, on the other hand, reject the entire foundation of historical evidence regarding the Holocaust, instead advancing these basic falsehoods: (1) "[The] gas chambers and crematoria in the concentration camps were used . . . [only] for delousing clothing and disposing of people who died of disease and overwork . . . [and] not for mass extermination"; (2) Only about 600,000 Jews rather than six million actually died; and (3) The deaths that occurred were "nothing more than an unfortunate byproduct of the vicissitudes of war" rather than a result of an intentional program of mass extermination (Shermer and Grobman 2000:3).

In the United States, deniers take advantage of their First Amendment right to freedom of speech and press.[25] The First Amendment protects everyone's right to question the existence of whatever they like—of God, of Elvis Presley's death, of O. J. Simpson's guilt or innocence, or of the Holocaust. Bradley Smith, for instance, gained considerable media attention in the 1990s when he took out full-page ads in U.S. college newspapers and widely distributed a pamphlet he wrote on "The Holocaust Controversy: The Case for Open Debate" (Anti-Defamation League 1993; Lipstadt 1993; Shermer and Grobman 2000). Smith, who is based in California, publishes a newsletter, "The Smith Report," which according to its subtitle is "America's only monthly Holocaust revisionist newsletter." He also operates a website, the Committee for Open Debate on the Holocaust (www.codoh.com). Smith appeals to students' natural skepticism and naïveté when he writes:

> No subject enrages campus Thought Police more than Holocaust Revisionism. We debate every other great historical issue as a matter of course, but influential pressure groups with private agendas have made the Holocaust story an exception. . . . Students should be encouraged to investigate the Holocaust story the same way they are encouraged to investigate every other historical event. (cited in Shermer and Grobman 2000:62)

Holocaust deniers strive for legitimacy by publishing professional-looking books and monographs, replete with footnotes and bibliographic citations. These writers are in fact very knowledgeable about particular aspects of the Holocaust and try to exploit ambiguities of historical detail, making it difficult for anyone who is not well-versed in these specifics to properly respond to their claims. The Institute for Historical Review (IHR), based in California, is arguably the most well-known denial organization. Founded by right-wing extremist Willis Carto in 1978, the IHR tries to present itself as a "think tank" of sorts, which holds pseudoacademic conferences and publishes pseudoacademic books and articles. The IHR first achieved notoriety in 1980 when it offered $50,000 to anyone who could prove that the Nazis had gassed Jews at Auschwitz. Holocaust survivor Mel Mermelstein accepted the challenge and provided the IHR with evidence in the form of his own and other survivors' testimony. When the IHR refused to pay him the money, Mermelstein filed a civil lawsuit. The judge ruled in favor of Mermelstein, noting that the court had taken "judicial notice" that Jews had been gassed at Auschwitz (cited in Shermer and Grobman 2000:43).

In 2000, Holocaust denial was on trial again in the British libel case of *David Irving v. Penguin Books Ltd. and Deborah Lipstadt.*

David Irving, best-selling author of some thirty popular history books, is perhaps the most knowledgeable and sophisticated Holocaust denier. Although he is British, he has forged ties with Holocaust deniers throughout Europe and North America, including the IHR. He is a self-described "moderate fascist" who has a great fondness for Germany (cited in Lipstadt 1993:161). Irving has written that Great Britain made a mistake in going to war against Germany and that the Allies and Germany committed comparable atrocities. In his 1977 book *Hitler's War*, he portrayed Hitler as a rather harried executive who was unaware of the campaign against the Jews that some of his minions had undertaken in the East. In the late 1980s he began claiming that gas chambers were never used for extermination (Anti-Defamation League 1993; Shermer and Grobman 2000).

In her book *Denying the Holocaust*, historian Deborah Lipstadt (1993) had accused Irving of being a Holocaust denier, as well as being a bigot and a deliberate falsifier of evidence. Irving chose to sue Lipstadt and Penguin Books (the publisher of her book in the United Kingdom) in Britain rather than the United States because libel laws in that country place the burden of proof on defendants to show that they did *not* libel plaintiffs. Lipstadt's side was required to demonstrate that the evidence that Irving was a denier was "so clear-cut that only a willful misreading or conscious distortion of the facts could account for [his] positions" (Guttenplan 2000:47). During the trial the defense amassed piles of Nazi documents and submitted lengthy reports by experts, including Christopher Browning, who when given an opportunity to testify in court "quickly made rubble of Irving's arguments" (Greif 2000:36). The judge ruled in favor of the defense, a testimony to the value of social science research.

Preventing and Researching Genocide

Arguably the greatest concern of social science is to contribute, in whatever way it can, to the prevention of genocide. This literature typically aims at clarifying the nature of genocide, as distinct from other atrocities and forms of mass murder, so that governments in a position to act, like the United States, can recognize it in a timely manner and take action to prevent it from coming to full fruition. Hence one finds books on this subject concluding with a call for action, which include efforts, in the spirit of Lemkin, to clearly delineate the atrocities and giving them a name—genocide—that creates a moral imperative for otherwise bystander governments to intervene and mitigate bystander collusion with the "standard form of genocide denial by perpetrators"—that what is occurring is "counter-insurgency warfare" (Shaw 2007:171). Others encourage the development of mechanisms of genocidal monitoring and early detection that can be used to guide policymakers, while at the same time admitting that not all situations are amenable to direct intervention (Fein 1993; Goldhagen 2009; Horowitz 2002; Power 2002).

Following Horowitz (2002), among others, I take genocide to entail the structural and systematic mass killing undertaken by a bureaucratic (typically totalitarian) state apparatus against a group of innocent people (see chapter 1). In the concluding pages of *Taking Lives: Genocide and State Power*, Horowitz identifies several of "the highest and thorniest issues that remain to be examined in genocide studies," which are worth mentioning by way of conclusion here as well (2002:403). These include, but are not limited to: (1) an examination of the relationship between genocide, on the one hand, and civil strife, ethnic conflict, and warfare, on the other hand; (2) the need for a more exacting specification of the "distinction between major genocides" and those that can legitimately be described as "Holocausts"[26]; (3) explaining why some totalitarian regimes, such as Hitler's Germany, commit genocides, while other regimes, such as Mussolini's Italy, do not (see chapter 1); (4) ascertaining the degree to which international law is "an operational reality or a fiction" when it comes to responding to genocides; and (5) evaluating the acceptable means of outside intervention for terminating genocidal regimes—for instance, "can the bombing and decimation of an 'evil' regime be viewed as a good, without regard to the damage inflicted on the innocents of the offender nation?" (p. 403).

That this research agenda will be multidisciplinary should go without saying, but sociology, as a disciplinary endeavor, cannot afford to be left behind. Whether the lessons to be learned from such scholarship are morally clear or ambiguous, we would all do well to heed Brzezinski's admonition about whether Holocaust remembrance is a "proclamation of a moral imperative" or a "pompous declaration of hypocrisy." Whatever the answer to the questions we have thus raised, one thing is certain, if anything is to be learned from the systematic and rigorous contemplation of an historical event like the Holocaust, that knowledge would benefit from a full engagement with all of its complexities and from all angles of inquiry. Sociology can benefit from historical studies; historical studies can benefit from sociology. Silence is no longer an option.

Notes

1. The GC "did not require the extermination of an entire group, only acts committed with the intent to destroy a substantial part. If the perpetrator did not target a national, ethnic, or religious group *as such*, then killings would constitute mass homicide, not genocide" (Power 2002:57). For a review of conceptual-definitional issues, see Chalk and Jonassohn (1990), Fein (1993), Horowitz (2002), and Shaw (2007). On the distinction between crimes against humanity and genocide, see Rothe and Mullins (2007).

2. "By 1953, the Eisenhower administration moved to avoid any loss of presidential authority by essentially making a negative commitment to human rights treaties" (Ronayne 2001:24). The American Bar Association, which initially opposed ratification, changed its position in 1976.

3. One of the GCs most ardent supporters was Senator William Proxmire, a Democrat from Wisconsin. "On January 11, 1967, Proxmire stood up on the Senate floor to deliver his first genocide speech. He casually announced his intention to begin a campaign that would not cease until the United States had ratified the pact" (Power 2002:79). As he said: "The Senate's failure to act has become a national shame. . . . I serve notice today that from now on I intend to speak day after day in this body to remind the Senate of our failure to act and of the necessity for prompt action" (quoted in Power 2002:79). Over the next nineteen years, Proxmire made 3,211 speeches in which he offered a "daily soliloquy to rebut common American misperceptions" (p. 83). In one speech he opined: "The true opponents to ratification . . . are not groups or individuals. They are the most lethal pair of foes for human rights everywhere in the world—ignorance and indifference" (quoted on p. 84).

4. Added to the objections was the view that the GC was anti-Christian. A legislative aid of the Liberty Lobby, E. Stanley Rittenhouse, announced that under the treaty "every missionary, both domestic and foreign, who attempted to convert anyone to Christianity would be guilty of attempting to destroy one's culture" (quoted in Ronayne 2001:30). He added: "Another case in point is the Jewish community. Since many of those within the Jewish and Zionist community hate Christianity and Christians, and since many of these folks consider as 'traitors' Hebrews who recognize Christ as the Messiah, any Christian who attempts to convert a Jew would be guilty of genocide under this treaty" (quoted in Ronayne 2001:31).

5. Pol Pot eluded capture until 1997, when he was tried and sentenced to "life imprisonment" under house arrest. He died in 1998.

6. On the role of the Serbian Orthodox Church in fomenting hostility, see Doubt (2007).

7. Muslim mosques and historic architecture were destroyed as well.

8. Under the leadership of the United States, the 1995 Dayton Peace Accords ended the three-and-a-half-year long war in Bosnia, although conflict later broke out in Kosovo. Milosevic was indicted by the UN International Court for crimes against humanity and arrested in 2001. He died while under detention at a UN facility in 2006.

9. The conflict spilled over into neighboring Burundi as well.

10. One exception was Paul Rusesabagina, a Rwandan hotel operator whose efforts to save more than a thousand Tutsi refugees were portrayed in the film *Hotel Rwanda*.

11. The peace-keeping mission that went awry in Somalia in 1993, which killed eighteen US troops and wounded seventy-three others, made the Clinton administration more cautious about intervening in Rwanda (Ronayne 2001).

12. In 1994, the UN established an international criminal tribunal to prosecute the perpetrators of the genocide, most notably, Rwanda mayor Jean-Paul Akayesu and former Prime Minister Jean Kambanda, who were convicted and given life sentences.

13. In 2003, the government of Sudan, collaborating with state-supported *Janjaweed* militias, launched a genocidal campaign against the six million people in the Darfur region of western Sudan. More than 400,000 people were killed (Hagan and Rymond-Richmond 2009; Rothe and Mullins 2007; Shaw 2007). In 2010, the International Criminal Court issued an arrest warrant for Omar Hassan al-Bashir, the president of Sudan, on multiple counts of genocide. At the time of this writing, he has yet to be brought to justice (Lynch and Hamilton 2010).

14. In 1990, the United Church of Christ's Theological Panel released a statement entitled "Message to the Churches," which acknowledged that the "Holocaust has sent Christians back to their texts and traditions to re-examine their theology and to ask about their own complicity in the anti-Semitism that gave rise to the horror" (cited in Eckardt 1997:142).

15. In addition to opening diplomatic ties between the Vatican and Israel in 1994, Pope John Paul II hosted a concert at the Vatican that commemorated the victims of the Holocaust (Braham 1999). But recall, on the other hand, the Pope's role in the controversy over the symbolic legacy of Auschwitz (see chapter 7).

16. Paul van Buren advances a more benevolent Christian theology that consists of a loving God who created us as free and responsible beings; thus God is unable to intervene in our lives "without ceasing to be the God of love and freedom," leaving Him with no choice but "to sit still and . . . suffer in agony . . . [and] in solidarity with His people" (1980:116, 119). This formulation, however, deviates from traditional Scripture, which postulates that "God's divine power far exceeds anything that humans can do. God is not bound by human freedom unless he chooses to be. . . . God is the One who ultimately sets the boundaries in which we live and move and have our being," and hence He is responsible for worldly events (Rubenstein and Roth 1987:298–99). Still another Christian view attributes evil in the world to the work of the devil; but if God cannot stop the devil, he is not all powerful (Jonas 2001).

17. German-Christian clergy have also drawn complaints over their willingness to offer mitigating testimony on behalf of accused Nazi war criminals in postwar legal proceedings (Buscher and Phayer 1988; Marcuse 2001; Phayer 2000; Webster 2001).

18. Like Christians, Jewish believers have faced a theological dilemma from the Holocaust. Richard Rubenstein and John Roth (1987) believe there is no escaping the conclusion that biblical Judaism purports God to be the ultimate author of the Jewish people's fate and hence of their misfortune. In traditional Jewish theology, God is believed to have entered into a special covenant with the Jews at the time He delivered the Ten Commandments to Moses (see chapter 2). At the same time, God is said to have warned of dire consequences if his chosen people failed to obey divine law. Some Orthodox Jews even hold non-Orthodox Jews responsible for their own misery, believing that the latter have erred in their ways and beliefs (Bauer 2001).

In this study of Holocaust survivors, Reeve Robert Brenner (1980) found that about 70 percent believed in God prior to the Holocaust. Among the prewar believers in Brenner's study, only a third remained unwavering in their faith, while about a tenth lost faith in God's existence altogether. Importantly, most of the believers rejected the idea that "those who perished in the Holocaust were being punished by God for their own sinfulness" or that God may have had some other purpose such as a test of their faith or a desire to "purify moral character through suffering" (Rubenstein and Roth 1987:295). Thus there was little agreement among Brenner's subjects with the traditional Jewish belief in a deity who actively intervenes in the affairs of humanity and who punishes those who ignore His commandments. Rather, most of the religiously inclined survivors believed in a God who granted people freedom of action and responsibility for their own actions. According to this view, as expressed by some Jewish theologians, God "created an imperfect world awaiting perfection. If we are to be full partners with God in perfecting the world's shortcomings, God must, of necessity, hide Himself . . . so that we can bring about our own redemption" (Hass 1995:145; Katz 2001). As Arthur Cohen puts it, "God is not the strategist of our particularities or our historical condition, but rather the mystery . . . [and] hope of our futurity" (1981:97).

Yehuda Bauer (2001) asks, however, if God has hidden Himself, is he not a callous God who chose to be absent and who could have stopped the Holocaust if He wanted? Hasn't He thus become irrelevant to humanity's affairs? Rabbi Irving Greenberg (1990) suggests that perhaps God is no longer all-powerful, even if He once was, and that He now requires human cooperation to redress the ills of the world. Although "God is no longer in a position to command, . . . the Jewish people are so in love with the dream of redemption that [they have] volunteered to carry out the mission" (cited in Berenbaum 2001:628).

Other Jewish theologians try to skirt the issue of God's responsibility for the Holocaust by claiming that God's ways are mysterious and beyond the realm of human comprehension. Or they assert that the Holocaust, like the flood of Noah's time, was an act of creative destruction designed to bring the Jews and the world into a new and better age. Still others argue that the Holocaust challenges Jews to resist the logic of destruction represented by the genocide and engage in acts of resistance and restoration that mend or restore humanity, what in the Jewish tradition is known as *Tikkun* (Bauer 2001; Berenbaum 2001; Maybaum 1965; Rubenstein and Roth 1987).

19. Social movements are typically the means by which core groups are convinced, cajoled, or coerced to accommodate the demands of marginal groups (Alexander 2006).

20. See chapter 8, note 19.

21. I derive this view, in part, from my Reform Jewish upbringing. The *Haggadah* that we read during our Passover Seders contained this passage, which had a marked influence on me: "We gather year after year, to retell this ancient story. For in reality, it is not ancient, but eternal in its message. . . . The struggle for freedom is a continuous struggle. . . . Each age uncovers a formerly unrecognized servitude, requiring new liberation to set man's soul free. . . . In every age, some new freedom is won and established, adding to the advancement of human happiness and security. . . . [T]he concept of freedom grows broader, widening the horizon of finer and nobler living. Each generation is duty-bound to contribute to this growth, else mankind's ideals become stagnant and stationary. The events in Egypt were but the beginning of a force in history which will forever continue" (cited in Berger 2011:202).

22. Sen (2000) notes that it is a natural and potentially benign part of social development to identify with some people and not others. This process is in fact integral to the creation of a subjective sense of self. A problem arises, however, when others become the object of our experience in a way that involves typifying them as persons endowed with negative symbolic meaning, as people to be feared and rejected, even removed from our midst. Sen does not think that to reverse the other-creating process of exclusion it is necessary that we identify our subjectivity with all people. Rather, we merely need to become capable of tolerating others and considering their interests and claims regardless of whether we can, as some say, "feel their pain."

23. Daniel Goldhagen (2009) takes a different tact, emphasizing that genocide is constituted by an "eliminationist" ideology that is of an entirely different order than other forms of exclusion (see also chapter 1, note 19). Conservative pundit George Will takes a different tact, too, viewing the common character of mass atrocities not in exclusionary practices but in the "disorder" that arises in the absence of "social restraints" (2001:68).

24. The original notion of historical revisionism (in its legitimate guise) is credited to the historian William Appleman Williams, who reinterpreted dominant views regarding U.S. foreign policy, particularly as it relates to the Cold War (Lipstadt 1993).

25. In many other countries around the world—including the democratic nations of Australia, Austria, Belgium, Canada, France, Germany, Israel, Italy, New Zealand, Sweden, and Switzerland—the legal system allows for the suppression of speech and printed material that denies the Holocaust (Shermer and Grobman 2000). Most Holocaust scholars in the United States do not favor legal restraints on Holocaust denial, but neither do they think, as some suggest, that the deniers should simply be ignored (Lipstadt 1993; Shermer and Grobman 2000).

26. See chapter 1, note 1.

References

Abel, Theodore. [1938] 1986. *Why Hitler Came to Power*. Cambridge, MA: Harvard University Press.

———. 1951. "The Sociology of Concentration Camps." *Social Forces* 30:150–55.

Abraham, David. 1981. *The Collapse of the Weimar Republic: Political Economy and Crises*. Princeton, NJ: Princeton University Press.

Adam, Uwe. 1989. "The Gas Chambers." In *Unanswered Questions: Nazi Germany and the Genocide of the Jews*, ed. Francois Furet. New York: Schocken.

———. 1990. "Anti-Jewish Legislation." In *Encyclopedia of the Holocaust*, vol. 1, ed. Israel Gutman. New York: Macmillan.

Adler, H. G. 1958. "Ideas Toward a Sociology of the Concentration Camp." *American Journal of Sociology* 63:513–22.

Alexander, Edward. 1994. *The Holocaust and the War of Ideas*. New Brunswick, NJ: Transaction.

Alexander, Jeffrey C. 1984. "Social-Structural Analysis: Some Notes on Its History and Prospects." *Sociological Quarterly* 25:5–26.

———. 1989. *Structure and Meaning: Relinking Classical Sociology*. New York: Columbia University Press.

———. 2004. "On the Social Construction of Moral Universals: The 'Holocaust' from War Crime to Trauma Drama." In Jeffrey C. Alexander, et al., *Cultural Trauma and Collective Identity*. Berkeley, CA: University of California Press.

———. 2006. *The Civil Sphere*. Oxford: Oxford University Press.

Allen, William Sheriden. 1984. *The Nazi Seizure of Power: The Experience of a Single German Town, 1922–1943*. New York: Watts Franklin.

Amato, Joseph A. 1990. *Victims and Values: A History and a Theory of Suffering*. New York: Greenwood Press.

Anheier, Helmut K., and Friedhelm Neidhardt. 1998. "The Nazi Party and Its Capital: An Analysis of NSDAP Membership in Munich, 1925–1930." *American Behavioral Scientist* 41:1219–36.

Anheier, Helmut K., Friedhelm Neidhardt, and Wolfgang Vortkamp. 1998. "Movement Cycles and the Nazi Party: Activities of the Munich NSDAP, 1925–1930." *American Behavioral Scientist* 41:1262–81.

Anti-Defamation League. 1993. *Hitler's Apologists: The Anti-Semitic Propaganda of Holocaust "Revisionism."* New York: Anti-Defamation League.

Arad, Gulie Ne'eman, ed. 1995. "Israeli Historiography Revisited." Special issue of *History and Memory* 7(1):5–172.

Arad, Yitzhak. 1987. *Operation Reinhard Death Camps: Belzec, Sobibor, Treblinka*. Bloomington, IN: Indiana University Press.

241

Arendt, Hannah. 1951. *The Origins of Totalitarianism*. New York: Harcourt, Brace & World.

———. 1963. *Eichmann in Jerusalem: A Report on the Banality of Evil*. New York: Viking Press.

Aronson, Shlomo. 1990. "Heydrich, Reinhard." In *Encyclopedia of the Holocaust*, vol. 2, ed. Israel Gutman. New York: Macmillan.

Aronson, Shlomo, and Peter Longerich. 2001. "Final Solution: Preparation and Implementation." In *The Holocaust Encyclopedia*, ed. Walter Laqueur. New Haven, CT: Yale University Press.

Art, Robert. 1993. "United Nations." *World Book Encyclopedia*. Chicago, IL: World Book.

Askenasy, Hans. 1978. *Are We All Nazis?* Secaucus, NJ: Lyle Stuart.

Auerbach, Jerold. 1990. *Rabbis and Lawyers: The Journey from Torah to Constitution*. Bloomington, IN: Indiana University Press.

Augstein, Rudolf. 1998. "The Sociologist as Hanging Judge." In *Unwilling Germans? The Goldhagen Debate*, ed. Robert R. Shandley. Minneapolis, MN: University of Minnesota Press.

Ausubel, Nathan. 1964. *The Jewish Book of Knowledge*. New York: Crown.

Avisar, Ilan. 1997. "Holocaust Movies and the Politics of Collective Memory." In *Spielberg's Holocaust: Critical Perspectives on* Schindler's List, ed. Yosefa Loshitsky. Bloomington, IN: Indiana University Press.

Aviv, Daryn, and David Shneer. 2007. "Traveling Jews, Creating Memory: Eastern Europe, Israel, and the Diaspora Business." In *Sociology Confronts the Holocaust: Memories and Identities in Jewish Diasporas*, eds. Judith M. Gerson and Diane Wolf. Durham, NC: Duke University Press.

Baehr, Peter. 2002. "Identifying the Unprecedented: Hannah Arendt, Totalitarianism, and the Critique of Sociology." *American Sociological Review* 67:804–31.

Baldwin, James. [1967] 1994. "Negroes are Anti-Semitic Because They're Anti-White." In *Blacks and Jews: Alliances and Arguments*, ed. Paul Berman. New York: Delta.

Baldwin, Peter, ed. 1990. *Reworking the Past: Hitler, the Holocaust, and the Historians' Debate*. Boston, MA: Beacon Press.

Bankier, David. 1990a. "Four-Year Plan." In *Encyclopedia of the Holocaust*, ed. Israel Gutman. New York: Macmillan.

———. 1990b. "Mischlinge." In *Encyclopedia of the Holocaust*, ed. Israel Gutman. New York: Macmillan.

———. 1992. *The Germans and the Final Solution*. New York: Oxford University Press.

Bannister, Robert. 1992. "Principle, Politics, Profession: American Sociologists and Fascism." In *Sociology Responds to Fascism*, eds. Stephen P. Turner and Dirk Käsler. New York: Routledge.

Barkai, Avraham. 1989. *From Boycott to Annihilation*. Hanover, MA: University Press of New England.

Baron, Lawrence. 1988. "The Historical Context of Rescue." In Samuel P. Oliner and Pearl M. Oliner, *The Altruistic Personality*. New York: Free Press.

———. 1992. "The Dutchness of Dutch Rescuers: The National Dimension of Altruism." In *Embracing the Other: Philosophical, Psychological, and Historical Perspectives on Altruism*, eds. Pearl M. Oliner, et al. New York: New York University Press.

Bartov, Omer. 1992. *Hitler's Army: Soldiers, Nazis, and War in the Third Reich.* New York: Oxford University Press.

——. 1997a. "German Soldiers and the Holocaust: Historiography, Research and Implications." *History and Memory* 9:162–88.

——. 1997b. "Spielberg's Oskar: Hollywood Tries Evil." In *Spielberg's Holocaust: Critical Perspectives on* Schindler's List, ed. Yosefa Loshitsky. Bloomington, IN: Indiana University Press.

Bartrop, Paul R. 2000. *Surviving the Camps: Unity in Adversity During the Holocaust.* Lanham, MD: University Press of America.

Batson, C. Daniel. 1991. *The Altruism Question: Toward a Social-Psychological Answer.* Hillsdale, NJ: Lawrence Erlbaum.

Bauer, Yehuda. 1987. "On the Place of the Holocaust in History." *Holocaust and Genocide Studies* 2:209–20.

——. 1989a. "Is the Holocaust Explicable?" *Holocaust and Genocide Studies* 5:145–55.

——. 1989b. "Jewish Resistance and Passivity in the Face of the Holocaust." In *Unanswered Questions: Nazi Germany and the Genocide of the Jews,* ed. Francois Furet. New York: Schocken.

——. 1991. "Who was Responsible and When? Some Well-Known Documents Revisited." *Holocaust and Genocide Studies* 6:129–49.

——. 1994. *Jews for Sale? Nazi-Jewish Negotiations, 1933–1945.* New Haven, CT: Yale University Press.

——. 2001. *Rethinking the Holocaust.* New Haven, CT: Yale University Press.

Bauman, Zygmunt. 1988. "On Immoral Reason and Illogical Morality." *POLIN: A Journal of Polish-Jewish Studies* 3:294–301.

——. 1989. *Modernity and the Holocaust.* Ithaca, NY: Cornell University Press.

——. 2004. "Categorial Murder, Or: How to Remember the Holocaust." In *Re-Representing the Shoah for the Twenty-First Century,* ed. Ronit Lentin. United Kingdom: Berghan.

Belkin, Aaron, and Geoffrey Bateman, ed. 2003. *Don't Ask, Don't Tell: Debating the Gay Ban in the Military.* Boulder, CO: Lynne Rienner.

Bell-Fialkoff, Andrew. 1999. *Ethnic Cleansing.* New York: St. Martin's Griffin.

Bellah, Robert, Richard Madsen, William M. Sullivan, Ann Swidler, and Steven M. Tipton. 1985. *Habits of the Heart: Individualism and Commitment in American Life.* Berkeley, CA: University of California Press.

Benner, Patricia, Ethel Roskies, and Richard S. Lazarus. 1980. "Stress and Coping Under Extreme Conditions." In *Survivors, Victims, and Perpetrators: Essays on the Nazi Holocaust,* ed. Joel E. Dimsdale. New York: Hemisphere.

Berbrier, Mitch. 2000. "Ethnicity in the Making: Ethnicity Work, the Ethnicity Industry, and a Constructionist Framework for Research." In *Perspectives on Social Problems,* vol. 12, eds. James A. Holstein and Gale Miller. Stamford, CT: JAI Press.

Berenbaum, Michael. 1987. "The Americanization of the Holocaust." In *Bitburg and Beyond: Encounters in American, German, and Jewish History,* ed. Ilya Levkov. New York: Sure Sellers.

—— ed. 1990. *A Mosaic of Victims; Non-Jews Persecuted and Murdered by the Nazis.* New York: New York University Press.

———. 1993. *The World Must Know: The History of the Holocaust as Told in the United States Holocaust Memorial Museum.* Boston, MA: Little, Brown.

———. 2001. "Theological and Philosophical Responses." In *The Holocaust Encyclopedia,* ed. Walter Laqueur. New Haven, CT: Yale University Press.

Bergen, Doris L. 1998. "The Ecclesiastical Final Solution: The German Christian Movement and the Anti-Jewish Church." In *The Holocaust and History: The Known, the Unknown, and the Disputed,* eds. Michael Berenbaum and Abraham J. Peck. Bloomington, IN: Indiana University Press.

Berger, Ronald J. 1995. *Constructing a Collective Memory of the Holocaust: A Life History of Two Brothers' Survival.* Boulder: University Press of Colorado.

———. 2002. *Fathoming the Holocaust: A Social Problems Approach.* New York: Aldine de Gruyter.

———. 2003. "It Ain't Necessarily So: The Politics of Memory and the Bystander Narrative in the U.S. Holocaust Memorial Museum." *Humanity and Society* 27:6–29.

———. 2011. *Surviving the Holocaust: A Life Course Perspective.* New York: Routledge.

Berger, Ronald J., Charles S. Green, III, and Kirsten E. Krieser. 1998. "Altruism Amidst the Holocaust: An Integrated Social Theory." *Perspectives on Social Problems,* vol. 10, eds. James A. Holstein and Gale Miller. Stamford, CT: JAI Press.

Berman, Paul, ed. 1994. *Blacks and Jews: Alliances and Arguments.* New York: Delta.

Bernston, Marit A., and Brian Ault. 1998. "Gender and Nazism: Women as Joiners of the Pre-1933 Nazi Party." *American Behavioral Scientist* 41:1193–218.

Bershtel, Sara, and Allen Graubard. 1992. *Saving Remnants: Feeling Jewish in America.* Berkeley, CA: University of California Press.

Bettelheim, Bruno. 1960. *The Informed Heart.* Glencoe, IL: Free Press.

Billstein, Reinhold, Karola Fings, Anita Kugler, and Nicholas Levis. 2001. *Working for the Enemy: Ford, General Motors, and Forced Labor in Germany During the Second World War.* New York: Berghahn.

Biondich, Mark. 1999. *Stjepan Radic: The Croatian Party, and the Politics of Mass Mobilization.* Toronto: University of Toronto Press.

Bivin, David. 2004. "Was Jesus a Rabbi?" *Jerusalem Perspective Online,* January 1, retrieved from http://www.jerusalemperspective.com.

Black, Edwin. 2001. *IBM and the Holocaust: The Strategic Alliance Between Nazi Germany and America's Most Powerful Corporation.* New York: Crown.

———. 2009. *Nazi Nexus: America's Corporate Connections to Hitler's Holocaust.* Washington, DC: Dialog Press.

Bloch, Herbert A. 1947. "The Personality of Inmates in Concentration Camps." *American Journal of Sociology* 52:335–41.

Błonski, Jan. [1987] 1990. "The Poor Poles Look at the Ghetto." In *My Brother's Keeper? Recent Polish Debates on the Holocaust,* ed. Antony Polonsky. London: Routledge.

Bloom, Harold. 2005. *Jesus and Yahweh: Names of the Divine.* New York: Riverhead Books.

Bloxham, Donald. 2009. *The Final Solution: A Genocide.* New York: Oxford University Press.

Bloxham, Donald, and Tony Kushner. 2005. *The Holocaust: Critical Approaches.* Manchester, UK: Manchester University Press.

Blumenthal, Max. 2009. *Republican Gomorrah: Inside the Movement that Shattered the Party.* New York: Nation Books.

Bock, Gisela. 1983. "Racism and Sexism in Nazi Germany: Motherhood, Compulsory Sterilization, and the State." *Signs: Journal of Women in Culture and Society* 8:400–21.

Bodemann, Y. Michal, ed. 1996. *Jews, Germany, Memory: Reconstructions of Jewish Life in Germany.* Ann Arbor, MI: University of Michigan Press.

Bondy, Ruth. 2001. "Thereisienstadt." In *The Holocaust Encyclopedia*, ed. Walter Laqueur. New Haven, CT: Yale University Press.

Botwinick, Rita Steinhardt. 2001. *A History of the Holocaust: From Ideology to Annihilation*, 2nd ed. Upper Saddle River, NJ: Prentice-Hall.

Botz, Gerhard, ed. 1991. *I Want to Speak: The Tragedy and Banality of Survival in Terezin and Auschwitz*, by Margareta Glas-Larsson. Riverside, CA: Ariadne Press.

Bower, Tom. 1997. *Nazi Gold: The Full Story of the Fifty-Year Swiss-Nazi Conspiracy to Steal Billions from Europe's Jews and Holocaust Survivors.* New York: HarperCollins.

Boyer, Paul. 2001. "Rapturous Tidings: The Holocaust, Bible Prophecy Belief, and Conservative American Christianity." *Dimensions: A Journal of Holocaust Studies* 15:3–8.

Braddock, David L., and Susan L. Parish. 2001. "An Institutional History of Disability." In *Handbook of Disability Studies*, eds. Gary L. Albrecht, Katherine D. Seelman, and Michael Bury. Thousand Oaks, CA: Sage.

Brady, Robert A. 1937. *The Spirit and Structure of German Fascism.* London: Gollancz.

Braham, Randolph L. 1989. "The Jewish Councils: An Overview." In *Unanswered Questions: Nazi Germany and the Genocide of the Jews*, ed. Francois Furet. New York: Schocken.

———. 1999. "Remembering and Forgetting: The Vatican, the German Catholic Hierarchy, and the Holocaust." *Holocaust and Genocide Studies* 13:222–51.

Breitman, Richard. 1991. *The Architect of Genocide: Himmler and the Final Solution.* Hanover, NH: Brandeis University Press.

———. 1998. *Official Secrets: What the Nazis Planned, What the British and Americans Knew.* New York: Hill and Wang.

Breitman, Richard, and Alan M. Kraut. 1987. *American Refugee Policy and European Jewry, 1933–1945.* Bloomington, IN: Indiana University Press.

Brenner, Reeve Robert. 1980. *The Faith and Doubt of Holocaust Survivors.* New York: Free Press.

Bresheeth, Haim. 1997. "The Great Taboo Broken: Reflections on the Israeli Reception of *Schindler's List*." In *Spielberg's Holocaust: Critical Perspectives on* Schindler's List, ed. Yosefa Loshitzky. Bloomington, IN: Indiana University Press.

Brodkin, Karen. 1998. *How Jews Became White Folks and What That Says about Race in America.* New Brunswick, NJ: Rutgers University Press.

Browning, Christopher R. 1990a. "Deportations." In *Encyclopedia of the Holocaust*, vol. 1, ed. Israel Gutman. New York: Macmillan.

———. 1990b. "Final Solution." In *Encyclopedia of the Holocaust*, vol. 2, ed. Israel Gutman. New York: Macmillan.

———. 1990c. "Nisko and Lublin Plan." In *Encyclopedia of the Holocaust*, vol. 3, ed. Israel Gutman. New York: Macmillan.

———. 1992. *Ordinary Men: Reserve Police Battalion 101 and the Final Solution in Poland.* New York: Harper Perennial.

———. 1996. "A Final Hitler Decision for the 'Final Solution'? The Riegner Telegram Reconsidered." *Holocaust and Genocide Studies* 10:3–10.

———. 1998. "Afterword." *Ordinary Men: Reserve Police Battalion 101 and the Final Solution.* New York: Oxford University Press.

———. 2000. *Nazi Policy, Jewish Workers, German Killers.* Cambridge, UK: Cambridge University Press.

———. 2004. *The Origins of the Final Solution: The Evolution of Nazi Jewish Policy September 1939–March 1942.* London: William Heinemann.

———. 2010. *Remembering Survival: Inside a Nazi Slave-Labor Camp.* New York: Norton.

Brumlik, Micha. 1996. "The Situation of Jews in Today's Germany." In *Jews, Germany, Memory: Reconstructions of Jewish Life in Germany*, ed. Y. Michal Bodemann. Ann Arbor, MI: University of Michigan Press.

Brunner, José. 1997. "Pride and Memory: Nationalism, Narcissism and the Historians' Debates in Germany and Israel." *History and Memory* 9:256–300.

Brustein, William. 1996. *The Logic of Evil: The Social Origins of the Nazi Party, 1925–1933.* New Haven, CT: Yale University Press.

———. 1998. "The Nazi Party and the German New Middle Class, 1925–1933." *American Behavioral Scientist* 41:1237–61.

Burg, Avraham. 2008. *The Holocaust is Over, We Must Rise from the Ashes.* New York: Palgrave.

Burleigh, Michael, and Wolfgang Wipperman. 1991. *The Racial State: Germany, 1933–1945.* New York: Cambridge University Press.

Buscher, Frank, and Michael Phayer. 1988. "German Catholic Bishops and the Holocaust, 1940–1953." *German Studies Review* 11:463–85.

Buszko, Jozef. 1990. "Auschwitz." In *Encyclopedia of the Holocaust*, vol. 1, ed. Israel Gutman. New York: Macmillan.

Calhoun, Craig, ed. 2007. *Sociology in America: A History.* Chicago, IL: University of Chicago Press.

Caplan, Sophie. 1993. "Polish and German Anti-Semitism." In *Why Germany? National Socialist Anti-Semitism and the European Context*, ed. John Milfull. Oxford: Berg.

Cargas, Harry J. 1986. "An Interview with Elie Wiesel." *Holocaust and Genocide Studies* 1:5–10.

Carpi, Daniel. 2001. "Italy." In *The Holocaust Encyclopedia*, ed. Walter Laqueur. New Haven, CT: Yale University Press.

Carter, Jimmy. 2006. *Palestine: Peace Not Apartheid.* New York: Simon and Schuster.

Chalk, Frank, and Kurt Jonassohn, eds. 1990. *The History and Sociology of Genocide: Analyses and Case Studies.* New Haven, CT: Yale University Press.

Chesnoff, Richard Z. 1999. *Pack of Thieves: How Hitler and Europe Plundered the Jews and Committed the Greatest Theft in History.* New York: Doubleday.

Clendinnen, Inga. 1999. *Reading the Holocaust*. Cambridge, UK: Cambridge University Press.

Cochavi, Yehoyakim. 1990. "Zentralstelle für Judische Auswanderung." In *Encyclopedia of the Holocaust*, vol. 4, ed. Israel Gutman. New York: Macmillan.

Cohen, Arthur. 1981. *The Tremendum: A Theological Interpretation of the Holocaust*. New York: Crossroad.

Cohen, Elie A. 1953. *Human Behavior in the Concentration Camp*. Westport, CT: Greenwood Press.

Cohen, Nava. 1990. "Medical Experiments." In *Encyclopedia of the Holocaust*, vol. 3, ed. Israel Gutman. New York: Macmillan.

Cohn, Norman. 1967. *Warrant for Genocide: The Myth of the Jewish World Conspiracy and the Protocols of the Elders of Zion*. New York: Harper & Row.

Cole, Tim. 1999. *Selling the Holocaust*. New York: Routledge.

Cooper, Abraham. 1996/1997. "Who Profited from the Nazi Genocide." *Response* 17(3):2–4.

———. 1998. "Switzerland's Unwanted Guests." *Response* 19(1):2.

Cooper, John. 2008. *Raphael Lemkin and the Struggle for the Genocide Convention*. New York: Palgrave Macmillan.

Corni, Gustavo. 2003. *Hitler's Ghettos: Voices from a Beleaguered Society 1934–1944*. London: Arnold.

Cornwell, John. 1999. *Hitler's Pope: The Secret History of Pius XII*. New York: Viking.

Crader, Kelly W., and William W. Wentworth. 1984. "A Structural Reinterpretation of Responsibility, Risk and Helping in Small Collectives of Children." *American Sociological Review* 49:611–19.

Davidson, Shamai. 1992. *Holding on to Humanity—The Message of Holocaust Survivors: The Shamai Davidson Papers*, ed. Israel W. Charny. New York: New York University Press.

Dawidowicz, Lucy S. 1976. *The War Against the Jews 1933–1945*. New York: Bantam.

———. 1981. *The Holocaust and the Historians*. Cambridge, MA: Harvard University Press.

Deák, Istvan. 1983. "What Was Fascism?" *New York Review of Books*, March 3:13–16.

———. 2000a. "Introduction." In *The Politics of Retribution in Europe: World War II and Its Aftermath*, eds. Istvan Deák, Jan T. Gross, and Tony Judt. Princeton, NJ: Princeton University Press.

———. 2000b. "The Pope, the Nazis and the Jews." *New York Review of Books*, March 23:44–49.

Deák, Istvan, Jan T. Gross, and Tony Judt, eds. 2000. *The Politics of Retribution in Europe: World War II and Its Aftermath*. Princeton, NJ: Princeton University Press.

De Felice, Renzo. 2001. *The Jews in Fascist Italy: A History*. New York: Bartleby.

DellaPergola, Sergio. 1996. "Between Science and Fiction: Notes on the Demography of the Holocaust." *Holocaust and Genocide Studies* 10:34–51.

Dershowitz, Alan M. 1991. *Chutzpah*. New York: Touchstone.

Des Pres, Terrence. 1976. *The Survivor: An Anatomy of Life in the Death Camps*. New York: Oxford University Press.

Dimsdale, Joel E. 1980. "The Coping Behavior of Nazi Concentration Camp Survivors." In *Survivors, Victims, and Perpetrators: Essays on the Nazi Holocaust*, ed. Joel E. Dimsdale. New York: Hemisphere.

Diner, Hasia R. 2004. *The Jews of the United States*. Berkeley, CA: University of California Press.

Domansky, Elisabeth. 1997. "A Lost War: World War II in Postwar German Memory." In *Thinking about the Holocaust: After a Half Century*, ed. Alvin Rosenfeld. Bloomington, IN: Indiana University Press.

Doneson, Judith E. 1987a. "The American History of Anne Frank's Diary." *Holocaust and Genocide Studies* 21:149–60.

———. 1987b. *The Holocaust in American Film*. Philadelphia, PA: Jewish Publication Society.

———. 1997. "The Image Lingers: The Feminization of the Jews in *Schindler's List*." In *Spielberg's Holocaust: Critical Perspectives on* Schindler's List, ed. Yosefa Loshitsky. Bloomington, IN: Indiana University.

Doubt, Keith. 2007. "Scapegoating and the Simulation of Mechanical Solidarity in Former Yugoslavia: 'Ethnic Cleansing' and the Serbian Orthodox Church." *Humanity and Society* 31:65–82.

Douglas, Mary. 1966. *Pollution and Danger: An Analysis of Concepts of Pollution and Taboo*. New York: Praeger.

Dov Kulka, Otto. 1990. "Theresienstadt." In *Encyclopedia of the Holocaust*, vol. 4, ed. Israel Gutman. New York: Macmillan.

Duffy, Peter. 2003. *The Bielski Brothers*. New York: HarperCollins.

Durkheim, Émile. [1893] 1964. *The Division of Labor in Society*. New York: Free Press.

———. [1915] 1965. *The Elementary Forms of Religious Life*. New York: Free Press.

Dutt, R. Palme. 1935. *Fascism and Social Revolution: A Study of the Economics and Politics of the Extreme Stages of Capitalism in Decay*. New York: International.

Dwork, Debórah, and Robert Jan van Pelt. 2002. *Auschwitz: 1270 to the Present*. New York: Norton.

Eban, Abba. 1984. *Heritage: Civilization and the Jews*. New York: Random House.

Eckardt, Alice L. 1997. "The Shoah-Road to a Revised/Revived Christianity." In *From the Unthinkable to the Unavoidable: American Christian and Jewish Scholars Encounter the Holocaust*, eds. Carole Rittner and John K. Roth. Westport, CT: Praeger.

Edelman, Murray. 1977. *Political Language*. New York: Academic Press.

Ehmann, Annegret. 2001. "Mischlinge." In *The Holocaust Encyclopedia*, ed. Walter Laqueur. New Haven, CT: Yale University Press.

Einwohner, Rachel L. 2003. "Opportunity, Honor, and Action in the Warsaw Ghetto Uprising of 1943." *American Journal of Sociology* 109:650–75.

———. 2009. "The Need to Know: Cultured Ignorance and Jewish Resistance in the Ghettos of Warsaw, Vilna, and Lódz." *Sociological Quarterly* 50:407–30.

Elder, Tanya. 2005. "What You See Before Your Eyes: Documenting Raphael Lemkin's Life by Exploring His Archival Papers, 1900–1959." *Journal of Genocide Research* 7:469–99.

Emirbayer, Mustafa, and Ann Mische. 1998. "What is Agency?" *American Journal of Sociology* 103:962–1023.

Engelmann, Bernt. 1986. *In Hitler's Germany: Everyday Life in the Third Reich.* New York: Pantheon.

Epstein, Helen. 1979. *Children of the Holocaust: Conversations with Sons and Daughters of Survivors.* New York: Penguin.

Evans, Bette Novit. 2010. "The Constitutions of Religious Pluralism in the United States." In *Religion and Democracy in the United States: Danger or Opportunity?*, eds. Alan Wolfe and Ira Katznelson. Princeton, NJ: Princeton University Press.

Evans, Richard J. 1989. *In Hitler's Shadow: West German Historians and the Attempt to Escape from the Nazi Past.* New York: Pantheon.

———. 1991. "German Unification and the New Revisionism." *Dimensions: A Journal of the Holocaust* 6:10–14.

Fackenheim, Emil L. 1978. *The Jewish Return into History: Reflections in the Age of Auschwitz and a New Jerusalem.* New York: Schocken.

Favev, Jean-Claude. 1990. "Red Cross, International." In *Encyclopedia of the Holocaust,* vol. 3, ed. Israel Gutman. New York: Macmillan.

Fein, Helen. 1979. *Accounting for Genocide: National Response and Jewish Victimization During the Holocaust.* New York: Free Press.

———. 1993. *Genocide: A Sociological Perspective.* Newbury Park, CA: Sage.

Feldman, Gerald D., and Wolfgang Seibel, eds. 2005. *Networks of Nazi Persecution: Bureaucracy, Business, and the Organization of the Holocaust.* New York: Berghahn.

Fenyvesi, Charles. 2001. "Raoul Wallenberg." In *The Holocaust Encyclopedia,* ed. Walter Laqueur. New Haven, CT: Yale University Press.

Finkelstein, Norman. 2000. *The Holocaust Industry: Reflections on the Exploitation of Jewish Suffering.* New York: Verso.

Fischer, Klaus P. 1995. *Nazi Germany: A New History.* New York: Continuum.

Fisher, Ronit. 2001. "Medical Experimentation." In *The Holocaust Encyclopedia,* ed. Walter Laqueur. New Haven, CT: Yale University Press.

Fleischner, Eva. 2001. "The Crucial Importance of the Holocaust for Christians." In *The Holocaust: Readings and Interpretations,* eds. Joseph R. Mitchell and Helen Buss Mitchell. New York: McGraw-Hill/Dushkin.

Fogelman, Eva. 1994. *Conscience and Courage: Rescuers of Jews during the Holocaust.* New York: Anchor.

Förster, Jürgen. 1986. "The German Army and the Ideological War against the Soviet Union." In *The Policies of Genocide: Jews and Soviet Prisoners of War in Nazi Germany,* ed. Gerhard Hirschfield. London: Allen and Unwin.

Fox, John P. 2001. "Holocaust Education in Europe." In *The Holocaust Encyclopedia,* ed. Walter Laqueur. New Haven, CT: Yale University Press.

Fraenkel, Daniel. 2001. "Nuremberg Laws." In *The Holocaust Encyclopedia,* ed. Walter Laqueur. New Haven, CT: Yale University Press.

Frank, Anne. [1952] 1958. *The Diary of a Young Girl.* New York: Simon and Schuster.

Frankl, Viktor E. 1959. *Man's Search for Meaning,* rev. ed. New York: Pocket.

Freedman, Samuel G. 2000. *Jew vs. Jew: The Struggle for the Soul of American Jewry.* New York: Simon and Schuster.

Freeman, Michael. 1991. "The Theory and Prevention of Genocide." *Holocaust and Genocide Studies* 6:185–99.

Friedlander, Henry. 1998. "The T$_4$ Killers: Berlin, Lublin, San Sabba." In *The Holocaust and History: The Known, the Unknown, and the Disputed*, eds. Michael Berenbaum and Abraham J. Peck. Bloomington, IN: Indiana University Press.

———. 2001. "Euthanasia." In *The Holocaust Encyclopedia*, ed. Walter Laqueur. New Haven, CT: Yale University Press.

Friedländer, Saul. 1989. "From Anti-Semitism to Extermination: A Historiographical Study and an Essay in Interpretation." In *Unanswered Questions: Nazi Germany and the Genocide of the Jews*, ed. Francois Furet. New York: Schocken.

———. 1993. *Memory, History, and the Extermination of the Jews*. Bloomington, IN: Indiana University Press.

———. 2009. *Nazi Germany and the Jews, 1933–1945*, abr. Orna Kenan. New York: Harper Perennial.

Friedrich, Otto. 1994. *The Kingdom of Auschwitz*. New York: Harper Perennial.

Gallant, Mary, and Jay E. Cross. 1992. "Surviving Destruction of the Self: Challenged Identity in the Holocaust." In *Studies in Symbolic Interaction*, vol. 13, ed. Norman K. Denzin. Greenwich, CT: JAI Press.

Gamson, William A. 1992. "The Social Psychology of Collective Action." In *Frontiers in Social Movement Theory*, eds. Aldon D. Morris and Carol McClurg Mueller. New Haven, CT: Yale University Press.

———. 1995. "Hiroshima, the Holocaust, and the Politics of Exclusion." *American Sociological Review* 60:1–20.

Gans, Herbert. 1979. "Symbolic Ethnicity: The Future of Ethnic Groups and Cultures in America." *Ethnic and Racial Studies* 2:1–20.

Garber, Zev. 1994. *Shoah: The Paradigmatic Genocide*. Lanham, MD: University Press of America.

Gebert, Konstanty. 2008. *Living in the Land of Ashes*. Kraków: Austeria Publishing House.

Gellately, Robert. 1988. "The Gestapo and German Society: Political Denunciation in Gestapo Case Files." *Journal of Modern History* 60:654–94.

———. 1997. "Denunciations in Twentieth-Century Germany: Aspects of Self-Policing in the Third Reich and the German Democratic Republic." In *Accusatory Practices: Denunciation in Modern European History, 1789–1989*, eds. Sheila Fitzpatrick and Robert Gellately. Chicago, IL: University of Chicago Press.

———. 2001. *Backing Hitler: Consent and Coercion in Nazi Germany*. New York: Oxford University Press.

Gerhardt, Uta. 1993. *Talcott Parsons on National Socialism*. New York: Aldine de Gruyter.

———. 2002. *Talcott Parsons: An Intellectual Biography*. Cambridge, UK: Cambridge University Press.

Gerson, Judith M., and Diane L. Wolf, eds. 2007. *Sociology Confronts the Holocaust: Memories and Identities in Jewish Diasporas*. Durham, NC: Duke University Press.

Gerth, Hans, and Saul Landau. 1963. "The Relevance of History to the Sociological Ethos." In *Sociology on Trial*, eds. Maurice Stein and Arthur Vidich. Englewood Cliffs, NJ: Prentice-Hall.

Gerth, Hans, and C. Wright Mills, eds. 1946. *From Max Weber*. New York: Oxford University Press.

Giddens, Anthony. 1971. *Capitalism and Modern Social Theory: An Analysis of the Writings of Marx, Durkheim, and Max Weber.* Cambridge, UK: Cambridge University Press.

Gilbert, Gustave M. 1950. *The Psychology of Dictatorship.* New York: Ronald Press.

Gilbert, Martin. 1998. *Israel: A History.* New York: William Morrow.

———. 2000. *Never Again: A History of the Holocaust.* New York: Universe.

———. 2006. *Kristallnacht: Prelude to Destruction.* New York: HarperCollins.

Gilman, Sander L., and Karen Remmler, eds. 1994. *Reemerging Jewish Culture in Germany; Life and Literature Since 1989.* New York: New York University Press.

Gitlin, Todd, and Liel Leibovitz. 2010. *The Chosen Peoples: America, Israel, and the Ordeals of Divine Election.* New York: Simon & Schuster.

Goffman, Erving. 1959. *The Presentation of Self in Everyday Life.* Garden City, NY: Doubleday.

Goldhagen, Daniel Jonah. 1996. *Hitler's Willing Executioners: Ordinary Germans and the Holocaust.* New York: Knopf.

———. 1998. "'*Modell Bundesrepublik*': National History, Democracy, and Internationalization in Germany." In *Unwilling Germans? The Goldhagen Debate*, ed. Robert R. Shandley. Minneapolis, MN: University of Minnesota Press.

———. 2004. *A Moral Reckoning: The Role of the Church in the Holocaust and Its Unfulfilled Promise.* New York: Vintage.

———. 2009. *Worse Than War: Genocide, Eliminationism, and the Ongoing Assault on Humanity.* New York: Public Affairs.

Goldstein, Eric. 2006. *The Price of Whiteness: Jews, Race, and American Identity.* Princeton, NJ: Princeton University Press.

Gonzales, Laurence. 2003. *Deep Survival: Who Lives, Who Dies, and Why.* New York: Norton.

Gouldner, Alvin W. 1970. *The Coming Crisis of Western Sociology.* New York: Avon Books.

Gouri, Haim. 1994. "Facing the Glass Booth." In *Holocaust Remembrance: The Shapes of Memory*, ed. Geoffrey H. Hartman. Cambridge, MA: Blackwell.

Greenberg, Irving. 1990. "History, Holocaust and Covenant." *Holocaust and Genocide Studies* 5:1–12.

Greif, Gideon. 2001. "Gas Chambers." In *The Holocaust Encyclopedia*, ed. Walter Laqueur. New Haven, CT: Yale University Press.

Greif, Mark. 2000. "The Banality of Irving." *American Prospect*, April 24:32–37.

Gross, Jan T. 2000. "Themes for a Social History of War Experience and Collaboration." In *The Politics of Retribution in Europe*, eds. Istvan Deák, Jan T. Gross, and Tony Judt. Princeton, NJ: Princeton University Press.

———. 2002. *Neighbors: The Destruction of the Jewish Community in Jedwabne, Poland.* New York: Penguin.

———. 2006. *Fear: Anti-Semitism in Poland After Auschwitz.* New York: Random House.

Gross, Michael L. 1994. "Jewish Rescue in Holland and France During the Second World War: Moral Cognition and Collective Action." *Social Forces* 73:463–96.

Gushee, David. 1994. *The Righteous Gentiles of the Holocaust: A Christian Inter-pretation.* Minneapolis, MN: Fortress Press.

Gutman, Israel. 1990a. "Ghetto." In *Encyclopedia of the Holocaust,* vol. 2, ed. Israel Gutman. New York: Macmillan.

——. 1990b. "Kovner, Abba." In *Encyclopedia of the Holocaust,* vol. 2, ed. Israel Gutman. New York: Macmillan.

——. 1990c. "Warsaw: Jews During the Holocaust" and "Warsaw Ghetto Uprising." In *Encyclopedia of the Holocaust,* vol. 4, ed. Israel Gutman. New York: Macmillan.

——. 1990d. "Youth Movements: General Survey." In *Encyclopedia of the Holocaust,* vol. 4, ed. Israel Gutman. New York: Macmillan.

——. 1990e. "Zyklon B." In *Encyclopedia of the Holocaust,* vol. 4, ed. Israel Gutman. New York: Macmillan.

Gutman, Israel, and Robert Rozett. 1990. "Estimated Jewish Losses in the Holocaust." In *Encyclopedia of the Holocaust,* vol. 4 (Appendix 6), ed. Israel Gutman. New York: Macmillan.

Gutman, Israel, and Avital Saf, eds. 1984. *The Nazi Concentration Camps.* Jerusalem: Yad Vashem.

Guttenplan, D. D. 2000. "The Holocaust on Trial." *The Atlantic Monthly,* February:45–66.

Habermas, Jürgen. 1998. "Goldhagen and the Public Use of History: Why a Democracy Prize for Daniel Goldhagen." In *Unwilling Germans? The Goldhagen Debate,* ed. Robert R. Shandley. Minneapolis, MN: University of Minnesota Press.

Hacking, Ian. 1986. "Making Up People." In *Reconstructing Individualism: Autonomy, Individuality, and the Self,* eds. Thomas C. Heller, Morton Sosna, and David E. Wellbery. Stanford, CA: Stanford University Press.

Hagan, John, and Wenona Rymond-Richmond. 2009. *Darfur and the Crime of Genocide.* New York: Cambridge University Press.

Halbwachs, Maurice. [1950] 1980. *The Collective Memory.* New York: Harper & Row.

——. 1992. *On Collective Memory,* ed. Lewis Coser. Chicago, IL: University of Chicago Press.

Hall, John R. 1992. "Where History and Sociology Meet: Forms of Discourse and Sociohistorical Inquiry." *Sociological Theory* 10:164–93.

Halpert, Burton P. 2007. "Early American Sociology and the Holocaust: The Failure of a Discipline." *Humanity and Society* 31:6–23.

Hamerow, Theodore S. 2008. *Why We Watched; Europe, America, and the Holocaust.* New York: Norton.

Hamilton, Richard F. 1982. *Who Voted for Hitler?* Princeton, NJ: Princeton University Press.

Hancock, Ian. 2009. "Responses to the Porrajmos: The Romani Holocaust." In *Is the Holocaust Unique? Perspectives on Comparative Genocide,* ed. Alan S. Rosenbaum. Boulder, CO: Westview Press.

Harel, Zev, Boaz Kahana, and Eva Kahana. 1988. "Psychological Well-Being Among Holocaust Survivors and Immigrants in Israel." *Journal of Traumatic Stress* 1:413–29.

Hartman, Geoffrey, ed. 1986. *Bitburg in Moral and Political Perspective.* Bloomington, IN: Indiana University Press.

Hass, Aaron. 1990. *In the Shadow of the Holocaust: The Second Generation*. New York: Cornell University Press.

———. 1995. *The Aftermath: Living With the Holocaust*. Cambridge, MA: Cambridge University Press.

Hayes, Peter. 1987. *Industry and Ideology: IG Farben in the Nazi Era*. Cambridge, UK: Cambridge University Press.

———. 1998. "State Policy and Corporate Involvement in the Holocaust." In *The Holocaust and History: The Known, the Unknown, and the Disputed*, eds. Michael Berenbaum and Abraham J. Peck. Bloomington, IN: Indiana University Press.

Haynes, Stephen R. 1998. "Holocaust Education at American Colleges and Universities: A Report on the Current Situation." *Holocaust and Genocide Studies* 12:282–307.

Helmreich, William. 1992. *Against All Odds: Holocaust Survivors and the Successful Lives They Made in America*. New York: Simon and Schuster.

Herberg, Will. 1955. *Protestant-Catholic-Jew: An Essay in American Religious Sociology*. Garden City, NY: Doubleday.

Herf, Jeffrey. 1984. *Reactionary Modernism: Technology, Culture, and Politics in Weimar and the Third Reich*. New York: Cambridge University Press.

———. 1994. "German Communism, the Discourse of 'Antifascist Resistance,' and the Jewish Catastrophe." In *Resistance Against the Third Reich: 1933–1990*, eds. Michael Geyer and John W. Boyer. Chicago, IL: University of Chicago Press.

———. 1997. *Divided Memory: The Nazi Past in the Two Germanys*. Cambridge, MA: Harvard University Press.

Herman, Burt. 1999. *Breakthrough: $5.2 Billion Settlement Reached in Nazi Slave Labor Case*. Associated Press. December 15, retrieved from http://www.abcnews.go.com.

Hertzberg, Arthur. 1968. *The French Enlightenment and the Jews: The Origins of Modern Anti-Semitism*. New York: Schocken.

Hervieu-Léger, Danièle. 2000. *Religion as a Chain of Memory*, trans. Simon Lee. New Brunswick, NJ: Rutgers University Press.

Higham, Charles. 1983. *Trading With the Enemy: The Nazi-American Money Plot, 1933–1949*. New York: Barnes and Noble.

Hilberg, Raul. 1961. *The Destruction of the European Jews*. Chicago, IL: Quadrangle.

———. 1985. *The Destruction of the European Jews*, rev. ed. New York: Holmes and Meier.

———. 1986. "Bitburg as Symbol." In *Bitburg in Moral and Political Perspective*, ed. Geoffrey Hartman. Bloomington, IN: Indiana University Press.

———. 1989. "The Bureaucracy of Annihilation." In *Unanswered Questions: Nazi Germany and the Genocide of the Jews*, ed. Francois Furet. New York: Schocken.

———. 1991. "Opening Remarks: The Discovery of the Holocaust." In *Lessons and Legacies: The Meaning of the Holocaust in a Changing World*, ed. Peter Hayes. Evanston, IL: Northwestern University Press.

———. 1992. *Perpetrators, Victims, and Bystanders: The Jewish Catastrophe, 1933–1945*. New York: HarperCollins.

———. 1996. *The Politics of Memory: The Journey of a Holocaust Historian.* Chicago, IL: Ivan Dee.

———. 2001. "Auschwitz." In *The Holocaust Encyclopedia*, ed. Walter Laqueur. New Haven, CT: Yale University Press.

Hindley, Meredith. 1996. "Negotiating the Boundary of Unconditional Surrender: The War Refugee Board in Sweden and Nazi Proposals to Ransom Jews, 1944–1945." *Holocaust and Genocide Studies* 10:52–77.

Hirsch, Michael. 1999. "A Nazi-Era Bill Finally Comes Due." *Newsweek*, February 22:40–41.

The History Place. 1999. "Genocide in the 20th Century: Bosnia-Herzegovina," retrieved from http://www.historyplace.com.

Hitchens, Christopher. 2001. "Wiesel Words." *The Nation*, February 19:9.

———. 2007. *God is not Great: How Religion Poisons Everything.* New York: Twelve.

Hitler, Adolf. [1925] 1943. *Mein Kampf*, trans. Ralph Manheim. Boston, MA: Houghton Mifflin.

Hoffman, Charles. 1992. *Gray Dawn: The Jews of Eastern Europe in the Post-Communist Era.* New York: HarperCollins.

Hofstader, Richard. 1959. *Social Darwinism in American Social Thought.* Boston, MA: Beacon Press.

Holstein, James A., and Gale Miller. 1990. "Rethinking Victimization: An Interactional Approach to Victimology." *Symbolic Interaction* 13:103–22.

Horowitz, Irving Louis, ed. 1964. *The New Sociology: Essays in Social Science and Social Theory in Honor of C. Wright Mills.* New York: Oxford University Press.

——— ed. 1967. *The Rise and Fall of Project Camelot: Studies in the Relationship Between Social Science and Practical Politics.* Cambridge, MA: MIT Press.

———. 1968. *Professing Sociology: Studies in the Life Cycle of Social Science.* Carbondale/Edwardsville, IL: Southern Illinois University Press.

———. 1972. "Political Bias and Social Analysis." In *Foundations of Political Sociology*, ed. Irving Louis Horowitz. New York: Harper & Row.

———. 1976. *Genocide: State Power and Mass Murder.* New Brunswick, NJ: Transaction.

———. 1993. *The Decomposition of Sociology.* New York: Oxford University Press.

———. 2002. *Taking Lives: Genocide and State Power,* 5th ed. New Brunswick, NJ: Transaction.

———. 2009. "Stages in the Evolution of Holocaust Studies." *Human Rights Review* 10:493–504.

Huener, Jonathan. 2003. *Auschwitz, Poland, and the Politics of Commemoration, 1945–1979.* Athens: Ohio University Press.

Hughes, Everett C. 1962. "Good People and Dirty Work." *Social Problems* 10:3–10.

Ibarra, Peter, and John Kitsuse. 1993. "Vernacular Constituents of Moral Discourse: An Interactionist Proposal for the Study of Social Problems." In *Reconsidering Social Constructionism*, eds. James A. Holstein and Gale Miller. Hawthorne, NY: Aldine de Gruyter.

Ignatieff, Michael. 2001. "Lemkin's Words." *The New Republic*, February 26:25–28.

Insdorf, Annette. 2003. *Indelible Shadows: Film and the Holocaust*, 3rd ed. New York: Cambridge University Press.

Irving, David. 1977. *Hitler's War*. New York: Viking.

Isaac, Jules. 1959. *Jesus et Israel*. Paris: Pasquelle Editeurs.

James, Harold. 2001. *The Deutsche Bank and the Nazi Economic War Against the Jews*. Cambridge, UK: Cambridge University Press.

Jay, Martin. 1993. "Postmodern Fascism? Reflections on the Return of the Oppressed." *Tikkun* 8:37–41.

Jelinek, Pauline. 2000. "Holocaust Glare Turns on U.S. Companies." *Wisconsin State Journal*, August 28:A1.

Jessop, Bob. 2002. *The Future of the Capitalist State*. Cambridge, UK: Polity.

Jewish Virtual Library. 2006. "The Jewish Population of the World," retrieved from http://www.jewishvirtuallibrary.org.

Joffe, Josef. 1998. "'The Killers Were Ordinary Germans, Ergo the Ordinary Germans Were Killers': The Logic, the Language, and the Meaning of a Book that Conquered Germany." In *Unwilling Germans? The Goldhagen Debate*, ed. Robert R. Shandley. Minneapolis: Minnesota University Press.

Johnson, Eric A. 1999. *Nazi Terror: The Gestapo, Jews, and Ordinary Germans*. New York: Basic.

Johnson, Paul. 1987. *A History of the Jews*. New York: Harper & Row.

Jonas, Hans. 2001. "The Concept of God: A Jewish Voice." *A Holocaust Reader*, ed. Michael L. Morgan. New York: Oxford University Press.

Jones, Priscilla Dale. 1990. "Trials of War Criminals: General Survey. In *Encyclopedia of the Holocaust*, vol. 4, ed. Israel Gutman. New York: Macmillan.

Judt, Tony. 2000. "The Past is Another Country: Myth and Memory in Postwar Europe." In *The Politics of Retribution in Europe: World War II and Its Aftermath*, eds. Istvan Deák, Jan T. Gross, and Tony Judt. Princeton, NJ: Princeton University Press.

Kahana, Boaz, Zev Harel, and Eva Kahana. 1988. "Predictors of Psychological Well-Being Among Survivors of the Holocaust." In *Human Adaptation to Extreme Stress*, eds. John Preston Wilson, Zev Harel, and Boaz Kahana. New York: Plenum.

Kaplan, Marion A. 1998. *Between Dignity and Despair: Jewish Life in Nazi Germany*. New York: Oxford University Press.

Kater, Michael. 1983. *The Nazi Party: A Social Profile of Members and Leaders 1919–1945*. Cambridge, MA: Harvard University Press.

———. 1984. "Everyday Antisemitism in Prewar Germany: The Popular Bases." *Yad Vashem Studies* 16:129–59.

Katz, Steven T. 2001. "Jewish Faith After the Holocaust: Four Approaches." In *The Holocaust: Readings and Interpretations*, eds. Joseph Mitchell and Helen Buss Mitchell. New York: McGraw-Hill/Dushkin.

Kaufman, Jonathan. 1994. *Broken Alliance: The Turbulent Time Between Blacks and Jews in America*. New York: Simon and Schuster.

Kellerman, Natan. 2001. "Psychopathology in Children of Holocaust Survivors: A Review of the Research Literature." *Israel Journal of Psychiatry and Related Sciences* 38:36–46.

Kelman, Herbert C., and V. Lee Hamilton. 1989. *Crimes of Obedience: Toward a Social Psychology of Authority and Responsibility*. New Haven, CT: Yale University Press.

Keneally, Thomas. [1982] 1993. *Schindler's List: A Novel*. New York: Touch-stone.

Kennedy, Michael D., and Miguel A. Centeno. 2007. "Internationalism and Global Transformation in American Sociology." In *Sociology in America: A History*, ed. Craig Calhoun. Chicago, IL: University of Chicago Press.

Kershaw, Ian. 1998. *Hitler: 1889–1936 Hubris*. New York: Norton.

———. 2000. *Hitler: 1936–1945 Nemesis*. New York: Norton.

Khalidi, Rashid. 2006. *The Iron Cage: The Story of the Palestinian Struggle for Statehood*. Boston, MA: Beacon Press.

———. 2008. "Palestine: Liberation Deferred." *The Nation*, May 26:16–19.

Kirkpatrick, Clifford. 1938. *Nazi Germany: Its Women and Family Life*. Indianapolis, IN: Bobbs-Merrill.

Klein-Parker, Fran. 1988. "Dominant Attitudes of Adult Children of Holocaust Survivors toward Their Parents." In *Human Adaptation to Extreme Stress*, eds. John Preston Wilson, Zev Harel, and Boaz Kahana. New York: Plenum.

Klug, Brian. 2007. "The State of Zionism." *The Nation*, June 18:23–30.

Koch, Hansjoachim W. 2000. *The Hitler Youth: Origins and Development 1922–1945*. New York: Cooper Square Press.

Kochan, Lionel. 1990. "Alfred Rosenberg." In *Encyclopedia of the Holocaust*, ed. Israel Gutman. New York: Macmillan.

Koehl, Robert Lewis. 1983. *The Black Corps: The Structure and Power Struggles of the Nazi SS*. Madison, WI: University of Wisconsin Press.

Koffler, Florette Rechnitz, and Richard Koffler. 1995. *Uncertain Refuge: Italy and the Jews During the Holocaust*. Urbana, IL: University of Illinois Press.

Koonz, Claudia. 1987. *Mothers in the Fatherland: Women, the Family and Nazi Politics*. New York: St. Martin's Press.

———. 1991. "Genocide and Eugenics: The Language of Power." In *Lessons and Legacies: The Meaning of the Holocaust in a Changing World*, ed. Peter Hayes. Evanston, IL: Northwestern University Press.

Kraft, Robert N. 2002. *Memory Perceived: Recalling the Holocaust*. Westport, CT: Praeger.

Krajewski, Stanisław. 2005. *Poland and the Jews: Reflections of a Polish Polish Jew*. Kraków: Wydawnictwo Austeria.

Krakowski, Shmuel. 1990a. "Chelmno." In *Encyclopedia of the Holocaust*, vol. 1, ed. Israel Gutman. New York: Macmillan.

———. 1990b. "Rumkowski, Mordechai Chaim." In *Encyclopedia of the Holocaust*, vol. 3. ed. Israel Gutman. New York: Macmillan.

Kreimeier, Klaus. 1996. *The Ufa Story: A History of Germany's Greatest Film Company, 1918–1945*. New York: Hill and Wang.

Krondorfer, Bjorn. 1995. *Remembrance and Reconciliation: Encounters Between Young Jews and Germans*. New Haven, CT: Yale University Press.

Kuper, Leo. 1990. "The United States Ratifies the Genocide Convention." In *The History and Sociology of Genocide*, eds. Frank Chalk and Kurt Jonassohn. New Haven, CT: Yale University Press.

Kurek-Lesik, Ewa. 1992. "The Role of Polish Nuns in the Rescue of Jews." In *Embracing the Other: Philosophical, Psychological, and Historical Perspectives on Altruism*, eds. Pearl M. Oliner, et al. New York: New York University Press.

Kuznick, Peter J. 1987. *Beyond the Laboratory: Scientists as Political Activists in 1930s America.* Chicago, IL: University of Chicago Press.

Langer, Lawrence L. 1991. *Holocaust Testimonies: The Ruins of Memory.* New Haven, CT: Yale University Press.

Lanzmann, Claude. 1985. *Shoah: An Oral History of the Holocaust.* New York: Pantheon.

Laqueur, Walter. [1972] 2003. *A History of Zionism: From the French Revolution to the Establishment of the State of Israel.* New York: Schocken.

———. 1980. *The Terrible Secret: Suppression of the Truth about Hitler's "Final Solution."* Boston, MA: Little, Brown.

———. 1996. *Fascism: Past, Present, Future.* New York: Oxford University Press.

———. 2000. "Auschwitz." In *The Bombing of Auschwitz: Should the Allies Have Attempted It?*, eds. Michael J. Neufeld and Michael Berenbaum. New York: St. Martin's Press.

Large, David Clay. 1994. "'A Beacon in the German Darkness': The Anti-Nazi Resistance Legacy in West German Politics." In *Resistance Against the Third Reich: 1933–1990*, eds. Michael Geyer and John W. Boyer. Chicago, IL: University of Chicago Press.

Lasch, Christopher. 1994. *The Minimal Self: Psychic Survival in Troubled Times.* New York: Norton.

Lee, Carol Ann. 2003. *The Hidden Life of Otto Frank.* New York: William Morrow.

Leichter, Sinai. 1990. "Kielce." In *Encyclopedia of the Holocaust*, vol. 2, ed. Israel Gutman. New York: Macmillan.

Lemkin, Raphael. 1944. *Axis Rule in Occupied Europe.* Washington, DC: Carnegie Endowment for International Peace.

Lengyel, Olga. 1947. *Five Chimneys*, trans. Clifford Coch and Paul P. Weiss. Chicago, IL: Zififi-Davis.

Lentin, Ronit. 2004. "Introduction: Postmemory, Unsayability and the Return of the Auschwitz Code." In *Re-Representing the Shoah for the Twenty-First Century*, ed. Ronit Lentin. United Kingdom: Berghan.

Levi, Primo. [1960] 1993. *Survival in Auschwitz.* New York: Collier.

Levine, Paul. 1998. "Bureaucracy, Resistance, and the Holocaust: Understanding the Success of Swedish Diplomacy in Budapest, 1944–1945." In *The Holocaust and History: The Known, the Unknown, and the Disputed*, eds. Michael Berenbaum and Abraham J. Peck. Bloomington, IN: Indiana University Press.

Levy, Daniel, and Nathan Sznaider. 2006. *The Holocaust and Memory in the Global Age.* Philadelphia, PA: Temple University Press.

Lewy, Guenter. 1999. "Gypsies and Jews Under the Nazis." *Holocaust and Genocide Studies* 13:383–404.

Lifton, Robert Jay. 1967. *Death in Life: Survivors of Hiroshima.* New York: Simon and Schuster.

———. 1980. "The Concept of the Survivor." In *Survivors, Victims, and Perpetrators: Essays on the Nazi Holocaust*, ed. Joel E. Dimsdale. New York: Hemisphere.

———. 1986. *The Nazi Doctors: Medical Killing and the Psychology of Genocide.* New York: Basic Books.

Linenthal, Edward T. 1995. *Preserving Memory: The Struggle to Create America's Holocaust Museum*. New York: Viking Press.

Lipset, Seymour Martin. 1960. *Political Man: The Social Basis of Politics*. Garden City, NY: Doubleday.

Lipset, Seymour, and Earl Raab. 1995. *Jews and the American Scene*. Cambridge, MA: Harvard University Press.

Lipstadt, Deborah E. 1993. *Denying the Holocaust: The Growing Assault on Truth and Memory*. New York: Free Press.

———. 2000. "The Failure to Rescue and Contemporary American Jewish Historiography of the Holocaust: Judging from a Distance." In *The Bombing of Auschwitz: Should the Allies Have Attempted It?*, eds. Michael J. Neufeld and Michael Berenbaum. New York: St. Martin's Press.

Litvak, Meir. 1994. "A Palestinian Past: National Construction and Reconstruction." *History and Memory* 6:24–56.

Loseke, Donileen R. 1999. *Teaching About Social Problems*. Hawthorne, NY: Aldine de Gruyter.

Loshitsky, Yosefa, ed. 1997. *Spielberg's Holocaust: Critical Perspectives on Schindler's List*. Bloomington, IN: Indiana University Press.

Lubetkin, Zivia. 1981. *In the Days of Destruction and Revolt*. Tel Aviv, Israel: Hakibutz Hameuchad.

Lukas, Richard C. 1986. *Forgotten Holocaust: The Poles Under German Occupation 1939–1944*. Lexington: University Press of Kentucky.

Lundberg, George A. 1944. "Sociologists and Peace." *American Sociological Review* 9:1–13.

Lynch, Colum, and Rebecca Hamilton. 2010. "International Criminal Court Charges Sudan's Omar Hassan al-Bashir with Genocide." *Washington Post*, July 13, retrieved from http://www.washingtonpost.com.

MacIver, Robert M. 1941. "Some Reflections on Sociology During a Crisis." *American Sociological Review* 6:1–8.

Maher, Thomas. V. 2010. "Threat, Resistance, and Collective Action: The Cases of Sobibór, Treblinka, and Auschwitz." *American Sociological Review* 75:252–72.

Maier, Charles S. 1988. *The Unmasterable Past: History, Holocaust and German National Identity*. Cambridge, MA: Harvard University Press.

Mannheim, Karl. 1936. *Ideology and Utopia: An Introduction to the Sociology of Knowledge*, trans. Louis Wirth and Edward A. Shills. New York: Harcourt Brace World.

Marcuse, Harold. 2001. *Legacies of Dachau: The Uses and Abuses of a Concentration Camp, 1933–2001*. New York: Cambridge University Press.

Markle, Gerald E. 1995. *Meditations of a Holocaust Traveler*. New York: SUNY Press.

Markle, Gerald E., Mary D. Lagerwey-Voorman, Todd A. Clason, Jill A. Green, and Tricia L. Meade. 1992. "From Auschwitz to Americana: Texts of the Holocaust." *Sociological Focus* 25:179–202.

Markovits, Andrei S. 1990. "Coping with the Past: The West German Labor Movement and the Left." In *Reworking the Past: Hitler, the Holocaust, and the Historians' Debate*, ed. Peter Baldwin. Boston, MA: Beacon Press.

———. 1998. "Discomposure in History's Final Resting Place." In *Unwilling Germans? The Goldhagen Debate*, ed. Robert R. Shandley. Minneapolis, MN: University of Minnesota Press.

Marrus, Michael. 1987. *The Holocaust in History*. New York: New American Library.

———. 1991. "The Use and Abuse of the Holocaust." In *Lessons and Legacies: The Meaning of the Holocaust in a Changing World*, ed. Peter Hayes. Evanston, IL: Northwestern University Press.

———. 1997. *The Nuremberg War Crimes Trial 1945–46: A Documentary History*. Boston, MA: Bedford.

Marrus, Michael, and Robert O. Paxton. 1981. *Vichy France and the Jews*. New York: Stanford University Press.

———. 1987. "The Nazis and the Jews in Occupied Western Europe, 1940–1944." In *Unanswered Questions: Nazi Germany and the Genocide of the Jews*, ed. Francois Furet. New York: Schocken.

Marx, Karl. [1852] 1963. *The Eighteenth Brumaire of Louis Bonaparte*. New York: International.

Marx, Karl, and Friedrich Engels. [1848] 1948. *Manifesto of the Communist Party*. New York: International.

Matthews, Rick A. 2006. "Ordinary Business in Nazi Germany." In *State-Corporate Crime: Wrongdoing at the Intersection of Business and Government*, eds. Raymond Michalowski and Ronald C. Kramer. New Brunswick, NJ: Rutgers University Press.

Maybaum, Ignaz. 1965. *The Face of God After Auschwitz*. Amsterdam: Polak and Van Gennep.

Mayer, Arno J. 1989. *Why Did the Heavens Not Darken? The "Final Solution" in History*. New York: Pantheon.

Mazian, Florence. 1990. *Why Genocide? The Armenian and Jewish Experiences in Perspective*. Ames, IA: Iowa State University Press.

Mazower, Mark. 2010. "God's Grief." *Times Literary Supplement*, September 17:7–8.

Mendes-Flohr, Paul, and Jehuda Reinharz, eds. 1995. *The Jew in the Modern World: A Documentary History*. New York: Oxford University Press.

Merton, Robert K. [1937] 1968. "Science and the Social Order." In Robert K. Merton, *Social Theory and Social Structure*. New York: Free Press.

Mierzejewski, Alfred C. 2001. "A Public Enterprise in the Service of Mass Murder: The Deutsche Reichsbahn and the Holocaust." *Holocaust and Genocide Studies* 15:33–46.

Miller, Ingo. 1991. *Hitler's Justice: The Courts of the Third Reich*. Cambridge, MA: Harvard University Press.

Miller, Judith. 1990. *One by One, by One: Facing the Holocaust*. New York: Touchstone.

Milton, Sybil. 1990. "The Context of the Holocaust." *German Studies Review* 13:269–83.

Mitchell, Alison. 2002. "Israel Winning Broad Support from the U.S. Right." *The New York Times*, April 21, retrieved from http://www.nytimes.com.

Mitchell, Joseph R., and Helen Buss Mitchell, eds. 2001. *The Holocaust: Readings and Interpretations*. New York: McGraw-Hill/Dushkin.

Moll, Christiane. 1994. "Acts of Resistance: The White Rose in the Light of New Archival Evidence." In *Resistance Against the Third Reich: 1933–1990*, eds. Michael Geyer and John W. Boyer. Chicago, IL: University of Chicago Press.

Mommsen, Hans. 1986. "The Realization of the Unthinkable: The 'Final Solution' of the 'Jewish Question' in the Third Reich." In *The Policies of Genocide: Jews and Soviet Prisoners of War in Nazi Germany*, ed. Gerhard Hirschfeld. London: Allen and Unwin.

———. 1998. "The Civil Service and the Implementation of the Holocaust." In *The Holocaust and History: The Known, the Unknown, and the Disputed*, eds. Michael Berenbaum and Abraham J. Peck. Bloomington, IN: Indiana University Press.

Monroe, Kristen R. 1996. *The Heart of Altruism: Perceptions of a Common Humanity*. Princeton, NJ: Princeton University Press.

Morris, Benny. 2008. *1948: A History of the First Arab—Israeli War*. New Haven, CT: Yale University Press.

———. 2009. "Derisionist History." *The New Republic*, Nov. 18:41–47.

Mosse, George L. 1978. *Toward the Final Solution: A History of European Racism*. New York: Howard Fertig.

Müller, Filip. 1979. *Eyewitness Auschwitz: Three Years in the Gas Chambers*. New York: Stein and Day.

Müller-Hill, Benno. 1998. "Human Genetics and the Mass Murder of Jews, Gypsies, and Others." In *The Holocaust and History: The Known, the Unknown, and the Disputed*, eds. Michael Berenbaum and Abraham J. Peck. Bloomington, IN: Indiana University Press.

Murray, Williamson. 2000. "Monday-Morning Quarterbacking and the Bombing of Auschwitz." *The Bombing of Auschwitz: Should the Allies Have Attempted It?*, eds. Michael J. Neufeld and Michael Berenbaum. New York: St. Martin's Press.

Mushkat, Marian. 1990. "Trials of War Criminals: Nuremberg Trial." In *Encyclopedia of the Holocaust*, ed. Israel Gutman. New York: Macmillan.

Nagel, Joane. 1994. "Constructing Ethnicity: Creating and Recreating Ethnic Identity and Culture." *Social Problems* 41:152–76.

Neufeld, Michael J., and Michael Berenbaum, eds. 2000. *The Bombing of Auschwitz: Should the Allies Have Attempted It?* New York: St. Martin's Press.

Nolte, Ernst. 1965. *Three Faces of Fascism*. New York: Holt, Rinehart, and Winston.

Nora, Pierre. 1986. *Les Lieux de Mémoire, La Nation*. Paris: Gallimard.

Novick, Peter. 1999. *The Holocaust in American Life*. Boston, MA: Houghton and Mifflin.

Offer, Dali, and Lenore J. Weitzman, eds. 1998. *Women in the Holocaust*. New Haven, CT: Yale University Press.

Olick, Jeffrey K., and Daniel Levy. 1997. "Collective Memory and Cultural Constraint: Holocaust Myth and Rationality in German Politics." *American Sociological Review* 62:921–36.

Olick, Jeffrey K., and Joyce Robbins. 1998. "Social Memory Studies: From 'Collective Memory' to the Historical Sociology of Mnemonic Practices." *Annual Review of Sociology* 24:105–40.

Oliner, Pearl M., et al., eds. 1992. *Embracing the Other: Philosophical, Psychological, and Historical Perspectives on Altruism*. New York: New York University Press.

Oliner, Samuel P., and Pearl M. Oliner. 1988. *The Altruistic Personality: Rescuers of Jews in Nazi Europe.* New York: Free Press.

Osiel, Mark. 1997. *Mass Atrocity, Collective Memory, and the Law.* New Brunswick, NJ: Transaction.

Paldiel, Mordecai. 1996. *Sheltering the Jews; Stories of Holocaust Rescuers.* Minneapolis, MN: Fortress Press.

Patterson, Orlando. 1991. *Freedom in the Making in Western Culture.* New York: Basic Books.

Pawełczynska, Anna. 1979. *Values and Violence in Auschwitz: A Sociological Analysis* Berkeley, CA: University of California Press.

Pawlikowski, John T. 1997. "Penetrating Barriers: A Holocaust Retrospective." In *From the Unthinkable to the Unavoidable: American Christian and Jewish Scholars Encounter the Holocaust,* eds. Carole Rittner and John K. Roth. Westport, CT: Praeger.

———. 1998. "The Catholic Response to the Holocaust: Institutional Perspectives." In *The Holocaust and History: The Known, the Unknown, and the Disputed,* eds. Michael Berenbaum and Abraham J. Peck Bloomington, IN: Indiana University Press.

Paxton, Robert O. 2004. *The Anatomy of Fascism.* New York: Vintage.

Payne, Stanley G. 1980. *Fascism: Comparison and Definition.* Madison, WI: University of Wisconsin Press.

———. 2001. "Fascism in Western Europe." In *The Holocaust Encyclopedia,* ed. Walter Laqueur. New Haven, CT: Yale University Press.

Penslar, Derek Jonathan. 1995. "Innovation and Revisionism in Israeli Historiography." *History and Memory* 7:125–46.

Petropoulos, Jonathan. 1997. "Co-Opting Nazi Germany: Neutrality in Europe During World War II." *Dimensions: A Journal of Holocaust Studies* 11:15–21.

———. 2001. "The Roller Coaster of Restitution: The United States Government's Involvement with Holocaust Victims' Assets." *Dimensions: A Journal of Holocaust Studies* 15:9–18.

Peyser, Marc. 2001. "Out of the Attic, At Last." *Newsweek,* May 21:57.

Phayer, Michael. 2000. *The Catholic Church and the Holocaust, 1930–1965.* Bloomington, IN: Indiana University Press.

Phillips, Kevin. 2006. *American Theocracy: The Peril and Politics of Radical Religion, Oil, and Borrowed Money in the 21st Century.* New York: Viking.

Piliavin, Jane, and Hong-Wen Charng. 1990. "Altruism: A Review of Recent Theory and Research." *Annual Review of Sociology* 16:27–65. Palo Alto, CA: Annual Reviews.

Pingel, Falk. 1990. "Concentration Camps." In *Encyclopedia of the Holocaust,* vol. 1, ed. Israel Gutman. New York: Macmillan.

———. 1991. "The Destruction of Human Identity in Concentration Camps: The Contribution of the Social Sciences to an Analysis of Behavior Under Extreme Conditions." *Holocaust and Genocide Studies* 6:167–84.

Piper, Franciszek. 2006. "Design and Development of the Gas Chambers and Crematoria at Auschwitz." In *Death by Design: Science, Technology, and Engineering in Nazi Germany,* ed. Eric Katz. New York: Pearson Longman.

Podeh, Elie. 2000. "History and Memory in the Israeli Educational System: The Portrayal of the Arab–Israeli Conflict in History Textbooks (1948–2000)." *History and Memory* 12:65–100.

Polonsky, Antony, ed. 1990. *My Brother's Keeper? Recent Polish Debates on the Holocaust.* London: Routledge.

Polonsky, Antony, and Joanna B. Michlic, ed. 2004. *The Neighbors Respond: The Controversy over the Jedwabne Massacre in Poland.* Princeton, NJ: Princeton University Press.

Poole, James. 1997a. *Hitler and His Secret Partners: Contributions, Loot and Rewards, 1933–1945.* New York: Pocket.

———. 1997b. *Who Financed Hitler: The Secret Funding of Hitler's Rise to Power, 1919–1933.* New York: Pocket.

Power, Samantha. 2002. *"A Problem from Hell": America and the Age of Genocide.* New York: Basic.

Prekerowa, Teresa. 1990. "Zegota." In *Encyclopedia of the Holocaust,* ed. Israel Gutman. New York: Macmillan.

Pressac, Jean-Claude, with Robert Jan van Pelt. 2006. "Engineering Mass Murder at Auschwitz." In *Death by Design: Science, Technology, and Engineering in Nazi Germany,* ed. Eric Katz. New York: Pearson.

Proctor, Robert. 1988. *Racial Hygiene: Medicine Under the Nazis.* Cambridge, MA: Harvard University Press.

Prosono, Marvin. 1994. "Symbolic Territoriality and the Holocaust: The Controversy over the Carmelite Convent at Auschwitz." In *Perspectives on Social Problems,* vol. 6, eds. James A. Holstein and Gale Miller. Greenwich, CT: JAI Press.

Prosono, Marvin, and Gary Brock. 1996. "The Holocaust and the Construction of the Sacred: The Emerging Mythos of the 'Crucified Clan.'" In *Perspectives on Social Problems,* vol. 8, eds. James A. Holstein and Gale Miller. Greenwich, CT: JAI Press.

Public Broadcasting Corporation. 1995. "Nazi Designers of Death." NOVA television documentary.

———. 1999. *The Triumph of Evil.* Frontline television documentary.

Rabinbach, Anson. 1997. "From Explosion to Erosion: Holocaust Memorialization in America Since Bitburg." *History and Memory* 9:226–55.

Ram, Uri. 1995. "Zionist Historiography and the Invention of Modern Jewish Nationhood: The Case of Ben Zion Dinur." *History and Memory* 7:91–124.

Rapaport, Lynn. 1997. *Jews in Germany after the Holocaust: Memory, Identity, and Jewish–German Relations.* Cambridge, UK: Cambridge University Press.

Redlich, Shimon. 2002. *Together and Apart in Brezezany: Poles, Jews, and Ukrainians, 1919–1945.* Bloomington, IN: Indiana University Press.

Reinharz, Jehuda, and Evyatar Friesel. 1997. "The Zionist Leadership Between the Holocaust and the Creation of the State of Israel." In *Thinking about the Holocaust: After a Half Century,* ed. Alvin H. Rosenfeld. Bloomington, IN: Indiana University Press.

Reiss, Albert J., Jr. 1971. *The Police and the Public.* New Haven, CT: Yale University Press.

Rempel, Gerhard. 1989. *Hitler's Children: The Hitler Youth and the SS.* Chapel Hill: University of North Carolina Press.

Reynaud, Michel, and Sylvie Graffard. 2001. *The Jehovah's Witnesses and the Nazis: Persecution, Deportation, and Murder, 1933–1945.* New York: Cooper Square Press.

Rhodes, Richard. 2002. *Masters of Death: The SS-Einsatzgruppen and the Invention of the Holocaust.* New York: Knopf.

Riemer, Jeremiah H. 1998. "Burdens of Proof." In *Unwilling Germans? The Goldhagen Debate,* ed. Robert R. Shandley. Minneapolis, MN: University of Minnesota Press.

Rittner, Carol, and John K. Roth, eds. 1993. *Different Voices: Women and the Holocaust.* New York: Paragon House.

Ritzer, George. 1992. *Classical Social Theory.* New York: McGraw-Hill.

Roiphe, Anne. 1988. *A Season for Healing: Reflections on the Holocaust.* New York: Summit.

Ronayne, Peter. 2001. *Never Again? The United States and the Prevention and Punishment of Genocide Since the Holocaust.* Lanham, MD: Rowman and Littlefield.

Rose, Paul L. 1990. *Revolutionary Anti-Semitism in Germany: From Kant to Wagner.* Princeton, NJ: Princeton University Press.

Rosen, Richard N. 2006. *Saving the Jews: Franklin D. Roosevelt and the Holocaust.* New York: Thunder's Mouth Press.

Rosenbaum, Alan S. 1993. *Prosecuting Nazi War Criminals.* Boulder, CO: Westview Press.

——. 1998. *Explaining Hitler: The Search for the Origins of Evil.* New York: Random House.

—— ed. 2009. *Is the Holocaust Unique? Perspectives on Comparative Genocide,* 3rd ed. Boulder, CO: Westview Press.

Rosenfeld, Alvin H. 1985. *Imagining Hitler.* Bloomington, IN: Indiana University Press.

——. 1991. "Popularization and Memory: The Case of Anne Frank." In *Lessons and Legacies: The Meaning of the Holocaust in a Changing World,* ed. Peter Hayes. Evanston, IL: Northwestern University Press.

——. 1997. "The Americanization of the Holocaust." In *Thinking about the Holocaust: After Half a Century,* ed. Alvin H. Rosenfeld. Bloomington, IN: Indiana University Press.

Rosenfeld, Gavriel. 1999. "The Politics of Uniqueness: Reflections on the Recent Polemical Turn in Holocaust and Genocide Scholarship." *Holocaust and Genocide Studies* 13:28–61.

Roth, Michael. 1993. "Politics, Piety, and Transformation." *Tikkun* 8:79–81.

Rothchild, Sylvia, ed. 1981. *Voices from the Holocaust.* New York: New American Library.

Rothe, Dawn L., and Christopher W. Mullins. 2007. "Darfur and the Politicization of International Law: Genocide or Crimes against Humanity?" *Humanity and Society* 31:83–107.

Rubenstein, Richard L., and John K. Roth. 1987. *Approaches to Auschwitz: The Holocaust and Its Legacy.* Atlanta: Westminster John Knox Press.

Rubenstein, William D. 1997. *The Myth of Rescue: Why the Democracies Could Not Have Saved More Jews.* New York: Routledge.

Ruckerl, Adalbert. 1990a. "Denazification." In *Encyclopedia of the Holocaust,* vol. 1, ed. Israel Gutman. New York: Macmillan.

———. 1990b. "Trials of War Criminals: West Germany." In *Encyclopedia of the Holocaust*, vol. 4, ed. Israel Gutman. New York: Macmillan.

Sachar, Howard M. 1992. *A History of the Jews in America*. New York: Vintage.

Salzman, Jack, with Adina Back and Gretchen Sullivan Sorin, eds. 1992. *Bridges and Boundaries: African Americans and American Jews*. New York: Jewish Museum.

Santner, Eric L. 1990. "On the Difficulty of Saying 'We': The 'Historians' Debate' and Edgard Reitz's *Heimat*." *History and Memory* 2:276–96.

Sarna, Jonathan D. 2004. *American Judaism: A History*. New Haven, CT: Yale University Press.

Schleunes, Karl. 1970. *The Twisted Road to Auschwitz: Nazi Policy Toward German Jews, 1933–1939*. Urbana, IL: University of Illinois Press.

Schmitt, Raymond L. 1989. "Sharing the Holocaust: Bitburg as Emotional Reminder." In *Studies in Symbolic Interaction*, vol. 10, ed. Norman K. Denzin. Greenwich, CT: JAI Press.

Schwartz, Barry. 1991. "Iconography and Collective Memory: Lincoln's Image in the American Mind." *Sociological Quarterly* 32:301–19.

———. 1996. "Memory as a Cultural System: Abraham Lincoln in World War II." *American Sociological Review* 61:908–27.

Segev, Tom. 1993. *The Seventh Million: The Israelis and the Holocaust*. New York: Hill and Wang.

Sen, Amartya. 2000. "Other People." *The New Republic*, December 18:23–29.

Sewell, William H., Jr. 1992. "A Theory of Structure: Duality, Agency, and Transformation." *American Journal of Sociology* 98:1–29.

Shandler, Jeffrey. 1997. "Schindler's Discourse: America Discusses the Holocaust and Its Mediation, from NBC's Miniseries to Spielberg's Film." In *Spielberg's Holocaust: Critical Perspectives on Schindler's List*, ed. Yosefa Loshitsky. Bloomington, IN: Indiana University Press.

Shandley, Robert R., ed. 1998. *Unwilling Germans? The Goldhagen Debate*. Minneapolis, MN: University of Minnesota Press.

Shapira, Anita. 1995. "Politics and Collective Memory: The Debate Over the 'New Historians' in Israel." *History and Memory* 7:9–40.

———. 1997. "The Holocaust and World War II as Elements of the Yishuv Psyche Until 1948." In *Thinking about the Holocaust: After Half a Century*, ed. Alvin H. Rosenfeld. Bloomington, IN: Indiana University Press.

Shapiro, Edward S. 1992. *A Time for Healing: American Jewry Since World War II*. Baltimore, MD: Johns Hopkins University Press.

Shaw, Martin. 2007. *What is Genocide?* Cambridge, UK: Polity.

Sherman, Franklin, and Helmut T. Lehman, eds. 1971. *Luther's Works*. Philadelphia, PA: Fortress Press.

Shermer, Michael, and Alex Grobman. 2000. *Denying History: Who Says the Holocaust Never Happened and Why Do They Say It?* Berkeley, CA: University of California Press.

Sherwood, Ben. 2009. *The Survivors Club: The Secrets and Science that Could Save Your Life*. New York: Grand Central.

Shirer, William. 1960. *The Rise and Fall of the Third Reich: A History of Nazi Germany*. New York: Simon and Schuster.

Siła-Nowicki, Władysław. [1987] 1990. "A Reply to Jan Błonski." In *My Brother's Keeper? Recent Polish Debates on the Holocaust*, ed. Antony Polonsky. London: Routledge.

Silk, Mark. 1984. "Notes on the Judeo-Christian Tradition in America." *American Quarterly* 36:65–85.

Simmons, Roberta G. 1991. "Altruism and Sociology." *Sociological Quarterly* 32:1–22.

Simpson, Christopher. 1988. *Blowback: America's Recruitment of Nazi War Criminals and Its Effects on the Cold War*. New York; Widenfeld and Nicolson.

———. 1993. *The Splendid Blond Beast: Money, Law, and Genocide in the Twentieth Century*. New York: Grove Press.

Skocpol, Theda. 1987. "Social History and Historical Sociology: Contrasts and Complementaries." *Social Science History* 11:17–30.

Smith, Helmut Walser. 2002. *The Holocaust and Other Genocides: History, Representation, Ethics*. Nashville, TN: Vanderbilt University Press.

Snow, David A., E. Burke Rochford, Steven K. Worden, and Robert D. Benford. 1986. "Frame Alignment Processes, Micromobilization, and Movement Participation." *American Sociological Review* 51:464–81.

Snyder, Sharon L., and David T. Mitchell. 2006. *Cultural Locations of Disability*. Chicago, IL: University of Chicago Press.

Spector, Shmuel. 1990a. "Einsatsgruppen." In *Encyclopedia of the Holocaust*, vol. 2, ed. Israel Gutman. New York: Macmillan.

———. 1990b. "Railways, German." In *Encyclopedia of the Holocaust*, vol. 3, ed. Israel Gutman. New York: Macmillan.

———. 1990c. "Yad Vashem." In *Encyclopedia of the Holocaust*, vol. 4, ed. Israel Gutman. NewYork: Macmillan.

Speier, Hans. 1986. *German White-Collar Workers and the Rise of Hitler*. New Haven, CT: Yale University Press.

Spielvogel, Jackson J., and David Redles. 2010. *Hitler and Nazi Germany: A History*, 6th ed. Upper Saddle River, NJ: Prentice-Hall.

Steinbacher, Sybille. 2005. *Auschwitz: A History*, trans. Shaun Whiteside. London: Penguin.

Steinweis, Alan E. 2001. "The Holocaust and American Culture: An Assessment of Recent Scholarship." *Holocaust and Genocide Studies* 15:296–301.

Sundquist, Eric J. 2006. *Strangers in the Land: Blacks, Jews, Post-Holocaust America*. Cambridge, MA: Harvard University Press.

Taraki, Lisa. 1990. "The Development of Political Consciousness Among Palestinians in the Occupied Territories, 1967–1987." In *Intifada: Palestinians at the Crossroads*, eds. Jamal R. Nassar and Roger Heacock. New York: Greenwood Press.

Taylor, James, and Warren Shaw. 1987. *The Third Reich Almanac*. New York: World Almanac.

Tec, Nechama. 1986. *When Light Pierced the Darkness: Christian Rescue of Jews in Nazi-Occupied Poland*. New York: Oxford University Press.

———. 1993. *Defiance: The Bielski Partisans*. New York: Oxford University Press.

Teveth, Shabtai. 1996. *Ben-Gurion and the Holocaust*. New York: Harcourt Brace.

Tilles, Daniel. 2008. *Passive Accomplices or Helpless Bystanders? British and American Responses to the Holocaust, 1941–5*. Kraków, Poland: Galacia Jewish Museum.

Todorov, Tzvetan. 2001a. *The Fragility of Goodness: Why Bulgaria's Jews Survived the Holocaust*. Princeton, NJ: Princeton University Press.

———. 2001b. "In Search of Lost Crime." *The New Republic*, January 29:29–36.

Turner, Henry Ashby, Jr. 1985. *German Big Business and the Rise of Hitler*. New York: Oxford University Press.

Turner, Stephen P. 1992. "Sociology and Fascism in the Interwar Period: The Myth and Its Fame." In *Sociology Responds to Fascism*, eds. Stephen P. Turner and Dirk Käsler. New York: Routledge.

———. 2007. "A Life in the First Half-Century of Sociology: Charles Ellwood and the Division of Sociology." In *Sociology in America: A History*, ed. Craig Calhoun. Chicago, IL: University of Chicago Press.

Unger, Michal. 1986. "The Prisoner's First Encounter with Auschwitz." *Holocaust and Genocide Studies* 1:279–95.

Vago, Bela. 1987. "The Reaction to Nazi Anti-Jewish Policy in East-Central Europe and in the Balkans." In *Unanswered Questions: Nazi Germany and the Genocide of the Jews*, ed. Francois Furet. New York: Schocken.

Van Buren, Paul. 1980. *Discerning the Way: A Theology of the Jewish Christian Reality*. New York: Seabury.

Vidich, Arthur J., and Stanford M. Lyman. 1985. *American Sociology*. New Haven, CT: Yale University Press.

Vital, David. 1991. "After the Catastrophe: Aspects of Contemporary Jewry." In *Lessons and Legacies: The Meaning of the Holocaust in a Changing World*, ed. Peter Hayes. Evanston, IL: Northwestern University Press.

Volkov, Shulamit. 1989. "The Written Matter and the Spoken Word: On the Gap between Pre-1914 and Nazi Anti-Semitism." In *Unanswered Questions: Nazi Germany and the Genocide of the Jews*, ed. Francois Furet. New York: Schocken.

Walker, Kizer. 1994. "The Persian Gulf War and the Germans' 'Jewish Question'?" In *Reemerging Jewish Culture in Germany*, eds. Sander L. Gilman and Karen Remmler. New York: New York University Press.

Webster, Ronald. 2001. "Opposing 'Victors' Justice': German Protestant Churchmen and Convicted Criminals in Western Europe After 1945." *Holocaust and Genocide Studies* 15:47–69.

Wehler, Hans-Ulbrich. 1998. "Like a Thorn in the Flesh." In *Unwilling Germans? The Goldhagen Debate*, ed. Robert R. Shandley. Minneapolis, MN: University of Minnesota Press.

Weinberg, Daniel. 2001. "France." In *The Holocaust Encyclopedia*, ed. Walter Laqueur. New Haven, CT: Yale University Press.

Weinberg, Gerhard L. 1998. "The Allies and the Holocaust." In *The Holocaust and History: The Known, the Unknown, and the Disputed*, eds. Michael Berenbaum and Abraham J. Peck. Bloomington, IN: Indiana University Press.

Weissberg, Liliane. 1997. "The Tale of a Good German: Reflections on the German Reception of *Schindler's List*." In *Spielberg's Holocaust: Critical Perspectives on* Schindler's List, ed. Yosefa Loshitzky. Bloomington, IN: Indiana University Press.

Weissman, Gary. 2004. *Fantasies of Witnessing: Postwar Efforts to Experience the Holocaust*. Ithaca, NY: Cornell University Press.

Weitz, Yechiam. 1994. "The Herut Movement and the Kasztner Trial." *Holocaust and Genocide Studies* 8:349–71.

Welch, David. 1993. *The Third Reich: Politics and Propaganda*. New York: Routledge.

Wendell, Susan. 1996. *The Rejected Body: Feminist Philosophical Reflections on Disability*. New York: Routledge.

Wiener, Jon. 1989. "Talcott Parsons' Role: Bringing Nazi Sympathizers to the U.S." *The Nation*, March 6:306–09.

Wiesel, Elie. [1958] 2006. *Night*. New York: Hill and Wang.

———. 1995. *All Rivers Run to the Sea, Memoirs, 1928–1969*, vol. 1. New York: Knopf.

Wilhelm, Hans-Heinrich. 1990. "Euthanasia Program." In *Encyclopedia of the Holocaust*, vol. 1, ed. Israel Gutman. New York: Macmillan.

Will, George. 2001. "July 10, 1941, in Jedwabne." *Newsweek*, July 9:68.

Wills, Garry. 2000. *Papal Sin: Structures of Deceit*. New York: Doubleday.

Wirth, Louis. [1936] 1985. "Preface to Karl Mannheim." In Karl Mannheim, *Ideology and Utopia: An Introduction to the Sociology of Knowledge*. New York: Harcourt, Brace.

Wistrich, Robert S. 1995. *Who's Who in Nazi Germany*. New York: Routledge.

Wolfe, Alan, and Ira Katznelson, eds. 2010. *Religion and Democracy in the United States: Danger or Opportunity?* Princeton, NJ: Princeton University Press.

Wolffsohn, Michael. 1993. *External Guilt? Forty Years of German–Jewish–Israeli Relations*. New York: Columbia University Press.

Wright, Erik O. 1978. *Class, Crisis, and the State*. New York: Schocken.

Wuthnow, Robert. 1989. *The Restructuring of American Religion: Society and Faith Since World War II*. Princeton, NJ: Princeton University Press.

Wyman, David S. 1984. *The Abandonment of the Jews: America and the Holocaust, 1941–1945*. New York: Pantheon.

Yaffe, Richard. 1980. "Intermarriage Abettors should be Ousted from Leadership, Roth Urges." *New York Jewish Week*, Manhattan ed., July 6:2.

Yahil, Leni. 1990. *The Holocaust: The Fate of European Jewry*. New York: Oxford University Press.

Young, James. 1993. *The Texture of Memory: Holocaust Memorials and Meaning in Europe, Israel, and America*. New Haven, CT: Yale University Press.

Zahn, Gordon C. 1962. *German Catholics and Hitler's Wars*. New York: Sheed and Ward.

Zald, Mayer N., and John D. McCarthy, eds. 1987. *Social Movements in Organizational Society*. New Brunswick, NJ: Transaction.

Zald, Mayer N., and Bert Useem. 1987. "Movement and Countermovement Interaction: Mobilization, Tactics, and State Involvement." In *Social Movements in Organizational Society*, eds. Mayer N. Zald and John D. McCarthy. New Brunswick, NJ: Transaction.

Zeitlan, Irving. 1990. *Ideology and the Development of Sociological Theory*. Englewood Cliffs, NJ: Prentice-Hall.

Zubrzycki, Geneviève. 2006. *The Crosses of Auschwitz: Nationalism and Religion in Post-Communist Poland*. Chicago, IL: University of Chicago Press.

Zuccotti, Susan. 1987. *The Italians and the Holocaust: Persecution, Rescue, and Survival*. New York: Basic.

———. 2002. *Under His Windows: The Vatican and the Holocaust in Italy*. New Haven, CT: Yale University Press.

Index

Abel, Theodore, 7
Abraham, 27
Abs, Hermann, 63
Adenauer, Konrad, 153-154
AEG, 77
African Americans, 58, 217; and Jewish Americans, 194, 198-200, 203; and *Schindler's List*, 200
Akbar, Nai'm, 199
Aktion 14f 13, 40, 89
Alexander, Edward, 185, 198
Alexander, Jeffrey, 1, 12, 19, 35, 191, 210 (n31), 229-30
Allianz, 77
Allies, 1, 114, 125, 144, 148; and denazification of Germany, 151; immigration policy of, 60-61, 98, 126-33; knowledge of Final Solution by, 134-37; negotiation for Jewish lives by, 138-42; postwar division of Germany and, 148, 152; postwar trials conducted by, 2, 148-50
Altruism, 119-21, 144 (n3); affective, 119; autonomous, 120; cognitive, 119; normative, 120; *See also* Helpers/rescuers; Resistance to Final Solution; "Righteous Gentiles"
Amato, Joseph, 147
American Jewish Congress, 129
American Jewish Joint Distribution Committee, 138, 142
American Sociological Association, 5
American Sociological Society, 5
Americanization of the Holocaust: 173; films and the, 184-90; museums/memorials and the, 190, 193-95, 200-1
Anheier, Helmut, 53
Anielewicz, Mordekhai, 106-7

Anschluss, 60
Anti-Jewish pogroms/massacres, 79, 168-70, 213; *See also* Kristallnacht
Anti-Semitism: and Christianity, 32-34, 225-28; of early American sociologists, 5-6; "eliminationist," 18, 161; Nazism and, 11-12, 19-20; origins of term, 31; in post-Communist societies, 225; racism and, 12, 27, 31, 36-37; "redemptive," 12; in relation to helping/rescue activity, 120; *See also* Germany; Poland; United States
Arab League, 176
Arabs: opposition to Israel by, 155, 176-77, 181-83; resistance to Jewish immigration by, 132-33, 175; and the United Nations, 176, 182; *See also* Egypt; Palestine
Arafat, Yasir, 182
Arendt, Hannah, 4, 10-11, 102
Armenian genocide (Turkey), 10, 196-97, 213, 215
Arrow Cross, 140-41
Aryanization. *See* Germany
Assimilation, 174, 229-30; of European Jews, 34; of Jewish Americans, 191, 204
Auschwitz, 68, 76-77, 91-92, 97, 142, 187-88, 233; bombing of, 143-44; Carmelite convent controversy at, 165-66, 168; gas chambers/crematoria at, 68, 76, 91; IG Farben and, 76, 109-10, 143; Polish martyrdom and, 163-65; State Museum at, 163; symbolic territoriality and, 165; War of Crosses controversy about, 166-68
Auschwitz-Birkenau, 76, 91, 107-8, 110-11, 143, 165

Auschwitz-Monowitz, 76, 91, 108-10, 143
Austria, 30-31, 44-45, 142; annexation by Germany of, 60; Nazi plunder of, 63
Avisar, Ilan, 189
Axis Rule in Occupied Europe, 214

Bain, Reid, 6
Baldwin, James, 198
Balfour Declaration, 132
Banality of evil, 4, 15, 18, 23 (n5)
Bankier, David, 81
Banks. *See* Nazism; Swiss banks
Barmen Declaration, 116
Barabbas, 29
Baron, Lawrence, 126
Bartov, Omer, 85, 188-89
Bauer, Yehuda, 3, 140, 142
Bauman, Zygmunt, 3, 8, 21, 32, 169, 225
Bayer, 75
BBC, 114
Begin, Menacham, 182
Belgium, 120
Bell-Fialkoff, Andrew, 224
Bellah, Robert, 21
Bełżec, 68, 89
Ben-Gurion, David, 174-75, 180-81, 210 (n26)
Ben Yosef, Shlomo, 204
Benner, Patricia, 102
Berenbaum, Michael, 195-97
Bergen-Belsen, 157, 186
Berger, Michael, 108-10
Berger, Sol, 99-100, 106
Bergson, Peter, 145 (n17)
Bermuda conference, 136
Bershtel, Sara, 204
Betriebsrats, 154
Bettelheim, Bruno, 100
Bialystock pogroms (Russia), 213
Bielski, Tuvia, 107
Biondich, Mark, 79
Bismarck, Otto von, 9
Bitburg affair, 157-58, 202
Blackshirts/Black Corps/Black Order, 77
Blatter für Deutsche und Internationale Politik, 161
Bloxham, Donald, 10
Bogardas, Emory, 6
Bonaparte, Napoleon/Bonapartism, 15
Bonhoeffer, Dietrich, 116

Book of John, 32
Borsig, Ernst von, 14, 50
Bosnia-Herzegovina, genocide in, 220-23
Botz, Gerhard, 100
Braham, Randolph, 227
Brand, Joel, 142
Breitman, Richard, 46, 61, 66, 126, 133
British. *See* Great Britain
British Foreign Office, 135-36
Bronfman, Edgar, 201
Browning, Christopher, 44, 67, 100-1, 234
Brustein, William, 48
Brzezinski, Zbigniew, 196, 224, 235
Buchenwald, 90
Budapest Relief and Rescue Committee, 142
Bulgaria, 120, 137; Orthodox clergy in, 121
Bureaucracy: of destruction, 17-19, 77-78; division of labor in, 17-18; Weber's view of, 17, 77
Burg, Avraham, 203
Bush, George H. W., 202, 221
Bystanders, 113, 124, 235

Calhoun, Craig, 8
Calvin, John/Calvinism, 122-23
Cambodia, genocide in, 220
Capitalism. *See* Nazism
Carter, Jimmy, 182, 193-94, 196, 218
Carto, Willis, 233
Carver, Thomas Nixon, 5
Catholic Youth League, 117
Catholica, 31
Catholics/Catholic Church: assistance to Nazi war criminals by, 153; and postwar Auschwitz controversies, 164-68; response to the Holocaust by, 116-18, 121, 226; *See also* Christian-Jewish coexistence; Christians/Christianity
Centeno, Miguel, 8
Central Office for Jewish Emigration, 61
Chelmno, 68, 88-89, 104
Chesnoff, Robert, 203
Christian Democratic Union, 153-54
Christian-Jewish coexistence/reconciliation, 164-65, 225-28; and Catholic Church, 225-27

Independent, 51
Institute for Historical Review, 233
Interhamwe militias, 223
The International Jew, 51
International law, 149-50, 213; *See also*
United Nations
International Military Tribunal, 2,
148-50
International Red Cross, 137, 139,
145-46 (n19)
Irving, David, 233-34
Isaac, Jules, 227
Israel/Israelis: vs. American/Diaspora
Jews, 175-76, 178, 193, 210 (n26);
collective memory in, 173-84; and
Egyptian peace accord, 182; and
Middle East conflict, 181-84,
192; "new historians" in, 183-84;
number of Jews in, 173; and Palestin-
ian peace accord, 183; Six Day War,
155, 181-82, 187, 192, 209 (n23);
United Nations partition plan for,
176-77, 203; War of Independence,
176; Yom Kippur War, 182, 192; *See
also* Eichmann, Adolf; Kasztner trial;
Palestine; Yad Vashem; Zionism
Italy: fascism in, 11, 124; response to
anti-Jewish policy in, 120, 124-25

J.A. Topf und Söhne, 76
Jabotinsky, Zev, 174-75
Jackson, Robert, 149
Jay, Martin, 11
Jedwabne massacre (Poland), 79, 168-70
Jehovah's Witnesses, 118
Jenninger, Phillip, 160
Jesus Christ, 29-30, 190; crucifixion of,
30, 165, 226
Jewish Agency for Palestine, 175
Jewish Americans: and African
Americans, 194, 198-200; assimila-
tion of, 191, 204; continuity of, 203-6;
discrimination against, 191; and
Holocaust memory, 173, 192-93; vs.
Israeli Jews, 190-93; religious faith of,
191, 204-5; response to the Holocaust
by, 129, 134-38, 142; success in Amer-
ica of, 191, 208 (n20); victim identity
of, 192-93; *See also* Judaism; United
States Holocaust Memorial Museum
Jewish Combat Organization, 106

Jewish councils, 83, 102-4
Jewish deaths. *See* Holocaust
Jewish emigration/immigration: postwar,
163, 175; prewar, 59-61, 98, 126-33
Jewish ghettos, 65; in Łódz, 104; man-
agement of, 18, 82-83; in Vilna, 95; in
Warsaw, 18, 83, 106-7, 177, 187
Jewish National Fund, 178
Jewish police force, 104
"Jewish problem": 5, 36, 46, 55, 90, 127;
emigration solution to, 59-61; Final
Solution to, 64, 68; legal solution to,
55-58
Jewish refugee problem, international
aspects of, 60-61, 131-33; *See also*
Allies; Displaced person camps
Jewish resistance, 104-6; in concentra-
tion camps, 107-8; in forests, 107,
123; in ghettos, 106-7, 177; Israeli
views about, 177-80
Jews: biblical history of, 28-29; and
the Enlightenment, 34-35; in Middle
Ages, 31-32; *See also* Christian-
Jewish coexistence; Israel; Jewish
Americans; Judaism
John XXIII, Pope, 226
John Paul II, Pope, 164-66
Johnson, Eric, 80-81, 114-15
Johnson, Paul, 176
Judaism: and continuity problem, 204-6;
and theological interpretations of
the Holocaust, 238 (n18); *See also*
Christian-Jewish coexistence; Jews;
Jewish Americans
Judas Iscariot, 29
Judenfrei, 44, 46, 142, 173
Judenräte. *See* Jewish councils
Judeo-Christian heritage, 191, 208
(n19), 229
Judt, Tony, 225

Kanin, Garson, 187
Karadzic, Radovan, 221
Karski, Jan, 136
Kasztner, Rezsö, 142, 179
Kasztner trial, 179
Kaunas pogrom (Lithuania), 170
Keneally, Thomas, 188
Kennedy, Michael, 8
Khmer Rouge, 20
Kielce pogrom (Poland), 168-69

Rosenfeld, Gavriel, 197
Roskies, Ethel, 102
Ross, Edward Alsworth, 5
Roth, John, 30, 118
Rozett, Robert, 98
Rubenstein, Richard, 30, 118
Rubenstein, William, 130, 138, 141
Rumkowski, Mordechai Chaim, 104
Russians. *See* Soviet Union
Rwanda, genocide in, 222-23

SA (Nazi Storm Troops), 49, 69(n4), 77
St. Louis (ship), 131
San Salvador, 140
Saul of Tarsus (Paul), 30
Schacht, Hjalmar, 62
Scheubner-Richter, Max Erwin von, 50
Schindler, Oskar, 188-90
Schindler's List, 188-90; reception in
  Germany of, 190; reception in Israel
  of, 208 (n17)
Schleicher, Kurt von, 54
Schluenes, Karl, 44
Schulte, Eduard, 135
Schumacher, Kurt, 154
Science, vs. religion, 28
SD (Nazi Security Service), 60-61, 77
Second Vatican Council, 226
Segev, Tom, 180
Sen, Amartya, 230
Serbia, genocide by, 221
Seti I, Pharaoh of Egypt, 28
Shapira, Anita, 177
Sherwood, Ben, 96
Shirer, William, 2
Shoah, 23 (n2)
Shoah Visual History Foundation, 96,
  190
Siła-Nowicki, Władysław, 169
"Silent Holocaust," 204, 211 (n37)
Silverman, Sidney, 141
Simon Wiesenthal Center, 200-2
Simpson, Christopher, 15, 154
Sinekiewciz, Henryk, 213
Sister Bendicta of the Cross, 165
Six Day War, 155, 181-82, 187, 192, 209
  (n23)
Skarzyska, Krystyna, 170
Slovakia, 118
Smith, Bradley, 232-33
Smith, H. Alexander, 218

Snyder, Sharon, 38
Sobibór, 89, 107
Social action, 11
Social Darwinism, 36-37
Social difference(s), 214, 230-31
Social movement theory, 46, 48, 95,
  103, 121-22
Social solidarity, 19, 21, 168, 192, 229
Social structure, 11
Socialism/socialists/social democrats,
  45, 51, 53, 123, 154, 156
Sociological theory/classics, 4, 12-13
Sociology/sociologists: anti-Semitism
  and Christian reformism in, 5-6;
  genocide research agenda for,
  235- 36; neglect of the Holocaust by,
  3-8, 232; response to fascism/Nazism
  by, 6-7
Sociology in America, 7
Sociology Confronts the Holocaust, 5
Sociology of knowledge, 4-5
Sonderkommando, 107
Sonderweg, 9-10
Southern Baptist Convention, 228
Soviet Union/Russians, 139, 151, 159,
  216, 218; collective memory in, 152,
  155, 163-64; German invasion of, 67,
  134; influence on postwar Poland
  of, 163-64; Jews in, 67, 163; killed by
  Nazis, 2; prisoners of war, 2, 107, 123,
  196; Tripartite Conference and, 141,
  143; *See also* Allies; Stalin, Joseph
Spain, 118, 126, 136, 140
Spector, Shmuel, 178
Speer, Albert, 143
Spielberg, Steven, 96, 188-90
SS (Schutzstaffel), 38, 61, 77-78, 113-14;
  Bitburg affair and, 157; businesses
  owned by, 74-75
Stalin, Joseph, 163-64, 216; pact with
  Hitler, 65, 67
Star of David insignia, 58, 158
Statue of Liberty, 126
Stauffenberg, Claus Schenk Count von,
  115
Stein, Edith, 164
Sterilization, compulsory: in Nazi
  Germany, 38-39; in the United States,
  38, 41 (n7)
Stier, Walter, 18, 84-85
Straaten, Werenfried van, 165

The Holocaust, Religion, and the Politics of Collective Memory

CPSIA information can be obtained at www.ICGtesting.com
Printed in the USA
BVOW08s1609030913

330076BV00004B/7/P